ADLERIAN COUNSELING

A PRACTICAL APPROACH
FOR A NEW DECADE

Third Edition

Thomas J. Sweeney

Professor
School of Applied Behavioral Sciences
and Educational Leadership
Ohio University
Athens, Ohio

ACCELERATED DEVELOPMENT INC.
Publishers
Muncie   Indiana

ADLERIAN COUNSELING
A PRACTICAL APPROACH FOR A NEW DECADE

Technical Development: Tanya Dalton
Sandra Gilmore
Delores Kellogg
Marguerite Mader
Sheila Sheward

Library of Congress Cataloging-in-Publication Data

Sweeney, Thomas John, 1936-
    Adlerian counseling: a practical approach for a new decade /
Thomas J. Sweeney. -- 3rd ed.
        p.   cm.
    Includes index.
    Bibliography: p.
    ISBN 0-915202-84-0
    1. Counseling. 2. Adler, Alfred, 1870-1937. I. Title.
BF637.C6S9   1989
158'.3--dc19   88-82676
                                                                CIP

LCN: 88-82676

ACCELERATED DEVELOPMENT INC., Publishers
3400 Kilgore Avenue, Muncie, IN 47304
Toll Free Order Number 1-800-222-1166
In Indiana Call (317) 284-7511

DEDICATION

To my children, Elizabeth, Ann, Tom, Kate, and Mike, in the hope that they will one day say of their parents, as I have said of my parents, Thomas and Sarah Sweeney, "They gave me the love and encouragement needed to be my best self—they inspired me to think of others' needs as well as my own, to have the courage to act when I was afraid, to try again when it was appropriate, to celebrate when I succeeded and, in all circumstances, to have the courage to be imperfect without the loss of self-esteem."

AUTHOR'S INTRODUCTION

This book is written with the practitioner in mind. It is about the practical applications of the psychology of Alfred Adler, a pioneer in what is sometimes referred to as a "common sense" approach to social living. It is used successfully by counselors and therapists of all types in a variety of settings with persons of all ages and capabilities. It is also applied successfully by parents, teachers, paraprofessional, peer counselors, and lay persons in homes, businesses, and educational settings.

Earlier editions of this work were reported to be useful, concise overviews of the theory and practice of what Adler called his Individual Psychology. Although revised and expanded significantly since the last edition, an effort has been made to retain these positive qualities. As a consequence, comparative theories and practices are held to a minimum.

Adler left a legacy which is well suited to the coming decade and beyond. As the balance of social and economic influence shifts from the young, white and Anglo-Saxon to an older, racially and ethnically mixed society, the old power structure will be tested. Those who understand the philosophy and practice of a psychology based upon equalitarian values will be able to assist in the transition which will inevitably take place within our society.

If this sounds radical, read on. A visionary in many respects, Adler nurtured the concept of social democracy at the turn of the century when few people would follow his lead. One who did follow and lived long enough to see the social evolution needed to help others appreciate its worth was Rudolf Dreikurs. Dreikurs patterned his efforts after those of Adler as a lecturer, consultant, counselor, and founder of child guidance and family education centers. He was especially interested in child guidance because Adlerians believe that in the early years is when life style or the characteristic way of making one's place is developed.

Unlike Adler, Dreikurs shared his experience through writing as well. He wrote practical, easily read papers and books concerned with Individual Psychology and its uses. He also was recorded and filmed on different occasions conducting family and teacher consultation and counseling sessions. Even before his death in 1972, ample evidence was being exhibited that his students and colleagues would and could continue the work which he helped begin. His books, *The Challenge of Marriage* (1946) and *Social Equality: The Challenge of Today* (1971), are prophetic statements about the social changes within our society. More importantly, he addressed what is needed for changes to be in the best interests of all persons. This book is intended as a contribution to the continuation of his mission.

The first chapter is a short introduction to the man, the movement, and psychology of Alfred Adler. For persons unfamiliar with the theory, it should serve as a basis for understanding the assumptions underlying methods discussed in subsequent chapters. Not infrequently, persons new to this literature are surpised by how much is known to them through other counseling approaches. On the other hand, each chapter will reveal some unique applications of this approach.

Chapter 2 is entirely new. I asked my long time friend and colleague, Dr. Mel Witmer, to draw upon his extensive research and teaching experience to give us a compendium of the latest research and practices on the characteristics of healthy persons as they related to Individual Psychology. They are focused around the major life tasks of work, friendship and love, spirit, and self. To the best of our knowledge, this is a unique contribution to the literature and should stimulate additional interest in such research and its implications.

Chapters 3 and 4 explain dimensions and uses of natural and logical consequences. Adlerians give particular attention to consequences as methods which follow the "ironclad logic of social living." We teach that within this approach, "rules are for everyone." All of us experience negative consequences when we ignore the laws of nature. Social convention and society's laws have a force which influence our behavior as well. When understood and used wisely, social "rules" can be powerful, positive methods in helping persons of all ages.

Nurturing courage is a key concept throughout Adlerian practice. It is a fundamental goal in all teaching and counseling practice. Chapter 5 addresses encouragement as an essential element in helping and methods for sharing it. Activities for self-appraisal of one's understanding are provided.

Chapter 6 is "must" reading for anyone who lives or works with young people. This chapter has been expanded to include research which supports both the philosophy and practice of Individual Psychology in its application to guiding young people. Research on effective methods in schools, not specifically identified as Adlerian per se, are both exciting and potentially controversial in their implications. For example, replacing competitive with cooperative learning methods could, as one source stated it, "revolutionize education" in this country. Adlerians have learned much from parents and teachers which resulted in rules of thumb, specific techniques, and useful methods which are shared for the benefit of present generations. The goals of disruptive behavior, how to identify the goals, and corrective actions which complement the encouragement process are illustrated with case examples.

Life style assessment is outlined and explained as an introduction to its uses. Seen by some as mystical in the demonstrations of masterful clinicians, the serious student of Individual Psychology discovers that no magic is involved. Chapter 7 provides a guide for discovering the simplicity and interrelatedness, for example, of early recollections and present behavior. Applicable to persons of all ages, it can be an excellent tool for quickly establishing rapport and overcoming counselee resistance.

Chapter 8 explains the Adlerian counseling process. Each stage is explained and illustrated. In addition to examples taken from my work with young people, the use of early recollections as a tool for helping older persons is presented. Because "life review" has been observed as a common phenomenon among older persons, some gerontological experts have encouraged workers in the field to capitalize upon this as a method for helping older persons.

At the conclusion of Chapter 8, life style assessment with particular attention to family constellation is illustrated from a teaching demonstration interview by Dr. Harold Mosak, one of the foremost Adlerians. As one more illustration of the versatility of this method, he wins the cooperation of a teenage girl in full bloom of rebellion and successfully aids her in reaching new understandings about herself and her relationship to her family.

Even though "work" was considered one of the most fundamental of life tasks by Adler, little systematic attention has been given to its practical implications for Adlerian counselors in working with counselees involved in the career decision process. Dr. Mark Savickas draws upon his substantial research and professional experience as a career counselor to add new and innovative dimensions to career counseling. "Life review counseling," as he illustrates in Chapter 9, is a significant addition to Adlerian literature on this topic.

Marriage counseling is one of the most challenging and, consequently, potentially satisfying relationships for counselors. Chapter 10 provides both a philosophical and psychological perspective to this process. It uses recent sociological research to disclose the pattern of "uncoupling" as a useful source for assessing the likelihood of successful marriage counseling throughout the process. A step-by-step case example is presented including specific techniques and methods potentially useful to facilitating goals of counseling.

Conflict resolution and work with families have received much attention in both popular and professional literature. Chapter 11 addressed both family counseling and consultation. Because the literature on various systems approaches to counseling has expanded rapidly since the previous edition of this book, I have included a section to illustrate some of the complementary aspects of systems theory and practice to Adlerian counseling.

Consultation, per se, is frequently not differentiated from other helping methods by Adlerians. For purposes of Chapter 11, a distinction is made between counseling and consultation. Underlying assumptions and strategies of the Adlerian consultant are outlined. In addition, stages of the consultation process as they apply to parent and teacher conferences are illustrated. Because Adlerians make a practice of working with all the children in a family, an illustration of the children's conference is used. In addition, suggestions are made on how group demonstrations are handled by the Adlerian consultant. Typical recommendations which most families find helpful illustrate how principles of Individual Psychology can be practically implemented in all families. Because recommendations do not always result in the outcomes intended, a few common errors which occur in implementation are discussed.

The last chapter is about group procedures. They are among the most compatible with Individual Psychology. Problems of social living are held in common. Discussion, consulting, and counseling groups, therefore are logical methods of the Adlerian counselor. In Chapter 12, each of these methods is discussed with reference to work with children and adults.

In each chapter, the reader will find a number of suggested references as guides to study beyond the scope of this work. One need not be an "Adlerian" to use and benefit from the ideas and methods described. Adler indicated that he was not bound by his own creation. Like those who followed Adler, we can further his work best by creatively adapting and adding to it.

February, 1989

Thomas J. Sweeney

CONTENTS

3. NATURAL CONSEQUENCES
Life's Rules Are For Everyone 81

4. LOGICAL CONSEQUENCES
Society's Lessons 93

LIST OF FIGURES

LIST OF FORMS

LIST OF TABLES

CHAPTER 1

INDIVIDUAL PSYCHOLOGY
The Man, the Movement, and the Psychology of Alfred Adler

The psychology of Alfred Adler had its beginning in Vienna at the turn of the century. He began private practice as an ophthalmologist in 1898, but later turned to general practice and then to neurology. His first psychological paper, "The Physician as Educator," was published in 1904. Its major theme was clearly applicable to all educators. Adler emphasized the importance of the "child's confidence in his own strength," particularly in relation to guiding sick or pampered children (Furtmueller & Wexberg, 1922). He believed that the child's greatest good fortune was the personal courage to cope with life. He instructed educators to help children develop discipline by allowing them to experience the natural consequences of their acts without fear of those who educate them. Throughout the remainder of his life, he was interested in child rearing practices and the instruction of parents and teachers in what he considered to be important principles of guiding children.

Mosak and Dreikurs (1973) traced the similarities and differences between Adler and various philosophers and psychologists over the years. To some, Adler appears to be no more than a student of Freud who became a dissenter and pursued variations on psychoanalysis (Fine, 1973). Adler, however, revealed the outline of this theory in a publication which predated his contact with Freud (Ellenberger, 1970). While Adler's reason for joining Freud is not entirely clear, Freud invited him to join his Wednesday evening discussion group in 1902 after Adler had written two defenses of Freud's theories. What now appears to be more accurate is to state that Adler was a colleague of Freud, for evidence exists that each influenced the other in some aspects of each other's theory.

From the perspective of visibility in history, Freud clearly has the greater renown. In some respects, this attainment has been a curiosity to followers of Adler. Differences between them were so significant that they eventually became antagonists. Adler viewed man as worthwhile, socially motivated, and capable of creative, independent action. The theory is so based upon the concepts of social democracy that only in recent history has it begun to have an impact in education and psychology. Even today, however, comparatively few persons are aware of the Individual Psychology of Alfred Adler.

Ellenberger (1970) has stated the circumstances quite succinctly:

> Any attempt to assess the influences of Adler's work brings about a paradox. The impact of individual psychology stands beyond any doubt. . .(but) it would not be easy to find another author from which so much has been borrowed from all sides without acknowledgement than Alfred Adler. (p. 645)

This tends to be true to such a degree that few persons who have ever studied child rearing practices, education, or psychology could be considered unaware of Adler's ideas. On the other hand, few would remember his name were they asked to identify the author of these ideas. For example, while many people see at least a superficial parallel between Eric Berne's theory of Transactional Analysis and Freud's concepts of id, ego, and superego, few individuals seem to know that this social interaction analysis is predicated on many of Adler's teachings concerning social living and psychological growth. Similarly, many persons actively are advocating the application of

Glasser's Reality Therapy a la *Schools Without Failure* to public education without the slightest notion that several of the most fundamental principles and techniques are Alderian in nature. Frankl, Lecky, and Rollo May were students of Adler and on occasion credit him as a source of some of their ideas. Similarly, Eric Fromm, Karen Horney, and H.S. Sullivan integrate Adlerian psychology into their own systems—so much so that Ellenberger (1970, p. 860) observed that Horney's psychology "combines Adlerian teachings with Freudian terminology."

Albert Ellis (1970), who identified Adler as "one of the first humanistic psychologists," is a member of the American Society of Adlerian Psychology and increasingly identifies with Adlerian principles. In addition, Phillips's Interference Therapy, Kelly's Psychology of Personal Constructs, Sartre's Existential Psychoanalysis, and Mowrer's Integrity Therapy all seem to reveal Adler's influence (Allen, 1971a). This influence in no way should be interpreted as a detraction from the individual author's own contribution to the theory and practice of counseling and psychotherapy. The comment is on the pervasiveness of Adler's influence without public recognition of this fact. As the reader will discover, however, this occurrence is consistent with Adler's theory and preference; i.e., for others to find his ideas useful was more important than for them to remember their origin.

Adler has been described as an essentially simple man, of great personal forcefulness and physical strength. His personal orientation was toward the betterment of the human condition (Ansbacher, 1969). Adler was the second of six children. Born on February 7, 1870, his father was a middle-class Jewish merchant and his mother a homemaker. His earlier years included poor health and being run over by a vehicle. His health improving as he grew older, his interest in medicine resulted in a degree from the University of Vienna in 1895.

Individuals create their own evaluations
and choices of how to respond to life events.

Adler's interest in why people respond differently to similar life events is reflected in his early attention to the study of

Organ Inferiority (1907). His later lectures, books, and articles illustrated even more clearly the realization that individuals create their own evaluations and choices of how to respond to life events. In a book of remembrances of those who knew the man, he obviously chose to enjoy life. Not one to miss a good time, he enjoyed telling stories and participating in a singing session around a piano.

After serving as a medical officer in World War I, he established a number of child-guidance clinics in the Vienna schools. Through these clinics, teachers, social workers, physicians, and others learned to understand children's behavior and how to help them. Through the clinics, which spread throughout Europe at that time, and his unique style of public lecture and demonstration, Adler developed a relatively small but significant following.

In 1935 when the Nazis began their oppression of Europe, Adler had to flee to America with his then radical, politically unacceptable ideas about a society of social equals. Although he had taught and lectured extensively in the United States, his death in 1937 while on tour in Scotland, left a significant void. His followers in the United States found great resistance by those who adopted Freud's Psychoanalysis. In addition, history shows that this country was far from truly accepting and practicing the equalitarian principles upon which Individual Psychology is based.

With this background, one only can admire all the more the persistence and resiliency of Adler and those who followed him. Probably his most noted student and colleague, Dr. Rudolf Driekurs, commands special mention. A prolific writer and founder of the Alfred Adler Institute of Chicago, through personal energy and talent he brought Adler's ideas into practical usefulness for thousands of parents, couples, and practitioners. His sense of urgency in teaching others how to live together was evident in his level of writing, lecturing, and counseling even until his death in 1972. Having recollections of him myself through lectures, counseling demonstrations, and informal talks, I can vouch for the fact that he lived what he taught. In their book on the life and works of Rudolf Driekurs titled, *The Courage to be Imperfect*, Terner and Pew (1978) help us know him better through many anecdotes recalled by friends and students. One of their quotes from Dreikurs may help the reader to understand the man better:

> . . . I don't mind the patient criticizing me. I don't mind admitting that I have made a mistake—I very often make mistakes.

> We should not be afraid of making mistakes . . . It is more important that we are human. It is unfortunate that one has to emphasize that today, because it is not the customary practice in psychotherapy to be human. Some psychiatrists wouldn't go to the elevator with the last patient of the day for fear of coming too close to him. They have to wait until the patient has gone down. "Don't come too close because that interferes with the therapeutic relationship." This is just the opposite of what I am saying. I want to function and to be recognized as a fellow human being. (p. 243)

Following Adler's conviction that our society was two generations removed from truly achieving equality, Dreikurs' (1946) book on marriage forecast the social revolution which we have experienced since World War II. Ridiculed and rejected by many of his peers in medicine and psychiatry, Dreikurs lived long enough to see his books best sellers among lay persons and professionals alike. Equally important, his work continues through his students and colleagues in this country and abroad.

In addition to the center in Chicago, Adlerian institutes offer certificates in child guidance, counseling, and psychotherapy in New York, Minneapolis, Berkeley, and Toronto. Satellite centers are growing in other locations, some with university connected programs. Newsletters, periodical, workshops, and conventions are available as sources of new developments, techniques, and research for interested persons. Adler's Individual Psychology is having an impact in its own right, particularly in the area of child rearing and classroom behavior, and increasingly in other areas including marriage and family counseling, industrial relations, correctional counseling, and human relations groups.

BASIC CONCEPTS

At the risk of oversimplifying Adler's theory, the following sections are offered as a foundation for subsequent chapters in which will be discussed the application of the Adlerian theory. Each chapter will elaborate further upon certain concepts as they apply to specific techniques or methods. The major thrust of this chapter, therefore, is to help the reader understand the significance of certain concepts without pursuing them in great detail or showing their application to specific methods or techniques.

Socio-Teleo-Analytic

A number of assumptions, propositions, and beliefs can be listed under Adler's theory of personality. The essence of his system can be captured in part, however, by defining it as socio-teleo-analytic. Adler perceived man as a *social being* with a natural inclination toward other people. Developmentally, human beings are among the most dependent of all creatures at birth. Someone must nurture and care for us if we are to survive.

From early dependent experience and throughout life, human beings can be understood best as they interact with others. As children begin discovering themselves, others, and the world, their first impressions of the world are predicated upon contact with and through other people. As shall be seen later, these early impressions develop into rules about life which individuals use to help them understand, predict, and manage their world.

Adler believed that man had a basic inclination toward being a part of the larger social whole, a striving to feel belongingness, a willingness to serve the greater good for the betterment of mankind. He called this *Gemeinschaftsgefuhl*. The closest interpretation of this word in English is social interest. An expression of this inclination is observed in each person's striving to make a place for himself/herself and to feel belongingness.

Parents, significant other adults, and siblings offer opportunities for individuals to fashion their own notions about how to make their places in a group. Because cognitive processes and life experiences are quite limited for children, many of these notions or rules have limited value or can be quite unsatisfactory when viewed externally by someone observing their behaviors. These rules are perceived, nevertheless, as helpful by individuals as they make choices, even though these processes and experiences remain largely unexamined in a critical manner.

The subjective or phenomenological view of individuals is necessary, therefore, if one is to understand their characteristic ways of moving through life. Adler referred to the basic notions which guide us through life as our style of life, or as more commonly referred to now, as *life style.* Adler characterized life style as ". . . unity in each individual—in his thinking, feeling, acting; in his so-called conscious and unconscious, in every expression of his personality. This (self-consistent) unity we call the style of life of the individual" (Ansbacher & Ansbacher, 1967, p. 175).

Our life style is not determined by heredity or environment but both are important antecedents. For example, individuals decide how they think, value, and feel about being female, the oldest, or without the presence of a father. There is no ideal right or wrong life style. Quite to the contrary, each life style is unique.

Although Adler wished to emphasize the necessity for viewing man holistically, i.e., not in parts when he coined the term *Individual Psychology,* he also helped to underscore his belief in the uniqueness of each person. A superficial study of Individual Psychology might lead one to conclude that conformity was one of its objectives in practice. Not only would this conclusion be inaccurate, but also Adler would have stated that it is not even probable. In the same sense that finger and voice prints are unique. Adler observed that every individual fashions a unique way of moving through life.

Obviously, a psychology of personality which revealed no general or nomothetic rules of behavior upon which to base practice would be of little utility. As will be seen in subsequent chapters, Adlerian principles do indeed provide many useful guidelines. The significance of idiographic factors, however, is equally important. Adler stated:

> I believe that I am not bound by any strict rule or prejudice but prefer to subscribe to the principle: Everything can also be different . . . . General rules-even those laid down by Individual Psychology, of my own creation—should be regarded as nothing more than an aid to a preliminary illumination of the field of view in which the single individual can be found-or missed. (Ansbacher & Ansbacher, 1967)

Adlerians are sometimes described as soft determinists; while freedom is not absolute, neither is determinism absolute. Predictions of human behavior must be stated in terms of probabilities of occurrence. Perfect correlations between what Adlerians refer to as antecedents and specific behaviors are elusive for many reasons. Not the least of these reasons is the belief that each individual has a creative capacity to transcend even standardized research conditions.

Therefore, Adler believed that individuals can be understood best within the social context of their transactions with others. He emphasized, however, the uniqueness of individuals determines their own movement through life, i.e., their life style.

Teleo

Teleo denotes the goal-striving nature of human beings. Behavior is purposive even though this facet may be obscure to the observer. Individuals choose to act or not act because it serves some purpose and utility for them.

Behavior is purposive.

Adler believed that man was not driven by instincts or molded by heredity, experience, or environment. Instead, he envisioned man as moving toward goals perceived as important to him.

> The science of Individual Psychology developed out of the effort to understand that mysterious creative power of life—that power which expresses itself in the desire to develop, to strive and to achieve—and even to compensate for defeats in one direction by striving for success in another. This power is *teleological*—it expresses itself in the striving after a goal. (Ansbacher, 1969, p.1)

Much has been written about the significance of inferiority. Ansbacher (1969) noted that Adler did not give a clear answer as to which had primacy in the development of the human being, goal striving or inferiority feelings. Ansbacher believed that goal striving should have primacy although he could not be conclusive in supporting this position. However, Adler believed in the purposive nature of man's striving. He observed that an individual's behavior could be understood best in relation to what he/she valued and moved toward achieving.

The teleological aspect of Adler's theory reveals the optimistic, encouraging nature of his position. Goals of behavior can be understood and anticipated. Individuals may choose to change the valuing of their goals and/or behavior which they use in their striving. Individuals are not victims of circumstances beyond their control in an absolute way.

Analytic

The analytic orientation to Individual Psychology is derived from the observation that most behavior is based upon that which is unconscious or nonunderstood (Mosak & Dreikurs, 1973, p. 39). Individuals frequently report that they do not understand their behavior or motives. Closer inspection reveals that individuals often understand more than they willingly admit. In a helping relationship, they more readily accept direct confrontations on the purposes of their behavior including some purposes previously unknown to them.

Adler and his followers have developed techniques for helping individuals to discover basic notions about themselves, others, and life. He was influenced by Vaihinger's (1965) "philosophy of 'as if.'" He concurred with Vaihinger that individuals behave "as if" circumstances were absolutely true. e.g., life is dangerous, I am weak, or others cannot be trusted. While some notions of individuals are stated clearly and believed beyond reproach, other notions are far more subtle and yet powerful influence upon behavior. Adler referred to them as fictive notions.

So long as individuals function fairly well in their daily life, their notions remain unexamined. When their notions are challenged or proved ineffective in maintaining feelings of belonging, what is often termed as an "emotional" crisis develops. Such are the times when counseling or psychotherapy are needed. Try as they may, individuals cannot truly discover and change their mistaken ideas and behaviors without assistance. Behavior may change and show accommodation to varying circumstance including age, cultural milieu, and similar factors. Life style is not believed to change, however, except through psychotherapy, personally powerful life experiences, or causes such as brain injury, drugs etc.

Early Development

As a means of studying Adler's psychology further, the development of personality as it unfolds from childbirth may be helpful. The child, thought totally dependent at birth, is by no means helpless in the strict sense of the term. From the Adlerian point of view, even infants begin training adults far better than many parents train their children.

Love and parental interest are
important ingredients to
personality development.

On the assumption that infants typically receive attention and care from the moment of their birth, they are the cause of activity. They begin learning about life, themselves, and others in the most fundamental ways. Bodily functions contribute to much of this activity in the early hours and days of life. As feeding, elimination, and other comforts become routine, the babies's attention may turn to sounds, touch, vague sights that intervene in their lives. Coping with these many involve crying, smiling, or any of a number of responses. Infants learn by their interpretation of the natural and social consequences which they experience with individuals around them. Adlerians often cite the example of perfectly healthy babies who do not cry, do not use their vocal capabilities. These cases have been babies born to deaf parents. These babies learn early that crying aloud serves no useful purpose, therefore, they simply wiggle, shed tears, and become red in the face.

Overconcerned or overprotective parents often lose an unnecessary amount of sleep and energy attending to noises coming from the baby's room. As will be seen in later sections, Adler definitely believed that love and parental interest are important ingredients to personality development. Unfortunately, pampering and overprotecting beyond what is reasonable, can be very dangerous. Babies under such circumstances may perceive that they are not able, that others must take care of them, or that terrible things may happen when their parents are away. If corrective training is not instituted during their early years, such notions or variations on them may become a part of their life style.

In most instances, children begin developing a sense of their strengths and weaknesses while attempting mastery over those aspects of being which seem within their reach. They also are beginning to make observations about their place in events around them. As their psychomotor capabilities develop, others' behavior toward them will change and they must decide how they will behave. If they are convinced of their belongingness and assess their capabilities as adequate, they will require less attention, service, and outward encouragement from those around them than previously.

Whether children make accurate assessments or not, they will behave according to their assessments. Adlerians believe that children usually are excellent observers, but they often are poor evaluators and interpreters of their experiences. As a consequence, feelings of inferiority are believed to be common because of their initial experiences as dependent, small, and socially inferior persons. Feelings of inferiority are not inherently good or bad. The individuals, for example, often move toward mastery and competence in compensations for these feelings. Through social interaction they further nurture their social interest and become persons others describe as full-functioning (Rogers, 1961), self-actualizating (Goldstein, 1939), and high in social interest (Adler, 1938). Children's responses to early experiences within the family unit, then have implications for how they approach their life tasks.

Family Constellation

Adler placed considerable importance upon the family constellation.

Family constellation is a term used to describe the socio-psychological configuration of a family group. The personality characteristics and emotional distance of each person, age differences, order of birth, the dominance or submission of each member, the siblings, and the size of the family are all factors in the family constellation and affect the development of the personality . . . certain behavior types can be characterized by examining the individuals's place in the constellation. Thus, the first born, the second born, and the only child have certain characteristics which render their personality predictable in terms of attitudes, personality traits and subsequent behavior. (Shulman & Nikelly, 1971, p. 35)

Children's position in the family has special significance. They derive impressions of their place in the family, their world at the time, by comparing themselves with whoever is closest to them. While much is often said about birth order or ordinal position in relation to the family constellation, Adlerians are aware that the individual's *psychological* position must be studied. A boy and girl in a family may be treated as two only children. Similarly, two children born ten years apart may be reared like only children.

The perceptions and recollections of our first six to eight years of life will reveal our psychological position, because during these years, Adler believed, the life style was established. Discussions with the children and parents also can reveal a child's psychological position.

With the qualification on family position noted, the ordinal descriptions of the position deserve identification. Adlerians typically list five ordinal positions: oldest, second, middle, youngest and only child. With each ordinal position is associated certain classical characteristics, but these characteristics are nomothetic impressions which are to be quickly set aside when idiographic data about a given individual refutes validity of the classical characteristics.

The oldest children can be typified as "king for a day." They are first and undisputed rulers of the family, the cause of glad tidings and happily the center of attention. One day a stranger appears in the house. Depending upon the proximity in months or years, parental attitudes, sex, and other such variables, the oldest children evaluate the threat to their position in the family. On the average, they learn to take the newcomer in stride, especially if parents are not too impressed with some likely acting-out behavior and provide encouragement for their oldest children to recognize their place as secure within the family.

Oldest children generally are able to relate well to adults, subscribe more readily to adult expectations and values, help at home particularly with the younger children, assume social responsibility, and develop socially acceptable ways of coping with life's tasks. The tendency of oldest children is to strive for perfection as a goal, which can have serious negative consequences to them.

The second children arrive to find someone already ahead of them. When within six years of the older child, and again depending upon age and similar variables, second children typically will pursue their place in ways opposite to the older child. They may be less responsible, more independent, more demanding of service, and more interested in whatever the oldest does not pursue or master. Second children often strive to be number one. The competitions, referred to as sibling rivalry, can be quite intense in families which encourage comparisons between children. They can be portrayed by the illustration of persons in a foot race. First children hear footsteps behind them and race to keep ahead. The second children see the person in front and feel that if they just try harder, maybe they can overtake them. Some individuals give up the race in discouragement. Others become admired as socially productive, although in some cases, they may gain only slight satisfaction from their efforts.

Middle children acquire an added condition to their existence, a younger sibling. Often in families of three, the middle children feel squeezed in their position. They perceive themselves as singularly disadvantaged. They have few, if any, advantages of the oldest youngster and now their position as baby has been supplanted. To help really convince them of their predicament, the oldest children often help take care of the youngest, thereby establishing for themselves an ally. The oldest may be seen as "bossy" toward the other children as well.

Middle children will likely still move in directions opposite to the older youngster. They may be more independent, rebellious, sensitive, and overtly seek assurances of their place with the parents. As is true with each position in the family, children can transcend these early perceptions through compensatory behavior which eventually works to their benefit. Each child often perceives his/her position as the most burdensome to bear.

Youngest children enjoy positions which they perceive as the center of attention. Not only do they have parents but also older siblings to entertain and provide them service. While the youngest children might be troublesome at times, they have a protector to care for them. In fact, as youngest children get a little older, it's even fun to start something with the middle child and watch the older ally and the parents run to save the "baby". They are often described as cute, a charmer, and the family's baby, no matter how old they become.

They may choose to use this charm and manipulative ways to just get by and enjoy life's many pleasures. On the other hand, with family values by both parents on achievement, they might be the hardest runners and greatest achievers of them all if they perceive that as a way to make their place.

The only children may have the perceptions of the oldest child with one important exception. They are never dethroned and are less likely to feel the pressure of a close competitor. The only children may be perceived as quite mature for their age, comfortable with adults, responsible, cooperative, and developing mastery in cognitive skills. Their most likely perceived deficiency will be in relating to their peer group. Unlike the other youngsters, they may have little or no intimate give and take with other children. This can make early school experiences more difficult for these children as they begin coping with new life situations involving a peer group.

Life Tasks

Adler believed that everyone is confronted by at least three major life tasks: work, friendship, and love (Dreikurs, 1953). In addition, Mosak, and Dreikurs (1967) have identified a fourth and fifth task only alluded to by Adler. The fourth task is man's dealing with spiritual self in reaction to the universe, God, and similar concepts. The fifth task concerns the individual's success in coping with self as subject, I, and as object, me. Only those discussed by Adler are presented here, although the next chapter addresses the others as well.

Work. Equipped with their unique rules or guidelines about life, themselves, and others, individuals move from childhood to preadolescence, adolescence, and adulthood with a societal expectation that they will become more responsible, cooperative, and able to cope with life situations. Lack of success in the work task is fundamental to the most discouraged people in society. Although gainful employment is not required, persons who find difficulty sustaining employment are in all probability individuals who lack confidence in their worth and ability.

In the school situation, failure and dropping out are tantamount to demotion and unemployment, i.e., loss of confidence and a sense of worth. Dreikurs (1968) believed that children who failed were not bad or lazy but, instead, discouraged. To face and fulfill one's life tasks requires the courage to be imperfect, to make mistakes, to fail occasionally but to try again. For too many children, school becomes a confirmation of their private assessment, i.e., they are not adequate. In later life, many of these individuals will be found consistently unemployed, welfare recipients, or institutionalized. Although it appears difficult for persons to change in later life, Adler believed that we always have that capability.

Friendship and Love. Dreikurs (1953) indicated that discouragement generally was not limited to one life task area. For example, most individuals can cope with the daily requirements of work whether by gainful employment or through services to others. Doubts, reservations, and fears may reveal themselves only at times. Friendship and intimate love relationships tend to be more demanding of cooperation, give and take and respect. If an individual has persistent difficulties in either or both of these life tasks, discouragement is present which probably can be noted in the other areas as well. As will be noted in Chapter 8, not all life task difficulties can be traced to psychosocial origin. Dreikurs (1946) has observed that whenever individuals persistently complain, blame, make excuses, report fears, or discuss disabilities, they are revealing discouragement.

Of life tasks, love relationships require that greatest courage and faith in self and the other party. Our weaknesses, concerns, and peculiarities come under closer scrutiny than in most other life situations. Adlerians have observed, for example, that the very characteristics which attract individuals to one another also contribute to their friction in marriage. Frequently, our cultural "it's a man's world" orientation which Adler discussed under the concept of masculine protest, encourages stereotyped notions such as a "real" man brings home the family income and the woman cares for the children and serves the husband. Problems of partners do not normally surface openly until the relationship becomes quite disturbed, even though they could have been predicted on the basis of life style analysis.

Not all such complementary, yet friction-producing, qualities can be stereotyped by societal circumstances. For example, in one case a husband always had the greatest regard for his wife's opinion, so much so that he depended upon her to make most of the major family decisions because he doubted the reliability of his own decisions. On the other hand, she had admired his industriousness and goal-oriented attitudes toward life. After three children and several years of married life, the wife felt isolated from him. He never participated in family decisions; in fact, he was so busy with his work that she felt she meant hardly anything to him.

He initially felt threatened by her confrontations and somewhat confused by what seemed to be happening. She wanted him to work less and to participate more in family decisions. Through counseling they came to understand and anticipate their conflicts by establishing a new agreement for working together.

As Adler had noted, once these individuals understood their own movement through life, they could decide to change their attitudes and behavior with renewed respect for themselves and one another. They were able, in this case, to establish behavioral ways of short-circuiting old expectations, including the husband's low estimate of his decision-making ability.

Function of Emotions and Feelings

Emotions are multifaceted. Izard (1977) in a scientifically oriented exposition, describes three levels of emotion as neurophysiological, neuromuscular, and conscious and intuitive. In the first level, electrochemical activity is described. At the second level, the facial-muscular response is explored. The meaning and significance of an emotion is at the third level. While aware of the importance of the first two levels, counselors are most concerned with the third level, that which helps discern intentions and goals.

Frequently, counselors will be told in a variety of ways that individuals cannot help themselves—they just feel so angry, sad, bored, or whatever that they must behave as they do. Adler, of course, would not accept these evasions of responsibility. While excuses take many forms, emotions often are identified as central to the problems which individuals bring to counselors.

We record our impressions,
including feelings, for
future reference.

Because confusion often surrounds the terms "emotion" and "feelings," Gaylin's (1979) definitions may be helpful:

> Emotion—is the general term which encompasses the feeling tone, the biophysical state, and even the chemical changes. . .[that] underline the sensations we experience.

> Feeling—is our subjective awareness of our own emotional state. It is that which we experience; that which we know about our current emotional condition. (p. 1)

Witmer (1985) provided an excellent chapter on feelings and their purpose. He noted that they are internal indicators, external signals, and motivational directives. They reveal the internal impact of external events upon the mind and body. When danger exists, they can help with defense or survival. In cases of growth and enhancement, they provide pleasurable sensations which reinforce and further continued nurturing. They function as external signals by communicating intentions to others.

Adler conceptualized emotions and feelings in much the same way. He perceived emotions as tools necessary to the execution of behavior. Emotions are not considered entities unto themselves. Love, joy, anger, sadness, guilt, and fear do not come to us out of a vacuum. We must first perceive, value, feel, and then, act.

Remembering that much of our valuing in regard to life, ourselves, and others is a blueprint already stored in our unconscious thought processes, much of what is attributed to instant love, fear, or anger can be traced back to one's life style data bank. Harris (1969) referred to the individual's "tapes" from early experiences. As we grow and experience, we "record" our impressions, including feelings, for future reference.

Many counselees will wish to discredit this concept of emotions because it places responsibility on them for their present decisions and actions. As will be seen in subsequent chapters, Adlerians are very much interested in emotions but more as signposts to the individual's mistaken notions and their intentions. As Dreikurs (1967) and Ellis (1962) have explained, messages we send ourselves build the energy we use to act. We do not "fall in love" as struck by a cupid's arrow.

Our blueprint helps us process impressions of others to which we respond rather automatically, sometimes quite incorrectly. In the absence of knowledge or experience, we do not feel anything until we can fit it into our system of expectations.

Observers of the Adlerian counselor might conclude that he/she is very insensitive to the anger, complaining, blaming, tears, or affection expressed in a counseling session. If the emotions are tools used by the counselee to distract or otherwise manipulate the counselor from the goals for counseling, he/she indeed may seem unimpressed by their presence. The less visible feelings and attitudes are what the Adlerian will pursue, e.g., isolation, lack of confidence, and insecurity.

Holistic View

The indivisibility of a person is a fundamental belief of Adlerian psychology. At a time when holistic approaches to medicine, mental health, and rehabilitation are coming into the forefront, the practitioner will find its usefulness apparent. When dealing with a wide range of people and circumstances, the probabilities of any one science or discipline being able to adequately explain, diagnose, or prescribe treatment for all the ills of people are nil. The author, therefore, continually seeks and incorporates new knowledge of human behavior into this approach.

In the most basic form, one recognizes the interaction between physical and psychological well being. Biofeedback research and its application in stress management has helped to corroborate Adler's assumption that what one thinks can produce physiological symptoms similar to those of other origin. Infection, disease, and other injury to the body are potentially mood modifying. Fatigue, particularly due to distress, is symptomatic of the interaction of mind and body. In short, even personal experience suggests the validity of such position.

Adler was not first as a proponent of this point of view. As Witmer (1985) noted:

> The concept of health and wellness as encompassing mind-body unity reaches back thousands of years to middle eastern religions, the ancient Greeks, and Far Eastern philosophies. Greek medical tradition like the Jewish healing tradition exemplified in Christ, treated the whole person. Mind and body were not separated but seen as interrelated and interdependent. (p.43)

Another area of study which tends to support the usefulness of a holistic view of human behavior concerns nutrition. Smith (1976) and Reuben (1978) represent different points of view but serve to illustrate the growing interest and study of nutrition and its impact on human behavior and attitudes. While most persons recognize the deleterious effects which drugs can have on their mind and body, far fewer are conscious of how excesses of sugar or preservatives can do violence to them or their children.

For years women have used various contraceptives not knowing that their systems were experiencing significant nutritional losses which affected other aspects of their being (Seaman & Seaman, 1977). With such knowledge, we are now able to integrate this into a broader framework for understanding behavior. Teamwork among disciplines and practitioners is based upon such a point of view.

Adlerian practitioners also are aware that samples of an individuals behavior can help counselors to understand a more global life plan and direction of movement. Such behaviors, however, are only an approximation of the total and must be kept in proper perspective as such. One can anticipate, for example, that difficulty in sustaining friendships because of excessive demands for attention or unreliability would contribute to problems in marriage or love relationships. The greater intimacy, give and take, and equalitarian nature of love would be under even more stress than friendships. The fact than one chooses not to marry, however, would not necessarily indicate a lack of capacity for personal commitment, empathy, and courage required in a loving relationship.

Holism, then, is a point of view from which to understand others as dynamic, self-directed, interrelated mind and body moving through life with a unique plan for having significance in relation to others. Helping counselees change how they think and feel in their relationships with others, for example, can result in better physical health, greater satisfaction with their work, and increased joy and interest in other aspects of their lives.

Value System

Adlerians occasionally are charged with being manipulative in their practice. Dreikurs believed that this was true in the sense that when anyone influences another, he/she is manipulative. Dreikurs (1971) has helped to open the Adlerian value orientations to critical analysis. Adlerian presuppositions for practice rest upon a belief that individuals who are high in social interest will think of themselves and others as equals and behave accordingly. Dreikurs believed that if individuals valued themselves as equal to everyone else, the major problems of society would be virtually eliminated. He observed that in approximately 8,000 years of man's social existence, we have tried to function on the mistaken premises of authoritarian systems which continually fail to solve the problems of man.

As early as 1946, Dreikurs (1946) predicted that women, blacks, children, and other minorities would progressively demand equality, the unfulfilled American dream. Anyone reading his book on marriage would be inclined to believe it was written in this decade rather than in the 40s. Adler, predating the world wars, similarly was far ahead of his time in this regard. Those who perceive themselves as being in power do not relinquish it readily. The upheaval of the last decade is evidence, however, that large groups of minorities, including children, no longer intend to tolerate disregard and inequality from the traditional "superiors." Authority from on high is questioned. Power among the few is suspect. Dreikurs was concerned, however, that without education to a more satisfactory agreement among mankind, the underdogs would simply strive to overcome the top dogs and repeat the cycle at some further time.

In the same sense that many individuals strive toward goals of superiority, power, wealth, or position, groups similarly seek to be in control of others. The great emphasis in our society on competition and the external signs of superiority is further testimony to the preoccupation with control and influences. In such circumstances, cooperation too often becomes compromise of a temporary nature.

The values which Dreikurs (1971) proposed in lieu of those now found in society include:

Present	Proposed
ambition	enthusiasm
righteousness	friendliness
	understanding
obligation	belongingness
	participation
conformity	self-respect
	self-improvement
perfection	courage
rugged	mutual help
individualism	cooperation

Adlerians believe that you cannot make others do anything which they do not consider useful to them. Therefore, in spite of many efforts, some individuals will not change their behavior or attitudes even in the face of discomfort or inconvenience. This is predicated on the concept that all behavior is purposive, i.e., it serves a use for individuals to pursue their goals. From their unique perceptions of life, individuals may consider changing as dangerous or at least difficult.

On the other hand, Adler made a distinction between the behaviors which move individuals toward others, i.e., high social interest, and those which move them against or away from others (Adler in Ansbacher & Ansbacher, 1967, p. 158). The latter behaviors were denoted as socially useless, self-defeating behaviors. While all behaviors are "useful" from the individual's point of view, the Adlerian value system would note that some attitudes detract from the individual's self-esteem and, consequently, social interest.

Attitudes and behaviors which result in an individual's avoiding or failing to meet basic life tasks would be considered on the useless side of life by Adler. Because this is a "psychology of use and not inventory," Adlerians do not typically label these behaviors in categories according to symptoms. One way of conceptualizing the relative movement of an individual in the direction of social interest is depicted in Figure 1.1.

Low Social Interest:

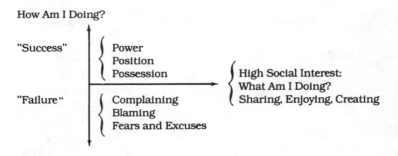

Figure 1.1. Social Interest Continua: Vertical (Low) vs Horizontal (High).

Persons moving primarily on a vertical plane are most concerned about how they are doing in their endeavors. They constantly are evaluating and comparing their efforts to others or to a fictive notion of perfection which they strive to attain. Persons who actively move in this direction often are identified as productive, "successful" people in their field. They are typified by the driving, Type A personality (Friedman & Ulmer, 1984). A sad commentary on their striving is that they rarely gain much satisfaction from their efforts or the outcome because of a nagging concern that what was gained may be lost. The "can you top this" feeling may persist long after evidence substantiates the person's competence or adequacy.

The horizontal plan in Figure 1.1 denotes movement toward enjoyment and participation in life activities. Persons evaluate their activities on the basis of the satisfaction they and/or others gain from them. This portrayal of movement should not be construed to indicate that high social interest individuals do not enjoy competition or that the low social interest persons gain no satisfaction from their work. Actually most persons are somewhere in between the two directions of movement.

The difference might be observed, for example, in a competitive game or sport. High social interest persons may play very hard to win but will have enjoyed the game, win or lose. Low social interest individuals who lose, if they play at all, will in contrast feel defeated, possibly even disgusted with themselves, until they can reestablish themselves as winner. As will be illustrated in Chapter 6, Adlerians are conscious of this distinction particularly with regard to the application of behavior modification related techniques in school situations. The indiscriminate use of rewards to reinforce achievement or social behavior also can reinforce the individual for moving vertically (extrinsic motivation) rather than horizontally (intrinsic motivation) (Greene & Lepper, 1974).

Validation

Adlerian theory and practice are validated primarily by use and incorporation into several other systems or approaches to counseling. Allen (1971a) and Mosak and Dreikurs (1973) identified virtually every major personality approach to counseling and psychotherapy with the notable exception of traditional psychoanalysis, as incorporating Adlerian principles and techniques into its system. These authors compared the major premises and techniques of Adler with Rogers, Maslow, Phillips, Horney, Glasser, Sullivan, Ellis, Fromm, Frankl, May, and others. While some authors have credited Adler with holding similar ideas or as a foundation for certain of their practices, others seem unaware of his works or at least do not acknowledge them.

Many studies have been made of birth order over the years. Data from these have been conflicting due in large measure to methodological shortcomings and insufficient insight by the investigators concerning the difference between psychological position and birth order. Nevertheless, some interesting observations tend to confirm the experience of Adlerian practitioners that eldest children tend to be leaders. For example, eight out of nine presidents of the United States who were elected or served during a time of war were oldest or only sons. The ninth president was elected two years before the war suddenly took place. In quieter times, only eight of twenty-one presidents were first born sons or only sons.

Overall, Stewart (Goodall, 1972) reported that 52% of all presidents were first sons and 32% were third sons. Of some importance was the observation that 45% of presidents were from families with four or more sons. He reported similar findings when studying the birth order patterns of vice-presidents, defeated presidential and vice-presidential candidates, and sixty-four prime ministers of Great Britain. Other studies tend to affirm the special position of first born children but always with qualifications which only corroborate the Adlerian emphasis upon both idiographic and nomothetic considerations.

Because Alderians have tended to work and be trained in nonuniversity settings in the past, the paucity of research on Adlerian methods is not surprising. Mosak and Dreikurs (1973) predicted that more research would be conducted by Adlerians in university settings and would be found in the literature more frequently in the future. There is some evidence that they predicted accurately.

What follows are some reports on the effectiveness and validity of Adlerian theory and methods. An early study by Platt (1971) established the effectiveness of Adlerian methods in the elementary school classroom. A study by Taylor and Hoedt (1974) reported the effectiveness of parent and teacher groups compared to electic group counseling with elementary school children in effecting changes in the children's behavior. The authors of the latter study concluded that working with adults was more effective than working only with the children.

A similar result was found by Hoffman (1975) in a study involving high school students and their teachers. In this case, the greatest change was observed in student behaviors in which the teacher participated in a consultation group led by the school counselor and students received group counseling concurrently. Next most effective was the teacher consultation group and finally the counseling group for students. All treatment groups received the assistance of an Adlerian trained counselor. All treatment groups resulted in significant positive change in target student classroom behaviors after a nine week period. Control group students made no significant change in the same period.

A variety of studies have been reported (Burnett, 1988; Sweeney & Moses, 1979) which document the usefulness of parent and teacher study-consultation groups. Burnett (1988) concluded:

The research studies . . . strongly support the effectiveness of Adlerian parenting programs. Changes in a positive direction were noted on measures of children's behavior, children's self-concept, parental behavior, and parental attitude. The studies were, one the whole, methodolically sound. (p. 74)

The evaluation of multimedia approaches have been added to the more traditional study group methods (Kerney, 1980; Kibler, Rush, & Sweeney, 1985; McKay & Hillman, 1979; Rush, 1978). One of the promising aspects of these study group methods is the capability of assisting parents or others in child care without the requirement that they must read in order to understand the methods. Films, audio-tapes, and poster illustrations supplement the leader's material.

In studies of a different nature, early recollections were used to predict counselor empathy (Altman, 1973) and counselor effectiveness based on expert judgements of counselor social interest (Zarski, Barcikowski, & Sweeney, 1977). In both cases, significant positive correlations were found between counselor social interest scores and dependent variables. These findings tend to corroborate Adler's concept of social interest as a global description of positive mental health. The higher the social interest scores, the greater the empathy and effectiveness as a counselor based on counselee outcome measures. Unfortunately, subsequent studies using similar methods have been unsuccessful in corroborating the findings regarding social interest and counselor effectiveness. This seems to be due in part to difficulties in developing appropriate instruments, easily used and interpreted.

Kern, Matheny, and Patterson (1978) provided a critical analysis of research on Adlerian theory and methods. They noted that Adlerian techniques have been applied most often with teachers, parents, and students in educational settings and with parents and young children in parent study groups and family education centers. At the time of their review, they concluded:

> Clients more positively affected by the approach are pre-adolescent and adolescent youth experiencing difficulty with classroom behavior, school achievement or interpersonal relationships. Adults benefiting most from the approach are classroom teachers and parents of young children . . . There is scant evidence . . . with clinical populations such as social offenders, alcoholics and other drug abusers, severely emotionally disturbed, and psychosomatic patients. . .We feel certain that Adlerians counselors are working with these populations. It is disappointing that so little has been done to demonstrate the effectiveness of the approach in working with these clients. (p. 89)

Kern et al. also cite studies which support such constructs as life style, goals of misbehavior, private logic, social interest and the techniques of logical consequences, encouragement, class meetings, and disengagement.

Subsequent chapters will cite other relevant research which pertain to specific topical areas. More studies are needed, however, to add to the theory and practice of Adlerian psychology. Although Adlerian practitioners, including hundreds of lay group leaders and Family Education Center volunteers, are satisfied with its utility and face validity, experimental data will no doubt increase its credibility with publics of a different persuasion.

SUMMARY

The Individual Psychology of Alfred Adler is enjoying recognition and use unprecedented in its history. Even as other systems incorporate or independently discover principles and methods essentially Adlerian in nature, Adlerian institutes, study groups, and practitioners increase in number. Central concepts to this approach include:

1. Human beings are social beings who are essentially self-determining, purposive, and creative (idiographic) in their approaches to making a place for themselves in life.

2. Individuals are best understood holistically in their functioning from a phenomenological (subjective) point of view.

3. The life style, the individual's unique set of convictions about himself/herself, life and others, is the map or outline which he/she uses to guide him/her in approaching basic life tasks: work, friendship, love, self, and spirit. Established by the age of six to eight, it remains basically unexamined and unchanged under normal circumstances.

4. Unsuccessful coping with basic life tasks is a sign of discouragement. Discouragement can be overcome early in life relatively easily; however, it always can be overcome at anytime in life if the individual chooses to do so.

5. Social interest is Adler's conceptualization of a quality in human beings which constitutes their proclivity for being responsible, cooperative, and creative members of

humankind. Persons high in social interest enjoy and like themselves, others, and life. Social interest must be nurtured, however, or the individual's faulty perceptions of himself/herself can result in discouraged, self-defeating behaviors.

6. Adlerians tend to subscribe to a value system based upon social democracy with equality of people at the core. Their approach to helping other people is basically educative and preventative in nature, although remedial and crisis intervention work is also carried out.

Further elaboration upon these and related concepts will be found in succeeding chapters in the discussion of methods and techniques of Individual Psychology with individuals and groups.

STUDY QUESTIONS

Directions: Respond to the following in the spaces provided.

1.(a) Explain the concept of goal directed behavior, i.e., behavior is purposive.

(b) Do you agree? _____ If not, why?

2. What is meant by "socio-teleo-analytic" as descriptions for this approach?

3.(a) What is the function of emotions?

(b) Where do emotions originate?

(c) In what ways can emotions be useful or disruptive socially?

4.(a) Which of the life tasks is most easily met?

(b) Which of the life tasks is most difficult to meet?

(c) Why are the responses to "a" and "b" as they are?

J. MELVIN WITMER
College of Education
Ohio University
Athens, Ohio 45701

J. Melvin Witmer, Ph.D., is a Professor of Counselor Education at Ohio University. He is a Licensed Professional Clinical Counselor, a Psychologist, and a National Certified Counselor. He has been a professor, consultant, and workshop leader in counseling and human development for more than 20 years. His being a teacher in elementary, secondary, and higher education gives him a developmental perspective on how people grow and learn. Experience in school counseling, school psychology and a private practice continue to motivate him to search for barriers that inhibit growth and the beliefs and behaviors that develop human potential.

For the last decade, Mel has been directing research in stress management, conducting stress workshops, and through teaching and professional organizations, working to improve the quality of counseling services by licensing and ethical means. Currently, he is interested in the application of health psychology and behavioral medicine to the treatment of stress-related illnesses and the quality of life. Recent presentations at professional conferences and continuing education workshops include the use of imagery in counseling, the magic of metaphors in counseling, and the characteristics of psychologically healthy people and wholeness. In his 1985 book, *Pathways to Personal Growth,* he described the process of developing one's potential, striving for wellness, understanding emotions, encouraging others, teaching values, and coping with stress. More than 45 dissertations have been directed, 15 of them related to the nature of stress and its intervention. Mel has received seven awards from various professional organizations for his leadership and service to the profession of counseling.

Personal interests include photography, indoor and outdoor gardening, jogging, sailing, traveling, and vacationing with the family. Occasionally, he escapes to his fantasy island off the South Carolina coast where his favorite pastime is walking along the beach.

CHAPTER 2

REACHING TOWARD WHOLENESS

J. Melvin Witmer, Ph.D.
College of Education
Ohio University

Health to you! The Greek people use this as a greeting and farewell expression. The Greek word **yiasoo** which means "health to you" has its historical origin with Hygea, the goddess of health. She was an expert on teaching the ways of living in harmony with nature in order to prevent disease. The Hebrew word **shalom** has historically been used as a greeting and farewell to express a personal wish of peace and "completeness" or a sense of wholeness to another person. In German, **Gesundheit** is used to wish health and wholesomeness. **Health** is an Old English term that shares a root meaning with the words hale, heal, and whole. The above terms all infer a wish for a soundness of body, free from disease or infirmity, in which inner harmony, balance, and wholeness may exist. Many cultures have language expressions that convey a message of well-being for greeting another person.

What is the origin and nature of this wholeness? Does a single motivating force move and direct the organism in a given direction? Adler (1954) in his writings to acquaint the general public with the fundamentals of Individual Psychology, observed that, "The psychic life is a complex of aggressive and security-finding activities whose final purpose is to guarantee the continued existence on this earth of the human organism, and to enable him to securely accomplish his development" (p. 28).

Maslow (1970) in his pioneerning work that led to the development of humanistic psychology, studied the characteristics of healthy persons. He noted that:

> Human life will never be understood unless its highest aspirations are taken into account. Growth, self-actualization, the striving toward health, the quest for identity and autonomy, the yearning for excellence (and other ways of phrasing the striving "upward") must by now be accepted beyond question as a widespread and perhaps universal human tendency. (pp. xii and xiii)

Maslow appears to be drawing heavily from Adler in describing the single purpose of life as striving to be "fully human," a process of self-actualization.

In this reaching toward human potential or the possibilities in being human, two counteracting forces function to sustain life and fulfill the individual's potential for health and happiness (Witmer, 1985). One force strives to protect and defend the organism against harm, the other strives to nurture and enhance its well-being.

> One force strives to protect and defend the self, both the physical and psychological self. This protective force clings to safety and defensiveness, tending to provide security, afraid to move away from that which is known. It is afraid of independence, freedom, separateness, and newness. The other force impels the individual toward wholeness and uniqueness of self, toward a fuller functioning of pleasures and capacities. It moves forward and outward to create and enhance existence. One force provides safety and satisfaction, the other growth and satisfaction. (Witmer, 1985, p. 15).

Human behavior, then, is directed toward a goal. "The psychic life of man is determined by his goal" (Adler, 1954, p. 29). This teleology, striving toward a future goal, is ever-present in the movement and activities of an individual. Therefore, to understand the goal of an individual we must note the present activities. Instead of looking to the past for causality in explaining human actions, consciously and subconsciously motivated actions are viewed as reflecting the intent or outcome desired by the person.

In order to achieve the genetic destination to develop and protect the growth and well-being of the organism, the individual formulates a *life plan.* Out of this life plan develops a *life style,* an orientation toward life that is powered by a *fictional goal* (Dinkmeyer, Pew, & Dinkmeyer, 1979). In early childhood, the person develops a *fictional image* of what he/she has to do to enhance and protect existence. This fictional image becomes a **central goal** of the person's life style, guided by subjective notions of what one has to be like or do to be safe, to feel a sense of belonging, or to be superior. All of these notions are perceived by the individual as essential to well-being.

However, the fictional goal may be **self-defeating** as well as **self-enhancing** because of mistaken notions shaped by the person's private logic, and influenced by genetic, cultural, and family factors, as well as early experiences. Discovering what these fictional goals are becomes an important process in eliminating self-defeating behavior or facilitating self-enhancing behavior in reaching toward wholeness.

The individual in playing out the drama of life so that the ultimate purpose may be achieved also is confronted by *life tasks.* Adler (Dreikurs, 1953) proposed that as a member of the human community, we must engage in at least three life tasks—*friendship, love,* and *work.* The extent to which one is successful in these is an indicator of the individual's level of maturity. Adler alluded to fourth and fifth life tasks (Mosak & Dreikurs, 1967). The fourth task is the individual's dealing with a *spiritual self* in relation to the cosmos, God, and universal values. Fifth is the task of *defining and affirming one's self,* both in a subjective and objective way. The life plan with its private logic and fictional goal becomes the *cognitive map* for beliefs and behaviors the individual uses to negotiate the life tasks. This plan ideally ought to nurture a healthy life style in quality of life as well as for longevity of life.

Considerable research has accumulated in the last two decades that describes the characteristics of the healthy person, especially the psychological dimensions of wholeness. A classical and landmark study was that done by Maslow (1968; 1970) in which he identified the characteristics of self-actualizing people whose nature constituted a high level of psychological health. These characteristics, summarized as 14 dimensions by Witmer (1985), range from superior perception of reality, to spontaneity and naturalness, to genuine social interest and identification with the human race. Numerous disciplines are now contributing to our expanding knowledge about the healthy person: humanistic psychology, anthropology (neoteny), developmental stage theory, quality of life and well-being research, longevity research, personality and behavior, behavioral medicine, psychosomatic medicine, stress research, and health psychology.

Wholeness is an integral part of the "changing consciousness" as described by Willis Harman (1988) in his new book, *Global Mind Change: The Promise of the Last Years of the Twentieth Century.* He has characterized the changing internal image of reality as having five aspects: search for wholeness, search for community and relationship, search for identity, search for meaning, and sense of empowerment. Wholeness is an integral part of all of the "reperception" that has been taking place in the United States and to some extent throughout the world in the last 20 years. In a variety of ways the perception is being expressed that life is whole and something is wrong with a society that breaks it into fragments (Harman, 1988).

Chapter 2 is a summarization of the literature that describes the nature of health, well-being, and wholeness. Ten characteristics emerge. They are noted metaphorically in Figure 2.1 according to the life task that is engaged. The life tasks and characteristics might be conceptualized as a wheel of wholeness with spirituality as the hub and the other nine dimensions as spokes in the wheel. With spirituality as the center, the other nine are integrated to perform the life tasks which constitute the tread or rim which makes contact with the road of life.

SPIRITUAL CENTEREDNESS

"The destiny of man lies in his soul." Herodotus

From the earliest known recordings of human activity, evidence is abundant of a belief in a force or being greater and

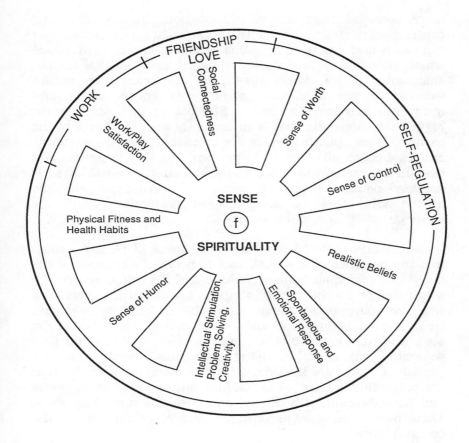

The world is a wheel and it will all come round right.   Old Proverb

Figure 2.1. Life tasks and the characteristics of the healthy person that make up wholeness. The hub and the rim of the wheel make up the four life tasks: sense of spirituality, self-regulation, work, and friendship and love. Spirituality in the hub and the nine spokes constitute the ten characteristics of wholeness.

more powerful than oneself. Throughout history including contemporary times, every civilization, culture, or nation has expressed and practiced religious beliefs that represent values which reflect what is considered sacred and essential for the sustenance of life. With some this has focused on nature worship, others a divine person who knows about and intervenes in human activities. Still others seek an inner or higher consciousness that is in harmony with the forces of the cosmos. These spiritual beliefs are translated into ethical, moral, and legal codes, all of which in part are intended to protect and sustain the sacredness of life. Individual character and life style are developed in a way that is thought to nurture the soul while at the same time be acceptable or harmonious with the supreme being/force of the universe.

Adler (1954) noted that the uniqueness of human beings was the presence of a soul. A soul is necessary because of the individual's freedom to move. Reason and the will to act require a spiritual or psychic life to interact with the environment in a way that guarantees existence and achieves fuller development. He seemed to use the concept of soul as a way to describe the sum and substance of the "psychic life," which makes us separate from all other living organisms. Faculties of the psychic life that are important to the development of the soul are perception, memory, imagination, fantasy, dreams, empathy and identification with others, and hypnosis and suggestion. These psychic faculties serve to give shape and meaning to the cosmic picture.

Purposiveness

Purposiveness (teleology) in the psychic life is central to Adlerian psychology. *"The psychic life of man is determined by his goal.* No human being can think, feel, will, dream, without all these activities being determined, continued, modified and directed toward an ever-present objective" (Adler, 1954, p. 29). Thus all phenomena of the soul life may be seen as preparation for some future situation. All manifestations of the human soul are therefore understood as directed toward a goal.

Purpose or meaning in life has been the primary concern of all the world's great religions. Serving God, a creator, or recognizing a life force, respecting one's fellow human beings, and achieving an inner state of harmony and God-consciousness are aspects of religious emphases. Beliefs, rituals, and lifestyles have been developed to assign a certain sacredness to life. These spiritual beliefs and practices are intended to sustain and enhance life, even beyond one's existence in life on Earth.

This valuing of life was eloquently described by Albert Schweitzer (1965), renowned theologian and missionary doctor. He taught that reverence for life was the fundamental principle of ethics upon which the ethics of civilization depends. If life is not regarded as intrinsically valuable, humankind's relationship to God, nature, and fellow-beings dissolves. "The principle of reverence for life includes an elemental sense of responsibility to which we must submit with all our being" (p. 32).

> The essence of Goodness is: Preserve life, promote life, help life to achieve its highest destiny. The essence of Evil is: Destroy life, harm life, hamper the development of life . . . The fundamental principle of ethics, then, is reverence for life. (Schweitzer, 1965, p. 26)

Purposiveness is found through the different life tasks. However, if a healthy spiritual self is not developed, lasting satisfaction is not likely to be found. The soul continues to seek an inner peace and joy that can be found only in confronting oneself and connecting with a cosmic spirituality of harmony, beauty, and justice. Pleasure and satisfaction can be achieved through success in the other three life tasks but until the spiritual self is affirmed, the center of wholeness is incomplete.

Longevity research seeks to explore the biological and psychosocial factors that contribute to an extended life expectancy while maintaining optimum health. Pelletier (1981) in summarizing the longitudinal studies of longevity reported the single most accurate predictor is life style. Factors relating life style to longevity are work satisfaction, happiness and overall life satisfaction, being married, positive religious attitudes, being physically and mentally active, and being creative. In studies of centenarian communities, Pelletier (1981) reported that the psychological dimensions that make up the social environment that contributes to their long life include "prolonged and productive involvement in family and community affairs, an acquired status of dignity and wisdom, and an enduring sense of the meaning and purpose of life itself" (p. 306).

Stress research is another source of data for understanding the characteristics of the healthy person. In studying 670 male telephone company executives in Illinois, Kobasa (1979) found that psychological hardiness could decrease chances of becoming ill by as much as 50%. Her study of life events, health, and personality has pinpointed "three C's" that preserve good health even amidst great stress—challenge, commitment, and control. The high-stress, low-illness executives showed more hardiness, that is, held a stronger commitment to self, an attitude of vigorousness toward the environment, a sense of meaningfulness, and an internal locus of control. Kobasa found that the three hardiness factors of challenge, commitment, and control accurately predicted well-being regardless of exercise and family medical history. A second study of the same population with a prospective design was continued over a five year period by Kobasa, Maddi, and Kahn (1982). Their results demonstrated that hardiness decreased the likelihood of symptom onset.

The commitment factor was described by Kobasa (1979) and Maddi and Kobasa (1984) as the opposite of alienation with persons involved in whatever they were doing. It is expressed as a tendency to involve oneself in (rather than experience alienation from) whatever one is, does, or encounters. Such persons have a generalized sense of purpose that allows them to identify with and find meaningful events, things, and persons of their environment. They involve themselves in the activity wholeheartedly, are rarely at a loss for things to do. In contrast, alienated people find things boring or meaningless and hang back from involvement in the tasks they have to do. Often they are at a loss about what to do with leisure time.

The meaning that people ascribe to their life experiences appears to influence their psychological and physical health, even when the event is a negative or threatening one. Several studies have shown that any answer to the question "Why me?" is better than no answer (Affleck, Pfeiffer, Tennen, & Fifield, in press; Bulman & Wortman, 1977; DuCette & Keane, 1984). Finding positive meaning in the face of adversity may have its origin with one's religious or spiritual beliefs. The search for or creation of meaning for understanding life events appears to be a powerful motive. Associated with these beliefs may be a sense of general optimism, an aspect of the spiritual self to be discussed next.

Optimism

Adler (1954) described optimism as a belief and a feeling-tone that enables children to express power with confidence in solving the problems which they meet. They grow up with the characteristics of individuals who consider the tasks of life within their power. "We see the development of courage, openness, frankness, responsibility, industry, and the like. The opposite of this is the development of pessimism" (p. 330). In understanding human beings, Adler stated that one criterion to use is the manner in which they approach difficulties, and noted that optimists and pessimists approach difficult tasks differently. Optimists are individuals whose character (personality) development, by and large, progressed without serious delays.

> They approach all difficulties courageously and do not take them too seriously. They maintain their belief in themselves and assume a happy attitude toward life with comparative ease. They do not demand too much of life because they have a good evaluation of themselves and do not consider themselves neglected or insignificant. Thus they are able to bear the difficulties of life more easily than others who find difficulties only further justification for believing themselves weak and inadequate. In the more difficult situations the optimists remain quiet in the conviction that mistakes can always be rectified. (p. 142)

Hope and optimism are eternal to the human spirit wherever humankind is found. The meaning of the events present and past may be unclear or discouraging. Future events are unpredictable. Yet the inclination of the psyche, Adler would say the soul, is to have hope, which is a wish or desire that is anticipated or expected. Optimism is the expression of hope that with a certain degree of confidence one can expect either the best possible outcome or to dwell upon the most hopeful aspects of a situation. Both dimensions of optimism are important, the expectation of a desirable outcome and focusing on the positive aspects of the situation. When a disposition to expect positive outcomes is present, beliefs and behaviors of the individual tend to motivate the person to create and seek opportunities for the hopes to come true.

Hope springs internal as well as eternal. Hoping for the best may have a biological origin. Lionel Tiger (1979) in his book, *Optimism: The Biology of Hope,* develops a strong argument that optimism is a biological phenomenon. Human beings are made happier by optimistic thoughts than despairing ones. Optimism as an attitude, mood, or strategy for anticipating outcomes and undecided situations "is as much a part of human nature, of the human biology, as are the shape of the body, the growth of children, and the zest of sexual pleasure" (p. 15). It is as necessary as air for the long-range well-being of the individual. Tiger cites numerous studies of the neurochemistry of internal opiates and argues that

> these findings are directly relevant to the possibility that there is a location in the brain for the good feelings about the future. For the first time we may be on the way to finding a specific source for notions of personal well-being and for the sense of optimism in one's life. (p. 151)

Tiger also argues that religion, since it is deeply intertwined with optimism, is a biological phenomenon (p. 40). Although religions around the world have great differences, they all support communal social bonds and all offer people opportunities to organize their concerns about their future in this life and in a life hereafter. Through religion the brain constructs notions of the future called *imaginal thinking.* The positive thoughts and the optimistic feelings caused by endocrine secretions motivate people to plan and act in ways that provide survival and security for the future. The popularity of the book, *The Power of Positive Thinking* by Norman Vincent Peale (1956) is one example of how optimism through religion in the last quarter century has had such a broad appeal.

Another source of information supporting optimism as part of human nature is *neoteny,* an aspect of anthropology which emphasizes early childhood traits that are retained into later stages of individual development. Of much interest from a developmental perspective is Asley Montagu's (1981) *Growing Young*, a treatise on extending and retaining early traits into adult life. "The child is the forerunner of humanity—forerunner in the sense that the child is the possessor of all those traits that, when healthily developed, lead to a healthy and fulfilled humanity" (p. 130). If we wish to know what traits should be extended into adulthood for a healthy human being, we have only to watch children to see them displayed.

Montagu has compiled from scientific writings a list of 26 needs or drives observed in the very early life of children. One of these is optimism. He noted that children are natural optimists for the future appears to them to be full of promises that will be fulfilled with growth. Living in a world of rising expectations, the child puts the self-fulfilling prophecy to good use. Being optimistic about expected outcomes, children are likely to do that which is necessary to make them come true. Hence optimism serves a biological and social function, enabling the individual to develop as a person and grow in socially useful skills.

Only in recent years has scientific attention been devoted to the possibility that optimism may have beneficial effects. Researchers are interested in establishing a link between optimism and health, both physical and psychological well-being. Steingiser (1981) in studying optimism as a mediating variable in the management of stress, randomly sampled 181 male faculty and their spouses in a midwestern university. Results showed that those who were most optimistic had less anxiety, less arousal of negative emotions, and fewer physical illnesses in the two previous years.

Witmer, Rich, Barcikowski, and Mague (1983) studied a nonclinical, general adult population of 363 persons aged 18 to 63. In looking for psychosocial characteristics associated with the stress response, optimism was found to be one of the primary variables which characterized the good copers who had less anxiety and fewer physical symptoms. In a second study, three measures of optimism were used with an adult sample that was screened to include only those who were undergoing stressful life events. Again optimism was a characteristic associated with the good copers. They had less anxiety and fewer physical symptoms than the poor copers (Witmer, Rich, Barcikowski, in preparation).

The influence of an optimistic orientation, that is a generalized expectation that good things will happen, was reviewed by Scheir and Carver (1987). From their own research and that of others reported by them, optimism was found to be negatively associated with physical symptom reports. One study looked at the relationship of optimism upon recovery from coronary bypass surgery. The findings strongly suggest that optimism exerted a strong and pervasive positive effect on the patients' physical well-being, both during and immediately following surgery. Optimists seemed to show fewer signs of intraoperative complications and to evidence a faster rate of recovery than pessimists. With this same sample optimists reported being less hostile and somewhat less depressed than did pessimists just prior to surgery. Their base rate of social support seemed stronger and they reported greater satisfaction with their environments at work. In reviewing other studies, the authors reported that optimists tended to have less cardiovascular response to stressful events than pessimists. Optimism also appears to have positive links to immunological functioning.

Oneness and the Inner Life

Individual psychology takes its name from the basic tenant of the unity of the personality (Dreikurs, 1953). The concept is derived from the Latin word individuum, which literally means "undivided," "indivisible." From an Adlerian perspective the person's life style is based upon consistent purposiveness, which in the mind of the individual can even transcend what appears to the observer at times as a contradiction. When a pattern of inconsistencies and ambivalence is a style in coping with life events, the person usually has no intentions of proceeding openly toward the goal, but through deception, secrecy, or manipulative ways. In reality this makes maintaining a sense of wholeness more difficult.

Spiritual dimensions were present in the self-actualizing people studied by Maslow (1970). Although their spiritual beliefs were not necessarily orthodox, mystical experiences were fairly common among them. He used the term **peak experiences** to describe mystical or natural experiences of life in which occurred an intense pleasant emotion, a loss of self, sensuality, a feeling of being whole, at peace with oneself, and very much in the present moment. An openness to such experiences transcended reason and everyday routines. Secondly, not only did the healthy people in Maslow's research accept themselves and others, they felt very much akin to nature and the universe. A third dimension was the need for solitude and privacy. They sought a certain quality of detachment when the occasion called for it, remaining calm and serene emotionally during disturbing events. They turned inward drawing upon inner reserves available for acting upon the situation.

Both Eastern and Western religions tend to recognize the oneness of the person and the desire to attain an inner peace and sense of wholeness, free from inner conflict and fragmentation. Sources of spirituality likely come from within as well as outside the person. Inner voices, inner wisdom, higher consciousness, or the Spirit of God are all forms of the spiritual side of wholeness. Traditionally religion and spirituality have sought peace, guidance, and contact with the universal force through meditation, prayer, worship, contemplation, or introspection. All these forms of inner-directed activities allow for aspects of self-examination whether in the context of religious doctrine or a personal philosophy. The importance of self-examination was noted many centuries ago by Socrates when he said, "The unexamined life is not worth living."

Although the spiritual side of life will never be fully explained by science in terms of physiological processes, Herbert Benson has made a significant contribution in understanding the relationship between certain religious or spiritual practices and the scientific knowledge of the mind, physiological responses, and the benefits. As a cardiologist, teacher, researcher, and clinician at the Harvard Medical School, he identified a response that quiets the mind/body, renews energies, and opens up the mind for new insights and potential change (Benson, 1975; 1987). He labeled this phenomenon the **Relaxation Response.** His medical and clinical research demonstrates that it "shuts off the distracting stressful, anxiety-producing aspects of what is commonly called the 'fight-or-flight' response" (p. 36).

Benson with Proctor (1984) also combined this simple technique with a person's deepest personal beliefs to create other internal environments that could help the individual reach enhanced states of health and well-being. He referred to this as the **Faith Factor** in the Relaxation Response. This simple technique involves: "(1) finding a quiet environment; (2) consciously relaxing the body's muscles; (3) focusing for ten to twenty minutes [once or twice a day] on a mental device, such as the word **one** or a brief prayer; and (4) assuming a passive attitude toward intrusive thoughts" (p. 5). The focus word or phrase is silently repeated over and over for ten to twenty minutes. Neutral, religious, or philosophical words or phrases can be used, e.g., "The Lord is my shepherd," "shalom," "one," or "peace." This mechanism is what Benson (1987) in his latest work, *Maximum Mind,* calls Phase One of the Principle of the Maximum Mind. Phase One opens up the mind to the forces of renewal.

Phase Two follows immediately with another five to twenty minutes directed to thinking, pondering, or allowing an inner dialogue about the topic from as many angles as possible. Moving to Phase Two of the Principle of the Maximum Mind, a more directed form of thinking is used with the information. Nonjudgmental thinking may focus on an image, word, phrase, or short reading. New information may be introduced for Phase Two. The mind will be more open to receive it and allow it to have a positive effect. This second phase enhances the potential for creativity, healing, and change in beliefs. It is a time when one is most receptive to altering established mental circuits. "This more directed thought process will help you to rewire circuits in your brain in more positive ways" (p. 69).

Religious practices and worship services of the world's great religions have elements that appear in a more complex fashion to elicit at least in part the Relaxation Response discovered by Benson. In the absence of such religious practices, opportunities for regular self-examination become more dependent upon incidental life experiences rather than the ever-present admonition and questioning engendered in the context of religious values regarding the moral responsibilities of life.

Religious practices tend to support the importance of oneness, the inner life, and self-examination for developing the spiritual self.

Several frontiers of research into this aspect of relaxation and meditation are predicted by Benson (1987). "These include the self-controlled 'marshalling' of brain chemicals and an expansion of the understanding and use of the placebo effect, and a broader use of the Principle. . .as an aid to spiritual, intellectual and athletic development" (p. 213). Spiritual and scientific evidence can be combined to enhance our capacity to break through old bad habits, alleviate many illnesses, alter unproductive ways of thinking and realize fuller potential, and embark on a truly transformed way of living.

Values and Character Development

"The state of being without a system of values is psychopathogenic, we are learning. The human being needs a framework of values, a philosophy of life, a religion or religion-surrogate to live by and understand by in about the same sense that he needs sunlight, calcium or love" (Maslow, 1968, p. 206). Valuelessness leads to value-illnesses, illustrated by Maslow as apathy, alienation, hopelessness, and cynicism. Such conditions can become physical illnesses as well as lead to psychological and social ills. "The cure for this disease is obvious . . . a validated, usable system of human values we can believe in and devote ourselves to (be willing to die for)" (p. 206). The values of the healthy self-actualized person differ from the average or pathogenic. They have profoundly different interpretations of the physical, social, and the private psychological world. Unhealthy people tend to see the world as a dangerous place or a place to selfishly exploit without much concern for the well-being of others. Healthy (self-actualized) people in Maslow's research were strongly ethical with definite moral standards. However, their notions of right and wrong and of good and evil were often not the conventional ones. They were confident about their values and rarely showed the confusion, conflict, or inconsistency so common in the average person's dealings. Their values tended to be universal in nature, transcending time and culture, with the ability to distinguish between means and ends. When conflict does occur between the two, means are usually subordinated to ends. The importance of the "rightness" and stability of values for effectively coping with stress was explored by Witmer et al. (1983) in a study mentioned earlier. Good copers, those who had less anxiety and physical symptoms, reported feeling confident that their guiding values were right for them and would last.

Values important to the spiritual self are those that are moral in nature. *Moral values* are those that guide our behavior in acting for our own well-being and demonstrating respect and compassion for the good of others (Young & Witmer, 1985). They have two basic functions. First, they are a source of meaning anchored in purpose and hope. Secondly, values help us in decision making and problem solving. They direct us in the use of our space, time, energy, material resources, and human relationships. The home, school, and religious affiliations are primary sources for developing values that facilitate decision making and problem solving.

In Adler's (1954) discussion of the science of character, he seemed to be considering more of what psychology today calls personality. He speaks of character as the behavior pattern according to which one's striving for significance is elaborated in terms of social feeling. Character traits are acquired for the purpose of achieving significance (striving for power) and the expression of social interest for bonding with others. Together they constitute fitting in or making a place for oneself. "The character of the human being is . . . an index of the attitude of this human being toward his environment, and of his relationship to the society in which he lives" (p. 153). The character traits of a person reflect the human soul. We acquire our impressions of the soul in another person by observing how an individual stands toward society, how one expresses fellowship in humanity, and how one makes existence fruitful and vital.

After years of moral drifting and attempts to be neutral on values issues. American schools appear to be renewing efforts in a generic spiritual development under the concept of character education. An example is the curriculum developed by the *American Institute for Character Education* (1986) in San Antonio, Texas. The main goal of the *Character Education*

Curriculum is to develop **responsible citizens** with healthy self-esteem. The aim of the program is to indicate to children those values which are generally accepted by members of our society, such as honesty, patriotism, generosity, and responsibility. The curriculum is now used in more than 24,000 classrooms in 44 states.

SELF-REGULATION

The life task of self-regulation is used in this chapter to include a majority of the characteristics of the healthy person: sense of worth; sense of control; realistic beliefs; spontaneity and emotional responsiveness; intellectual stimulation, problem solving, creativity; sense of humor; and physical fitness and health habits. More global than self-esteem and self-efficacy, self-regulation is the process involved in how an individual regulates relatively long-term patterns of goal-directed behavior (Bandura, 1986; Heppner & Krauskopf, 1987; Mischel, 1981). It embodies the appraisal and action components of thinking and behaving. Included are a range of cognitions related to monitoring, planning, initiating, maintaining, and evaluating behavior (Heppner & Krauskopf, 1987).

The concept of self has been given a prominent role in the development of personality theories and has been central in several for understanding personality traits and the process of change (e.g., Adler, 1954; Allport, 1955; Rogers, 1951). From an Adlerian point of view, the striving for significance is motivated by the individual's subjectively conceived goal of success, sometimes called the **self-ideal** (Dinkmeyer, Pew, & Dinkmeyer, 1979). Inferiority feelings result from perceptions of inadequacy and unimportance (low self-esteem). The push toward a unique identity involves compensation and self-actualization. This movement toward a unique identity is seen by Adlerians as the master motive (Dinkmeyer et al., 1979).

What are the healthy traits that enable the individual to regulate the self successfully on the pathways to wholeness? In this section we shall see what the health and wellness literature suggests for effective self-regulation.

Sense of Worth (Self-Esteem)

Although separate headings are being used for Sense of Worth and Sense of Control, they comprise what is frequently cited in the literature as self-esteem. *Self-esteem* is a very general appraisal, which, beyond physical and safety needs, is the greatest single factor that affects individual growth. Accepting oneself as a person of worth and having a sense of competence or control corresponds to the Adlerian striving for significance. When these two aspects of self are perceived as inadequate, feelings of inferiority arise. These feelings are frequently a result of faulty self-evaluation. Healthy self-actualizing people see themselves as worthy and able, liked and acceptable. Our review of these topics under two separate headings is for convenience, not because they are discrete entities.

Developing a sense of identity and sense of worth has been left largely to happenstance in American education. Except for those who strongly believe that education is more than academic learning, interests, attitudes, feelings, and values have been ignored. At school as well as in the home, relationships are fraught with negative interactions, alienation, and discon-nectedness. We value the esteem of others in defining our own self-identity.

The healthy individuals of Maslow's (1970) research had a strong acceptance of themselves and their own nature. They accepted their own weaknesses and imperfections without being upset or disturbed. Closely related to acceptance of self and others was a lack of defensiveness and a distaste for artificialities. Relatively free of such chronic negative emotions as anxiety and guilt, they seemed to enjoy who and what they were.

In a national study done by Campbell (1981), twelve domains of life were considered for their contribution to satisfaction with life. Satisfaction with self which included a sense of worth and control had the strongest relationship. Those who scored highest had extraordinarily positive feelings of well-being. This satisfaction with self seemed to depend rather little on objective circumstances of life such as education, income, or place of residence.

Positive self-esteem was one of the factors identified with good copers by Witmer et al. (1983) in the study noted previously. Items on meaning in life and a sense of realness or authenticity clustered as self-esteem. Poor copers had lower self-esteem and a greater amount of anxiety and physical symptoms.

Sense of Control (Self-Esteem)

Adler (1954) seemed to equate the goal of superiority with power, presumably for the purpose of significance, which is the ultimate goal of human behavior. If power, not necessarily perceived as a negative dimension, is comparable to control, then much scientific evidence is accumulating to support its potency for wellness. Beliefs about personal control have to do with feelings about mastery and confidence. We shall continue with a discussion on control or as it is sometimes described in the literature as competence, locus of control, or self-efficacy. *Powerlessness* is a condition in which the individual perceives self as having little or no power to influence events or regulate one's own emotions.

Self-esteem was significantly related to physical and mental health in a survey conducted by the *California Department of Mental Health* (1979). Interviews were conducted with a sample of 1006 persons 18 years of age and older. Those who had high self-esteem reported having better mental and physical health than those with low self-esteem. Low self-esteem also went along with more self-reported physical illness and with disturbances such as insomnia, anxiety, and depression. Low self-esteem was also related to higher frequencies of marital problems, financial problems, emotional problems about illness and problems with self. Persons who felt they had a high degree of control over their lives were more likely to feel good about themselves mentally and physically, and report fewer ailments.

Control is sometimes defined as a sense of competence as in the research by Witmer et al. (1983) that included 363 adults from a general population. One factor that described the good copers was competence, which included items on optimism, control, and perceived overall ability to cope with stress. Those who had perceived life as being manageable had less anxiety and fewer physical symptoms.

Control along with challenge and commitment made up the three dimensions that Kobasa (1979) found to characterize the factor of psychological **hardiness** in her study of several hundred telephone company executives. She observed that psychological hardiness could decrease chances of becoming ill by as much as 50%. These dimensions accurately predicted well-being regardless of exercise and family medical history. **Control** was defined as the opposite of powerlessness; more in control of events; expressed as a tendency to feel and act as if one is influential (rather than helpless) in the face of varied contingencies of life; perception of oneself as having a definite influence through the exercise of imagination, knowledge, skill, and choice.

Continuing with a second study of the same population over a five year period, Kobasa, Maddi, and Kahn (1982) looked at health and happiness. Results confirmed the findings of the first study. **Hardiness** decreased the likelihood of symptom onset. **Control** in conjunction with **challenge** and **commitment** served as a resistance resource in buffering the effects of stressful events.

Hardiness can be developed and nurtured to assist people in staying healthy (Maddi & Kobasa, 1984). Important are early parent-child interactions in a family atmosphere that builds commitment, control, and challenge. When intervention is necessary, individual and group counseling can assist in helping an individual move from a sense of alienation to commitment, powerlessness to control, and seeing life events more as a challenge than a threat.

Control can be general beliefs one has about control of events and outcomes (Rotter, 1966; 1975) or a specific belief that a particular situation can be shaped or influenced (Bandura, 1977). It can also be viewed as beliefs about internal control and external control. Those with **internal control** believe that events are contingent upon ones's own actions and as such yield more effort and persistence in achievement situations (Lazarus, 1984). An **external locus of control** refers to the belief that events are contingent upon luck, chance, fate, or powers beyond their control. In a review of research on locus of control and health attitudes and behavior, Strickland (1978) cited studies which indicated that persons with a sense of internal control were more likely to collect information about disease and health maintenance, take action to improve their health habits, and engage in preventive care.

Although general beliefs about having overall control seem to be important, situational control is just as important. Believing that one is capable of engaging in a certain behavior to achieve a particular outcome influences how the individual behaves and enables the person to cope more effectively. Recent research at *Stanford's Arthritis Center* has indicated how powerful beliefs and expectations are for improving health (Lorig, Holman, O'Leary, & Shoor, 1986). Persons who improved the most were those who had a positive outlook and felt a sense of control regarding their arthritis. The key difference between those who improved and those who didn't was the person's **perception** of his or her ability to control or change the arthritic symptoms. The quality, self-efficacy, reflects a person's own conviction that he/she can or will be able to perform a specific action. It is a belief in one's capacity to perform, not necessarily what abilities one has at the present (Bandura, 1977).

What are the boundaries for control? Through such modalities as imagery, meditation, and biofeedback, the boundaries of what we can control internally have been extended beyond what was thought to be possible only a decade ago. Scientific evidence shows us that the mind is capable of overriding the autonomic nervous system, the automatic pilot that regulates all vital body processes such as blood flow, muscle tension, brain waves, emotional arousal, and production of immunity agents. **Imagery,** for example, gives us the potential and capability to influence every system in the body and consciously override the automatic pilot. While boundaries we set do limit the potential for control, they are necessary for our own peace of mind by recognizing what can be changed and what is beyond one's direct influence or control (Antonovsky, 1987).

Realistic Beliefs

Whatever we believe about ourselves and the world around us is what we become. (Witmer, 1985)

Healthy people have a keen perception of reality, seeing reality more as it actually is, not as one might want or desire it to be. They recognize that which is rational and logical as well as that which is distorted or wishful thinking. The superiority in the perception of reality leads to a superior ability to reason, to perceive the truth, to come to conclusions, to be logical and cognitively efficient (Maslow, 1968).

Each individual constructs his/her views of reality. This set of beliefs or "personal truths" guiding the individual is spoken of by Adlerians as the *private logic* (Dinkmeyer et al., 1979). Since it is the person's subjective view of reality, it is not necessarily in line with the objective reality of how things actually are. Therefore, the person behaves on the basis of the personal meaning given to an event. The greater the discrepancy between the private logic and reality, the more maladaptive will be the behavior. Coping effectively with life events depends upon a positive, but realistic perception of the situation and one's resources to cope.

Unhealthy persons who have mood disturbances are not emotionally sick, but cognitively wrong. That is, they are thinking irrational thoughts, doing faulty reasoning, or living by maladaptive rules made up of unrealistic or inappropriate "shoulds" and "oughts" or "do's" and "don'ts." Research and clinical evidence have documented that negative thoughts which cause emotional turmoil nearly always contain gross distortions or unrealistic expectations. Ellis (1962) identified 12 irrational beliefs that create self-defeating behavior and neurotic anxiety. Beck (1976, 1984) in working with depressed persons has noted that depressed persons have a constellation of negative perceptions of the self, the world, and the future.

The relationship between rational-irrational beliefs and effective coping was studied by Witmer et al. (1983). Good copers who had less anxiety and fewer physical symptoms than poor copers, tended to score lower and disagree with the following statements: (1) the past continues to influence me so much that it is hard for me to change or prevent bad things from happening; (2) I can't help getting down on myself when I fail at something or when something goes wrong; (3) it is very important for me to be liked and loved by almost everyone I meet; (4) I must be perfectly competent, adequate, and achieving in all that I do to consider myself worthwhile; and (5) I have little control over my moods which are caused mostly by events outside myself.

Perhaps Kobasa's third characteristics of hardiness, **challenge,** is an aspect of realistic thinking (Kobasa, 1979). Those executives who tended to view change as a challenge rather than a threat were more hardy and only half as subject to illness as the less hardy people confronting similar stressors. Such differences in appraisal, originating in part from beliefs about oneself and perceived reality, can result in significant differences in responding to events. For example, the hardy person is more likely to view loss of a job as an opportunity to seek out better employment rather than as a catastrophe and confirmation of one's own worthlessness. Challenge in the hardy people was expressed as a belief that change rather than stability is normal in life and that the anticipation of changes is an interesting incentive to growth rather than a threat to security.

Spontaneity and Emotional Responsiveness

Self-actualizing people were described by Maslow (1970) as relatively spontaneous in behavior and far more spontaneous than others in their inner life, thoughts, impulses, emotions, desires, and opinions. Their behavior is spontaneous and natural, frequently unconventional when great issues are involved. A childlike simplicity and authenticity is in their responsiveness to events. Their relationships are essentially free of defensiveness and deceptiveness. However, they are sensitive to the hurt and embarrassment of others. Self-actualizing people count their blessings. They retain a continued freshness of appreciation with a wonderful capacity to experience the "newness" of things and events, a flower, sunset, piece of music, a child. They are open to their own emotions, both positive and negative, and willing to self-disclose in a spontaneous way.

If we look to the young child for traits in this area, Montagu's (1981) list includes a sense of wonder, playfulness, joyfulness, laughter and tears, dance, and song. **Wonder** has a certain interest and excitement that motivates the person to explore the known and unknown for new perceptions. **Genuine play** is at its best when done "for the fun of it." "The ability to play is one of the principal criteria of mental health" (Montagu, 1981, p. 156). **Laughter and tears** are uniquely human traits, not because we might have more cause to do both, but because of their physiological and social benefit to the organism. The fun of **joyfulness** appears to be as strong a biological drive as any other. We need only observe the romping and sheer delight of children when they are playing. Much of the Western world seems to have neglected to recognize the importance of joy as a developmental need. Children also express their emotions spontaneously through **dance** and **song.**

Adler (1954) referred to emotions as **psychic movements** and like **character traits,** have a definite goal and direction. Accompanied by a physiological dimension they function as physical and psychic energy for the benefit of the person. Love, joy, sadness, anger, and fear are tools necessary for acting on our perceptions and values. Holistically they are part of the pattern we develop for a given lifestyle that will achieve our goals in life.

Behavioral medicine, psychosomatic medicine, and psycho-neuroimmunology have established a relationship between thoughts, feelings, and illness. When certain negative emotions become chronic or are suppressed, they can be destructive to our well-being. For example, if one engages in hostility as a way of life, one's health may be at risk. In the hard-driving, competitive Type A personality, hostility appears to be the most likely characteristic that contributes to high blood pressure, coronary artery disease, and death (Ornstein & Sobel, 1987). Anxiety, loneliness, and depression can suppress the immunity system thus increasing the chances for an illness to occur (Locke, Kraus, Leserman, Hurst, Heisel, & Williams, 1984). Relaxation and positive emotional states appear to enhance immune function (Dillon, Minchoff, & Baker, 1985; Kiecolt-Glaser, Garner, Speicher, Penn, Holliday, & Glaser, 1984; McClelland, Ross, & Patel, 1985). The influence of daily events, moods, and the secretory immune system (antibody agents in saliva) was demonstrated by Stone, Cox, Valdimarsdottir, Jandorf, and Neale (1987). Not only did a negative mood result in lower antibody response, but a positive mood was associated with a higher antibody response.

Intellectual Stimulation, Problem-solving, and Creativity

Thinking when reduced to its basic elements is primarily a problem-solving process (Montagu, 1981):

> Strangely enough, it is not generally understood that the ability to think soundly is almost as vitally necessary as the ability to breathe soundly . . . Unsound thinking leads to unsound conduct: unsound conduct adversely affects health, especially mental health, and results in human as well as socially destructive effects. Thinking soundly leads to the understanding of the necessity of feeling soundly . . . The brain, as we have already seen, is a problem-solving organ; as such it requires constant exercise. That exercise is largely of a problem-solving kind . . . Unsound thinking leads to unsound "solutions." and . . . is not likely to . . . produce or contribute to a healthy human environment. (p. 139)

Thinking and the traits that constitute intellectual functioning begin very early in life. Children have an innate hunger to think and problem-solve. The need to think soundly, according to Montagu (1981), is accompanied by a cluster of traits characteristic of the developing child and will continue into adulthood unless severely handicapped or discouraged by the environment. These traits are the need to know, the need to learn, the need to organize, curiosity, and a sense of wonder. Explorativeness, experimental-mindedness, flexibility, open-mindedness, imagination, and creativity are additional intellectual conditions and characteristics that enable the person to master the environment, pursue mental, artistic, and productive activities that challenge thinking and produce satisfaction.

Creativeness was a universal characteristic in all of the self-actualizing people studied by Maslow (1970). Self-actualizing people show in one way or another a special kind of creativeness, originality, or inventiveness. They have a creativeness that seems to be akin to the naive and universal creativeness of children. It appears in many different forms. This creativeness, as an expression of a healthy personality, is projected into activities in which the person engages.

In recent years researchers and personnel working with older persons have noted how engaging them in intellectually stimulating activities and creative tasks such as arts and crafts have the effects of regeneration and rejuvenation. Renewing those traits which are present very early in life tends to extend one's longevity. *Being mentally active and creative enhances the quality of life along with the longevity* (Pelletier, 1981).

Creativity functions in several ways to enhance the well-being of the person (Witmer, 1985). The process (1) facilitates holistic development of human potential, (2) contributes to psychological health and wellness, (3) enhances social and cultural life, (4) enlarges possibilities for vocational success, and (5) enriches leisure and recreational life.

Our task in education and psychology is primarily one of nurturing the innate capacity children have to be creative, and rekindle this process in adults for whom barriers, real or imagined, have stifled their creativity. When a counselor assists another person to explore, discover, and define life's meaning, a creative process is involved. The teacher who inspires, models, and intuitively facilitates new learning in students is being creative. Norman Cousins (1979) noted the lives of Pablo Casals and Albert Schweitzer to illustrate his conviction "that creativity, the will to live, hope, faith, and love have biochemical significance and contribute strongly to healing and to well-being" (p. 86).

Sense of Humor

> A merry heart doeth good like a medicine; but a broken spirit drieth the bones. Proverbs 17:22

The use of **humor** as medicine was highlighted by Norman Cousins in his 1976 account of a recovery from a serious connective tissue illness seen as an incurable disease. Cousins, a well-known writer and at that time editor of *Saturday Review,* devised a plan to use massive doses of humor and mega-doses of vitamin C to combat his painful, worsening condition in the hospital. Knowing that negative emotions produced negative chemical changes, he questioned whether positive emotions wouldn't produce positive chemical changes. By using episodes from *Candid Camera,* old *Marx Brothers* films, and humor books, Cousins discovered that 10 minutes of genuine belly laughter had an anesthetic effect and would give him at least two hours of pain-free sleep. With humor and vitamin C being administered, recovery began. Today 24 years after his illness, Cousins is living an active personal and professional life. Although a case of one does not establish sufficient scientific evidence, his case does continue to inspire scientific researchers, health practitioners, and laypersons to further explore the possibilities of humor and positive emotions for health benefits. Cousins (1979) chronicled his story in a book called *Anatomy of an Illness As Perceived by the Patient.*

Humor is as old as humankind. It is innate to our nature, unique to us as human beings. We are the only living creatures that appear to have a sense of humor, at least that which is shown on facial expression. Humor, particularly when it is accompanied by laughter, creates physiological, psychological, and social changes. The skeletal muscles become more relaxed, breathing changes, and possibly the brain releases certain chemicals that are positive to our well-being. Psychologically, humor overrides negative emotions, dissipating them at least for the time being, and then leads to perceptional changes in our thinking.

The social power of humor is well known. It is a potent force to reduce interpersonal conflict, tension, or unpleasant situations. It is also a mode of communication, often permitting the expression of ideas or feelings that would otherwise be difficult to express. Humor is a powerful means for expressing love or rejection. Non-joggers now have a good alternative if they take the advice of Norman Cousins (1979) "that hearty laughter is a good way to jog internally without having to go outdoors" (p. 84).

A consistent characteristic in Maslow's (1970) study of self-actualized persons was a sense of humor but not of the ordinary type. Self-actualized persons do not laugh at humor which ridicules people or makes someone else look inferior. A philosophical or cosmic humor is preferred. It consists largely of poking fun at human beings in general or when they are foolish or take themselves too seriously. The humor of the psychologically healthy person is a thoughtful, philosophical humor that may elicit a smile more than a laugh, that is intrinsic to the situation, and that is spontaneous rather than planned.

Humor is described by Montagu (1981) as one of our earliest and greatest natural resources. Babies as early as six weeks of age respond with a smile or laughter to the sound and facial expression that goes with the humor being expressed by the other person. "It is natural for children to laugh and to see the humor in all sorts of things, whether they be real or imagined, or of their own creation" (p. 175). Humor enlarges our perspective of ourselves and the world, tends to preserve our equilibrium, serves as a good defense against pain and disappointment, and adds a rich flavor to our day as we see "opportunities to respond to what we may alone perceive as funny, either about ourselves, things, or other people" (Montagu, 1981, p. 175). Playfulness, imagination, and creativity are closely allied with the sense of humor discussed above.

The use of humor as an effective method for adaptation to life was one of the mature defenses that Vaillant identified in the on-going followup study of more that 200 Harvard graduates over a 30 year period. Health surveys were correlated with psychological tests each year. Those with the best adjustment used more humor than those with the poorer adjustment. Humor is seen as an antidote for distress, but healthy because it allows both the idea and the affect to co-exist in consciousness (Vaillant, 1977).

Adler (1954) emphasized the therapeutic use of humor. He felt that therapists in addition to specific training should have "a jovial attitude . . . blessed with cheerfulness and good humor . . ." (p. 201). The benefits of humor in counseling and psychotherapy have been recently summarized by Mosak (1987) and Fry and Salameh (1987). Humor is seen as being useful in establishing a relationship, assessment and diagnosis, turning the client around, and as a criterion for termination.

The client's capacity for humor is related to lifestyle. Certain lifestyles do not permit humor, e.g., people who believe that suffering builds character (Mosak, 1987). Appropriate humor from the counselor communicates a certain "human-ness," a friendliness that may suggest safety in the relationship.

Humor can be used during the sessions to reduce anxiety or depression, put a situation in a more realistic perspective, or perhaps through a humorous metaphor, image, or twisted adage confront the client's pattern of thinking in a way that turns the thinking around, thus a little different pattern of thinking emerges.

Across therapy sessions the counselor can be alert to the presence and emergence of a sense of humor. Such behavior is one indicator of progress. However, humor can be used defensively to avoid facing painful content and feelings. As such, the client and counselor must break through the protective facade to deal with genuine feelings and beliefs. When the counselor uses humor, it should be *with* the client not *at* the client.

In the Adlerian view, "humor always involves some kind of incongruity. It may be an exaggeration, a contradiction, an understatement, a reversal, a surprise, something ludicrous or totally unreal, but humor always involves some kind of cognitive discrepancy" (Mosak, 1987, p. 25). Whatever type of humor is used by the counselor, it should always be done with respect for the client as a person and the intention to move the client toward the goals of therapy.

If humor has an effective role in counseling and psycho-therapy and is good medicine for treating illnesses, how much more important might it be for enhancing wellness? As LeShan (1982) has noted, it permits us to laugh at ourselves, binds us to others, makes life's problems easier, heals, and is a part of wholeness.

Physical Fitness
and Health Habits

The body along with the mind is equally important for maintaining the health and wholeness of the individual. **Exercise** and **nutrition** are critical for the optimal functioning of the body, and furthermore for efficient intellectual performance. Exercise and nutrition affect our moods, thinking, and behavior.

The mind performs better when the body is fine turned. The benefits of exercise and nutrition to total well-being are summarized by Cooper (1982), nationally known for his work in revolutionizing America's exercise habits with his aerobics exercise program specifically designed to strengthen the heart and lungs. They appear very convincing to anyone who is interested in total well-being. For the less enthusiastic, the list of benefits is hard to ignore:

more personal energy;

more enjoyable and active leisure time;

greater ability to handle domestic and job-related stress;

less depression, less hypochondria, and less "free floating" anxiety;

fewer physical complaints;

more efficient digestion and fewer problems with constipation;

a better self-image and more self-confidence;

more attractive, streamlined body, including more effective weight control;

bones of greater strength;

slowing of the aging process ;

easier pregnancy and childbirth;

more restful sleep;

better concentration at work and greater perseverance in all daily tasks; and

fewer aches and pains, including back pains. (p. 12)

A landmark study showing a relationship between positive health habits, health, and life expectancy was conducted with approximately 7000 adults in Alameda County, California (Belloc, 1973; Belloc & Breslow, 1972). From their research seven factors are significantly related to health and life expectancy; (1) three meals a day at regular times and no snacking; (2) breakfast every day; (3) moderate exercise two or three times a week; (4) adequate sleep (seven or eight hours a night); (5) no smoking; (6) moderate weight; (7) no alcohol or only in moderation.

Followup data indicated that each of the seven health practices contributed to health and life expectancy. For example, 45 year-old men who practiced at least six of the seven positive lifestyle behaviors lived an average of 11 years longer than those who practiced only two or three. Each of the practices are behaviors that can be changed. Although such an approach to prevention is simple in concept, actual changing of behavior is problematic because of patterns established and the lack of environmental support for good health habits.

Exercise. The body was made for physical activity. Inactivity leads to lowered resistance to stress and disease, perhaps a shorter life span, and in general a deterioration of the vital body functions. A person is physically fit if capable of performing in three ways: cardiorespiratory endurance, flexibility in muscular movement, and strength and endurance in the use of the muscles. Considerable evidence now exists as to the physical benefits of exercise for cardiovascular efficiency and health, metabolic improvements, and muscular flexibility and strength. Heart rate and blood pressure tend to decrease, arteries and capillaries are extended for increased blood flow. Cholesterol and triglycerides are decreased. Catecholamines, stress related hormones, are decreased. The heart and other muscles throughout the body are strengthened. The lungs become more efficient in extracting oxygen from the air.

A definitive study which shows how exercise is a determinant of health was a followup study of 17,000 male alumni of Harvard University (Paffenbarger, Hyde, Wing, & Hsieh, 1977). Paffenbarger studied the exercise habits of these men, whose ages ranged from 35 to 74, for over a decade and concluded that mortality rates were significantly lower among the physically active. The exercises included walking, stair-climbing, and various sports and physical activities. Those alumni who exercised little, defined as burning fewer than 2,000 calories per week, ran a 64% greater risk of a heart attack than did those who were more active. Furthermore, the more a person exercised up to an optimal level, the better his/her chances to outlive peers. Life expectancy improved steadily starting at 500 calories per week expended on exercise (a 150-pound man burns off about 500 calories walking six miles) and continued upward to 3,500 calories a week.

Exercise was found to have a protective effect even if the men had other serious risk factors such as cigarette smoking, high blood pressure, more parental heart attacks. Those who burned 2,000 calories or more per week had death rates one-fourth to one-third lower than less active men. Based on the Harvard alumni study a middle-aged male can expect to live an extra two hours for every hour of exercise. What makes this exciting is that more life is being added to the years, not just years to life.

Psychological benefits are associated with exercise although no direct causative relationship has been confirmed. Sime (1984) considers the influence of the body on the mind in his review of the research on the psychological effects of exercise. He concluded that the evidence strongly suggests an association between exercise and state of mind, although the physiological pathways for doing this are not yet understood. Such associations show (1) a positive relationship with mental well-being, (2) a decrease in state and trait anxiety, (3) a decrease in mild to moderate depression, and (4) a decrease in muscular tension along with anxiety.

A majority of the studies using a self-concept measure show an improvement by increased feelings of self-worth and competence. The beneficial emotional effects of exercise tend to hold up across all ages and both sexes. The antidepressant effect of exercise is likely to be greater if combined with traditional counseling and psychotherapy. An important principle learned here as in other types of exercise programs is self-responsibility. The responsibility for prevention, treatment, and wellness is shifted from another person or institution to the client.

The value of physical activity throughout a lifetime is supported by the studies conducted with centenarian individuals and communities. In communities where persons typically live beyond 100 years of age, physical activity is a part of the lifestyle, usually required of men and women in the performance of their daily work tasks in an agricultural economy. Pelletier (1981) reviewed the factors that contribute to longevity of centenarian communities and proposed that it may be the most important factor in longevity and optimum health. Evidence is cited by Pelletier that persons in occupations such as postal delivery and farm work have a protective factor in preventing cardiovascular disease, thus contributing to a greater life expectancy.

Scientific studies conducted by health-related professionals show overwhelming positive results in favor of exercise for physical and mental health, longevity, and quality of life. It is a factor we have control over and can change in a way that it contributes to wholeness.

Nutrition. Six nutrients are necessary for good health—proteins, carbohydrates, fats, vitamins, minerals, and water. When serious deficiencies or imbalances occur in any of these, optimal health is sacrificed and diseases are likely to occur. Eating habits and food preferences are established early in life, consequently become difficult to change with increasing age. *What we eat not only affect our health but also our moods and performance.*

Human nutrition is an exceedingly complex and contro-versial area for research and clinical application. Controversy arises not over whether nutrition influences life expectancy and optimum health, but over what specific dietary factors have a causative effect on body processes. The human body is the most complex chemical factory known. Social, political, and economic issues also charge the issues emotionally.

Brain chemistry and function can be influenced by a single meal according to extensive research at the *Massachusetts Institute of Technology* (MIT) (Pelletier, 1981). Diet has a marked effect upon the primary neurotransmitters in the brain. MIT research scientist Judith Wurtman (1986) argued that diet is a major determinant of mood and attitude. Certain foods stimulate the production and activities of chemicals in the brain which influence mood and feelings that are related to performance ability and energy levels. Protein-packed foods such as fish and meats spur production of alertness chemicals, dopamine and norephinephrine. Carbohydrates, the starchy and sweet foods, induce the manufacture of serotonin, the calming chemical. Carbohydrates and proteins are most effective when taken alone and in their purest forms. Fats take so much longer to digest that it diverts blood away from the brain to the stomach, thus slows down the release of alertness chemicals.

Two diseases which have dietary components are heart attacks and cancer. Cholesterol and fats are the main culprits in causing heart attacks and strokes. When fatty deposits build up on narrowed artery walls, they may break loose, float a little way, and then block off an artery, resulting in damage to the heart, vessel, or brain. Death often ensues.

Coupled with a high-fat diet is a low-fiber diet since fat does not contain fiber. Persons who eat a high-fiber diet have a low incidence of cancer of the colon. People on high-fiber diets digest and eliminate a meal in 14 hours compared to the 48 hours it takes to move the high-fat meal through the colon. They have fewer intestinal problems including colon cancer, the number two cancer killer in the country.

Nutritional scientists agree that a balanced diet is the most important rule. In eating a variety of foods in order to get the full variety of more than 40 nutrients, one should select foods low in fat, low in sugar, and high in fiber.

For good health and maximum personal energy, a 50-20-30 percent balance is recommended among the three main food types Cooper (1982) recommended that daily caloric intake be distributed so that approximately 50% come from complex carbohydrates, 20% from protein sources, and 30% from fat. This combination provides a proper balance and availability of energy and nutrients. Reducing the fat intake to less than 30% may lower the chances of cancer of the colon, breast, pancreas, prostate, ovaries, and rectum (Cooper, 1982).

Dietary Guidelines for Americans, a booklet published by the *U.S. Department of Agriculture* (1985), provides sensible guidelines for nutrition and health. Based on the best nutrition information we have available now, they are (1) eat a variety of foods; (2) maintain desirable weight; (3) avoid too much fat, saturated fat, and cholesterol; (4) eat foods with adequate starch and fiber; (5) avoid too much sugar; (6) avoid too much sodium; and (7) if you drink alcoholic beverages, do so in moderation.

WORK SATISFACTION

Work As a Lifespan Task

Work as a life task was thought by Adler as the most important for the maintenance of life. Inability to fulfill this task was regarded as being a symptom of a serious illness (Dreikurs, 1953). Most people somehow fulfill this task and only the most discouraged people evade it. Social interest motivates cooperation in fulfilling the occupational task. However, few people devote their whole personality to their work and are able to maintain a certain distance in relationships and personality. The more demand that work makes on relationships and personality, the more clearly any defects in personality will show through.

Adler defined occupational work as any work which is useful to the community whether for monetary gain or not. Included are the work of a housewife (or househusband) and voluntary work to the community that is done on some regular basis. The test is whether work is done for the public good or welfare.

The **play** of children was considered by Adler (1954) as preparation for the future. Attitudes and relationships are developed and manifested. Games which develop competencies are stimuli for the spirit, for the fantasy, and for the life tasks of the child. Engaging in the play of games reflects social feeling and satisfies the child's need for social contact. Montagu (1981) noted that play is "among the clearest of neotenous behavioral traits" (p. 156). It is at its best when it is not restricted to the attainment of particular goal. Playing "for the fun of it" leads to broadening of perspectives, new discoveries, exploration, and mastery of the environment. The creative ability to play is one of the criteria of mental health (Montagu, 1981).

The role of work and **leisure** in life tasks is somewhat debatable. While technological advances have freed people to engage in more leisure activities, these advances have also taken much of the personal pride out of work performance. Leisure-time activities, therefore, are necessary to satisfy the social and psychological needs to be meaningfully involved. How does leisure contribute to the quality of life? Can leisure provide the self-esteem potentially available from work? The meanings of work and leisure are changing. Work ethics in our society are changing toward a greater emphasis on self-actualization and well-being.

Perhaps in today's changing world as we approach Toffler's (1980) *Third Wave* of civilization, we need to look at work more broadly. If work is a meaningful process in which one engages over a lifespan, all such activity must be considered as emphasizing an internal career process. A useful concept that includes work and leisure activities has been proposed by Miller-Tiedeman (1988) in what she calls *lifecareer.* It appears to be an extension of Adler's view of work as a life task. She describes it as "the path of open and individually understood self-organizing life process which is holistically at work in each moment" (p. 2). The lifecareer process is guided by inner knowledge, not according to another's view and vision, but to the timing and rhythm of one's own mission or reason for being. One's physical, mental, emotional, and spiritual needs tend to come into balance as one actively engages in the process. Realizing the interconnectedness of all things contributes to greater consciousness and growth in understanding the lifecareer process. Persons must use their career compass of experience, intelligence, and intuition. "As they do, each individual takes a potential quantum leap into living his or her *Lifecareer* as a willed process" (Miller-Tiedeman, 1988, p. 55). Play is an integral part of this process. Any activity that contributes to the growth and sustenance of the individual is in the broad context of work or career. Good work is seen as engaging the soul and the spirit (Schumacher, 1981).

Psychological, Social, and Economic Benefits

The different purposes that work can serve have been summarized by Herr and Cramer (1988). Psychological purposes include self-esteem, self-efficacy (control), identity, a feeling of mastery or competence, and commitment (meaning in life). Social benefits include a place to meet people, a feeling of being valued or needed by others, social status, and potential friendships. A work group is a sort of miniculture where social needs are met and its own set of values and norms are developed (Tart, 1986). Economic purposes include the obvious resources to purchase goods and services, evidence of success, and assets to purchase leisure or free time.

Those who are happy with their jobs are happier in general. In Freedman's (1978) study of happy people. Clearly satisfaction with one's job "is one of the most important factors, surpassed only by love and marriage, and equalled by various social and personal growth considerations" (p. 157). In *Psychology Today* (1978) a survey conducted on work attitudes relating to the importance of various job aspects, revealed that the top items were self-growth, chances to do something that makes you feel good about yourself, chances to accomplish something worth-while, and chances to learn new things.

What creates job satisfaction? Freedman's (1978) analysis of the data from several independent surveys adding up to over 100,000 responses, identified "five characteristics of the job [that] stand out as most important for people: the interest level of the work, chance for advancement, financial considerations, security, and whether the work seems worthwhile" (p. 160). Values that became more important to workers in the 1970s were "being recognized as an individual person" and "the opportunity to be with pleasant people with whom I like to work" (Yankelovich, 1978, p. 49).

Another value change that emerged in the 1970s was the pursuit of leisure (Yankelovich, 1978). When work and leisure were compared by Yankelovich as sources of satisfaction, only 21% stated that work meant more to them than leisure. This was true even though a majority (60%) said that while they enjoyed their work it was not their major source of satisfaction.

Work, Mental Health, and Well-Being

Over a period of 20 years Campbell (1981) conducted five national surveys that assessed 12 domains of life related to a sense of well-being. Consistently, **work** was one of the top six domains having the greatest influence in accounting for the level of satisfaction people felt with their life in general. The fact that a large majority of men and women believe they would prefer to continue to work even if their economic needs were taken care of demonstrates that work has a broader meaning than financial return.

As mentioned previously, Kobasa (1982) found that the telephone executives in a mid-western state who had the fewest illnesses and greatest resistance to the negative effects of stress included those who had expressed a sense of commitment, one of the three **hardiness** factors. Hardy executives found what they were doing to be interesting and important. Persons high in commitment involved themselves in whatever they were doing, having an overall sense of purpose.

Job satisfaction combined with meaning in life was one of five factors characterizing persons who coped effectively with stress in a study conducted by Witmer et al. (1983). Satisfaction with one's job and meaning in life clustered together as a separate factor. Those who had greater job-life meaning reported less anxiety and fewer physical symptoms related to medical conditions of a psychosomatic nature.

Despite the sophistication of genetic and biochemical research, the single most accurate predictor of longevity is *lifestyle* (Pelletier, 1981). Psychosocial dimensions are paramount. One particularly important such predictor is *work satisfaction* (Brill, 1978). Early longitudinal research conducted by Palmore (1969) examined the relationship of 39 variables to longevity for 268 community volunteers with ages 60 to 94 at the beginning of the study. He concluded that work satisfaction was the best single predictor among men aged 60 to 69. The work-satisfaction findings of Palmore are consistent with the prolonged and productive involvement through work roles and social roles of persons living in centenarian communities (Pelletier, 1981).

Research by two Dutch cardiologists (Danner & Dunning, 1978) examined the lifestyle and genetic factors contributing to the longevity of 100 persons who were at least 90 years of age. Genetic endowment was not the most significant factor for longevity. They concluded that overall a life of hard work without the hazards of affluence was typical of people who lived to a healthy old age. Pelletier (1981) in his review of lifestyle and longevity reported that meaningful involvement in the work and life of the community and the family was an essential factor for increasing life expectancy.

The relationship of mental health and well-being to work can be inferred by examining the impact of unemployment. Pelletier (1984) reported a study by Cobbon and Kasl indicating a suicide rate 30 times the national average in communities hit hard by layoffs. The literature demonstrates that "During periods of economic slump there is a marked increase in murder, suicide, mental illness, heart disease, alcoholism, divorce, domestic violence, family fights, and child abuse" (p. 129). Over the last decade a consensus has emerged that unemployment provokes or uncovers physical and mental illness (Ferman, 1982). If unemployment is not the direct cause of disease and disability, it undoubtedly aggravates or intensifies existing disorders.

The relationship between health and worker productivity is being recognized by the business community. One of the megatrends cited by Naisbett (1982) is the shift from institutional help to self-help. This new health paradigm has found a strong ally in the business community. Two driving forces appear to be behind this trend (Pelletier, 1984). The economic imperative is whether it increases performance, productivity, and profits. Early studies of cost/benefit analysis are suggestive of payoff in this respect. The other motivating force is a sense of social conscience and responsibility that is related to the image and attractiveness of the company of employees. However, over time programs must be at least self-sustaining and even profitable. New health programs emphasize personal responsibility and habits. Wellness programs in the workplace commonly include one or several of these components: exercise, smoking-cessation, a healthy diet and control of obesity, control of alcohol and substance abuse, stress management and relaxation, noise reduction, and control of toxic substances (Naisbett, 1982; Pelletier, 1984).

Although periodic declines in the work ethic are indicated, Pelletier (1984) reported that numerous surveys have given clear evidence that the "work ethic" ideal is alive, well, and growing stronger. Perhaps for several reasons American workers have a new perspective on the value of the "work ethic" and increased productivity. American business has learned from the Japanese style of management a "new spirit of working together" and the importance of the "people factor" to job satisfaction and performance. The high-tech/high-touch trend noted by Naisbett symbolizes the need for balance between our physical and spiritual reality. The human touch, the need to be together, and personal responsibility are critical components in the overall ingredients for work satisfaction. "We must learn to balance the material wonders of technology with the spiritual demands of our human nature" (Naisbett, 1982, p. 40).

FRIENDSHIP AND LOVE

> Some day, after we have mastered the winds, the waves, the tides
> and gravity, we shall harness for God the energies of love. Then for the
> second time in the history of the world, man will have discovered fire.

Teilhard de Chardin

Social Interest and Connectedness

Fundamental to understanding human behavior is the meaning that *social interest* has for each individual in seeking life satisfaction and maintaining well-being. Adler (1954) considered "social interest" or "social feeling" as innate to human nature, i.e., we are all born with the capacity and need to be connected with each other and in a cosmic relationship. Therefore, the broad meaning of social interest is a "sense of fellowship in the human community" (p. 38). This awareness of universal interconnectedness and interrelatedness of human beings combines to form a willingness to cooperate with others for the common good. Thus seeking to belong or making a place for oneself in relationship to others is a primary motivation for human behavior.

The social interest observed by Adler in studying human behavior is affirmed in the highest ideals of ethical codes and the world religions. In recent years, it has been confirmed by anthropological and psychological research. The research findings in stress management, health psychology, psychosomatic medicine, and behavioral medicine confirm social support as a factor in good health and longevity. Evidence is mounting to support Adler's use of social interest as a criterion for mental health.

Montagu has been explicit in his regard for Adler's concept of social interest. He applies this concept in support of his own view that "life is social and man is born to be social, that is cooperative—an interdependent part of a whole" (Montagu, 1955, p. 185). In his work on the neotenous traits of the child, Montagu (1981) noted that "The child is born not only with the need to be loved, but with the need to love others" (p. 131). The essence of this *love* is giving and caring. By being loved the power is released to love others. A second trait is **friendship** which is love of personal intensity. Love and friendship are what makes us human in the best sense of the word. Closely related to love is a third trait, **compassionate intelligence.** This trait is exhibited by involvement in the desire to help in some practical way.

When Maslow (1970) studied the characteristics of psychologically healthy persons, he found that one of the characteristics was social interest. The self-actualizing persons had "for human beings in general a deep feeling of identification, sympathy, and affection . . . a genuine desire to help the human race . . . members of a single family" (p. 165). Other social characteristics of this group were (1) deeper and more profound interpersonal relations than any other adults, and (2) acceptance of others as well as acceptance of self and nature.

Hans Selye, father and pioneer of stress research, proposed a natural code of ethics based upon the principle of altruistic egoism (Selye, 1974). Acting primarily for one's own good, the individual also manifests "love, goodwill, gratitude, respect, and all other positive feelings that render him useful and often indispensable to his neighbors" (p. 120). "Love thy neighbor as thyself" has been the basis of most religions and philosophies of conduct throughout the ages. Our long term survival is dependent upon maintaining an inner well-being and living in harmony with the environment. Earning our neighbor's love helps assure our own stability and happiness. This is necessary for protecting us from the stresses of life.

The strength of social relationships and their importance to our health is explained by psychologist Robert Orstein and physician David Sobel (1987). They conceptualize the brain as the center of a marvelous health-care system. The need for community is proposed as part of our genetic makeup.

> People need People. Not only for the practical benefits which derive from group life, but for our very health and survival. Somehow interaction with the larger social world of others draws our attention outside of ourselves, enlarges our focus, enhances our ability to cope, and seems to make the brain reactions more stable and the person less vulnerable to disease. (p. 202)

The warmth and good feelings that come from doing good may well come from endorphins—the brain's natural opiates. These opiates that have been linked to running and meditation may turn out to modulate altruism (Growald & Luks, 1988).

Human renewal and restoration along with the creation of wholeness have their roots in the characteristics of community. Health and healing are dependent upon the experience of a true community (Peck, 1987). In a society where lack of community is so often the norm, Peck sees community-building as a prerequisite to peace and wholeness at all levels, starting with the person and the neighborhood, then extending to international relationships.

Social Support, Interpersonal Relations, and Health

Social support has three types of functions (Schaefer, Coyne, & Lazarus, 1982). These consist of (1) emotional support—attachment, reassurance, being able to rely upon and confide in a person; (2) tangible support—involving direct aid such as loans, gifts, and services such as doing a chore or caring for someone who is ill; and (3) informational support—providing information or advice, and feedback.

Social skills are an important coping resource for adaptation to life events. Communication and social skills are important for working in cooperative relationships with others. A trend is evident in therapeutic, community and organizational training programs to improve interpersonal communication skills, establish social networks, and maintain social support (Lazarus & Folkman, 1984).

In looking at the benefits of friendships longitudinally, Vaillant (1977) examined the linkages between loving and health in following 200 Harvard graduates for 30 years. Better mental health in the men was reflected in a more friendly disposition, closer relationships with their children, being happily married over time, and better marital sexual adjustment. A more powerful predictor of poor mental health than sexual dissatisfaction in marriage was the overt fear of sex.

Besides the above associations between love and mental health, men who were classified as "friendly" were much more likely to be free of chronic physical illness as well as mental illness by age 52, and less likely to abuse drugs or alcohol. Vaillant concluded from the men in the study that being able to love one's friends, wife, parents, and children were predictors of good mental health. Among this same population, he found that **altruistic behavior** was associated with better mental health, proving especially helpful during stressful times in their lives.

In quality of life research directed by Flanagan (1978), spouse, children, and friends were found to be the top three contributors to overall satisfaction of life for women and men. Well-being research by Campbell (1981) in a national survey affirmed that marriage and friends significantly contributed to satisfaction with life. A recent story by USA Today (1988) reported several studies demonstrating the added satisfaction and health for the male in a marriage relationship. Married men were almost twice as likely to outlive never married men and three times more likely to live longer than divorced men. Husbands had a lower depression rate than people of any other marital status. The mental health of men improves unbelievably when they marry according to University of Michigan sociologist Ronald Kessler, who recently completed a study of 1,000 Detroit-area couples. Men consistently gave higher ratings to their marriages than did wives and men were much more affected than women if the marriage ended.

Men and women experience friendships differently. Very early in life females establish close one-on-one relationships. Whereas men tend to establish these friendships around activities, women have more close friends and share with them more intimately—feelings, revelations, nurturing (Rubin, 1985). Women do more social networking than men and are much more likely to be able to name a best friend.

Evidence continues to accumulate in showing the importance of social ties for health and life expectancy. In a large study by Berkman and Syme (1979), two epidemiologists, 7,000 residents of Alameda County, California were surveyed and then observed over a nine-year period in an attempt to identify the factors that protect people from illness and death. Over the nine years, they found that those who were single, widowed, or divorced, those with few close friends and relatives, and those who tended not to join or participate in community organizations died at a rate two to five times greater than those with more extensive social ties. This was true regardless of income, gender, race or ethnic background, age, and other lifestyle factors.

Further, a ten-year University of Michigan study followed 2,754 adults in Tecumseh, Michigan to observe among several factors the participants' personal relationships, group activities, and health (House, Robbins, & Metzner, 1982). Even though no medical differences were present at the beginning of the study, those with least social contacts had two to four times the mortality rate of the well-connected. The social support findings were found to be independent of such traditional risk factors as smoking, alcohol consumption, exercise, and obesity. Researchers also found that doing volunteer work dramatically increased life expectancy. Men who did no volunteer work were two and one-half times as likely to die during the study as men who volunteered at least once a week.

The relationship between human companionship and death due to coronary disease was studied by Lynch (1977). He examined medical data available from numerous studies over several decades and found that in addition to the traditional risk factors for coronary heart disease, the lack of human companionship may shorten a person's life. He concluded that, *"At all ages, for both sexes, and for all races in the United States, the nonmarried always have higher death rates, sometimes as much as five times higher than those of married individuals"* (p. 52). Not just for heart disease, but for all causes of death, the U.S. mortality rates are consistently higher for divorced, single, and widowed individuals of both sexes and all races.

The importance of stable social relationships or maintenance of social ties is documented by evidence from the study of such communities as Roseto, Pennsylvania and the pattern of social relationships by Japanese migrants. When Wolf and Goodell (1976) began their study in the 1960s, the population of Roseto was stable and the 1,630 residents were largely

Italians. Even though their diet was not unlike the surrounding communities, they had only one-third as many heart attacks as surrounding communities. Wolf and Goodell noted that, "The most striking feature of Roseto was its social structure . . . unlike most American towns Roseto is cohesive and mutually supportive, with strong family and community ties" (p. 79). In a study of migrants from Japan, the Japanese who maintained strong links to the traditional community had less heart disease that those who didn't in spite of diet and smoking (Marmot & Syme, 1976). They had one-fifth the rate of heart disease as those who adopted a Western pattern of social relationships.

Self-centeredness and one's attitudes toward others can affect the heart. Scherwitz, Graham, and Ornish (1985) reported that self-involved people tended to have more severe artery disease, even after the researchers controlled for other risk factors. They were more likely to have a heart attack including a second one. More self-involved patients were also more depressed and anxious. Self-centered people likely have stronger emotional and physical reactions to events. Orstein and Sobel (1987) have observed that we may well break our hearts by cutting ourselves off from the normal give-and-take of social intercourse. A deeper need within our brains than we know about may be motivating us to maintain "a stable connection with the larger 'organism' of humanity as a whole" (p. 185).

In his intriguing book, *The Language of the Heart,* Lynch (1985) reported a relationship between talking and the heart. He found that people who did not listen well but waited for a chance to answer back tended to have higher blood pressure. It also would rise most when talking to someone of a higher social status or addressing a group of unfamiliar persons. Blood pressure was lowest, when not talking at all or when talking with someone with whom they were intimate, like a spouse.

Research is also suggesting that social relationships affect our immune system. *Loneliness* as well as mild upsets are associated with decreased activity of natural killer cells. Kiecolt-Glaser and her colleagues (1984) compared 38 married women with an equal number of women who were separated or divorced. They found that married women had better immune function than the unmarried and women who reported they were happily married had the healthiest immune system of all the groups.

Weiss (1988) in his article on loneliness reported that loneliness of any kind is bad for health. "Among both students and psychiatric inpatients, the lonely have been shown to be more likely to have impaired immune system functioning; they definitely catch more colds and are probably more vulnerable to every sort of illness" (p. 5).

Doing good or even *thinking* about altruistic action may give the immune system a boost. In an exploratory study at Harvard by McClelland (Borysenko, 1985), students watching a film of Mother Teresa ministering to the poor and sick in Indian showed a temporary change in immunity agents in their saliva. Tests revealed an immediate increase and elevation for an hour later of Immunogobulin A, an antibody that helps defend the body against respiratory infections. The same phenomenon was observed when students visualized and focused upon someone else caring for them as well as their caring for someone else.

Sharing sorrow with someone else protects people from the stress of life. Siegel (1986) summarized the work of Pennebaker at Southern Methodist University where he found that "those who bore their grief alone had a much higher than average rate of illness, while those who could talk over their troubles with someone else had no increase in health problems" (p. 187).

The benefit of social relationships in a general non-clinical population of 363 persons was studied by Witmer et al. (1983). Having a confidant, a circle of friends, and liking people were items that went together in identifying those who coped best with stress. Those who were strongest in having a *social support system* had less anxiety and fewer physical symptoms.

Although the research is in its infancy, potential links between social support and various health dimensions have been summarized by Cohen (1988). He has noted the potential connections between social support and health behaviors, positive and negative affect, self-esteem and personal control, neuroendocrine response, and the immune function.

A line of a popular song says, "People who need people are the luckiest people in the world." Beyond the joy of relationships and the practical benefits we derive from group life, our very health and survival appear to be linked to the community. In almost all societies and in most religions emphasis is upon the virtues of caring for others, being generous to others, and serving them. Our future is inextricably bounded and bonded with others.

Loving one's neighbor as oneself is the essence of the wisdom Christ gave for what is necessary to live a more abundant life. Our own well-being and that of others are at stake when social interest, so insightfully observed by Adler, is not nurtured and valued. Perhaps we can see hope in research trends noted in persons seeking closer social ties with others. Yankelovich (1981) with his annual measures of "Search for Community" noted a large jump over an eight-year period. "People feel good about themselves when they believe what they are doing is good for others as well as for themselves—when they believe it is morally right" (p. 249).

SUMMARY

Reaching toward wholeness is a natural, unfolding process that is innate to us as human beings. This striving from within is strong yet easily influenced toward beliefs and behaviors that are self-destructive or exploitative of the well-being of others. Although this seeking of wholeness is cross cultural and across ages and generations, it ebbs and flows. Cultural forces and the consciousness of the times often flow counter to the nurturing of the individual's movement toward wholeness. A mind change that in recent times began in the 1960s seems to be crystallizing as we approach the 1990s. Valued in this new consciousness are wholeness, search for meaning, search for community and more intimate relationships, search for identity, and a sense of empowerment.

Review of the literature from multiple disciplines referred to in this chapter leads to some exciting yet not surprising conclusions. The characteristics of the healthy person, physically, psychologically, and spiritually, were described as 10 dimensions which can be likened to a wheel of wholeness. At the center of wholeness is the life task and dimension of spirituality with purposiveness, optimism, oneness, and values making up the different facets of the center.

The other nine dimensions of wholeness are spokes which extend outward in making contact with life events. Self-regulation is the second life task which includes the dimensions of a sense of worth, sense of control, realistic beliefs, spontaneity, intellectual stimulation, sense of humor, and physical fitness.

To Adler the life task of work was the most important for the maintenance of life. As the third life task it affords economic sustenance but of equal importance are its psychological and social benefits.

The fourth life task is friendship and love. Social interest is the altruistic motivation that enables us to reach out and form connections with others. These 10 dimensions, the hub and the spokes in the wheel, are the characteristics of wholeness that enable us to effectively move through the life tasks.

Future research will continue to extend our knowledge and even alter some of the current beliefs we have about wholeness. However, the knowledge now available to us has impelling implications for education, counseling, parenting, and community-building. Teachers, counselors, parents, and health and human development specialists in our society need to form a conspiracy. This is, we need to literally "breathe together" in uniting with community leaders to create a climate in which the inner striving toward wholeness can reach optimal potential. For any individual desiring to maximize human and spiritual potential, the paths toward wholeness are evident.

STUDY QUESTIONS

1. Critique the author's conceptualization of spirituality. What are the limitations and what are the affirmations according to your views in this area?

2. What in a child and young person's development contributes to healthy self-esteem?

3. From a developmental perspective, identify and discuss how counseling and education can enhance the dimensions of self-regulation.

4. How do work and leisure contribute to wholeness and psychological health?

5. Discuss Adler's concept of "social interest" and the relationship of friendship and love to health and well-being.

6. How might the four life tasks and 10 dimensions of wholeness be used in counseling and the development of treatment plans to remediate dysfunctional behavior and improve personal adjustment?

ACTIVITIES

1. In a small group discuss your striving toward wholeness. Informally evaluate your beliefs and behaviors according to the four life tasks and the 10 dimensions of wholeness. What changes would you like to make? What barriers are there to your achieving a healthier lifestyle? What do you need to do to enhance what Adler called a "fictional image" in your striving toward wholeness?

2. Select several of the 10 dimensions of wholeness and a healthy lifestyle. Discuss how these dimensions might be fostered in educational, work, and community settings.

CHAPTER **3**

NATURAL CONSEQUENCES

LIFE'S RULES ARE FOR EVERYONE

Have you ever

—locked your car keys in the car,

—found in the checkout line that you had left your cash and checkbook at home,

—stubbed your toe while walking without shoes, or

—lost or broke something of value because of carelessness?

All of these events can be powerful influences upon our behavior. All have certain characteristics in common. For one, each results in an undesirable, sometimes painful, consequence regardless of who you are. Each is the result of short-sightedness with respect to possible outcomes. A negative consequence occurs regardless of who you are. In each case, no one else is involved, i.e., the natural consequence follows without the intervention of anyone else.

Such experiences prompt comments about "experience is our best teacher" or "learning through the School of Hard Knocks!" Much can be said about the value of personal experience as a guide to learning how to cope with life. Such learning has its disadvantages, however. For example, real bodily harm or even death can be a result of a serious oversight. In other cases, an individual may overreact to possible consequences and develop fears which impede other areas of personal development. Also some consequences take an indefinite period of time to have an effect, e.g., not brushing teeth eventually develops cavities or unhealthy gums. In short, natural consequences already affect how we learn to cope with life but intelligent use of them is important for such consequences to have a positive influence.

ACTION DIMENSIONS

The action dimensions—natural consequences, logical consequences, and encouragement—of the Adlerian approach are the foundation of the educative process.

Natural Consequences

This consequence is the result of an ill-advised behavior which will follow without the intervention of another person. For example, if we neglect to take our clothes to the laundry, they do not get cleaned; if the children do not place their dirty clothes in the laundry hamper, they do not get cleaned.

Logical Consequences

This consequence is the result of an ill-advised behavior which can follow logically even though it requires the purposeful intervention of another person. For example, if others must pick up our belongings, they also may decide where to place them. A logical consequence would follow that we would have to do without their use during this period of time.

Encouragement

This dimension denotes the process by which one develops the faith and self-confidence needed to cope successfully with any predicament, any defeat, or any task; whatever the circumstance, the individuals know that they have a place, they belong, and they will survive.

EXPERIENCING NATURAL CONSEQUENCES

Natural consequences are the negative outcomes of an ill-advised behavior which follow without the intervention of another person. These are among the great social levelers in nature. Regardless of one's social stature, violate "common sense" rules about life and nature has its own recourse! You can be sure that heads of government sometimes stub their toes while fumbling around their bedrooms in the dark. Likewise, the most expensive automobile will not run unless the operator remembers to keep fuel in its gas tank! We can see in these examples how each person's equality is reinforced by recognition that nature's laws apply to all persons regardless of sex, age, race, etc. Such rules are for everyone!

From an historical perspective, the use of natural consequences as an aid to child rearing is by no means new. Spencer (1885) supported Rousseau's concepts of another hundred years earlier and condemned the harsh treatment accorded many children by parents and other adults. Spencer believed that punishment debased children rather than prepared them for the demands of adult life. As a more proper alternative, he discussed what Dreikurs and Grey (1968) identified as a natural consequence:

> When a child falls or runs his head against a table, the remembrance of which tends to make it more careful; and by repetition of such experience, it is eventually disciplined into proper guidance of its movements.

> . . . So deep an impression is produced by one or two events of this kind, that no persuasion will afterwards induce it thus to disregard the laws of its constitution . . . they are simply the unavoidable consequences of the deeds which they follow: are nothing more than the inevitable reactions entailed by the child's actions. (Spencer, 1885, pp. 161-163)

Everyone has learned important lessons about the natural order from such experiences. We have, therefore, a very useful tool in helping others to accept responsibility for their actions. Without explaining, nagging or pleading, you can "let nature take its course" and allow natural consequences to enforce the order which impinges on everyone.

PRACTICAL IMPLICATIONS

So many illustrations of natural consequences are operating that only a few should help you begin a list of your own. Carelessness in watching where you are going can result in bumps and bruises. Most children have ignored admonitions to "not run so fast" and fallen hard enough to hurt themselves. Touching hot plates, kettles, and so forth contributes to continued caution even when you are mature enough to discriminate between those items which may be dangerous and those which are not. Some adults pay little attention to their automobile fuel gauges or "idiot" light for oil. Inconveniences and costly repair bills are a result of such carelessness. Likewise, oversleeping, overeating, working to a point of exhaustion, forgetting tools needed to do a job, or allowing work to accumulate beyond a reasonable point, all constitute situations which contribute to natural consequences.

Self Study Situations

Now try to select one *or* more consequences to each action by asking the question: *What happens if no one intervenes in a positive or negative way?*

1. Never pick up clothes
   - ___ a. they remain dirty
   - ___ b. they get more soiled
   - ___ c. you run out of clothes
   - ___ d. someone else must pick them up

2. Go to a store late
   - ___ a. store is closed
   - ___ b. someone must open it for you
   - ___ c. you may be inconvenienced
   - ___ d. you become angry

3. Do not complete your work
   - ___ a. someone else does it for you
   - ___ b. you may have to do it at another potentially less convenient time

       ___ c. you have more to do
            the next time

       ___ d. you may lack the
            knowledge, skill, or
            experience needed for
            a future task.

4. Ignore the natural laws   ___ a. you may get bruised
            or injured

       ___ b. someone must pro-
            tect you

       ___ c. you run into, over,
            etc., that which is
            around you

       ___ d. your insurance rates
            go up

To help fully understand some of the subtleties of discriminating among the alternatives, find someone with whom to compare responses if possible. Having done this, the appropriate answers are given at the bottom of this page.

Frequently someone will indicate that a natural consequence is anger or similar emotional reaction. Emotions, however, are not an **unavoidable consequence** or **inevitable reaction** to an experience. People differ in their emotional reactions to identical events. Therefore, emotional reactions are not natural consequences. Likewise, to have an automobile accident while "ignoring the natural laws of motion" may result in higher insurance rates but this requires the intervention of someone else. Because of a number of circumstances, the insurance company may choose not to change your rates.

Occasionally the question of dangerous circumstances will arise. When we speak of this situation as a common sense approach, the need for judgement is implied. In fact, mastery of the subject can be determined in part by one's ability to discriminate in the use of general rules. **Knowing when appropriate time is to make an exception to a general rule connotes one evidence of mastery.** Sometimes you may

---

(Key: 1. a, b, c;   2. a, c;   3. b, c, d;   4. a,c)

choose not to intervene and protect a young person from a fall or bump because he/she has insisted on discovering the consequence for himself/herself. Likewise you may choose to stop providing a colleague, friend, or spouse with a way out of "forgetting" tools, supplies, appointments, etc. when you (and others) recognize that such behavior only serves to reinforce self-defeating and/or irresponsible behavior. On the other hand, no one could stand aside while a two or three year old ran into a busy thoroughfare or another adult proceeded to light a cigarette in an area of gas fumes.

The imagined prospect of youngsters maiming or killing themselves has been the enslavement of many adults. In discussions with many youngsters and on the basis of years of observation, a general truth seems apparent. On the average, no one chooses to seriously injure himself/herself purposely. Some may flirt with danger but generally with an expectation that they will not be injured. Some few young people and adults seem compelled to test themselves as "dare devils." These people are exceptions. More often, as one cartoonist noted in a discussion between two youngsters, they "have to plan their emergencies very carefully in advance!" in order to impress the adults in their lives.

Children plan their emergencies
to impress adults.

In one parent study group, a parent was convinced her son was "bound and determined to do himself in." Based on other information, the group questioned this assumption but the parent felt compelled to protect him from all manner of dangers. Two sessions later, the parent returned a believer in the group's admonitions. That week while the parent was in the process of preparing supper, the boy was seen walking on the peak of the garage roof. Suddenly he lost his footing and fell. Convinced that he had finally done it this time, the parent ran into the backyard. There behind the garage, sitting on top of a large carefully piled layer of leaves was the son, grinning from ear to ear. No one needed to explain his motivation and a more motivated parent study group participant could not be found!

Children are not the only ones whose behavior causes problems. When a family member, roommate, or co-worker **persistently** abuses common courtesy, allowing natural consequences to occur may be the solution. For example, many homemakers complain that their spouses tend to come home later than expected but looking for a fresh, still hot meal. The obvious consequence is a cold meal. In fact, when family members don't make it home and/or don't call to say that they will be delayed, some families agree that the late arrivers get leftovers. In such instances, no comments taunt the late arriver nor angry feelings because a good meal was not had by all. Silence is golden and friendliness an asset.

This last point is particularly important to understand. Because many people are accustomed to the use of punishment as a method of discipline, they want the offender to suffer! They believe that it isn't enough to no longer be in conflict, they want revenge or retribution! When in such a mental state, some natural consequences may seem mild indeed. Revenge and desire for retribution tend to escalate a conflict while natural consequences do not. Because no one needs to intervene, the force of reality is the teacher. You can remain friendly and unperturbed by what *formerly* had been an annoying situation. Statements of "I told you so" or "now you'll know better than to do that" are unnecessary, if not also unkind. They increase the probability of further conflict. Be patient and recognize that more responsible behavior will follow as the consequences prove their own value as a source of learning.

On a more serious note, the literature on alcohol and other substance abusers supports the position that often family and friends enable loved ones to continue in their self and other destructive behavior by excusing them from the consequences of their behavior. Whether the expectation is to clean up after vomiting (natural consequence) or not being allowed the use of the car (logical consequence), the enforcement of reasonable but firm rules is essential to any intervention program. Better that such intervention begin sooner rather than later for the benefit of all parties involved. Such "tough love" can save lives and relationships. Obviously, in such situations, other therapeutic interventions will also be necessary.

SUMMARY

This chapter was designed to heighten awareness of life's methods of teaching responsible behavior and attitudes. By studying how each of us has learned through the experiencing of natural consequences, we are better able to implement them as methods for allowing others to accept responsibility for their behavior. Subsequent chapters help illustrate natural consequences use and usefulness. The next chapter is particularly valuable as a further extension of consequences into the social domain.

STUDY QUESTIONS

Direction: Respond to the following in the spaces provided.

1. Why does the title to this chapter include "Rules Are For Everyone"?

2. Cite two or three illustrations from your experience which were important lessons based upon natural consequences.

3. Give one example of how you might allow someone you know to experience a natural consequence that could contribute to more responsible behavior on his/her part.

4. Under what circumstances might you choose to allow natural consequences to take place?

5. Under what circumstances might you choose to intervene to prevent someone else from experiencing a natural consequence?

ACTIVITIES FOR INDIVIDUALS AND GROUPS

Definition of Natural Consequences: this consequence is the result of an ill-advised behavior which will follow without the intervention of another person.

A. Check those of the following which could be examples of natural consequences:

Action	Natural Consequences
1. You forget to water plants	___ a. they die
	___ b. they lose leaves or blooms
	___ c. they may need re-placed
	___ d. someone else must do it
2. Lock your keys in the car	___ a. you may miss an appointment
	___ b. someone else must open it for you
	___ c. you may be inconven-ienced
	___ d. you become de-pressed
3. Don't tie your shoe laces	___ a. someone else does it for you
	___ b. you trip on your laces
	___ c. your shoes fit badly and may hurt
	___ d. in an emergency, you can't move quickly enough to reach safety
4. Go on vacation without money	___ a. you must borrow and pay interest
	___ b. someone must give you money

_____ c. you cannot do some
of the things you
planned to do
_____ d. you lose time trying
to get funds for the
things you want to do

B. Now reach a consensus with your partner and/or group members upon consequences which you agree are appropriate.

C. Check your responses with those of the key.

   (1. a,b,c;   2. a,c;   3. b,c,d;   4. c.d)

Listing Natural Consequences

A. List one or more *natural consequence to each of the following if another person does not intervene.*

Action	Natural Consequences
1. Misplace needed materials:	
2. Forget dental appointment:	
3. Careless with tools:	

4. Do not bathe:

5. Do not get enough sleep:

6. Miss one or more meals:

7. Abuse belongings:

8. Forget to bring clothes, equipment, or materials which are necessary:

B. Share your list of natural consequences with your group by having person take one of the actions, share his/her list, and invite others to add or modify as appropriate.

Sharing Personally Experienced
Natural Consequences

A. Now identify three or more natural consequences which you
    have experiences, even vicariously, that remain as important
    influences upon your behavior.

When you did this (ill-advised) . . .	**This (unfortunate) consequence followed . . .**

1.

2.

3.

B. Share with the other participant(s) one or more of the
    responses listed in Part A. do the other participant(s) agree
    that the consequences you listed are natural ones? Share
    and discuss other participants' responses.

CHAPTER 4

LOGICAL CONSEQUENCES

SOCIETY'S LESSONS

As noted in the previous chapter, natural consequences are powerful influences upon our behavior. They do have limitations. For this reason, social conventions in the form of understandings, mores, rules, and laws have an impact of their own. A lack of understanding or ignorance of these contributes to difficulties among people of different ethnic or national origin. Western businessmen, for example, are only beginning to appreciate the subleties to conducting business with Arabs, Chinese, or Japanese businessmen. Likewise, agreements within and between families will differ so much so that arrangements for a wedding can be tantamont to war!

For those who ascribe to the rules and mores of a given group, to violate them is to invite the social consequences as a result. Such consequences generally will be accepted as a logical outcome of the ill-advised behavior of one of its members. The influence of peer opinion and consensus contributes to the power of the rules upon individuals. While individuals probably will not like the consequences, they tend to accept the consequences because they apply to all members and the rules are intended to contribute to the betterment of individuals as well as the group. Unlike natural consequences, logical (social) consequences are not unavoidable consequences of the deeds which they follow. Their definition and application, therefore, are more complex and require a context in which they operate.

COMPARISONS OF CONSEQUENCES AND PUNISHMENT

Logical consequences are the negative outcome of an ill-advised behavior which can logically follow even though the consequence requires the purposeful intervention of one or more other persons. For example, if you leave your belongings in places that cause inconvenience to others, others may move them to places inconvenient to you. A logical consequence would follow in that you may have to do without the use of the belongings during this period of time.

Some persons new to the concepts of natural and logical consequences will equate them with punishment. This conclusion is an error which is well illustrated by Dreikurs and Grey (1968, pp. 71-77). The comparison in Table 4.1 can help distinguish between consequences and punishment.

ASPECTS OF LOGICAL CONSEQUENCES

Certain aspects contribute to the successful implementing of consequences. Three of these aspects are attitudes, choices, and actions.

Attitudes

The importance of maintaining a *friendly attitude* and helping to establish *choices* cannot be overemphasized. Angry feelings can be evoked in conflict for a variety of reasons. At such times, personal power gets translated into an ultimatum, "you do it my way or else!". Conflicts are escalated into major wars and cooperation goes right out the window!

Friendly attitudes can be maintained when (1) you can perceive other alternatives to your behavior besides arguing and (2) you are not preoccupied with winning or losing. Angry feelings can be facilitative when they are expressed without disrespect to oneself or the other person. They *even* may be encouraging as illustrated in Chapter 5. On the whole, however, Adlerians recommend that you extricate yourself from power struggles.

TABLE 4.1
Comparison Of Consequences And Punishment

Consequences	Punishment
Expresses the reality of the social order of the situation not of the person	Expresses the power of a personal authority—*Authoritarian*
Logically related to the disruptive behavior	Not logical, only an arbitrary connection between disruptive behavior and consequences
Involves no element of moral judgment	Inevitably involves some moral judgment
Concerned only with what will happen now	Concerned with the past
Relationship and atmosphere are friendly. Resentment is minimized	Often anger is present either overtly or covertly. Resentment is frequent
Develops intrinsic motivation and self-discipline	Depends on extrinsic motivation
No submission or humiliation	Often requires submission or humiliation
Freedom of choice within limits	No alternatives or choice
Consequences are acceptable	Punishment is at best only tolerable
Thoughtful and deliberate	Often impulsive
Person feels important	Person feels belittled
Choice given once only	Often involves endless nagging
Uses action	Uses talking and coercion

Because at least two people are required to have a fight, Dreikurs (1968) recommended that you take "the sail out of their wind." When angry feelings have subsided, a discussion of what transpired and why, i.e., what purpose was served, may be helpful in re-establishing a friendly relationship. This discussion does not mean giving in. Rather you side step the power struggle until calmer circumstances prevail. One simple technique is to go to the bathroom, i.e., the bathroom technique. As comical as it may sound, parents, children, and spouses report that it does indeed bring greater harmony to the family! Occasionally persons in work settings report equally good results with co-workers and bosses!

Extricate yourself from struggles.

Logical consequences inflicted in anger increase the probability that the recipients will perceive them as revenge or punishment. If the recipient is prone to conflicts with power or revenge as a goal, logical consequences as a method may be ineffective in any case. As a method, however, it gives you a recourse if no natural consequences are available or reasonable (waiting for the roof to fall in may take too long or inflict damage of too permanent a nature!).

Choices

Choices are another aspect of successfully implementing logical consequences. The magic in giving choices sometimes astounds persons unfamiliar with these methods. No one appreciates an ultimatum, particularly when there is personal tension between the parties involved. Sometimes, however, simply perceiving that one has some degree of influence and choice is sufficient to allay defensiveness and resistance. One such case was shared by a parent study group member who applied this principle in her work as receptionist for an ophthalmologist.

Occasionally patients would balk at having medication put into their eyes. She asked the physician if he would like a suggestion during one such episode. He followed her advice and asked the patient if he would like both drops at the same time or prefer to have them one at a time. The patient made his choice and the physician was forever grateful because it proved effective with other patients as well. Persons preoccupied with control are particularly open to being more cooperative when given choices.

The magic in giving choices
astounds persons.

Teachers and parents have reported similar results with youngsters. One such illustration comes from a teacher who was bothered by a pupil who persistently rocked back on his chair. In spite of warnings about school rules, and so forth, the pupil would tip the chair back on the two legs. Eventually the teacher asked if he would like to sit on all four legs like the other pupils or sit on just the two legs. He indicated that he would prefer to use just two. She took two books, placed them under the front legs so that the chair tilted back at a safe but uncomfortable angle. After a time, he removed the books and there was no further problem during the remainder of the year. In this case, the teacher wisely offered a choice and creatively established a logical consequence.

Action Not Words

Another important aspect to the successful implementation of natural and logical consequences is that action, not words, helps insure that fewer misunderstandings will follow. In the last example, once the choice was made, the teacher said no more. Especially when the boy decided to remove the books and be seated properly, her attention to other matters made it clear that she was not concerned about having her way. Had she made any comments, she could have run the risk of being misunderstood even though she may have meant well. Adults, no less than children, appreciate being allowed to cooperate quietly without fanfare when they decide it is once again in their best interest.

STUDY QUESTIONS

Direction: Respond to the following in spaces provided,

1. List four or more major distinctions between consequences and punishment.

2. Cite two or more illustrations from your experiences which you can now distinguish as natural vs. logical consequences.

3. Why should logical consequences apply to everyone in a common social group, i.e., what problems develop if they aren't?

4. When are logical consequences likely to be least effective?

ACTIVITIES FOR INDIVIDUALS AND GROUPS

Definition of Logical Consequences: A logical outcome of an ill-advised act and requires the intervention of another person to insure its impact. Normally, the individual has one or more alternative choices to a given situation. The logical relationship of the act to outcome helps the individual to accept responsibility for the misjudgment and its subsequent correction.

Examples:

Action	Logical Consequence
child does not get dressed in the morning	no breakfast if adult must use time to help with dressing instead of making breakfast
you leave clothes lying in hallway	others may put them where they please

Listing Logical Consequences

A. List one or more logical consequences to each of the following; *ask yourself, what happens if someone intervenes? Or what happens if that becomes a rule for everyone, i.e., what if the logic of how to behave is mimicked?*

Action	Logical Consequence
1. using others' materials, equipment, or clothes without permission	
2. neglect to inform others where he/she is going, will return, etc.	

3. persistently allows supplies to run low, e.g., car low on gas when it is returned

4. comes to regularly scheduled activities late, e.g. reading circle, class, or family meetings

5. does not listen to instruction first time

6. regularly solicits assistance after bedtime or at other times inconvenient to others

7. when called to come in, etc., never comes the first time

8. does not carry out trash, cut grass, etc., without being nagged or threatened

B. Share your list of logical consequences with your group by having each person take one of the actions, share his/her consequence list recommendation, and invite others to add theirs or modify yours as appropriate.

Sharing Personally Experienced Logical Consequences

A. Now identify three or more logical consequences which have been used successfully to help you or others experience the outcome of ill-advised behavior. Did others intervene? Was a "new rule" adopted?

Ill-advised Behavior   **Logical Consequence Experienced**

1.

2.

3.

B. Share with your partner or group members the responses listed in Part A. Does your partner or do your group members agree that the consequences you listed are logical consequences? Do the other members respond in the same way as you? Why or why not?

CHAPTER 5

ENCOURAGEMENT

THE ESSENTIAL ELEMENT IN HELPING

In John Kennedy's *Profiles in Courage* (1956), he described events surrounding acts of courage by legislators who found themselves at significant moments in history, unpopular with the constituents who had voted them into office. In each case, Kennedy illustrated how these men rose above partisan politics and the prevailing social practices of the day to act on principles fundamental to better society. Not all of these men had been true to the public trust throughout their careers, quite the contrary. On the other hand, several faced certain defeat and potential bodily harm if they acted counter to the popular opinion. When they did speak out, for example, against slavery, all of the negative consequences one would expect befell them. Kennedy believed that everyone has such opportunities in their lives when they must look into their own souls to determine how they shall act.

The cultivation of that quality which prompts one to act responsibly, deliberately, and with conviction is the subject of this chapter. Sometimes, as is evident, when faced with negative consequences, you act to serve a greater good than personal advantage. Equally important, it frees one to live fully in the world as an active participant each moment of each day.

The essential element in the concept of encouragement is *courage.* Ghandhi (Nehru, 1958) said,

> Courage is the one true foundation of character. Without courage there can be no truth, no love or religion. For one subject to fear can pursue neither truth nor love. (p. i)

The quality of approaching life courageously is what raises one's consciousness to the beauty all around us, to the intrinsic value in a new experience, to the satisfaction in making a new discovery, or in the mastery of a new skill. Optimally, everyone would greet each day as a new opportunity with an expectation that regardless of temporary negative circumstances, he/she would not only survive but thrive in the future. Not because of some good fortune but, because they choose to perceive life in this manner, it would be true for them.

We create our expectations of
how life will treat us and how
well we will respond.

Increasingly, research and clinical experience tend to corroborate the observations of Adler. He noted that each of us creates our expectations of how life will treat us and how well we will respond. Basically, people tend to place themselves in one of two broad categories. One group perceives themselves as captains of their ship or masters of their own destiny. By contrast, others deny that they can do much more than avoid a catastrophe from circumstances beyond their control. The latter group may take either passive or active attitudes and behavior, i.e., accepting their fate or challenging whatever force(s) they perceive as creating constraints. Persons in the passive group tend toward a disruptive behavior goal of inadequacy. Other such goals are discussed in Chapter 6.

Even as adults, some people deny responsibility for meeting life's tasks. They ask innocently, how could I assume responsibility for events over which I have no control? The active group by contrast tests for the limits. Daredevils, gamblers, and criminals of various sorts all tend to have a desire to "beat the odds," to experience a personal triumph in the face of a compelling force. In their discouragement, they have mistaken the meaning of their acts as something noble or necessary in order to be somebody of worth in an otherwise oppressive environment.

Obviously, matters of degree exist in the two broad categories. Witness the number of persons who subscribe to horoscope services or carry good luck charms. Many of these same people ostensibly believe in "free will" as a gift of the Creator. We are not surprised, then, by the variety and degrees of behavior which reflect discouragement in one's attitude toward coping with new or difficult life situations.

Early childhood experiences increase the probability but *do not determine* the orientation which a person assumes toward life. For example, the socialization process includes teaching children what is inappropriate or harmful. Adlerians believe that in order for children to develop into self-confident, healthy adults, they also need to know that you have faith in their abilities and that you accept them for who they are, not only what they do.

Children tend to be reminded constantly of their limitations. Consider the four-year old who can't reach the faucet, see the top of the counter, needs help cutting his food and can't quite snap his pants after going to the bathroom. As adults, we expect him to need help and know that he will soon be able to take care of himself. In the child's eyes, never having experienced full self-reliance, these temporary limitations can be perceived as signs of inferiority.

Given consistent encouragement, you increase the probability that a child will accept these shortcomings for what they are and keep trying to do his best. He will decide that, although he sometimes fails at what he attempts, this does not mean that he is a failure. By contrast, the child whose limitations are exaggerated through comparison to siblings, who experiences overprotection or other responses which impart a lack of respect and faith in him as an individual, may grow up feeling that he is inferior or otherwise unequal to the business of life.

ON BELIEVING

Recent literature on biofeedback research and stress management clearly demonstrate the capacity each of us has to create these moods and emotions that we wish to experience

(Witmer, 1985). They also lend empirical data to Adler's assumption that emotions are our tools to help us achieve our goals. By purposely practicing body relaxation and positive mental images, individual's learn to overcome debilitating stress resulting from real or imagined circumstances. In fact, research has established that the body does not distinguish between vicarious and real experiences. The body responds in the same way, for example, to imagined or real stressors if the individual *believes* that a real threat is imminent. Likewise, application of these same principles helps persons who experience chronic pain to overcome its negative impact on other aspects of their lives.

Simonton and Matthews-Simonton (1978) have helped terminal cancer patients to utilize the power of positive thinking to mobilize the body's natural healing forces to attack and overwhelm the cancer cells in their bodies. While the results of the methods are still under careful scrutiny and are by no means a replacement for more conventional medical treatment, the fact that some persons have responded favorably and others report greater comfort in coping with their condition lends support to the need for more openness about the capacities and interactions of the human mind and body. One must remember, too, that these are the patients upon whom all other methods have failed. Any remission is encouraging to the patient, for whatever length of time.

The author noted with interest the results of an investigation of race drivers heart beats, at rest, before leaving the pit area and while in time trials. As might be expected, the experienced drivers tend to be less excited than the "rookie" drivers. Likewise, the younger drivers tend to have a lower heart beat while relaxed at home. However, one young driver was noted to have a consistent, moderately low heart rate (110) throughout one time trial run even though he narrowly missed hitting the wall on two of the four turns. For whatever reason, he did not perceive a real threat to himself and continued to perform in a relatively nonstressed condition throughout the trial. As a consequence, he also experienced less fatigue and all its concomitant affects while actually on the track.

Many other life situations are less dramatic than these cited to which individuals respond as stressers. Significant life changes, even those considered socially positive such as promotions, marriage, and birth of child can contribute to situations which tend to correlate with physical and/or mental illness. Each of these circumstances has a potential for both positive and negative affects but in the eye of the beholder is where each is determined. Discouraged persons will point to the "lucky" person who was in the right place at the right time. Case studies reveal that more often, the "lucky" person had worked for years, sometimes against great odds, and recognized an opportunity or discovery for what it was because of the earlier experience.

Persons with what Adler called high social interest, tend to be purposely goal oriented. They believe that by setting goals, they increase the probability of achieving what they desire. Research on college student self-concepts and decision making strategies suggest that the high self-concept students are more deliberate and, consequently, successful in their planning than low self-concept students (Burnett, 1988). Research somewhat similar to that conducted with school age youngsters is still needed to determine if, through a program of encouragement, low self-concept college students could not only improve their self-concept but their decision making ability as well.

In the author's experience, discouraged persons have difficulty setting goals and having faith in themselves to do what the situation requires for them to be successful. Existing are what I consider situational or temporary conditions to which individuals respond with discouragement. The loss of a loved one, illness, prolonged fatigue, lack of proper nutrition, and such contribute to discouragement. The high social interest person tends to become less discouraged, i.e., less depressed, less prone to persist in withdrawal, and more likely to begin helping others as a means of overcoming their grief. They choose to redirect themselves, to establish new goals, new expectations, and regain satisfaction in the relatively simple, readily available satisfactions in life.

The low social interest person tends to *use* the situational or temporary conditions as an excuse for not acting responsibly and, when called for, with courage. A societal consequence of this circumstance is millions of dollars each year spent on sustenance for persons who psychologically have dropped out of society as a contributing member. Not everyone on welfare is low in social interest any more than everyone who is gainfully employed is high in social interest. As an imperfect society, although still better than many, it has yet to secure social equality for all of its people and, thereby, contributes to the very discouragement which we wish to ameliorate. A practical social consequence of this lack of equality is lost talent, lawlessness, and expenditure of resources for corrective purposes rather than prevention.

The remainder of this chapter is devoted to methods and techniques of encouragement. Fundamental to encouraging others is the need to encourage oneself. Wrenn (1980) addressed this concept in his article for counselors on "The Importance of Believing in Yourself or Building a More Positive Self-Image." The three elements he expounded upon in building a more positive self-image are as follows:

1. Recognizing and stressing your personal assets.

2. Developing a core of positive beliefs about others and about life.

3. Demonstrating a sense of caring for others.

The adage "physician heal thyself" speaks to the need for persons in the healing/helping profession to practice what they preach. Maltz (1960) provides a practical guide for this purpose. Discovering many of the same insights shared by Adler, he drew upon his experiences as a plastic surgeon to give serious students a means of avoiding "burn out" while meeting their own life tasks. Some researchers estimate that we humans "self-talk" at a rate of 800 words per minute and that we are talking to ourselves 70% of the time. If we are to help others obtain and sustain positive self-talk, we, too, must be careful what we mentally digest through our senses.

DEFINITION AND ASSUMPTIONS

Encouragement inspires or helps others toward a conviction that they can work on finding solutions and that they can cope with any predicament. Some basic assumptions about encouragement are extensions of the concepts presented in Chapter 1 concerning high and low social interest.

Encouragement includes the following seven actions. An example of a desirable statement is given followed by one that is not desirable.

1. **What** one is doing is more important than how one is doing.

    Ex: That's a beautiful shine on your car, what did you do to get it that way?

    Vs: I'll bet you take better care of your car than anyone else in town. (comparing)

2. The **present** is the focus more so than with the past or future.

    Ex: It's obvious that you're really enjoying this project by the time and energy that you're giving to it.

    Vs: Now why don't you work this hard all the time!

3. The **deed** is what is important rather than the doer.

    Ex: I really appreciate your help, thanks!

    Vs: You're such a good boy, you always do the right thing!

    or when correcting

    Ex: I really feel angry when you ask for food and then don't eat it.

    Vs: You're always wasting food—you're just plain irresponsible.

4. The **effort** is to be emphasized rather than the outcome.

    Ex: By golly, I enjoyed that game. If I can just learn to be more patient and not rush the ball, next time I should be able to give you a better match! (emphasis on progress, what to do, and enjoying increased competence)

Vs: You were lucky this time but you can be sure I'll beat you for sure next time, no matter what it takes! (it's winning that counts!)

5. **Intrinsic** motivation, (i.e., satisfaction, enjoyment, challenge) is to be expressed rather than extrinsic.

Ex: I spend hours taking pictures, nothing gives me more pleasure than capturing a moment in time which reflects the beauty in life!

Vs: What do I get for doing it? What's in it for me?

6. What is **being learned** is more important than what is not being learned.

Ex: You've just about mastered addition and subtraction. That will be very helpful to you in learning division and multiplication. Now let's look at a couple of problems which give you difficulty and get you help mastering them.

Vs: We're going to have to go on and you'll need to get help at home or division's going to be hard for you.

7. What is **being done correctly** is more important than what is not being done correctly.

Ex: You got 84 out of 100 correct on addition and subtraction. With just a little more effort, I know that you'll be able to go on to division and multiplication.

Vs: You missed 16 out of a 100.

The encouraging person practices these behaviors until they are given genuinely and spontaneously. Conversely, many people are prone to discourage others quite unconsciously. I am reminded of a television sports interview which captured the essential difference with respect to intrinsic vs extrinsic motivation as it relates to competition. In this instance, a downhill skier had just lost the championship by literally fractions of a second. Immediately after the results were announced, a commentator interviewed the skier and asked, "You lost the championship by only fractions of a second, knowing that now, how would you run the race differently?" The skier replied: "I wouldn't. It was a good run. I gave it my best effort and everything went as planned." The commentator continued "But you lost by only fractions of a second, might you have pushed off a little harder at the start or attack the track a little differently?" The skier, "Not really. It was an exhilarating run. I did my best. The other fellow just went a little faster!"

The commentator tried again in disbelief to elicit a regret or disappointment from the skier. The skier was comfortable, however, that it *was* a good run, he had done his best and to be second, third, or whatever was not his primary criteria. No doubt he would prefer to win. His goal does include winning but factors exist over which he does not have control, e.g., the other skier going a little faster! This brings us to another aspect of encouragement which I believe is a unique contribution to an understanding of helping others.

ESSENCE OF ENCOURAGEMENT

Life circumstances are subject to many factors beyond the control of individuals. Attitudes, expectations, and self-beliefs, however, are within the control of the individual. Assisting individuals to minimize the impact of noncontrollable factors and to maximize their use of controllable factors in enriching their own life experiences is of the essence in helping them.

Uncontrollable factors include, for example, the family into which one is born, the school system, neighborhood, economic environment, talents, handicaps, and physical characteristics shaped by genetic contributions of parents. Many others might be considered accidents of nature or man.

Among the controllable factors, on the other hand, are attitudes toward environmental circumstances, knowledge about self, others, and behavior which supports one's attitudes, expectations, and self beliefs. Concerning the basic life task of work, for example, Sweeney and Shafe (1978) outlined a strategy that teachers can use to assist in the career development of youngsters.

We define career development as the process individuals experience throughout life in acquiring knowledge, skills, and attitudes useful to them in both gainful and non-gainful work. Career choices (Chapter 9), like other personal choices, are in the realm of controllable factors.

Maximizing one's control over career choices includes

- encouraging positive work habits;

- teaching the value of purposeful attention to physical appearance;

- teaching how to locate, assess, and use career information; and

- developing knowledge and skill with valuing, decision making, goal setting, planning and follow through.

Minimizing the impact of noncontrollable factors includes

- acquiring information about economic trends and job requirements,

- raising consciousness to social attitudes and practices which can be unnecessary constraints such as sex stereotyping, and

- providing examples of individuals with similar handicaps who overcame them to pursue their career choices.

All people start out life with a desire
to discover, develop mastery, and enjoy life.

In short, a major thrust of encouragement is toward helping individuals' establish goals, attitudes, and competencies needed to cope with life as they experience it. Sometimes adults express concern that we are fostering mediocrity in performance. Nothing could be further from the truth. All people start life with a desire to discover, develop mastery, and enjoy life. Through encouragement, you feed these inclinations and bring them to consciousness to be enjoyed all the more. What parent hasn't experienced a young child saying "no, I want to do it myself." Who can't recall the deep satisfaction at developing mastery of a new task or problem, whether in tying one's shoe or solving a geometry problem?

I am often struck by adults' preoccupation with toilet training, eating habits, and bed times. All of these activities involve intrinsic satisfiers, i.e., pleasure, relief, and self assertiveness. With five children to help rear, I have had many occasions to pick up a tired, grumpy young one and begin carrying him or her to bed. On the way, with a head against my shoulder, I speak of how good its going to feel between the cool, clean sheets—stretching out, curling up and thinking pleasant thoughts—and, oh how good it will feel to be rested and what fun you will have when you get up rested! All of our children enjoy a good rest!

Likewise, toilet habits are no particular problem. When a youngster is ready to assume responsibility, a little help is all that's needed. Being too impressed with when the baby book says it might happen prompts anxious parents, and kids who know how to use it! On the other hand, asking how they feel when they finish, heightens awareness of the relief and pleasure involved. You also can talk about the good feelings associated with taking care of oneself.

When one is working on a new task or problem, help in insuring success is always appreciated. How much help is needed varies with individuals but success does encourage further effort. Inch by inch anything is a cinch! Regardless of age, people enjoy discovery and mastery. I remember well the experience of helping a thirty-five year old Catholic nun learn to water ski. For a nun at that time, to even be seen in public in other than the traditional habit was quite novel. She had been excited, however, by the prospect of learning to water ski since she was a young girl.

Not athletically inclined and also now accustomed to a more sedate life, she struggled time after time to bring herself out of the water. Finally, after many tries, she succeeded in a relatively short but significant ride. The expression of exhilaration on her face could not be explained adequately. Even now, one of her happiest recollections is the day she mastered water skiing. Some may say, "but she never became a champion water skier" and that's quite right, however, that was not her goal. The same "true grit" with which she attacked water skiing could be found in other areas of her interests.

The definition of success that I use corresponds to this philosophy. In this case:

> Success is the progressive realization of predetermined, worthwhile goals and a well balanced life.

Success, therefore, is a process not an event. Students in school can consider themselves already successful as they progress through school. Not only when they graduate. Parents can consider themselves successful even as they see their children struggling with life's challenges. Not only when the "children" graduate from colleges, get jobs, or whatever other events they might otherwise set as goals. By this definition, planfulness is deliberate. Setting goals and milestones to their achievement is deliberate. Valuing is central to the process as goals are determined to be "worthwhile" by the individual. Finally, a balance exists to such a life, i.e., physical health, mental health, and so forth are maintained through loving family relationships, attention to good eating habits, hygiene, cooperative work relationships, and so forth. With this definition, anyone can be helped to see themselves as successful.

If each of us enjoys life, enjoys learning and strives to be the best we can at what we choose, can anyone ask more? With proper encouragement, more young people will grow up like the skier in our earlier illustration, capable of being champions in their own minds because they enjoy doing their best at whatever they choose.

COMMUNICATING ENCOURAGEMENT

Research and experience have revealed that most people are not particularly effective listeners or communicators when others need their help. Being able both to reflect others feelings and to communicate your own effectively, increases the probability that better interpersonal relationships will be established. Most neophyte helpers believe that advice, information, or questions for more specific details are the main tools for helping others. While these techniques have a place, too, they are what can be called "action" dimensions of helping. When used early in response to others, these techniques actually have been found to be subtractive rather than helpful. They instead discourage the person further. Empathic (feeling) understanding as well as communicating same appear to be central, necessary conditions in a helping relationship. The facilitative dimension of helping, then, is prerequisite to the action dimension.

A vocabulary of feeling terms is listed in Table 5.1. A review of these terms can be helpful in developing more effective communication skills. Note, for example, which terms you use most comfortably and often. As you review the terms, consider how some are more specific and state feelings of greater intensity. For example, instead of "upset," you might say more accurately, "I feel embarrassed," "disappointed," or "angry." Improving your vocabulary helps provide greater resource for you as a facilitative listener and communicator. In the author's experience, many people lack an adequate vocabulary for this purpose.

When communicating that you have listened and understand what someone else is experiencing, accuracy, specificity, concreteness, and immediacy are important ingredients. A choice of terms is a major tool in this process. For example, "Even now you feel pleased that you made the proper choice" compared to "well that's nice, it sounds like you're pretty happy about it."

Study the set of discrimination categories and responses listed. At the end of the chapter, rate the responses in the self-practice activities. The purpose of these activities is to provide practice in discrimination between responses which are subtractive, interchangeable, and additive.

TABLE 5.1
Feelings Vocabulary List

absurd	daring	fulfilled	numb	suspicious
adequate	deflated	gallant	obsessed	terror
adventuresome	dejected	gay	odd	thankful
affectionate	delight	ghastly	offended	timid
afraid	depressed	gladness	overjoyed	tormented
aggravated	desirable	gleeful	overcome	tremendous
agony	despair	good	pang	triumph
agreeable	desperate	grateful	peaceful	troubled
amused	disagreeable	great	perturbed	trustful
angry	disappointed	grief	phoney	undesirable
anguish	discontented	grouchy	pleasure	uneasy
animosity	disgust	guilty	plucky	unfortunate
anxious	disheartened	happy	proud	unhappy
apprehensive	dislike	heartbroken	queer	unnerved
ardent	disquieted	hopeless	regret	valiant
arrogant	disturbed	hopeful	relaxed	voluptuous
ashamed	distrustful	horrible	relieved	warm
astounded	downcast	humble	repelled	weary
awful	eager	humiliated	resentment	winsome
bewitching	earnest	hurt	resignation	wistful
bitter	ecstasy	impatient	resolute	witty
blessful	elated	indignation	restless	wonderful
bold	emotional	indifferent	revealing	worried
bored	encouraged	insecure	ridiculous	
bothered	enraged	insincere	sad	
breathless	enthusiastic	inspired	satisfied	
buoyant	excited	intimate	scared	
captivated	exhilarated	intimidated	secure	
charming	fantastic	joy	seductive	
cheerful	fascinated	jubilant	self-reliant	
close	fearful	mad	sentimental	
comfortable	fervent	marvelous	skittish	
complacent	fidgety	meek	sorrow	
confused	fine	melancholy	special	
confident	flabergasted	merry	splendid	
contented	flustered	miserable	stricken	
contempt	forlorn	mortified	stunned	
crushed	fortunate	nervous	sulky	

Discrimination Categories and
Response Examples for Communications

Stem: I really want to do well in school (pause) . . . I mean I really try but (pause) . . . I just can't seem to keep up (pause) . . . you know, it's just so hard . . . knowing how to study, doing well on tests, and now writing reports! It really worries me . . .

Subtractive

1. Definitely hurtful, to sense of belonging, adequacy, or security.

   Response Example: "You're the kind of person who is always talking but never gets to work. Take your talk somewhere else, I'm busy."

   May simply change the subject making further subject exploration by speaker difficult or impossible.

   Response Example: "Yeah, well, that's how it goes. Say did you see the game last night?"

2. Type and/or intensity of feeling ignored; content oriented although not necessarily accurate even in this area, e.g., asks for more information or makes specific suggestions without indicating awareness of what was stated.

   Response Example: "So you don't know how to study effectively. . ." or "Have you talked to your teacher about it?"

Interchangeable

3. Restates content and feeling or, in many cases, reflects feeling tone with only necessary content included; even without the speaker's comments, a third party could determine essentially what was conveyed.

   Response Example: "You're really worried cause you can't keep up with your school work no matter how hard you try . . ." or "Doing well is really important to you but no matter how hard you try, you still can't seem to do well enough . . ."

Additive

4. Clarifies content and feelings expressed often stated more succinctly and increases probability of further exploration by individual; immediacy and specificity are often present in the communication.

   Response Example: "You want to do well but it's really discouraging and kinda scary because it seems to be getting more difficult all the time . . ."

5. Definitely adds new dimensions to exploration of feeling and content by speaker; enhances for example, speaker's capacity to deal with thoughts and feelings of belonging, adequacy or security; may be confrontation or action oriented but always within a context of nonpossessive regard and empathy.

   Response Example: "To do well seems so important but now you're wondering, can I really do it . . . do I have what it takes . . ."

**Activity 5.1 Communication Skills
Discrimination Activity**

Directions: Rate each of the following responses in their helpfulness to the individual speaking. Use the following:

S = subtractive

I = interchangeable, or

A = additive

Excerpt 1: *My husband comes home tired, complains about how hard he's worked all day and then proceeds to criticize what I haven't got done! With three kids and my mother-in-law dropping in several times a week, I'm absolutely beside myself!*

_____ a. Is your mother-in-law aware of how her visits upset your work schedule?

_____ b. Sounds like you need to talk with someone!

_____ c. Your husband's attitude really is insensitive to your situation; just thinking about it makes you angry.

_____ d. I can remember feeling that way myself.

Excerpt 2: *I went into see my supervisor about a problem I'm having with one of my coworkers. Before I knew what was happening, she was asking me what I'd done to bring this on! After working here for fourteen years with no problems, I felt hurt and betrayed.*

_____ a. You really feel betrayed by your supervisor—she completely missed the point of your conference— you must wonder, can you trust her?

_____ b. How long has she been with the company?

_____ c. In fourteen years, you never had other problems?

_____ d. That must really hurt. After all those years of good service, she questions you!

Excerpt 3: *We had such a really good time at the beach that all my problems seem inconsequential now!*

_____ a. That was some great trip to the beach! No problem seems too big or important that it can't be handled!

_____ b. Which one did you go to?

_____ c. How can you say that after all the money you must have spent!

_____ d. Sounds like you're still enjoying it, even your problems seem less important!

Excerpt 4: *After living with us almost as a member of the family for over a dozen years, our dog died this weekend and I still keep looking for him-expecting him to greet me when I come home. I feel so bad and yet I know he was just an animal.*

_____ a. It seems hard to explain but that dog was a member of the family. You miss him and really feel bad not having him there when you come home.

_____ b. I know how you feel. I once had a parakeet I felt that way about.

_____ c. Was he hit by a car or something?

_____ d. There must be a lot of people who feel that way; haven't you heard about animal cemeteries?

Direction: Check your responses with the following key:

	a.	b.	c.	d.
1.	S	S	A	S
2.	A	S	S	I
3.	I	S	S	I
4.	I	S	S	S

Activity 5.2 Communication Skills
Discrimination Exercise

Directions: Rate each of the following responses in their helpfulness to the individual speaking. Use the following:

S = subtractive

I = interchangeable, or

A = additive

Pupil to adult

Excerpt 1: *Boy, is she ever a great teacher! I mean she really makes coming to school fun. She even makes me feel that trying the problems is the best part!*

_____ a. Wow, she sure is some kind of great teacher! I even feel like I'd like to be in her class, too!

_____ b. How does she do that?

_____ c. She's so great that even the toughest problems seem like fun . . . it must be really exciting to be in her class!

_____ d. Do you think the other kids like her class, too?

Excerpt 2: *I don't ever get a chance to talk about the things I like. The other girls always pick their friends as discussion leaders. It isn't fair and they just don't care, either.*

_____ a. Why don't you tell them how you feel?

_____ b. The other girls really make you feel bad when they purposely leave you out of the discussion.

_____ c. It really doesn't seem fair for the other girls to exclude you from the discussion by always talking about their interest.

_____ d. Aren't you being a little over sensitive? You have the same vote as the other girls and the same opportunity.

Adult to Adult

Excerpt 3: *The things we talked about at the last team meeting really worked! I can't get over it! Only one day later and already I can see an improvement. I really think we've hit a bonanza!*

_____ a: Hey, that's wonderful! Sounds like you're right on top on this situation and really enjoying it.

_____ b. Well, don't be too disappointed if things don't go as well tomorrow.

_____ c. You'll have to tell us more about it at the next meeting.

_____ d. What a great feeling! Only one day and things are already going better! Let's share it with everyone else!

Excerpt 4: *I really don't understand what's happened to Mary lately. She seems distant . . . unwilling to talk with me like we used to . . . with drugs and such so much in the news now. I don't know what to think.*

_____ a. You feel worried about Mary's reluctance to confide in you as she use to . . . you're not at all sure what it could mean.

_____ b. You really shouldn't worry; girls Mary's age all go through that stage.

_____ c. Would you like me to get you a copy of a new government booklet on drugs? Maybe that would put your mind at ease.

_____ d. It's upsetting to have Mary being distant with you . . . you feel somewhat powerless to help her at a time when she may benefit most from your guidance.

Excerpt 5: *I'm sick and tired of always having to make do with second rate materials. If they don't think enough of us as teachers, the least they could do is think of the kids. It's the same old story every year. "Well, you know we're on an austerity budget"!*

_____ a. Yeah, it was that way at the last school I taught, too.

_____ b. I agree with you.

_____ c. It's really frustrating to try doing a decent job of teaching with second rate materials . . . the least they could do is think of the kids.

_____ d. It really is sad to think of how this affects the kids school experience and no one in authority even seems to care . . .

Direction: Check your responses with the following key:

	a.	b.	c.	d.
1.	A	S	I	S
2.	S	I	I	S
3.	I	S	S	A
4.	I	S	S	A
5.	S	S	I	I

Another aspect of verbal communication which deserves mention relates to minimizing the negative aspects of sharing angry or confrontative feelings. The basic principles involves "I messages" instead of "you messages" (Dinkmeyer & McKay, 1976; Gordon, 1975). In lieu of nagging, complaining or blaming, simply communicate the feelings that another's specific behavior tends to prompt in you. "I messages" (1) describe the behavior which is bothersome, (2) state your feeling about the consequence the behavior produces for you, and (3) include the consequence to you. An example is as follows:

- Behavior: **When** you don't fill the car up with gas after using it,

- Feeling: **I feel** angry

- Consequence: **because** I am delayed in getting to my office or appointment when I leave in the morning.

Compare the preceeding statement to the following: "Well, you did it again! When are you going to start acting responsibly? I was late to work because the car had no gas in the tank!"

I Messages

Not unlike logical consequences, to use the "I message" formula while angry and visibly upset, decreases its effectiveness. If your goal, however, is to maintain respect among all parties involved, you increase the probabilities that a successful solution can be found. As will be noted in those chapters on child guidance (Chapter 6) and family consultation (Chapter 11), being able to express our genuine feelings, even angry feelings, can be facilitative when respect is inherent in the relationship. The fact that you are angry (or really happy) reflects your level of genuine interest and valuing. To show a continuing desire to work toward a satisfactory solution without warfare actually contributes to greater trust, intimacy, and respect.

I believe that the truly successful resolution of differences and conflict builds stronger, better relationships whether at work, among friends, or in marriage. In fact, differences can be seen as an opportunity instead of a threat, to closer relationships. The practice of these methods and techniques of encouragement and conflict resolution increase our likelihood of healthier, more satisfying relationships.

Further Application

As noted at the beginning of this chapter, as many applications of these methods exist as the number of social conflicts. With respect to adult relationships, the same steps are followed although techniques will vary. The most commonly violated aspect of conflict resolution concerns the first step, mutual respect. When we believe that someone else is mistaken or has done something wrong, we tend to begin our interaction by asking accusatory questions, blaming, or pointing out the error. In short, we tend to undermine the other persons sense of belonging, security, or adequacy. Action statements follow as to what should be done to correct the situation. Even though the suggestions may address what the situation requires to correct it, the violation of step one almost precludes successful resolution. Winning and losing become the outcome of such situations.

On the other hand, if mutual respect is established through active listening, good eye contact, and empathic communication, the other steps may not be executed optimally but the situation can still be resolved satisfactorily. When others perceive openness, flexibility, and respect as elements of efforts to solve differences, a much greater probability of success exists in achieving a satisfactory outcome.

Another way of expressing our concern about another's behavior and/or attitudes can be characterized as facilitative confrontations (Carkhuff & Berenson, 1967). On occasion, sharing perceptions can be growth producing and helpful even though the perceptions speak to aspects of the person's being which one may find uncomfortable. I recall one such instance when an undergraduate in my human relations class had distinguished herself as the class clown. She was always good for a laugh. After getting to know her during the quarter, we had a conference concerning her relatively poor performance with the class assignments. I had noted that often she was the butt end of her pranks and jokes. I asked:

Co: I wonder why you end up being the one everyone looks to for a laugh. Do you know?

St: No, I really don't.

Co: I wonder, could it be that so long as you're good for a laugh, no one needs to take you seriously . . . that they keep you in your place as sorority or class clown because they feel more comfortable not considering your opinions, how you feel, what makes you happy . . . or sad . . .

St: (silent but pensive) . . . I've never quite put it that way before but I have wondered . . . do they really like me, no, do they respect me as a person. You think, "hey, does anybody care that I might not be here next quarter cause I'm flunking my courses?" . . . Yeah, that's it! (smiles) . . . so I'm the court jester, good for a laugh . . . I'll be darned!

Co: Quite a discovery, but you know what . . .

St: No

Co: It isn't their fault either . . .

St: What do you mean?

Co: Well, who said you had to be what they wanted?

St: Oh, I see.

Co: Now the question is, what do you want to do about it? Would you like to change?

St: You bet!

In this case, change was not so easy. As we pursued the situation further, I pointed out that because she lacked confidence in herself, she had developed many habits which earned her the reputation she now wanted changed. People expected her to perform, so to speak, as she always had. When one begins changing, others can become uncomfortable. All of a sudden you seem unpredictable! The combination of self-doubt and others' expectations are always a factor in such instances. She was able to accept my observations, even though they were psychologically distressing to her, because she experienced genuineness, nonpossessive caring, and empathic under-standing in our relationship. Equally important, I helped her understand the purpose of her behavior. How it masked her fear of being a failure and gave her an excuse for not exploring her real capabilities and talents was revealed. This "hidden reason," as Dreikurs called it, would no longer be as useful to her in avoiding her life tasks. More importantly, she was now free to have a good laugh and joke around or not, as she chose. She also began practicing behaviors which prompted others to perceive her as a more serious minded, responsible student, and friend.

Effective verbal communication, then, involves several components. Most often the words we use are the least important factors although they, too, contribute to the overall effect. Key concepts include

1. **reflective listening** which reveals an awareness of the kind and intensity of feelings expressed;

2. **non-judgmental attitudes** which show respect for the individual even though we may not like what they have done;

3. **accepting responsibility** for our feelings and avoiding blaming, complaining and nagging; and

4. **understanding the purpose of behavior** and how it may be self-defeating to the other person and/or ourselves in finding solutions to life circumstances.

In a presentation on behavioral techniques for improving classroom behavior of children, Madsen and Madsen (1970) reported that they and their research associates had visited the classrooms of several thousand teachers. Based on their observations, they concluded the 8% of the teachers were positive in their interactions with the young people 50% or more of the time. In the author's experience as a lecturer in the U.S. and abroad, workshop participants, including teachers, generally guessed fairly close to this 8% when asked their opinion. What this suggests is that the most powerful learning methods we have, i.e., modeling and example, are absent in the one environment where learning to cope with life is an expected outcome. Based upon readings in health professional journals, similar results between nurses and physicians also could be found. In short, the most important mission is to model, teach, and perfect methods of encouragement if we are to cope successfully with the problems of our time.

ON BEING ENCOURAGING

Attention to only verbal methods of encouragement leaves a significant gap in what is required. Adlerians stress the significance of action, not words, when coping with discipline problems. The same principle can be espoused for encouragement. All of us look for evidence that what others say is revealed also in their behaviors. Nonverbal communication can be as simple as smiling or as involved as planning and conducting events specifically designed to reflect love, respect, and genuine caring for others.

Remembering and celebrating birthdays, anniversaries, and graduations, all constitute nonverbal messages of encouragement. At such times, the recipients may not remember exactly what was said or what was given to them but they will remember the manner in which it was given.

Some illustrations of acts of encouragement include the following:

1. helping someone do a job that might otherwise be done alone;

2. listen to someone describe a hobby, a vocation, or event which she/he wanted to share;

3. keep busy and remain patient while someone else completes a task she/he found difficult;

4. complete or do another's task in order to let her/him have more leisure time;

5. share with a friend a book or record of value to you;

6. offer to do a favor without being asked;

7. send letters of appreciation, thanks, or remembrance, especially when it might easily be overlooked; and

8. intervene on another's behalf to help others appreciate his/her capabilities or contributions for a job to be done or were to be given.

Virtually any act which is given genuinely as an expression of appreciation, recognition, or acceptance of an other person's qualities, talents, or behavior can be encouraging. Sometimes individuals will question why Adlerians tend to avoid reference to praise. Several explanations can be given for this tendency. First, most often, we are working to help overcome evidence of discouragement in other persons. Referring to the explanation in Chapter 1 of the vertical and horizontal planes on which people tend to move, praise by our definition tends to bring attention to how one is doing more so than what one is doing, e.g., "you're a good painter, you've done that well!" Because discouraged persons tend to be preoccupied with how they are doing, we prefer to deemphasize it.

In the earlier case of the skier interviewed after losing a competition by only fractions of a second, to say he'd done a good job probably would have made little difference to him. In spite of the commentator's prompting, he already believed that he'd done his best! A good respected friends' praise for his run down the hill could be encouraging as *an affirmation of what he already believed.* When in doubt about another's level of self-confidence. We believe that it is better not to praise.

By dictionary definition, to praise is to express approval. In an authoritarian society or system, praise is a means of influence. Superiors "approve or disapprove" subordinates' work or behavior. Praise, then, is not an appropriate method for an equalitarian society. Praise also tends to bring attention to the person and not the act.

The personal tragedy of many persons can be traced to their early mistaken notions that in order to be somebody of importance they must perform to the satisfaction of others. On the one hand, some people decide what they will or will not do according to how it will please others, while some people will act only to displease others. In either case, the constants are equally stifling. We also have many examples of businessmen, writers, actors, music stars, and others who excelled in the eyes of their publics only to die from overdose of drugs, personal abuses to their health, and various other behaviors of a discouraged person. In these instances, success with power, position, and possessions all proved shallow and depressing. Some people will argue that success ruined these individuals. The influence of fame and money corrupted the persons. Demands of their public life were too great. These arguments may seem compelling if you accept the premise that these individuals could exercise no influence over their time, their friends, and their associates.

By contrast, we have examples of other successful, high visibility public figures, who in some cases in spite of personal tragedy in their private lives, are excellent examples of high social interest persons. Bob Hope has used his quick sense of humor and personal charm to lift the spirits of servicemen and less fortunate all over the world. He has been generous with his time, talent, and personal resources on behalf of many charities and causes. Never one to miss the humor in a situation, his humor is never purposely hurtful to anyone. As is noted in the chapters on consultation and counseling, helping others to laugh at the predicaments in life is therapeutic in itself. On the basis of that criteria, he could well be called Dr. Bob Hope!

Attention to appropriate touching
can be an important process
of encouragement.

One last observation about encouragement concerns touching. For a variety of reasons, touching others in our society seems to have acquired a kind of taboo (Thayer, 1988). Among certain ethnic groups, hugging and kissing men and women alike is an accepted expression of love, friendship, and warmth. No greeting or celebration is complete without it. And yet, Victorian attitudes and practices seems to coexist in a society charged with pornography, moral shifts, and preoccupation with sexual performance. This fact is particularly striking as new data accumulates that in the absence of fondling, cuddling, picking up, touching, and other signs of physical caring, animals experience all manner of maladies, including evidently, death in some situations. Case studies of human beings are likewise quite striking with respect to neglect in this area. For this reason, I believe that attention to appropriate touching can be an important factor in the process of encouragement.

In most instances, a simple but firm handshake, a touch on the arm or back, a kiss on the cheek, a hug or a holding of hands is sufficient. Early in courting, couples hold hands, kiss, caress, and fondles as an expression of their affection. Babies tend to receive similar treatment early in their young loves. As children grow older, they tend to pull away from parental touching but generally about the same time that they discover opposite sex attractiveness. Cultivating appropriate social expressions of interest, caring, and support among same sex and opposite sex without erotic overtones or connotations is desirable. Parents especially have many opportunities to model this with and for their children. Teachers working with young children likewise have many occasions when gentle touching to obtain attention or expressions of support would be helpful.

Nonverbal communication also can be attained by physical approximation, i.e., standing nearby or leaning over a table or desk to observe at close hand a piece of work or object. In each case, one's presence can be felt in a positive way by the other person.

SUMMARY

This chapter reviews various aspects of the most important element in promoting significant positive attitudes toward coping with life. Believing in oneself is influenced but not determined by others. In order to encourage others most effectively, you must believe in yourself. To have the courage to find solutions to life's predicaments is to have one of life's greatest assets.

Specific methods and techniques are available and, with practice, will make a difference in how you relate with others. Because encouragement is fundamental to Adlerian interventions, additional illustrations and explanations will be found in subsequent chapters. In addition, completing the study questions and the activities at the end of this chapter can be quite helpful. In conclusion, the persons who encourages

1. *respects* the individual as she/he is (even though you may not approve of specific behaviors);

2. *shows faith* that enables the person to have faith in himself/herself;

3. has an *expectancy* that the person's ability will be sufficient to function satisfactorily;

4. *recognizes effort* as worthwhile;

5. *works through* and with groups (family, classmates, co-workers) to free and enhance the development of individuals;

6. *helps* each person experience a sense of *belonging* in the group;

7. *helps develop skills and attitudes* needed by others for coping through sequencing and pacing of experiences and knowledge to insure success;

8. *utilizes the individual's interests* and assets to further her/his development; and

9. *volunteers encouragement* to others without any effort or behavior necessary on their part.

STUDY QUESTIONS

Direction: Respond to the following in spaces provided.

1. List qualities of an act of encouragement, e.g., more concerned with effort rather than outcomes.

2. Why do you think Adlerians teach that you should cultivate the courage to be imperfect?

3. Give two or more illustrations which represent

    a. someone approaching life tasks on the vertical plane and

    b. someone approaching life tasks on the horizontal plane.

4. Briefly describe "words which encourage" and give two examples.

5. Briefly describe "acts which encourage" and give two examples.

ACTIVITIES FOR INDIVIDUALS AND GROUPS

Definition of Encouragement

To inspire or help others; particularly toward a conviction that they can work on finding solutions; and, that they can cope with any predicament.

Rules of Thumb

Actions which encourage are more concerned with

a. **what** one is doing more so than with how one is doing,

b. the **present** more so than with the past or future,

c. the **deed** rather than the doer,

d. the **effort** rather than the outcome,

e. **intrinsic** motivation (e.g., satisfaction, enjoyment, or challenge) more than with extrinsic motivation (e.g., reward or punishment),

f. **what is being learned** more than with what is not being learned, and

g. **what is being done correctly** more than with what is not being done correctly.

Identifying Responses of Encouragment

A. Now try these four circumstances by selecting one or more actions which normally can be characterized as encouraging to others:

Circumstance	Encouragement Response
1. volunteers to help wash the dishes	_____ a. faint from surprise _____ b. tell them how to do it

_____ c. remain cheerful
and helpful no mat-
ter how it is done

_____ d. tell the person you
appreciated their
help and company

2. accidentally drops full
dinner plate on the floor

_____ a. clean it up for
them

_____ b. tell them to clean it
up

_____ c. ask if they would
like help cleaning it
up

_____ d. say nothing unless
it seems necessary

3. brings home a treat for
others

_____ a. express appreciation for the thought-
fulness

_____ b. ask where they got
it

_____ c. openly enjoy it

_____ d. reciprocate by sharing at another time
something that
they would enjoy

4. brings home report card

_____ a. explore with them
what subjects they
enjoy most

_____ b. sign it without
reading it

_____ c. give money for
good grades

_____ d. invite them to discuss what it means
to them

B. Now reach a consensus with your partner and/or group members upon consequences which you agree are appropriate

C. Check your responses with those of the Key

KEY

Responses to items 1 through 4 on pages 135 are as follows:

1. c.d.;   2. c.d.;   3. a.c.d.; and   4. a.d.

Listing Responses of Encouragement

A. Using the same procedures, list one or more encouraging responses (verbal or nonverbal) to each of the following assuming that someone else did the circumstance listed:

Circumstance	Encouragement Response
1. is unable to complete an assignment in the time allotted	
2. tends to be slow in motor skills	
3. volunteers to help with bothersome assignments	

Circumstance	**Encouragement Response**
4. washes the car	
5. loses an item of special value to you	
6. shares a common interest or hobby	
7. has a special talent	
8. takes a bath and goes to bed without being told (child)	

B. Share your list of encouraging responses with your group members or partner by having each person take one of the circumstances, share his/her list, and invite others to add or modify as appropriate

Sharing Personality Experienced Encouragements

A. Now identify three or more situations in which others have been encouraging to you when you really appreciated their support

Situation	**Encouragement Response**

1.

2.

3.

B. Think of one or more situations in which you feel more encouraged by what you do than by what others say or do (i.e., intrinsically motivated vs. extrinsically motivated)?

C. Under what circumstances do you find yourself feeling most discouraged? Can you identify the thoughts and feelings which influence your behavior at those times? Would you like to change those to an asset or to less importance?

D. Share the encouraging recollections which you have listed in Part A.

E. If you wish, you may share one of the circumstances in Part B.

F. Then if you wish, share one of the circumstances in Part C, asking the group and/or partner in what new ways you might approach such a situation, i.e., thoughts and actions as a means of overcoming it.

ENCOURAGEMENT ACTIVITY INVENTORY

DIRECTIONS: Simply check the frequency applicable to your own behavior for each time. Note that common activities can be used quite purposefully to encourage others.

Verbal *How often do you say something like:*	Daily	Weekly	Monthly	Yearly	Never or not applicable
1. I really enjoyed your company . . .					
2. I appreciated your help					
3. You seem to enjoy . . .					
4. I like your . . .					
5. I really like what I'm doing					
6. May I help?					
7. Thanks					
8. That's unfortunate, is there anything I can do?					
9. Can you tell me more about your hobby, trip, etc.?					
10. Would you teach me how to					
11. I feel good about myself . . .					
12. I'm really happy for you . . .					

Non-Verbal
How often do you:

	Daily	Weekly	Monthly	Yearly	Never or not applicable
1. Listen empathically to another share a concern or important event in his/her life.					
2. Send letters, get well cards, etc., to let others know you care about them . . .					
3. Remain patient when others are slow or less able.					
4. Remember birthdays, anniversary, or other important dates of loved ones and share them.					
5. Realize that you really enjoy what you are doing or whom you are with . . .					
6. Share a book, record, etc., of value to you with a friend.					
7. Offer to do a favor for another without being asked.					

CHAPTER 6

GUIDING CHILDREN TOWARD WHOLENESS

The predicament of teachers and parents in guiding the young is much like the proverbial iceberg. Even the casual observer will note that young people are more openly rebellious and independent than they were ten or fifteen years ago. Reports of violence against teachers have reached such proportions that some school boards have authorized teachers to carry weapons for defense and for police to be employed to patrol the halls. This plan at best is bankruptcy in guiding young people. More common, however, are the hundreds of small to large hassles teachers and parents face every day in their efforts to fulfill their most basic responsibilities. Under these circumstances, Adlerian methods and techniques have succeeded very well in correcting and preventing the conflict between adults and young people. The following review of research literature lays a foundation for supporting the general thrust of Adlerian child guidance.

RELEVANT RESEARCH TO SCHOOLS AND HOME

As noted in Chapter 5, encouragement is an essential element in any helping relationship. The need for more encouragement in schools is reinforced by a number of studies related to classroom interaction. For example, West et al. (1981) reported several studies that examined the reactions of 1500 adolescents to events that happened to them the previous five school days. They reported who did what to them and how pleasant it was. In one rural school, 37% of teacher actions were reported as pleasant and 63% were unpleasant (Eggleston, 1973). In a larger city high school, 41% of teacher behaviors were seen as pleasant while 59% were seen as unpleasant. Students were no more pleasant to one another than the teachers. In another study, the finding was that some eighth grade pupils were not spoken to individually by anyone all day long. Some youngsters only received reprimands or instructions.

As cited in the last Chapter, Madsen and Madsen (1970) reported that on the basis of several thousand classroom observations, only 8% of the teachers whom they observed were positive in their interactions with their pupils 50% or more of the time. This is not really very surprising when one considers the number of reminders, directions, and so forth that teachers typically voice in any given school period. In fact, rarely do the teachers or administrators in my workshops ever suggest that their classroom experiences would be better than that suggested by Madsen and Madsen's findings.

Other studies have estimated that students hear 15,000 negative statements in their 12 years of schooling. Reminders, reprimands, "naggings," and similar negative communications per year involve an estimated 22,000 minutes or the equivalent of 60 school days per year. This is nearly three times the number of positive comments that they hear. Clearly, the school environment can be hazardous to a healthy self concept! Similar interactive research data on what goes on in homes are more difficult to obtain among young people and their parents or guardians. We have no reason to doubt, however, that many homes have similar environments where young people receive more correction than encouragement and more punishment than logical consequences.

The challenge to teachers and parents is great. Both have important functions that are of the highest order in value within a democratic society. Fortunately, research evidence is available to suggest ways that both teachers and parents can effectively guide their young charges. In addition, evidence exists that individuals who possess the qualities desirable for young people will be more effective in their guidance.

Building Self-esteem, Achievement and Internal Orientation

Coppersmith (1967) is among those who reported that mothers high in self-esteem were more likely to have children also high in self-esteem. The homes of these youngsters were characterized as being more active, contentious, and interactive than children with lower self-esteem. Also of note, the homes of high self-esteem children have more and better defined rules by which to live than the children in the low self-esteem groups. The opportunity for the high self-esteem children, however, to discuss issues and differ with the opinion of the parents was also higher. Accommodation for the children's point of view was a hallmark within these families. In fact, these families tend to use more of what Adlerians call natural and logical consequences in lieu of coercive "punishment" and to use encouragement as a more effective way of winning cooperation than extrinsic rewards.

The parents of high self-esteem children apparently expect their children to strive and comply with the standards they establish. These expectations represent a belief in their child's adequacy and a conviction that they have the ability to perform in whatever way is required to succeed. These convictions, when set at a reasonable level, represent a parental vote of confidence. To the child they provide a clear indication that what is desired is attainable. As a result, they give courage as well as direction.

Adlerian like methods were the foundation used in building positive self-esteem in the children of the high self-esteem mothers in Coopersmith's studies. In summarizing his conclusions, Coopersmith states that:

> The most general statement about the antecedents of self-esteem can be given in terms of three conditions: total or near total acceptance of the children by the parents, clearly defined and enforced limits, and the respect and latitude for individual action that exists within the defined limits. (Coopersmith, 1967, p. 236)

Likewise, teachers who believe that what they do makes a difference in student outcomes are more likely to convey this attitude to their students. Rotter (1966) developed a measurement for "internal" and "external" locus of control orientations of individuals. Internal oriented individuals correspond to the horizontal movement characterized as high social interest in Chapter 1. Studies have shown that students taught by high internal teachers tend to achieve more than students taught by external teachers (Murray & Staebler, 1974; Rose & Medway, 1981; Vasquez, 1973). These teachers tend to encourage student goal setting, responsibility and self-confidence (Sadowski & Woodward, 1981). All of which are goals within Adlerian child guidance as well.

Some evidence has been obtained to show that children can be guided to change their internal beliefs (Dweck, 1975). While these changes in attitude have not yet been studied in relation to student changes in achievement, the evidence is that "internal" oriented students are higher achievers than "external" oriented students (Greene, 1976; Lefcourt, 1976; Stipek & Weisz, 1981).

Attributional theory (Weiner et al., 1971) has contributed to a large number of studies which relate to the concept of student locus of control. Like adults, internal oriented students believe that through their efforts and not "luck", they achieve success. Conversely, externals tend toward believing that ill fortune, circumstances over which they have no control, and related chance factors determine their destiny. While the results are not consistently the same for boys and girls (Crandall et al., 1962; Stipek & Hoffman, 1980), the research with elementary school age youngsters shows that internals have higher achievement than externally oriented children (Bar-tal, 1978; Bar-tal et al., 1982; Cauly & Murray, 1981; Cummingham, Gerard, & Miller, 1978; Kennelly & Mount, 1985).

A study by Mitchell (1979) found that low achieving students in grades 10 through 12 were once inclined to attribute their low achievement to bad luck or being disliked by their teachers than lack of effort. An interesting turn about on these kinds of findings, however, relates to how academically able students seem to process their successes and failures. Some studies have uncovered what researchers refer to as a "self-serving effect" (SSE) among these students (Marsh, 1986). Essentially what they have found is an inclination of the able students to accept responsibility for their successes but to attribute failure to external circumstances at a higher rate than the less able student.

Studies also have shown that students with positive self-concepts are likely to have the SSE tendency (Greene, 1985; Johnson, 1981; Marsh, 1984; Marsh, Cairns, et al., 1984). Stated another way, students who are high achievers and those with positive self-concepts tend to accept credit for their successes but deny accepting as much responsibility for their failures as compared to lower achievers and those students with lower self-concepts. The high self-concept students would seem to insulate themselves when low achievement is encountered. Conversely, the low self-concept students are more inclined to interpret the low achievement as a confirmation of what they already expected. Other special populations within the school also have this tendency.

Learning disabled students have an inclination toward being more externally oriented (Fahey, 1984; Pearl et al., 1980). Fahey (1984), drawing on the work of others as well, noted that "learning disabled children attribute their successes to external factors (task difficulty), while they attribute their failures to internal factors (ability) and not to difficulty of the task" (p. 436). As one might expect, students who are discipline problems in high school also tend to be externally oriented (Gnagey, 1981). This result was found with 12- and 13-year old school youngsters in Nigeria as well (Maqsud, 1980).

Krumboltz (1988) made the following observation after a review of related literature:

> So what have we learned? We know that internals achieve more and have fewer discipline problems than externals. We know that persons with good self-concepts tend to exhibit a strange inconsistency: They are responsible for their successes but not failures. We know that external beliefs can be changed to internal beliefs by persuasion, exhortation, goal setting exercises, cognitive restructuring, and telling the children, "you're good at this." We cannot be sure that changing beliefs changes academic achievement. (p. 41)

While research has not yet demonstrated that achievement will be affected by deliberate intervention to restructure the thinking of young people, from an Adlerian/cognitive point of view, this would seem to be a likely by-product of such a change. In this instance, certainly more is to be gained by moving ahead on faith than waiting for more research to be designed and conducted. The likely gains should far outweigh any possible shortcomings. More appropriate behavior, better feelings about themselves, and greater satisfaction with what they achieve are worthy enough goals when working with young people.

Cooperation as a Desirable Process and Goal

No more sacred "cow" may be in our society than the preoccupation with competition and the goal of "winning". Certainly, we do not wish to subscribe to a philosophy in which losing is better than winning or that failing is better than succeeding. As noted in Chapter 1, this is a win-win/no losers approach to human relations and life. As a consequence, we want to promote cooperative activities through which all youngsters can be "winners." For the doubtful, data are available to support such a position in the schools.

Johnson et al. (1981) report a meta-analysis based upon 122 studies dealing with the influence of cooperative, competitive, and individualistic goal structures on achievement. Their major findings deserve serious consideration by all educators.

Cooperation promotes higher achievement than does interpersonal competition. These results hold true for all subject areas (language arts, reading, math, science, social studies, psychology, and physical education), for all age groups (although the results are stronger for pre-college students), and for tasks involving concept attainment, verbal problem solving, categorizing, spatial problem solving, retention and memory, motor performance, and guessing-judging-predicting. (pp. 56-57)

In addition, they noted that cooperation promotes higher achievement and productivity than individualistic efforts. While less conclusive due to the number and types of studies conducted, to some extent the indication is that cooperation without intergroup competition promotes higher achievement and productivity than cooperation used in conjunction with intergroup competition (e.g., as in team sports). In conclusion, the authors noted,

> Given the general dissatisfaction with the level of competence achieved by students in the public school system, educators may wish to considerably increase the use of cooperative learning procedures to promote higher student achievement. (p.58)

Slavin (1980) found that in 14 of 17 studies, student achievement was highest under a team-learning approach compared to an individualistic control group. In the remaining three studies, no significant difference were found between groups on achievement. In another study involving more than 400 fourth and fifth grade students and 17 teachers, Slavin and Karweit (1981) found that the students in a cooperative classroom environment most of the day liked school more than control group students, named more friends in school and significantly increased their self-esteem. They also achieved significantly more on three academic tests of reading vocabulary, language mechanics. and language expression. No differences were found on four other tests of academic achievement. In short, the gains for the cooperative groups were in both academic and social-personal variables.

In light of the findings related to internal versus externally oriented students, Nowicki (1982) sought to determine if a cooperative learning environment favored one type of student over another. He found that both internals and externals achieved their best under the cooperative learning condition. However, when individuals were competing against themselves or other individuals, internals tended to improve more than externals.

When addressing the topic of encouraging teachers to experiment with forming cooperative classroom teams, Krumboltz (1988) went so far as to say:

> If we were to take these [research] findings seriously, we would drastically alter the way in which American education is conducted. Each student would be assigned to a team in every class, members would be expected to help each other, and the performance of the whole team would determine the grade of each individual member. (p. 55)

Krumboltz also noted that peer tutoring can be another effective way for schools to accomplish their purposes without greater funding or more professional staff. He cites studies that demonstrated peer tutoring produces both academic and social gains for the tutors as well as the tutees (Devin-Sheehan, Feldman, & Allen 1976; Feldman et al., 1976; Gartner, Kohler, & Riessman, 1971; McGee, Kauffman, & Mussen, 1977; Mize, Ladd, & Price, 1985; Paolitto, 1976). Chandler (1980) used 7th and 8th grade low achievers to tutor 2nd and 3rd grade children of similar temperament, academic achievement and type of problem. Each tutor spent 45 minutes a day, 4 days a week for 6 weeks at the tutees school. The tutor was responsible for developing quizzes and reporting progress to the program supervisor.

The young low achieving tutors were skeptical at first. Once they believed, however, that they were able to understand and help their tutees, they participated very willingly. At the end of the experiment, both groups had shown improvement in their academic subjects and in their attitudes toward school. Of interest as well was the finding that the tutors moved significantly toward an internal belief system.

A review of the literature by Schunk (1987) suggested that the age and sex of tutors may not matter so long as they are competent at the task to be learned. A same-age tutor may be more beneficial in those cases when tutees lack confidence in their ability to complete a task. Likewise, a same sex tutor may be more effective when the models are good examples of their sex role.

While much research still needs to be done, this brief review should be sufficient to corroborate some of what Adler and many of his followers have believed over the years. Through grassroots practice in vivo, they discovered that desirable outcomes in human relations could be realized with the attitudes, values, and practices described in this book. What follows are some of the principles and practices which related specifically to child guidance. They are just as applicable, however, to persons of later years.

PRINCIPLES OF CHILD GUIDANCE

Before one can presume to influence the behavior of another person, one must first establish premises upon which actions are based. Teachers and parents, for example, often subscribe to cultural expectations which remain unexamined and yet central to their discouragement as they find themselves unable to fulfill these expectations. Adlerians especially try to expose the folly of the "good mother" or the "good teacher" who has perfect control of his/her children and who sees to their every need.

> Each person, no matter how young,
> decides how he/she will
> approach life tasks.

Central to the development of personality is the concept that each person, no matter how young, decides how he/she will approach life tasks. Genetic factors, family, friends, and general environment definitely influence the individual's interpretations of what life means. What happens to the child or what he/she possesses genetically, however, is not as important to understand as how he/she values and consequently acts towards these circumstances. Respect for the child as a thinking, valuing human being is essential. As will be illustrated in later sections, all children are far more able than most adults credit them for being.

An important principle to understand is that one can influence another individual's behavior, but only under the most extreme circumstances can one control another's attitudes and behavior. Dreikurs often said, you cannot make others do anything they chose not to do! This is important for two reasons. First, adults can be freed of the burden to do the impossible—control another human being. Second, it clarifies the first step in attempting to influence someone else's behavior—we often must change our attitude and behavior first! This change is very hard for many teachers and parents to accept in practice. They ask, how can I teach or take care of my responsibilities if I cannot control the children? The answer is not so simple. The means is by helping the children to learn self-discipline.

If we can help adults to realize that children make the best choices of which they are capable from the perceptions they have of situations, the matter of changing our behavior can be more easily accepted. If what we are doing does not result in cooperation, continuing to do it will in all probability not help a problem situation, e.g., telling or spanking. Changing our behavior, however, changes the alternatives open to the child and then he/she must decide anew how to respond.

Only the most discouraged person will move away from participation with others. Even the angry person needs someone with whom to fight. Adler believed that people naturally are inclined to move toward other people and to make a place for themselves. Observe a new person assessing where he/she fits in a group, if at all, and how to establish himself/herself as a member. Everyone experiences these feelings, each with his/her own expectations of what probably will happen. Teachers and parents can use this understanding to help children find their place in new ways and to establish new expectancies for how they can participate.

Cooperation, not conformity, is the goal of Adlerian work with children, parents, and teachers. Cooperation requires respect for self and others, shared responsibility, and a commitment to the tasks at hand. Occasionally, the author has heard an adult say, "He is lazy," or "She isn't motivated." Closer inspection reveals quite the opposite is true. Children expend energy toward aggravating adults in very ingenious ways! Their goals are not toward cooperation with the adults, but they nonverbally agree to carry on a disagreement.

Cooperation Requires Mutual Respect and Understanding

Young children often say "no" even when they mean "yes." "No" is a statement of personal power to withhold cooperation. Too many adults become impressed with this expression and actually encourage children to use it more often by trying to correct it verbally. As children grow older they learn "no" can be expressed in many subtle ways. For a child's social interest to be nurtured, he/she requires opportunities to develop mastery in those aspects of social living suited to his/her capabilities. From getting up in the morning to learning to help with family activities, a child requires opportunities to participate, share, and benefit from labors of daily living. Too often, these opportunities are denied by the faulty notions of parents, on one hand, that they have an obligation to provide for the child's needs and, on the other, that they should assign to the growing youngster responsibilities which parents prefer not to do themselves. Such paradoxes are the foundation of many conflicts. Cooperation, then, requires mutual respect and understanding. Talking together with genuine regard for the other's opinions, suggestions, and concerns becomes an important activity for all parties involved. This kind of communication requires practice and a new understanding of one's role as participant. Adlerians use group activities extensively as a means of educating and encouraging others in this type of communication.

A summary of Adlerian thoughts for adults who guide children includes:

1. Freeing myself of the mistaken notion that I should control the child's behavior.

2. Accepting responsibility for changing my behavior first.

3. Respecting the child or adolescent for making the best choices he/she can under the circumstances, as he/she perceives them.

4. Realizing that children are attempting to make a place for themselves by whatever means seem available to them, i.e., socially useful or useless behavior.

5. Understanding that when children misbehave, it is an outward sign of their internal discouragement as participating members of our class or family.

6. Committing myself to helping children learn self-discipline and cooperation by friendly participation in the daily tasks we all must fulfill.

GOALS OF DISRUPTIVE BEHAVIOR

The assumption that all behavior is purposive opens a very interesting area for exploration when one observes the myriad of behaviors in a classroom or family. The naive observer may conclude that children simply are active and playful. New student teachers may feel that pupils are bent on driving teachers out of the classroom—and sometimes pupils are. Adlerians have determined that children's disruptive behaviors can be categorized by their goals, i.e., what the children expect to achieve by these behaviors either consciously or unconsciously. Normally these goals are most easily recognized in the disturbing behaviors of children up to the age of ten. After this age, they can still be observed in the behavior of adolescents and adults but these behaviors become less inclusive and other goals also are sought by the older persons.

The four goals of disruptive behavior are attention seeking, power seeking, revenge seeking, and inadequacy or assumed disability. Explanation of each follows.

Attention Seeking

To enjoy recognition is quite normal among children and adults. When attention seeking becomes an annoyance, however, it is a form of misbehavior and an early sign of discouragement. Dreikurs (1968) noted that attention-getting behaviors may be *active-constructive* (e.g., "perfect" child, bright sayings), *passive-constructive* (e.g., clinging vine, vanity), *active-destructive* (e.g., showing off, tyrant), or *passive-destructive* (e.g., speech impediments, fears). The two former types often are overlooked by adults because they are accompanied by "good" behaviors of the "model" child or "cute" behaviors of the charmer. Rarely are the persistent attention-seeking behaviors of the latter two overlooked. Tapping pencils, dropping books, forgetting instructions, coming in late, ad infinitum, distract adults every day and try their patience to the limit.

Power Seeking

Children discover at a very early age, generally by the age of two, the satisfaction of saying no. It is an assertion that "I can do what I want to do and you can't make me do anything I don't want to do!" This behavior also takes active- and passive-destructive forms. While some children will openly rebel, others will simply be quietly stubborn. In either case, the adult generally knows that he/she has been challenged.

Revenge Seeking

Adults often are most troubled by the active destructive behaviors of revenge because of the moral judgments which accompany lying, stealing, or hurting others. Adults do not realize that when they use their power to punish a child, they model the kind of behavior which the child may decide will work for him/her when attention and power fail.

Inadequacy or Assumed Disability

The most passive children can be the most discouraged and the most difficult to help. The child who withdraws from daily life tasks may be overlooked by some adults. His/her message is clear, however: "Don't expect anything from me because I don't have anything to give."

Not all behaviors will be easily classified into one goal area. For example, the more discouraged the youngster becomes, the more evidence of multiple goals will appear. The following case helps to illustrate this observation:

Example: Charles

Charles was a bright, handsome, healthy looking seven year old in the first grade. He demonstrated early in the year a readiness for reading and math. His home situation was quite unsettled because of the recent divorce of his parents.

His disruptive behavior initially was excessive attention seeking in every imaginable way. The teachers tried to be understanding, reassuring and generally sympathetic, but their time and patience had limits. Increasingly he resisted the teachers' instruction, spoke back to them (power), and began hurting children in the class (revenge). At this point, the author was asked to visit the class. In one ten-minute period, Charles was out of his seat behaving in disruptive ways fourteen times. Both teachers reported that on some days they were close to tears from trying to cope with him. He also was requesting to stay in during recess (inadequacy), attempting none of his school work (inadequacy), and potentially going to be denied the opportunity to ride the school bus because of his fighting.

As conscientious and well meaning as the teachers were, they were watching Charles become further removed from his classmates and convinced of his unworthiness. His insatiable attention-seeking behavior elicited a power response from the teachers; he responded to the challenge and ultimately was paddled by the principal. Threats of expulsion seemed only to strengthen his convictions. This process was reversed to an appreciable extent before the school year ended by encouragement and the use of logical and natural consequences. Lack of cooperation from his mother hampered a more satisfactory resolution of his problems. The kinds of corrective techniques which were used are discussed in a subsequent section.

IDENTIFYING GOALS OF CHILDREN'S DISRUPTIVE BEHAVIOR

Knowing the goals of misbehavior serve useful purposes. Being aware of goals can help adults to understand children better and to correct mistaken notions in pursuing these behaviors. To identify the goals and begin anticipating corrective actions, four questions should be asked:

1. What did the youngster do?

2. What did you do?

3. How did he/she respond to your action?

4. How did you feel?

Identify the goals of disruptive behavior
and begin anticipating corrective action.

An example will help to illustrate. The following excerpt is taken from a discussion between a teacher (Te) and a counselor (Co).

Te: Jimmy is constantly getting out of his seat, talking to other children, raising his hand, or talking out at the wrong time. He's really driving me up the wall!

Co: In your most recent encounter, what did he do and then what did you do?

Te: Well, just this morning I gave instructions for everyone to remain quiet while one of the children read from a book he had brought from home. Not two minutes later, Jimmy was singing to himself, looking out the window and tapping his pencil! When I told him to listen, he stopped but a short time later he was doing something else.

Co: In this case, would you say you were more annoyed than angry?

Te: Well, yes; most of the time he gets right back to work, but I just wish he'd stop bugging me.

In this case, we see a child who is active-destructively seeking attention. We know this goal by two pieces of information. First, when the teacher "corrects" him, he stops what he was doing. Second, she feels more annoyed by his behavior than anything else. This feeling is significant because children seeking power usually will not stop their behavior until they have clearly challenged the adult and provoked anger to some degree. Children seeking revenge will do what is necessary to elicit hurt, disappointment, or similar feelings. Children wishing to affirm their inadequacy will have succeeded when the adult finally says, "I give up, I can't do anything with her!" or "He's just not smart enough to cut the mustard." However said, the feeling most often expressed by the adult is one of defeat. In the previous case, attention appears to be the goal.

On the assumption that a mistaken conviction or notion about how they can make their place motivates their behavior, Adlerians note that children usually are saying approximately the following for each of the four goals:

Attention: I only really count when others notice and/or serve me.

Power: I only really count when others know I can do what I want to do.

Revenge: I can't be liked but I can hurt others and then they'll know I count, too!

Inadequacy: I'm stupid, inadequate, really hopeless, so why try—don't expect anything from me. Trying will only prove it to everyone.

Children generally are not aware of the purposes of their actions. Many children will stop their disruptive behavior when made aware of its purpose by a counselor. Teachers and parents should refrain from confronting children with these observations unless they have training and supervised experience in this process.

Persons not acquainted with Adlerian psychology are sometimes critical of the apparent oversimplification of these behaviors and question the validity of the assumptions behind the goals. In practice, counselors have ample opportunity to test these hypotheses as they talk with children. When confronted with "Could it be, Jimmy, that you want to keep your teacher busy with you to have her notice you," the counselor will see the recognition reflex, from a slight turning up of the lips to a broad smile or a knowing nod, that confirms that the counselor is on the right track. Whether or not the message is worded exactly right does not seem to be as important as presenting it in a friendly, caring manner.

Table 6.1 is not intended to be comprehensive, but it helps to illustrate the kinds of behavior which serve to achieve the child's goal. Occasionally, someone will question how one determines that striving for excellence or pleasing is a mistaken goal. Referring to the concept of social interest and the questions one asks concerning reaction to a child's behavior, persons moving on the horizontal plane with a goal of excellence in some area of interest are intrinsically motivated. They do not require praise, an audience, or persistent reassurance. They enjoy the activity and will perform for others but attention per se from others is nice, but not necessary. Anyone who has lived or worked with a person who demands attention can discern the difference quite readily. The person moving on the vertical plane constantly is assessing "how" they are doing. Evaluating their performance, seeking assurances,

TABLE 6.1
Typical Behaviors Associated With The Four Goals

Goal	Behaviors	
ATTENTION	Active Constructive	Passive Constructive
	cute remarks performing stunts strive for excellence, industriousness to exclusion of other activities	excessive pleasant- ness excessive charm exaggerated conscien- tiousness
	Active Destructive	Passive Destructive
	show off clown "infant terrible" unpredictable	bashfulness fearfulness untidiness eating peculiarities
POWER	Active Destructive	Passive Destructive
	argues contradicts exhibits "bad" habits temper tantrums dawdles	laziness stubbornness disobedience forgetful
REVENGE	Active Destructive	Passive Destructive
	viciousness stealing bedwetting fighting	obstructs undermines irresponsible
INADEQUACY		Passive Destructive
		indolence ineptitude stupidness

brooding over mistakes or making excuses, complaining or belittling others when circumstances don't suit them.

TYPICAL FAULTY GOALS OF ADOLESCENTS

Kelly and Sweeney (1979) identify eleven faulty goals of teenagers. Some of these goals are variations on the four mistaken goals of childhood. Basically they reflect a lack of one or more of the elements of self-respect, respect for others, shared responsibility, or constructive cooperation. Unlike goals of children, reactions of adults are all the more compounded by those of peers when responding to the disruptive behavior of adolescents. Perceived peer support, whether real or imagined, contributed to the faulty notions. In other instances, adult approval serves as a reinforcement to a mistaken notion of how to make one's place.

Typical faulty goals of adolescents
reflect a lack of self-respect,
respect for others, shared responsibility,
or constructive cooperation

All persons may exhibit evidence of one or more of these goals at various times in their lives. These goals are considered faulty only when the behaviors are used repeatedly despite being socially inappropriate or personally self defeating. On the other hand, defiance, conformity or withdrawal, for example, can be quite appropriate in certain situations.

Only when one is avoiding or denying responsibility for one or more life tasks (work, friendship, love) on a persistent basis is the faulty goal clearly identified. The experienced counselor can establish the validity of his/her observations by revealing what Dreikurs called the **hidden reason** to one's behavior in counseling. As is true of children, a recognition reflex such as a smile will help confirm the accuracy of your perceptions.

Superiority, Conformity, Popularity

The first three faulty goals involve some patterns of constructive behavior that often stimulate initial positive reactions from others. The goals nevertheless are faulty because they seriously constrain individual creativity and/or provoke competition at the expense of cooperation.

Superiority. Adolescents with the goal of superiority strive to be best at everything. They must get the highest grades, win school elections, or gather top honors to themselves. They often win high approval from adults. Their peers generally admire them, but also consider them with a mix of envy, even annoyance, at their competitiveness and success. If an adult tries to temper these superachievers, they usually react with a justification of their efforts. The general strategy for correcting or rechanneling these singleminded efforts involves avoiding blanket approval of achievements that are feeding the excessive need to achieve. Attention to enjoyment, satisfaction, and sharing with others in their activities and talents can refocus the individual's interest toward *what* they are doing rather than *how* they are doing. To foster the courage to be imperfect is essential so that these superachievers are not crushed by failures or defeats.

Conformity. Living up completely to the standards of established society (school, church, etc.) is the goal. These teenagers are literally young adults who have adopted the style and manner of establishment adults rather than peers. They receive consistent approval from adults but frequently evoke annoyance in many of their peers, except other adolescents with the same goal. Since they conform to adults, corrective action from adults will be received with courtesy and surface compliance, but with no real change. As with the previous two goals, complete approval of this behavior should be avoided. A program of corrective action will encourage both increased social activities with peers and independent activities.

Popularity. Teenagers with this goal are accumulators of friends and social contacts. They strive to be widely accepted and recognized by everybody. They join and are active in many school organizations. Like the superachievers, they also often win the approval of adults and peers, although some of the latter will react with envy and annoyance. The initial reaction to corrective efforts is usually a friendly, even outwardly agreeable response. No real change in attitude or behavior results however. To redirect these teenagers' behavior into more discriminating collaboration, corrective efforts should avoid blanket approval of popularity behavior and include strategies that encourage independent and personally self-assertive activities.

Defiance, Promiscuity, Inadequacy

The next three goals are more clearly disruptive or self-defeating and usually evoke negative reactions from adults.

Defiance. Defiant teenagers want to be in complete control or, at the very least, not controlled by adults. This goal is divided into three subcategories of defiant behavior, each with a characteristic pattern of behaviors and reactions. The first is the *independent struggle* in which there are innumerable arguments over dress, curfews, personal appearance and a whole array of other matters. In fact, anything, no matter how trivial, is a point of contention. Adults react with annoyance and anger to being constantly disputed. However, since disagreements are primarily with adults and not peer standards, peers usually react with approval and sympathy. Any direct attempt to correct will only fuel further resistance. The general corrective strategy involves an avoidance of arguing at times of provocation and, during pleasant moments, indirect suggestions that respect the teenager's right to choose for oneself.

The *aggression goal* is more extreme than the independence struggle. In this case, teenagers are striking out against others with fighting, vandalism, and delinquency. They evoke strong feelings of anger, hurt, and revenge in adults and are rejected by most of their peers. Corrective efforts that are built on angry efforts or punishment provoke more striking out. Although difficult, effective corrective efforts include control of the angry and hurt reaction and avoidance of angry striking back. What is needed is the patient building of a positive relationship, a mutual understanding of a positive relationship, a mutual understanding of reasonable limits, and a non-punitive use of natural and logical consequences (Dreikurs & Grey, 1968).

Effective corrective efforts include control
of your own anger and hurt reaction

Defiance also can be expressed by *attempted suicide.* In adults, they evoke a mixture of fear and concern, usually with some anger. They are usually out of touch with the pre-dominant peer group, and although they may receive some sympathy, are often treated with indifference. Their reaction to correction is a passive non-improvement. Effective correction blends avoidance of a hysterical reaction with a focused program of encouragement that uncovers and builds personal strengths. A useful explanation and illustration of Adlerian intervention with suicidal crisis clients will be found in an article by Messer (1973).

Sexual Promiscuity. Teenagers with this goal are seeking a feeling of belonging and selfhood by proving themselves sexually. They are not just sexually active, but are highly active in and defiant about their sexual behavior. Despite the greater openness about sex in our society, adults typically react with disgust and shock, and most teenagers react with disapproval and rejection. Corrective advice is defiantly rejected. Effective correction includes an avoidance of the shock or disgust reaction and a program of interaction that encourages a desire for personal self-respect and the respect of others.

Inadequacy. Teenagers with this goal enjoy the victim role and seek much consolation for their shortcomings. They give up early in all their endeavors and proclaim their deficiencies and lack of abilities. They tend to evoke an initial feeling of pity from others, with adults tending to feel hopeless and peers tending to be indifferent. Corrective efforts may spur some meager efforts at improvement, but surrender quickly takes over again. Effective correction builds on the avoidance of a discouraged or pitying reaction and provides a program of opportunities for small successes with encouragement for improvement and achievement.

Charm, Beauty, Sexism

The next three goals have a superficial appearance of being personally and socially constructive. They are closely related to one another.

Charm. Charmers find their place not through genuine cooperation or productivity, but with smooth talk and pleasing manners. Initially, others are often charmed and flattered by them. With some adults the veneer of charm may eventually evoke annoyance. Among peers, a successful charmer will provoke a mixture of admiration and envy. When corrected, the charmer will turn on more charm, and if this doesn't work, frequently will withdraw and sulk or pout. To redirect the charmer effectively, adults must not be taken in by the smooth behavior and must expect, with patience and without insult, productive behavior.

Physical Beauty or Strength. These teenagers rely completely on their good looks, physical strength, or abilities to define their place with others. They give excessive attention to these attributes and frequently evoke admiration, with some envy, in both adults and other teenagers. They ignore direct corrective efforts. For effective correction, the tendency to admire and praise physical attributes must be tempered, and a program of nonphysical activities, e.g., reading, volunteer charity work, art, and so forth, should be developed and encouraged.

Sexism. This goal is a variation on the previous two goals and involves an excessive overdevelopment of stereotypical masculine or feminine characteristics and behaviors. For teenage boys, it results in excessive macho behavior. In girls, it takes the form of clinging-vine behavior that combines an appearance of helplessness with underlying manipulation. Both adults and other teenagers generally are accepting of this behavior, although it eventually begins to grate or annoy after a while. Both males and females will reject direct corrective feedback. Alternative corrective strategies involve avoidance of blanket approval of the behavior and encouragement of positive attitudes and behaviors which are stereotypically associated with the opposite sex, e.g., child care, housework for males, and competence in auto mechanics for females.

Intellectuality and Religiosity

The final two goals have the appearance of positive directions for teenagers. However, they represent extremes that in reality inhibit full development.

Intellectuality. These teenagers gain their feelings of value and belonging completely from "book" learning, and discussing ideas. They are the very bookish students who study, read, or discuss ideas most of the time. They have the approval of adults but most of their peers are indifferent toward them. Corrective action usually is met with an intellectual argument. Effective correction avoids simple approval of the overintellectual approach to life and encourages nonbookish social and leisure activities, greater awareness and acceptance of feelings, and openness to nonintellectual values generally.

Religiosity. Teenagers with this goal seek belonging through an immersion in religious ideas and activities. They are regular and frequent church-goers, and religious themes pervade their conversations. Adults typically approve their behavior; however, they also may experience some annoyance. Their peers are mostly indifferent, but other religious adolescents will give approval. If corrected, they will defend their position and even pity their corrector. In effective corrections, both simple approval and arguments are avoided, and independent and exploratory thinking and conversations are encouraged.

Summary

In my experience, many people including teenagers do the right things for the wrong reasons. In the same manner that Berne, Perls, and Ellis help clients rid themselves of "shoulds" and "oughts", Adler recognized the counter productive nature of an overbearing conscience, the relentless demands of superiority, or the distructiveness of self-denial. While influenced by parents, peers, and others, thoughts and behaviors which serve these goals are, nevertheless, the self-made creation of the individual.

Your goal in counseling and guidance, therefore, does not require so much a change in behavior as a redirection of goals. For individuals who strive to please others, the reason for pleasing may be changed to one of intrinsic satisfaction. They are freed of the mistaken idea that not to please would be catastrophic. In the chapter on counseling, this will be illustrated. The concept of motivation modification is underscored because through it, changes in one area of life tasks tend to be transferred into other personal domains as well.

CORRECTIVE ACTION

Because you are most often confronted with a problem before determining that preventative measures are required, you need to develop competence with corrective methods.

As a consultant to adults working and living with young people, the author has found that summarizing what is required into four steps is helpful. These steps can be remembered easily by using the acronym CARE.

1. Catch yourself: don't act impulsively.

2. Assess goals—what goals are served by the behavior.

3. Respond with consequences and encouragement.

4. Execute with consistency, friendliness, and respect.

Dreikurs frequently emphasized that before the adult can begin doing something correctly, he/she must stop doing that which is incorrect. Parents and teachers alike tend to behave toward their children the way their parents and teachers behaved toward them. Increasingly, the old methods do not work because they were based on an authority from on high which was never questioned. We have been teaching social democracy so well that young people now believe its precepts and behave accordingly—these are trying times for the old methods!

Catch Yourself

Behavioral research on conditioning affirms the Adlerian notion that what most adults do impulsively when they respond to misbehavior is incorrect. Using the case of Jimmy who seeks attention, when the teacher was asked what she did in response to his behavior, she reported that she told him to stop his misbehavior. She gave him, then, the attention he sought. Not only did he receive the attention, he received reinforcement for misbehaving in a similar way again.

Upon telling adults that they must learn to catch themselves, they often believe that this will be difficult. In a manner of speaking it is difficult. On the other hand, much satisfaction can be obtained from observing the surprise our changed behavior elicits from the children. Initially, adults are unclear about what else to do. They should be forewarned that when they stop doing what they used to do impulsively, the attention-seeking behaviors of some children will increase before they decrease. Convinced that I only count when I have attention and/or service, children try desperately to reestablish the adult's part in their plan. This is one reason why preventative action is important, too.

Before proceeding to the other steps, a comment on talking deserves special note. In spite of some research which suggests otherwise (Mehrabian, 1968), most adults seem to behave as though words were the major means of communication. Whenever something does not suit them, they talk. They talk even though the children rarely listen.

Adults tend to talk too much! Establish a new rule: give instructions once and thereafter they are repeated only under exceptional circumstances or when it is convenient. Make action, not words, the principle means of conveying intentions.

Assess Goals

Disruptive behavior, in its simplest form, is evidence of feelings of discouragement. From the discouragement and lack of faith in themselves to meet life's daily tasks, people behave in ways which reinforce these notions. Adlerians refer to certain of these attitudes as *self-fulfilling prophesies.*

When one expects others not to like him/her and behaves as though they will not, other people generally do not like the person, but not for the reasons the individual imagines. Berne (1964), in *Games People Play,* described individuals who play games designed to fulfill their expectations and keep them from intimacy with others. Berne's descriptions are very well suited to similar observations made by Adler. To break this cycle of mistaken notions and expectations, adults must alter their behavior first. You may ask "How can I behave differently when I am angry?"

Often you become angry because you are judging and perceiving yourself as personally affronted. For example, you, a dad, think, "Look what Bill's doing now! I said he couldn't do that' who does he think he is? Well, I'll just fix his wagon right now!" Then you talk, threaten, and so forth. The thoughts flash in milliseconds, the feelings swell up simultaneously, you may not even realize what actually transpired. You do remember the feelings however. The feelings even linger after the episode and easily can be resurrected later in a discussion. The question is, can you develop new messages, new insights, and new alternatives to similar behaviors? The answer is "yes," with educational guidance, study and practice.

Behavior is secondary to attitude.

A part of the new thought process will include an initial recognition that the behavior is secondary to the attitude of discouragement. When moralizing and judging are removed from the process, feelings of righteous indignation typically associated with disruptive behaviors dissipate. If you consider first the discouragement, i.e., the message the other person is saying and feeling within himself/herself, your feelings will change in most cases as well.

Respond With Consequences and Encouragement

Having caught oneself and avoided doing the predictable, you will no doubt desire specific recommendations on how to proceed next. At this point, three major concepts in Adlerian methods presented in earlier chapters become the foundation of the responding action dimension of the guidance process. These are the following:

- Natural consequences (Chapter 3)

- Logical consequences (Chapter 4)

- Encouragement (Chapter 5)

Natural and Logical Consequences. The concept behind the effectiveness of natural and logical consequences is the logical order and pressure of reality. In the same sense that Adlerians believe a natural order of life exists, also a logical social order exists as well. Adults of all generations have tended to present these as rules and regulations to be accepted and followed without helping new generations to understand or discover the logic of social living. Some rules are illogical and arbitrary and children perceive this quickly. Such rules are fair game for conflicts in a power struggle. Patience in helping children and adolescents learn to experience the natural and logical order of daily living, however, is the keystone of effective guidance.

With social democracy as the basis for training methods, the adult can extricate himself/herself from the arbitrary exercise of power. As will be seen in some of the examples taken from actual experiences of teachers and parents, the use of democratic methods (including natural and logical consequences) will result in many immediate corrections of previously persistent problems. Why they work effectively seems associated with rules of thumb such as the following:

1. Natural consequences are sought first, before considering a logical consequence.

2. "New rules" of the class or family generally are presented and/or discussed before implementation.

3. "New rules" apply to everyone, including the adults.

4. Alternatives are always open to the individual, e.g., "you can stop crying or go to your room and return when you are through crying."

5. Consistency in implementing the "rules" consequences is followed with action, not words.

6. Logical consequences are avoided when power struggles are in process, i.e., angry feelings, evidence of power being exerted or challenged.

7. Friendliness prevails before, during, and after consequences are experienced from ill-advised acts of a family or class member, e.g., "I told you so" comments do not precede or follow, verbally or nonverbally.

8. Encouragement for the many positive ways individuals share, participate, and cooperate are highlighted. Everyone is made to feel and know that they have a place and belong especially when they reveal discouraged behavior.

9. Time for having fun together is an important part of the planning which takes place.

Knowing about these methods will not eliminate errors or the occasional satisfaction of being angry and full of righteous indignation. Frequently, when adults report that certain behaviors are still being pursued by the children, omissions or errors in one or more of the rules of thumb are present. On such occasions, adults should be aware that the consequences may not work and instead may backfire. A "logical" consequence inflicted in anger becomes a punishment.

Logical consequences do not work as effectively as natural consequences with power-oriented children because they tend to see the intervention by another as an exercise of power. If the adult is resentful or angry, the child is confirmed in his/her suspicion. Such lapses on the part of the adult can re-affirm the discouraged child's self-fulfilling prophesy.

Angry people are uncooperative.

Parents or teachers may rightfully wonder what to do when they are angry. They may ask, "Are angry feelings always bad?" To become angry is not unusual nor should it be "suppressed." How one expresses anger, however, is a different matter (Sweeney, 1973). When people become angry they also become uncooperative. This consequence involves power. Angry feelings can be expressed in ways which facilitate a relationship but only when the respect of each party is preserved and caring is a genuine foundation of the relationship.

As a general rule, Adlerians recommend that adults extricate themselves from power struggles. Because at least two people are required to have a fight, Dreikurs (1968) recommended that you take "the sail out of their wind." When the angry feelings have subsided, a discussion of what transpired and why, i.e., what purpose was served, may be helpful in reestablishing a friendly relationship. Saving bad feelings for another day can be equated with saving "brown stamps" as in Transactional Analysis. We cash them in for a fight over some other unrelated topic on which we feel unjustly treated. Adlerians believe, for example, that regular opportunities for classes and families to meet and discuss common concerns is necessary to help avoid brown stamp collecting. Such meetings are discussed in Chapter 11.

Coping with the goals of disruptive behavior, including examples of natural and logical consequences found in the next sections, can help eliminate the frustration and resultant anger some adults feel from not knowing what to do when action is required.

In Table 6.2 are summarized the probable responses of children to reprimands according to the goal sought by the child and presents some recommended alternatives to correct these behaviors. Likewise in Table 6.3 are summarized faulty goals of adolescents, reactions, of peers and adults, and alternatives to the expected responses.

The process of discovering natural and logical consequences is one which requires forethought and practice. Parent and teacher study groups which are discussed in Chapter 12 are particularly helpful in this regard. Remembering that the normal demands and logic of life are the source of these experiences, adults may ask three questions as a way of uncovering potential consequences which might be effective:

1. What will likely happen if no one intervenes?

   For example: don't remind; they'll be late
   don't pick up; their clothes won't get washed

(Continued on page 176)

TABLE 6.2
Corrective Action to the Four Goals
of Disruptive Behavior

Goal	Reprimand Results	Alternatives (Methods)
ATTENTION	Stops temporarily	Ignore small behavior, allow consequences to follow, do the unexpected, e.g., invite child to teach the class and give attention for positive behaviors
POWER	Intensifies with challenge or withdraws to fight another time	Extricate self, offer alternatives and look for natural consequences
REVENGE	Seeks ways to get even and be more disliked	Sidestep power struggle, maintain order with minimum restraint, work with counselor and parents, affirm positive behaviors, and expect the unexpected
INADEQUACY	If any behavior per se, withdraws	Be interested in them, encourages any effort and eliminate failure from their experience

TABLE 6.3
Typical Faulty Goals of Adolescents

I AM WORTHWHILE AND BELONG ONLY:

Faulty Beliefs	Goals	Examples	Adult Reactions	Peer Group Corrective Feedback	Reaction To Corrective Methods	Alternative Corrective Methods
When I am best	Superiority	Super striving for best grades, most honors first in the class, etc.	Approval	Admiration	Justifies striving	Avoid blanket approval Encourage courage to be imperfect Encourage social cooperation
When I have widespread peer social acceptance	Popularity (Social Climbing)	Constantly attempting to obtain widespread peer social acceptance	Approval	Acceptance Subgroup envy or annoyance	Superficial compliance Friendly disagreement	Avoid blanket approval Encourage independent activity
When I live up completely to all standards of established adult society	Conformity	Constantly tries to please particularly adults rather than peers, with good behavior, grades, etc.	Approval	Annoyance (with some envy)	Superficial compliance	Avoid blanket approval Encourage peer social activities Encourage individuality

Table 6.3 (Continued)

Faulty Beliefs	Goals	Examples	Adult Reactions	Peer Group Corrective Feedback	Reaction To Corrective Methods	Alternative Corrective Methods
I AM WORTHWHILE AND BELONG ONLY:						
When I am in complete control or not being controlled	Defiance: Independence struggle	Arguments over hair, dress, etc.	Annoyance Irritation	Acceptance Approval	Continue to argue Defiant compliance	Avoid arguing Suggestions at other times
	Aggression	Vandalism Fighting Delinquency	Anger Hurt Revenge	Rejection by most Subgroup acceptance	Strike back	Avoid hurt and anger Don't strike back Reasonable limits and use of consequences
	Withdrawal	Runaway Truancy Suicide	Fear Alarm	Indifference Some sympathy	Passive response No improvement	Avoid hysterical reaction Encourage social participation
When I prove and enjoy myself sexually	Sexual promiscuity	High level of intimate sexual activity with others	Disgust Shock Disapproval	Rejection by most Subgroup acceptance	Defiant rejection	Avoid shock and disgust Encourage desire for self-respect and respect of others
When I am completely supported and consoled in my shortcomings	Inadequacy	Gives up easily Displays	Pity Hopelessness	Pity Indifference	Meager effort, then give up again	Avoid discouraged reaction or pity Provide opportunities for small successes and encouragement

If I am...		Behavior				Guidance
When others find me completely charming and pleasing	Charm	Fascinating and pleasing with smooth talk and behavior	Charmed and flattered Sometimes mixed with annoyance	Charmed Flattered Pleased Envious	Steps up charm Pouting Withdrawal	Be unimpressed but friendly Remain courteous and insist on effort
If I am physically beautiful or strong	Beauty Strength	Excessive attention to and dependence on physical appearance	Admiration sometimes mixed with envy or irritation	Admiration sometimes mixed with envy or irritation	Ignoring	Avoid praise Encourage non-physical pursuits e.g., reading, art, music, etc.
When I am "super" man or "super" lady	Sexism	Boys: Macho behavior Girls: Clinging-vine behavior	General approval Some annoyance	General approval Some annoyance	Rejection	Avoid blanket approval Encourage contrasting "feminine" or "masculine" attitudes and behaviors
When I am completely involved in learning or discussing	Intellectualizing	Very bookish	Approval	Indifference Subgroup acceptance	Argue	Avoid blanket approval Encourage social leisure activities
When I am fully involved in religious ideas and activities	Religiosity	Deep involvement in religious ideas and activities Regular and frequent attendance at church	Approval Sometimes mixed with concern or annoyance	Ignored by most Subgroup acceptance	Pity Defensiveness	Avoid blanket approval or arguments Encourage exploratory thinking and talking

2. What can happen when "others" must intervene?

For example: adult moves belongings of children; children cannot find their belongings when they want them

adult prepares breakfast; however, children cannot have breakfast until they're dressed

3. What happens if "others" reciprocate or copy similar behavior?

For example: children wash dishes during TV commercials; mother cooks supper during TV commercials

children are persistently late coming home; parents lock house and remain unavailable when children want to come in.

Some examples of how each of these questions resulted in natural and logical consequences for the resolution of specific problems are summarized. These examples are taken from the experience of teachers, counselors, and parents who were participating in their first workshop or discussion group on consequences. Comments after each example will highlight the significance of those actions involved.

Example: "Others can reciprocate"

Each evening at 6 p.m. the parents like to watch the news, but it was often interrupted by the children. The daughter, 12, and son, 8, each of former marriages of the parents, managed to have a fight at that time frequently resulted in bad feelings between the parents as well as with the children.

In exasperation, the husband talked with a member of the class, who offered some suggestions including a copy of *Children the Challenge* (Dreikurs & Soltz, 1964). The problem was solved in two nights. At dinner the evening of the first day, the parents indicated that they would no longer enter into the fights of the children and that if the parents could not watch their programs, then the children should not be able to watch theirs either. The children offered no comments or objections.

That evening at six bedlam broke out! The children got into a loud argument in the bedroom and brought it into the kitchen. They finally ended up in the family room. The parents ignored it all and did not reprimand them. When the news program ended, the mother turned the television off and went to the bedroom. The father went to the bathroom to take a shower. The children howled, demanded to see their program, and even threatened to turn the television back on themselves. They did not, although both parents thought that they might. The hassle quickly subsided and the rest of the evening was quiet with everyone in his/her room.

Example continued: "No one intervenes"

The next evening as the fight progressed, they came to tattle on each other to the respective parent. Each parent responded, "We don't feel like fighting tonight. If you do, go back to Sarah's bedroom." (This room is farthest from the family room.) Each child gaped for a few seconds, turned, and went into the bedroom. They did not fight, but the parents could hear them talking. The third night, no hassle at six!

The parents in this case are excellent candidates for a parent discussion group. Evidently they caught on quickly to the elements necessary for successful use of these methods. First, they stayed out of the fights (did not intervene) thus allowing the natural consequence to occur—no parent attention, no interest in fighting; and second, they established that if the parents had no television then the children would have no television (reciprocated with a logical consequence). Much to their surprise, the children saw the logic of this, too, and did not challenge the parents on either issue.

Example: "Someone must intervene"

Each evening, Ann, a 14-year old, would deliver her newspapers after school. She developed a habit of preparing her papers in the foyer next to the front door. Paper, wire, wire cutters, and similar debris were consistently left behind for someone else to pick up.

After being reminded, coaxed, and reprimanded numerous times, the parents decided to intervene. Without any further comments, one or the other of the parents would simply pick up the wire cutters or the carrier's bag and place them in some out-of-the-way place. After several evenings of making do without these needed tools, they reappeared but without comment. No longer were reminders necessary! Occasionally, she would "forget" with a similar inconvenience the outcome.

Parents in this case were not removing the tools out of anger. They simply needed Ann's cooperation and she required theirs as well. Most workers cannot afford to leave their tools unnecessarily in others' way or in public places. Ann was learning an important lesson in social living through the use of a logical consequence.

For additional information and illustrations on logical and natural consequences, Dreikurs and Grey (1968) and Dreikurs, Grunwald, and Pepper (1971) are excellent resources.

Encouragement. A variety of books now are available in bookstores on how to be an encouraging person (Dinkmeyer & Dreikurs, 1963; Dinkmeyer & Losoncy, 1980; Losoncy, 1977; Witmer, 1985). They provide a very useful resource for discussion and illustrations of courage, encouragement, and discouragement as it applies to helping children and adults. Dinkmeyer and Driekurs (1963) indicate that

> What characterizes the courageous person is his conviction that he can work toward finding solutions, and, what is most important, that he can cope with any predicament. He is convinced that, as a person of integrity and worth, he can take in stride whatever may happen. The ability and willingness to accept anything that may come without feeling defeated and without giving up in despair, and the expectation that one will be capable of maintaining one's value and self-respect seem to be the outstanding features of a courageous person. (pp. 33-34)

Discouragement is so common that parents and teachers alike often do not realize that many of their smallest behaviors communicate a lack of faith in the child or adolescent. Dinkmeyer and Dreikurs (1963), Glasser (1969), Losoncy (1977), Neisser (1950), and Sweeney (1973, 1977, 1978) discussed attitudes and methods which facilitate the development of confidence in others. Among them are the following:

1. Accept and have faith in the individual as he/she is (not his/her potential).

2. Expect him/her to handle tasks and show this expectation by your actions.

3. When confronted with misbehavior, separate the deed from the doer.

4. Confirm the fact that mistakes, defeat, or failure are common to life and not catastrophic.

5. Emphasize the joy of doing and the satisfaction in accomplishment rather than evaluations of how one is doing.

6. Recognize progress and provide ample encouragement for genuine effort.

7. Show confidence in the child's ability to be competent and avoid comparisons with others.

8. Allow for differences such as rate of learning, patience, neatness, or interest.

9. Never give up on the child, no matter how persistently he/she tries to defeat the encouragement process.

The last point is particularly critical. Very discouraged persons also have a "private logic," i.e., assumptions and convictions about life, themselves, and others, which guide their general movement through life. As useless as these notions and behaviors may seem to an outside observer, they constitute their unique notions about how to make a place in life. They will not give these up readily, for as unsatisfactory as circumstances may seem, children are convinced that everything could be worse if they gave up their protective behaviors. They may think, for example, "Others know that I'm not trying and I fail. They want me to try but then everyone would know how really stupid I am—how terrible that would be!"

Such a person is not to be pitied, quite the contrary. Only superiors can pity inferiors. Glasser's (1969) chapter on involving students in valuing their misbehavior, i.e., how it helps or hurts them and others and contracting with them for new behaviors, deserves careful reading and use. He shows how small approximations of the behaviors desired by the pupil are often more realistic than requiring promises beyond the probability of being kept. Until repertoire of even small successes is obtained, failure is to be precluded whenever possible. We can begin reinforcing success experiences by what we say and do.

Statements which tend to be encouraging include

You seem to enjoy . . .

I enjoyed your company . . .

The others seem to appreciate your help . . .

Getting started is difficult . . .

What do you think . . .?

If I can help, let me know . . .

Mistakes can be helpful . . .

Acts of encouragement are at least as important as words of encouragement. When our intention is to help others have confidence in themselves, to be self-reliant and to have the courage to be imperfect—we can show this by what we do. The following are some examples of acts of encouragement:

1. When children are trying to accomplish something on their own for the first time, allow them to learn by their mistakes as well as their successes without comment, evaluation, or intervention unless they request it. Give assistance willingly when requested but without taking over. If verbal encouragement is appropriate afterward, try to capture and reflect their feelings toward this endeavor without evaluation of how they did.

2. When children are slower, less neat, doing or being different from adults, be patient, be kind—keep busy with other matters until they catch up or finish what they were doing.

3. When others err or cause an accident, allow them to correct the mistake, clean up the mess, and try again without reprisal. For very discouraged children, volunteer in a friendly manner to help them if they would like assistance but refrain from taking over or doing it all. Show them friendliness and cooperation by example.

4. When discouragement is revealed, help individuals know that they have a place in the class, the family, or the group by giving them helpful jobs that they can do or by actions others do for them (e.g., asking them to help with a task, saving special stamps for the stamp collector, buying a charm for another's bracelet, taking time to watch or join them in something they enjoy.)

5. When an adult enjoys a child's company or appreciates his/her assistance, the adult can show this by a smile, a pat, or other nonverbal behavior which the child, too can understand.

6. When playing a competitive game, adults can check their motives, i.e., are these to win at all costs or to do the best they can and enjoy the event, win or lose. The latter motives model an encouraging attitude and behavior. The former reinforces a discouraged attitude in which only winning counts.

Physicians, school nurses, and teachers often hear parent concerns which relate for example to eating, sleeping, and toilet habits of children. When no medical reason for these behaviors are evident, the physicians' guide found in Table 6.4 can be useful. In certain instances medical and dietary factors can precipitate bed wetting, grouchiness, or withdrawal behaviors. When no such reason seems plausible, understanding the social value of the behavior takes on special meaning. You will note that in each case, encouragement is an essential element in restoring more appropriate behavior.

(Continued on page 185)

TABLE 6.4
Physicians Guide To Some Typical Nonmedical Behavior Problems

Parents' Common Concerns	Child's Goal	Typical Adult Responses	Corrective Action[1]	Preventative Action[2]
Won't eat what's prepared	Attention	Annoyed, coax, or bribe	No special preparation of food, eat or not—his/her choice	Enjoy food yourself, make meal time pleasant—talk, sharing, etc.
Won't dress	Attention	Annoyed, coax, bribe, reprimand	Take as is to sitter or dress but no other service, e.g. breakfast	Look for opportunity to reflect satisfaction in caring for self, feeling more comfortable when warm, etc.
Fighting	Attention	Referee, annoyed	Stay out—go to bathroom or send to their room to settle it	Give attention at times when cooperation is evident—read, play games, or share a snack
Toilet Training	Attention	Annoyed, commotion	Relax, remain friendly	Emphasize intrinsic satisfaction, e.g., reflect relief and satisfaction in elimination with attention to caring for self, i.e., personal mastery

Table 6.4 (Continued)

Parents' Common Concerns	Child's Goal	Typical Adult Responses	Corrective Action[1]	Preventative Action[2]
Can't Sleep "needs" water, lights on, has "fears"	Attention	Annoyed, coax, bribe	Be pleasant at bedtime, ignore any calls including out of bed behavior	In morning or after naps, ask about good rest feelings; when bedtime approaches (child's tired) reflect how good it will feel to lie down, relax, have pleasant thoughts, etc.
Masturbation	Power	Angry, reprimand, punish	Be unimpressed, relax	Avoid moralizing, allow open, candid discussions about sexual development, encourage questions by simple, honest answers
Temper Tantrum	Power	Angry, reprimand	Remain calm; if public place—remove and indicate that he/she is welcome to accompany you only if cooperation is given; if home, go to bathroom until behavior stops—avoid talking	Give youngster a job or activity in which he/she can help or participate

Table 6.4 (Continued)

Parents' Common Concerns	Child's Goal	Typical Adult Responses	Corrective Action[1]	Preventative Action[2]
Disobedience	Power	Angry	Indicate a desire to be cooperative but choice is their's, too. Use natural or logical consequences as an alternative to punishment, e.g., doesn't wash dishes, you don't cook supper	Family or classroom meeting to discuss members strong points, how these can help others, plan entertainment, picnics, etc., and establish ground rules for cooperation of group to live by
Stealing	Revenge	Hurt, punish	Be unimpressed, expect some restitution and ask youngsters to make suggestions—use consequences not punishment	Don't give up, know youngster doesn't expect to be liked, give them a place by being helpful, expect cooperation, show faith

[1]General Principles for Corrective Action: Do the unexpected, don't talk, don't act impulsively, give up idea of controlling, use natural and logical consequences.

[2]General Principles for Preventive Action: Remain friendly, be firm, consistent and positive, encourage responsible behavior with attention to youngster and intrinsic satisfaction with helping, sharing, and enjoying new competence and independence. Help them know that they have a place in the family, class, etc., by actions, not just words.

Another important dimension to encouragement was noted in Chapter 5 concerning the value system underlying Adlerian methods and techniques. Adlerians attempt to help others move on a horizontal plane toward behaviors and attitudes which free them to think, feel, and act as equals to others, capable of meeting any circumstance, any consequence, in a manner suited to the situation. This value orientation caused Adlerians to question the effect of corrective recommendations which might be construed as rewards or punishment (i.e., not a logical outcome of their behavior) by the children involved. In some cases, the child's prerogative to misinterpret the intention of others is unavoidable. On the other hand, when groups of children are similarly affected, then the methods or the intentions of those using them must be examined.

Behave so as to think, feel, and
act as an equal to others

Greene and Lepper (1974) reported on a series of studies which led them to conclude that ". . .these studies show that the use of extrinsic rewards and controls can undermine the intrinsic interest of a child in the activities for which he received a reward" (p. 54).

These authors reached this conclusion by offering children rewards for participating in activities already known to be of intrinsic value to the children. When the rewards stopped, the children's interest in the activities waned. Greene and Lepper cautioned against the use of extrinsic rewards except under carefully considered circumstances. This author agrees with Greene and Lepper and believes that even efforts to provide encouragement can be misconstrued as rewards by those for whom it is intended. Because of this possibility, efforts to empathize with the child's feelings and attitudes are important.

For example, a teacher had been attempting to encourage a low achieving girl whose records indicated above average ability. One afternoon, the pupils were doing independent projects and the teacher noted that this girl had been unusually busy working on her project for over an hour without seeking help or bothering others. She watched the girl a few moments and then commented that the girl was doing a good job. The girl looked up, began to cry and ran out of the room. At first bewildered, the teacher later approached the girl:

Teacher: Mary, what I said upset you. . .do you want to talk about it?

Mary: I don't know what to say. . .you didn't say anything wrong.

Teacher: Hmm, I think maybe I did. . .I think, Mary, that no matter how hard you try, it doesn't seem good enough. . .and that really makes you feel bad.

Mary: Well. . .it doesn't seem to matter how hard I try (starts to cry). . .

Teacher: . . .you were really intent on what you were doing . . .really into it. . .could you show me what you have planned. . .

Mary: Uh-huh, it really isn't finished but. . .

In this case, the teacher had overlooked the guideline that she not comment on **how** the pupil was doing but upon **what** she was doing. The teacher, however, used her knowledge of the girl to empathize with her discouragement and to re-orient her to what she planned to do.

The girl seemed intrinsically motivated, so that the comment by the teacher was not necessary. The comment could have been more helpful, however, if it had simply reflected the youngster's satisfaction, brought it to consciousness, and was shared by the teacher.

Not all children are discouraged in the same way. Some seek adult assurance of their place by doing everything as perfectly as possible. Teacher comments on how they are doing are solicited regularly. In some cases, not to get 100% on a test is almost catastrophic. Parents often feel great pride in such children. Gold stars, dollars for an A, ad infinitum, only add to the discouragement.

> Through encouragement help others
> appreciate their intrinsic worth,
> their equality, their place in the world.

The world of these persons, as children and adults, is a constant climb for success, a constant need for assurances, an unrelenting demand on energy. They can be helped, however, to appreciate their intrinsic worth, their equality, their place in the world with the appropriate use of encouragement.

Execute with Consistency, Friendliness, and Respect

In the author's experience, adults have a tendency to seek relief only from the immediate problems that they are having with children and adolescents. When a reasonable amount of success is attained and the crisis of the moment has passed, further counseling or consultation ends.

A new agreement is sometimes reached between adults and children which is premature and falls far short of what is required to prevent future crises of the same type again. For this reason, an understanding with adults and children to follow through on the preventative aspects of the counselor's recommendations (Chapter 11) should be stressed. For purposes of execution in implementing corrective procedures, a few observations can help increase the probability of their effectiveness.

First, consistency is very important in taking corrective actions. Each time adults make exceptions to the agreed upon rules, they invite further hassles on modifying other rules on other occasions. This is a testing game which every parent or teacher has experienced. Friendliness will take the harsh edge off the firmness which is necessary to maintain order.

Second, be aware that some children will cry "foul" when they finally realize the new rules have a force of their own. They will claim that something is unfair about their implementation. If the rules apply to everyone, then they will see the logic in their application. They still may try to avoid the consequences by argument. In such cases, silence is golden. Respect is reinforced by the equality inherent in these methods.

I'm imperfect and I'll accept you
as being imperfect.

Third, do not be afraid to make a mistake—have the courage to be imperfect. Occasionally an adult will feel overwhelmed by the possibilities of doing the "wrong" thing. Such notions are counter-productive to the kinds of strategies Adlerians use to help others learn. We learn by doing, by our mistakes as well as successes. If we dwell on negative thoughts, we tend to revert to the old methods and feel defeated in the process as well.

Fourth, implement only one or two recommendations at a time. Work on correcting one type of behavior at a time. Success experiences for the adults are important as well. When adults are new to these methods, they can become confused or disappointed by attempting too many adjustment, too quickly.

SUMMARY

This chapter has outlined major principles, methods, and techniques of Adlerian child guidance. Several excellent books have been written on this topic. The reader desiring a more thorough explanation of these concepts will want to peruse some of the references.

One final note concerns the applicability of these methods to all people regardless of age or station in life. As will be seen in subsequent chapters, Adler's observations about the "iron-clad logic of social living" impinge upon all of us. It is further evidence of our equality. As we discover the order and harmony which can be found in living with young people, other aspects of our social lives improve as well. Marriage discussion groups often are the next activity after a parent study group because participants have experienced its value and want to enrich their lives further. As one studies the holy books of the world, similar themes about living together become apparent. An order and meaning to social living exist; this discovery is an adventure which will bring its own satisfactions.

STUDY QUESTIONS

Directions: Respond to the following in spaces provided.

1. Give one illustration of each of the four goals of misbehavior and the child's "private logic" in each situation. What are the adult feelings and traditional responses in each illustration?

2. List four faulty goals of adolescents discussed within the chapter which adults tend to reinforce. Do you agree that these are faulty goals? Why or why not?

3. Isolate one child-adult incident which you observed or in which you were involved, and apply the four steps represented by **CARE.** How might the results have been different had you done so?

4. Why is talking too much a shortcoming in the corrective dimension of discipline?

ACTIVITIES FOR INDIVIDUALS AND GROUPS

A. You have had an opportunity to study the principles and methods of Individual Psychology in relation to guiding young people. The concept of goal directed behavior is an exciting one when first fully understood. Initially, persons new to this approach want to apply their knowledge immediately. Naturally, successful application of this approach takes practice, creativity, and flexibility. The following exercises are designed to give you practice in recognizing the goals of misbehavior and to encourage you to begin to create alternative responses which can be applied to counseling and consultation.

1. Identifying Feelings and Behavior

   The following paragraphs are vignettes of everyday living. On Form 6.1, Feelings and Behaviors, identify the goal of misbehavior illustrated, the adult's usual reflexive response, and the result of this intervention. Also, propose an alternative response to the child's misbehavior. Please provide a specific response or action, e.g., mother leaves the room where the children are fighting. *Hint: try doing the unexpected.* Complete Form 6.1 on the next 2 pages. Then after completing the form, compare your responses to those in the Key to Form 6.1 which is shown on page 193.

Vignette 1: Mary is a cute little 2-year old *who has just dropped her plate of spaghetti on the floor* for the second time, gleefully laughing and saying, "All gone!"

Vignette 2: Jim and Joe are twins *who seem to fight all the time.* Father has just told Jim to share his construction set with his brother. Jim screams, "You can't make me!" to which replies, "I don't want to play with that old thing anyway!"

Vignette 3: Four-year-old Jessica brings her mother's church group meeting to a screeching halt when she *loudly and clearly curses* at the dog in the next room.

Vignette 4: Angered by her brother's refusal to take her along to the movies, Judy methodically *tears up his baseball cards* and sprinkles the pieces around his room.

Vignette 5: Although his achievement tests indicate he is able to complete the assignments, Steven rarely *attempts the more difficult mathematics problems.* He even refuses help from his own brother.

The main purpose of this activity is to help the student see the purposiveness of behavior. Your attention is drawn to the goals of misbehavior, the adult's feelings and thoughts and the normal responses. You will see in later lessons that new behaviors and attitudes by adults can change the relationships from fighting to friendliness.

FORM 6.1
Feelings & Behaviors

Situation	Child's Goal of Misbehavior*	Adult Typical Response	Outcome	Alternative Action
Vignette 1: Mary drops her plate of food on the floor.				
Vignette 2: Twins, Jim and Joe, fight all the time.				
Vignette 3: Jessica curses at the dog.				
Vignette 4: Judy tears up her brother's baseball cards.				
Vignette 5: Steven rarely attempts more difficult mathematics problems.				

*The predominate goal is most easily identified by the feelings evoked in the adult or others involved. If the adult feels annoyed, the child probably wants attention; if angry—power; if hurt/disappointed—revenge; if the adult gives up, the child's goal is inadequacy.

Key to FORM 6.1—Feelings & Behaviors

Situation	Child's Goal of Misbehavior*	Adult Typical Response	Outcome	Alternative Action
Vignette 1: Mary drops her plate of food on the floor.	attention	annoyed, and cleans up	child watches	say nothing, get clean up material and let the child help clean up
Vignette 2: Twins, Jim and Joe, fight all the time	power	angered, reprimands, referees	kids continue fights, Jim continues to challenge adults	sidestep power struggle, stay out of fights, boys to their rooms to fight or at least leave immediate area (preferably with no talk from adults)
Vignette 3: Jessica curses at the dog.	revenge	hurt, embarrassed, scolds, paddles	calls names, fights back.	remove firmly but without comment, let it be known later that she cannot go to church and disrupt others, you enjoy her company and would like her to go, "can she attend

				without disrupting others?" if yes, no more is said; if no, she cannot go until she is ready. No lectures or "what a good girl" pep talks later for cooperation—be pleasant, etc., and help make going fun, etc.
Vignette 4: Judy tears up her brother's baseball cards	revenge	hurt/angry	enjoys commotion	needs encouragement (future lessons)
Vignette 5: Steven rarely attempts more difficult mathematics problems	inadequacy	give up	Steven withdraws further	needs encouragement (future lessons)

2. Describing Personal Experiences

Describe at least two situations from your own experience in which you were dealing with a misbehaving
child. Include your response and how the child reacted.

—What were your feelings during and after the episode?

—With your current understanding of the purposiveness
of behavior, indicate what you believe was the child's
goal. How might you have responded differently?

*Personal Experience 1:*_____

_____

_____

_____

● Your Response _____

_____

● Child's Reaction _____

_____

● Your Feelings (during & after) _____

_____

● Child's Goal _____

_____

● How could you have responded differently? _____

_____

_____

Personal Experience 2: _____

_____

_____

- Your Response _____

    _____

- Child's Reaction _____

    _____

- Your Feelings (during & after) _____

    _____

- Child's Goal _____

    _____

- How could you have responded differently? _____

    _____

    _____

3. Sharing Experiences

Share your responses to the vignettes and your personal experiences as a group, with your study partner or an interested friend. Feel free to express any concerns or doubts you have about specific interventions described. Which suggestions would you be the most uncomfortable in attempting? Each person needs to be aware of his/her own feelings in working with this approach. Compare your responses on Form 6.1, Feelings and Behavior, with those in the Key to Form 6.1.

B. In previous lessons, you have had opportunities to study the principles and methods of Individual Psychology. In this lesson you have read about some of the mistaken or faulty goals of adolescents. The following exercise provides an opportunity for you to apply the Adlerian methods to the problems associated with teenagers' disruptive behavior.

1. Listing Adolescent Disruptive Behavior

   a. Based upon your experience and study, list three or more specific disruptive behaviors of adolescents on the chart provided on page 200.

   b. Now share your examples with other members of the class or your study partner. (You may list the examples on a chalkboard if you are in a classroom. Don't worry about spelling, have the courage to be imperfect!)

   c. Think about the examples listed:

      1) Are all the behaviors generally considered "bad" behavior, i.e., talking back, being irresponsible, etc.

      2) If so, think about some which are more accep- table to adults but nonetheless faulty goals as identified in Table 6.3 earlier in this chapter. List others on your form as necessary.

2. Discussing the Behaviors

   a. Divide into groups of three or four persons and each person in the group select one or two disruptive behaviors from her list to discuss. Use the form provided to determine as a group, the appropriate response for each category. As nearly so as possible, the members should select behaviors which relate to different goals in order to benefit from greater variety within the group discussion.

3. Completing the Chart

a. Following the group discussion of the selected teen problem behaviors, each member should complete the other items in Form 6.2, on the chart, Typical Teenager Disruptive Behavior, relating them to the specific behavior of interest to his/her (i.e., adult reactions, goals, thoughts, corrective responses). You may wish to refer to Table 6.3., again.

b. When all members are finished, discussion in the small groups can begin with what each person has listed and why. Maybe others know of a youngster like that, too, and can make suggestions for successful interventions. The group members also can help insure that goals, and thoughts, are consistent with the behavior and corrective methods.

FORM 6.2
TYPICAL TEENAGE DISRUPTIVE BEHAVIOR

Disruptive Behavior	Adult Reactions	Goals	Thoughts	Potential Encouraging Corrective Responses

C. In previous activities and lessons, we have presented and discussed the principles and methods of guiding young people. At this point in your studies, you realize that a persistently misbehaving person is pursuing a mistaken private logic that such behavior is necessary for them to be "somebody," to be recognized. We occasionally experience an almost spontaneous change in attitude and behavior of a very discouraged person. More often, however, time, patience, and consistency in the reasoned use of these methods is necessary to effect significant change.

In an earlier lesson, you gave thought to identifying a misbehaving young person to determine his/her goal and what consequences and encouragement might help. In most instances, we tend to think of the youngsters pursuing the first two goals, attention and power. This is natural because they are commonly pursued goals and they annoy or anger us.

The behavior and goals of revenge and inadequacy, however, discourage us. We tend to avoid or ignore such people. Our task in this activity is to identify a youngster(s) who persistently pursues the third or fourth goals. Then using the resources of other members in a small group (4 to 6) or with a study partner, develop a specific plan of intervention designed to reorient the mistaken goals and behavior of the youngster. (While it may go without saying at this point, the discouraged adolescent or adult also can benefit from such a plan.)

1. Developing a Positive Intervention Plan

    Identify a youngster whom you think pursues the goals of revenge or inadequacy. Using Form 6.3., Positive Intervention Plan, develop a plan. For an example, see Sample to Form 6.3. When you have a general outline, discuss your plan as a group or with your study partner. Each member should help the others to

    a. establish what *specific* behaviors are bothersome and might be changed,

b. identify the *goal and likely faulty private logic* the individual is thinking.

c. pinpoint a time or times when a discussion of natural/logical consequences might be *utilized to establish non-punitive rules* for everyone in relation to disruptive behavior (Remember that logical consequences are more easily misconstrued as punishment by the person pursuing the third goal.),

d. suggest specific methods and techniques of *verbal and non-verbal encouragement,*

e. establish *times and situations* for implementation of the plan, and

f. establish *guidelines for assessing progress* (small steps in the desired direction are often more useful than overly ambitious outcomes).

2. Sharing Experiences in Applying Adlerian Methods

At this point, you may wish to share some of your experiences in applying the methods of Individual Psychology in situations at home, school or work. The experiences of friends, etc., also can be shared even though names or other identifying information should be limited.

FORM 6.3
POSITIVE INTERVENTION PLAN[1]

Case Information

A. Description of youngster
- Age • Sex
- Physical Bearing (posture, cleanliness, mannerisms)

- Siblings: Brothers/ages
  Sisters/ages
- Ordinal Position

- Other Information

B. Disruptive Behavior(s)
-
-
-
-
-

C. Adult/Others Reactions
- Behavior

- Feelings

D. Predominate Goal of Misbehavior
(based on predominate feeling evoked in adult or others involved)
-

E. Private Logic (what the child is thinking)
-

F. If no change
- What misbehavior would you expect?

- What would the youngster expect from you?

[1]Non-evaluative, focus on satisfaction in activity and relationships.

Form 6.3 (Continued)

Preventive Intervention Action[1]

A. Verbal Encouragement
- I can
- When Given

B. Nonverbal Encouragement
- I can
- When Given

[1]Non-evaluative, focus on satisfaction in activity and relationships.

Form 6.3 (Continued)

Corrective Intervention Action[2]

A. Natural Consequences

B. Logical Consequences

[2]Remember, "do the unexpected, don't talk, don't act impulsively, give up the idea of controlling." The consequences should be rules upon which you have agreed after the discussion. Unlike punishment, they are logical, promote order, respect individual and group rights and are non-punitive in nature. Note that they involve alternative choices, not ultimatums.

Remain friendly, firm, consistent, and positive.

SAMPLE OF FORM 6.3   POSITIVE INTERVENTION PLAN[1]

Case Information

A. Description of youngster
- Age __11__   • Sex __M__
- Physical Bearing (posture, cleanliness, mannerisms)
  Avoids direct eye contact, slouches, bites fingernails
- Siblings: Brothers/ages __10__
    (younger brother is a charmer)
  Sisters/ages __13__
    ("model" oldest sister)
- Ordinal Position __2nd child__
- Other Information __Tom was recently transferred into my class because he was doing progressively poorer in his school work and the kids in the other class did not like him. His mother doesn't know what to do with him.__

B. Disruptive Behavior(s)
- Known to lie, steal
- Fights, hits others
- Easily discouraged
- Easily off task in class—not completing work

C. Adult/Others Reactions
- Behavior
  - Reprimand him, send to office
  - Make him apologize to others
  - Nag about work, tell him he can do better
  - Classmates avoid him
- Feelings
  - Hurt, Resentful

D. Predominate Goal of Misbehavior (based on predominate feeling evoked in adult or others involved)
- Revenge, because his behavior hurts others

E. Private Logic (what the child is thinking)
- Others don't like me. Life really isn't fair, but I'll show them. I can hurt them back!

F. If no change
- What misbehavior would you expect?
  Continued behavior problems described in "B" but, would look for the behavior to intensify—ways of hurting others more—seeking ways to get even and be more disliked.
- What would the youngster expect from you?
  - Increased nagging about work habits.
  - Not trust him, accuse him first
  - Call his parents
  - Many trips to the principal's office

[1]Non-evaluative, focus on satisfaction in activity and relationships.

Form 6.3 (Continued)

Preventive Intervention Action[1]

A. Verbal Encouragement

• I can	• When Given
Let him know that I'm glad he's in my class	1st day and periodically
Express appreciation for his help	Each time he helps
In an individual conference let him know that it must seem hard to him to have a sister who seems so good to others, but that doesn't matter in my class because I think he's showing us how really helpful and able he is.	As needed, if discouragement shows up consistently
Greet him with a smile and cheery hello and inquire about what's happened since yesterday.	Each day

B. Nonverbal Encouragement

• I can	• When Given
Introduce him through our classroom meeting and let him tell about his interests, etc.	1st day of class
Have him help collect papers.	1st day of class and periodically
Smile at him.	Each morning and periodically
Send home a note expressing positive observations about his help in my class and soliciting parents encouragement.	1st day and periodically
Give him extra or individualized lesson task if skills are not up to rest of class.	As needed
Invite him to help someone else with a job or task for which he has competence.	Periodically, but especially when he seems emotionally down

[1] Non-evaluative, focus on satisfaction in activity and relationships.

Form 6.3 (Continued)

Corrective Intervention Action[2]

A. Natural Consequences	B. Logical Consequences
In Tom's case, logical consequences may be the only alternative	In our class, we do not "hear" requests not prefaced with "please" or otherwise disrespectful. We ignore these without comment.
	• Persistently disruptive behavior results in removing oneself to the "time out" table and returning when ready to join back in.
	• Must complete work before recess or while others play but can join in recess when finished.
	• Cannot play with others when in a fighting mood but can rejoin us when ready to have fun.
	• Must compensate for broken or stolen items or not have access to them in the future.

[2]Remember, "do the unexpected, don't talk, don't act impulsively, give up the idea of controlling." The consequences should be rules upon which you have agreed after the discussion. Unlike punishment, they are logical, promote order, respect individual and group rights and are non-punitive in nature. Note that they involve alternative choices, not ultimatums.

Remain friendly, firm, consistent, and positive.

Chapter 7

LIFE STYLE ASSESSMENT

UNCOVERING THE UNCONSCIOUS

Adler characterized life style as the ". . . unity in each individual—in his thinking, feeling, acting; in his so called conscious and unconscious, in every expression of his personality. This (self-consistent) unity we call the style of life of the individual" (Ansbacher & Ansbacher, 1967, p. 175). Life style analysis or assessment is an effort to make explicit the attitudes, beliefs, and convictions which one uses in approaching or avoiding life's tasks. While the scope of this work does not provide a comprehensive introduction to methods and techniques of life style assessment, an overview is appropriate. For a more complete discussion see Shulman and Mosak (1988b) book, *Manual for Life Style Assessment.*

The best way to validate the usefulness and reliability of life style assessment is through personal experience as a subject of an assessment. You may become more aware of your own perceptions with the aid of a counselor. In the past only a few counselors may have been interested in the use of life style in counseling because only recently has emphasis been focused on life style assessment. This circumstance is changing as practitioners have access to useful references, courses and workshops, emphasizing life style. The following sections will provide an introduction to the rationale and methods utilized while other chapters contain life style information application in career and marriage counseling.

DATA GATHERING

Experienced counselors learn to observe behavior as a means of understanding the motivation which makes such behavior useful to an individual. Lombardi (1973) indicated, for example, eight possible ways to know or learn about another's life style:

1. case history

2. psychological interview

3. expressive behavior

4. testing

5. family constellation

6. early recollections

7. group interaction

8. symptomatic behavior

Adler in the *Problems of Neurosis* (1964) wrote that many ways are available to detect indications of another's life style. Among his early observations were those revealed through organic problems. Suggested in recent stress research is that individuals tend to respond to similar stressful circumstances with particular physiological reactions unique to their coping skills. When some individuals say that they can't "stomach" a situation, they literally mean it! Stomach ulcers, gall bladder attacks, nausea, and other symptoms are a result

Extensive life style information generally would not be necessary in cases such as the following.

1. Individual is seeking assistance with a situational problem within the person's capability of solving without such data.

2. Child whose behavior clearly reflects classical discouragement and for whom corrective action can be taken in the home and/or classroom.

3. A major theme or movement through life is apparent and recognizable when presented by the counselor as a result of observing and attentive listening.

4. Testing information, symptomatic behavior, family constellation, early recollections, or similar data already are available to the counselor in written form or report by the individual.

SOURCES OF DATA

When appropriate to proceed with a life style assessment, at least three sources of data are the following: (1) family constellation questionnaire (Dreikurs, 1954; Mosak & Shulman, 1971; Shulman, 1962), (2) early recollections (Dreikurs, 1954; Eckstein, Baruth, & Mahrer, 1978; Gushurst, 1971; Mosak, 1958), and (3) observations. In each instance, the trained interviewer is prepared to formulate hypothesis, test them, discard, modify, or confirm them as the case may be. Questioning techniques vary as do styles in conducting psychological investigations. Experienced practitioners are able to integrate sources of data into free flowing dialogue with a client while systematically elliciting responses from which formulations are derived.

Life style assessment underscores
the holistic nature of one's being.

The usefulness of life style assessment further underscores the holistic nature of one's being. Virtually every behavior is a small but significant piece of a larger plan or gestalt of interrelated parts. Our choice of clothes, body posture, and movement, all reveal underlying attitudes and convictions.

Essentially, life style assessment allows us to reveal the private logic which the individual follows. On one hand, most people acquire and accept certain motions of what is appropriate or inappropriate in socially living with others. Agreement on such matters may be called common sense. When individuals ignore or violate what the situation may demand as perceived by others, then these individuals are following their private logic.

Your private logic contributes to a belief that what you do is the appropriate course of action for you. Because it is a result of your earliest experiences in life and basically reinforced by selective perceptions of what you expect for life, others, and yourself, this private logic goes fairly unchallenged. Much like an invisible road map, you chart your goals, plans, and actions without an awareness of the rationale which you follow.

Your unconscious assumptions are on "automatic" so long as you are content with them and you make choices without asking, is there another way? Each of us acts "as if" his/her perceptions are the only ones possible or correct.

Adler noted that while one's life style is established by age six years or so, it can be changed whenever an individual considers it useful to do so. Actually most people do not require a significant change in their basic goals and learn to use their creative self-direction to accomodate to others' expectations in the many social contexts that they experience.

Understanding what Dreikurs called one's hidden reason in pursuing specific behavior contributes to the kind of understanding which counselees report as useful and comforting. Dreikurs would say, "Tell a person what he is (e.g., lazy, manic-depressive) so what? Tell a person how he feels, so what? But tell a person what he intends, what is his goal? Now that, the person can change!" Equally important, counselees feel encouraged by the knowledge that someone else understands their logic and can truly empathize with some of their predicaments.

FAMILY CONSTELLATION

The counselor attempts, then, to understand the individual's private logic on how to be somebody, how to have a place, how to be important. We look first at siblings and family for evidence of how life seems to be, how others are, and how we can make our place. Dreikurs noted that the youngster closest in age and most different from us had the greatest influence on our personality.

Research and clinical experience seem to corroborate this simple rule, that whatever one child likes or excels at, the other will be opposite. If one is artistic, the other will likely be athletic. An exception is when family values help to moderate the overt differences, for example, such as an expectation that everyone must do well in school. Differences between youngsters in those areas' in which they choose to excel, nevertheless, can be discerned. Early recollections are another rich source of material. For the beginner or infrequent user of life style assessment, some structure for data collection is useful. Fortunately tools are available to assist you.

The family constellation questionnaire requires that the individual think about his/her perceptions and feelings as a child of six to eight years old or younger. Some individuals can respond to this task very readily while others require some assistance in recapturing the childhood neighborhood, home, friends, or favorite things to do which are a touchstone of experiences for them as a child. Most persons become quite interested in recalling earlier times and self-disclose without hesitation. Many persons find this is a very enjoyable experience.

The counselor is guided by a series of questions which help discover such information as the individual's ordinal position in the family, comparative characteristics with other members of the family, interaction patterns within the family, family values, and adjustment to physical and socioeconomic conditions. The following are from among the questions often asked in these interviews (Dreikurs, 1967, pp. 125-52; Shulman & Mosak, 1988a, pp. 2-9 , 1988b, pp. 61-178).

A. Ordinal Position—List all the children in the family in their birth order and list their ages plus or minus years compared to the counselee's age, including siblings now dead and/or miscarriages which were known to the person as a child. For example:

       Bob + 2

       Tom 28 (counselee)

       Mary -2

       girl baby -3 (stillborn)

       Susan -10

In this example, Tom is a middle child in a two family constellation, i.e., Susan is more likely to have the characteristics of the only child because she is more than six to eight years younger than the next youngster.

B. Description of Siblings—Be specific in description

1. Who is most different from you? In what respect? (likely competitor)

2. Who is most like you? In what respect? (possible ally)

3. What kind of kid were you?

4. Describe the other siblings.

C. Comparative attributes—Rate self and siblings on each of the attributes by indicating who you believed was highest or most, who was lowest or least, and if you were neither one, indicate to which sibling you were most similar.

1. Intelligence
2. Hardest worker
3. Best grades in school
4. Helped at home
5. Conforming
6. Rebellious
7. Tried to please
8. Got own way
9. Sense of humor
10. High standards
11. Most spoiled
12. Most punished

D. Sibling Relationship

1. Who took care of whom?

2. Who played with whom?

3. Who was favorite of mother? Father?

4. Who got along best and who fought most?

E. Parent

    1. Parent ages

    2. What kind of person was each?

    3. Which child liked father most? Mother most? In what ways?

    4. What kind of relationship existed between father and mother?

    5. Who was more ambitious for the children? In what ways?

    6. Did any other persons live with or significantly influence you?

Dreikurs (1967, pp. 125-52) and Shulman and Mosak (1988b) discussed the significance of questions like these and others in much greater detail. The influence of early social experiences on one's biased apperceptions is the focus of attention. From the counselee's review of these early perceptions, the counselor can begin to develop a word portrait of the individual. Allen (1971b), Mosak (1972) and Shulman and Mosak (1988b) gave illustrations of this process from actual cases.

Early Recollections

Typically, early recollections are recorded as a part of the interview process following the family constellation. Individuals frequently will begin sharing early recollections before the counselor even suggests that they do so; Adlerians believe what is remembered is done so selectively because it has significance to the individual in understanding, managing, and controlling life experiences. Specific early recollections are those recalled to approximately age eight or nine years.

Early recollections are cues for
understanding present behavior.

The difference between a significant early recollection and a report must be noted. Many people recall family routines, frequent interactions, or general descriptions of early experiences. For example, one individual reported that every Sunday afternoon in the summer her family made ice cream as a pasttime. Even with more detail, it is not to be confused with a recollection. A useful recollection would be more specific and would bring attention to a particular incident. For example, the individual went on to say:

> I remember one Sunday afternoon it was a very pleasant outside and the older kids were running around ignoring the ice cream churn. I decided that I would make the ice cream and began to crank the handle. No one particularly noticed that I had seen the job to the end. They enjoyed the ice cream and so did I. I really felt pleased with myself and have liked ice cream especially well ever since (laugh).

In the previous example, no one in the family may have remembered her helping with the ice cream. In fact, it may never have happened. What is significant is that she remembers it as though it did happen. The counselor might hypothesize from this recollection that the individual believes:

> Among life's greatest satisfactions is seeing a job to the end, whether others realize who the source of giving is or not. When others shirk their responsibility, I can be depended upon to see that the job gets done. I can and do enjoy contributing to others' pleasure.

Specific childhood dreams can be treated as early recollections. Recurring dreams often stand out but they are considered as reports rather than early recollections.

The question which is asked to begin the process can have particular significance, i.e., what is your earliest recollection? In the author's experience, when the earliest recollection is recalled easily, a tendency is for it to contain major themes or patterns of belief fundamental to the individual's movement through life. This can be confirmed or refuted, however, by noting the content and affect in subsequent recollections.

Recording the approximate age of recollection can be helpful, especially as the counselor may observe, for example, that the individual recalled no recollections until a significant event occurred in the family, e.g., a birth or death, a family move, another person joined the family.

Whether the earliest recollection is remembered first or not, themes or patterns reveal themselves in a series of recollections. Some persons may remember only a few while most persons can recall six to ten or more recollections without difficulty.

Some Adlerians have the individual respond to a family constellation and recollection questionnaire in writing. The questionnaire is then supplemented by an interview to elaborate on or clarify written responses.

Among the activities and questions which the counselor considers as he/she seeks to understand the individual are in the next paragraph. This part of the process is completed after the interview in which the counselor listened, clarified, and recorded as accurately as possible the exact descriptions shared by the individual.

In these recollections:

Is the individual active or passive?

Is he/she an observer or participant?

Is he/she giving or taking?

Does he/she go forth or withdraw?

What is his/her physical posture or position in relation to what is around him?

Is he/she alone or with others?

Is his/her concern with people, things, or ideas?

What relationship does he/she place himself/herself into with others? Inferior? Superior?

What emotion does he/she use?

What feeling tone is attached to the event or outcome?

Is detail and color mentioned?

Do stereotypes of authorities, subordinates, men, women, old, young, reveal themselves?

Prepare a "headline" which captures the essence of the event; for example, in relation to the woman's recollection of ice cream: Girl Gets Job Done! (Mosak, 1972)

Look for themes and an overall pattern.

Look for corroboration in the family constellation information.

To the author's knowledge, no single, universally established set of questions or procedures exists which standardizes the life style process. Most practitioners modify or otherwise use their experiences as a means of deriving information needed to assist the individual. Gushurst (1971) and Eckstein et al. (1978) described the general process in more detail for persons interested in gaining greater familiarity with using these data.

The process of summary generally results in statements which can be as shown in the following, (Mosak, 1958, 1987; Shulman, 1962; Shulman & Mosak, 1988a, 1988b):

A. I am . . .

    1. Self-concept: Who I think I am, what I do, like, and so forth.

       a. For example: I am woman
                         I am short
                         I am honest

b. These may not be objectively true (i.e., a very short person may not feel short while a tall person may feel short); it is the subjective evaluation of the person that must be understood.

c. Listen for missing modifiers particularly when evident in the ratings and recollections, e.g., I am only a woman, I must be honest, I am very short.

2. Self-ideal: What I want, should be, or should do in order to have my place.

a. For example: I want to be rich
I should be generous
I should work hard
I should be a real man (woman)

b. Family values and atmosphere can be seen to have an influence on the self-ideal, e.g., you must get a good education to get ahead, always work to win, love cures all.

B. Others are . . .

1. General: People generally are kind, dependable, and trustworthy.

2. Specific: Women are good servants; men are strong; children should be seen but not heard.

C. Life:

1. General: Life is full of dangers, "a great big circus," a challenge to be met.

2. Specific: Things are as they seem, nature is very unforgiving of the weak persons like me; each day is a new opportunity for me.

From combinations of I am, others are, and life is, inferences can be made—"therefore, I. . .."

I am a child but I can do what I want to do.

Adults, i.e., those in authority have advantages over children which are unfair.

Life is a daily struggle in which only the strong survive.

Therefore, I must show adults that they cannot defeat me.

The method of operation is revealed by the "therefore, I" statement of conviction. This does not allow the observer to predict the specific behavior of the individual, e.g., will talk back or openly rebel. With each life style a number of possible behaviors exist. An individual may "defeat" the adults in his/her life by being superior to them in some positive quality or ability he/she judges significant. One may choose to challenge adults on the basis of their inconsistency to help demonstrate to the world how they are unfair.

To modify one's behavior does not require that the life convictions change. In fact, as individuals experience natural and logical consequences as well as punishment and reward, they modify their behavior. Adlerians simply believe that when a new, strange, or stressful situation occurs without the benefit of known clues, individuals resort to their earliest convictions.

OBSERVATIONS

Matthews (1972) discussed personality change in old age. She noted, with optimism, that Butler (1968) posited the universal occurrence in old people of an inner experience that he called the life review, i.e., recall of early childhood rearing practices in the home, struggles with conscience, first loves, aspirations of life. Adlerians believe such observations serve further to confirm the belief that while one's behavior does change, the orientation, i.e., characteristic way of moving through life, does not change except under unusual circumstances.

As each of us faces later years and/or death, we are confronted with a new, potentially stressful life task. A review of our basic life experiences and convictions would seem to be a likely course to follow in attempting to cope with later years and/or death from the Adlerian point of view (Sweeney & Myers, 1986).

This reviewing is not to suggest that one is "determined" by his/her life style in an absolute way. Adlerians have observed that while people fashion their own convictions, they also tend to hold to them in the face of new data, and actually establish expectencies to prove or affirm that they were accurate all along. Adlerians, therefore, are referred to these as "soft determinants" because they have noted changes in persons as a result of psychotherapy only when it would serve individuals better, or because of an usually significant event and/or brain damage. Generally, Adlerians do not expect life style changes, per se.

In the cases where life styles are reported to have changed, persons are observed to have different perceptions of their early years and even their early recollections have changed or were forgotten, i.e., they have new interpretations of similar events or they recall "new" incidents.

One's life style remains consistent
unless. . .

Life style analysis can involve a rather extensive review of an individual's life perceptions including family relationships and recollections, or less extensive exploration to simply help uncover an individual's characteristic movement through life. The emphasis is upon movement and motivation. Attempting to discover how and toward what goal an individual is moving is the counselor's objective. Whether or not the individual chooses to change his/her behavior or motivation is clearly the counselee's responsibility.

For further information on the research and practical use of this method, Baruth and Eckstein (1978) provided an overview which included illustrations of its use with children and adults under a variety of circumstances and applications. To assist the reader further in understanding the basics of this method and its application, you are referred to an Interviewer's Life Style Inventory which is included in this chapter following the "Summary." Also, an edited typescript and commentary of an interview between a seventeen year old "hippie" looking young woman and Dr. Harold Mosak are provided in Chapter 8. As is a common practice in demonstrations, Dr. Mosak conducted this interview before an audience of more than two hundred persons interested in learning about this method. The counselee is a volunteer who, at the time, was dressed in blue jeans, sandals, hippie style shirt and wore her long brown hair in a free flowing style.

SUMMARY

This chapter provides an overview of life style assessment as used in Adlerian counseling and psychotherapy. While much more can be addressed regarding this method, the reader should have an understanding of how this method is an outgrowth of the principle that all behavior is useful to individuals as they strive for a place of significance among others. With a knowledge that behavior is purposive and interrelated through one's life style, discovering another's private logic becomes a matter of guess or hypothesizing about the significance of specific behavior in relation to the whole. Through this process, you can help others in both small and large ways to understand and modify their behavior and/or motivate them to the mutual advantage of themselves and others. Persons inexperienced in projective techniques and their use will need supervised experience and practice in these techniques.

INTERVIEWER'S
LIFE STYLE INVENTORY*

FAMILY CONSTELLATION

Start with your oldest sibling and give his or her name and how many years older or younger he or she is than you are. Then the next oldest, etc. Also include deceased children and note miscarriages if you know them. List all siblings in descending order, including yourself. Give your siblings' ages in terms of plus (+) number of years older or minus (-) number of years younger.

		Name	Age (+ or -)	Comments
Siblings:	1 (Oldest)	_____	_____	_____
	2	_____	_____	_____
	3	_____	_____	_____
	4	_____	_____	_____
	5	_____	_____	_____
	6	_____	_____	_____

The following questions are to be answered *as you would have responded when you were a young child* of three to eight years of age. This is quite important and may require a little *relaxed reflecting* on where you lived, whom you played with as a child, etc. If closing your eyes for a moment would help, think back to the old neighbor, your favorite toys, etc.

---

*The questions are in large measure those in Dreikurs (1967, pp. 125-52) and found in various format in both published and unpublished literature. With experience and an understanding of the potential significance of these questions, an interviewer will learn to innovate somewhat on these subject areas.

A. Description of Siblings

1. Who is most different from you? _____In what respect?

_____

_____

_____

2. Who is most like you? _____? In what respect?

_____

_____

_____

3. What kind of kid were you? _____

_____

_____

_____

4. Describe other siblings.

Sibling 1 (oldest) _____

Sibling 2 _____

Sibling 3 _____

Sibling 4 _____

Sibling 5 _____

Interviewer's Life Style Inventory (continued)

Sibling 6 _____

B. Ratings of Attributes

Write in the space provided the name of the sibling (include consideration of yourself) whom you rate as being highest on each attribute. Then write the name of the sibling lowest on each attribute. If you are at neither extreme on an attribute, then draw an arrow (◄ or ►) in the middle column toward the sibling most like you. If you are an only child, how would you rate yourself on each attribute in relation to other children?

	Sibling Highest	Self ◄ or ►	Sibling Lowest
1. Intelligence	_____	_____	_____
2. Hardest Worker	_____	_____	_____
3. Best grades in school	_____	_____	_____
4. Helping around the house	_____	_____	_____
5. Conforming	_____	_____	_____
6. Rebellious	_____	_____	_____
7. Trying to please	_____	_____	_____
8. Critical of others	_____	_____	_____
9. Considerateness	_____	_____	_____
10. Selfishness	_____	_____	_____
11. Having own way	_____	_____	_____
12. Sensitive—easily hurt	_____	_____	_____
13. Temper tantrum	_____	_____	_____

Interviewer's Life Style Inventory (continued)

	Sibling Highest	Self ◄ or ►	Sibling Lowest
14. Sense of humor	_____	_____	_____
15. Idealistic	_____	_____	_____
16. Materialistic	_____	_____	_____
17. High standards of			
a. Achievement	_____	_____	_____
b. Behavior	_____	_____	_____
c. Morals	_____	_____	_____
18. Most athletic	_____	_____	_____
19. Strongest	_____	_____	_____
20. Tallest	_____	_____	_____
21. Prettiest	_____	_____	_____
22. Most masculine	_____	_____	_____
23. Most feminine	_____	_____	_____

24. In the case of females, determine when menarche began, who explained this phenomenon to them, when, how they felt about it, etc. Acceptance of one's sexuality, attitudes toward men, other women, etc., can be understood better in relation to attitudes associated with this event _____

_____

_____

_____

Interviewer's Life Style Inventory (continued)

25. Who was the most spoiled, by whom, how, and for what?_____

_____

_____

26. Who was the most punished, by whom, how, and for what? _____

_____

_____

27. Who had the most friends? _____What kind of relationship-

leader, exclusive, gregarious? _____

_____

C. Siblings' Interrelationship

1. Who took care of_____

_____

2. Who played with _____

_____

3. Who got along best with whom? _____

_____

4. Which two fought and argued the most? _____

5. Who was father's favorite?_____

6. Who was mother's favorite? _____

D. Description of Parents

1. How old is father? _____ Mother? _____

2. What kind of person is father? _____

   _____

   _____

   _____

   Kind of job? _____

3. What kind of person is mother? _____

   _____

   _____

   Kind of job? _____

   _____

   _____

4. Which of the children is most like father? _____. In

   what way? _____

   _____

5. Which of the children is most like mother? _____. In

   what way? _____

   _____

Interviewer's Life Style Inventory (continued)

6. What kind of relationship existed between father and mother? _____

_____

_____

    a. Who was dominant, made decisions, etc? _____

_____

    b. Did they agree or disagree on methods of raising children? _____

_____

    c. Did they quarrel openly? _____. About what?_____

_____

    d. How did you feel about these quarrels. Whose side did you

       take? _____

7. Who was more ambitious for the children? In which way? _____

_____

8. Did any other person (grandparent, uncle, aunt, roomer, etc.) live
   with the family? Were there any other significant figures in your
   childhood?

Describe them and your relationship to them. _____

_____

_____

_____

EARLY RECOLLECTIONS

How far back can you remember? Report recollections of specific incidents with as many details as possible, including your behavior and feelings at the time up to age eight or nine years. Make sure that this is a recollection and not a report that has been told to you by your parents or others. Specific childhood dreams are early recollections. Recurring dreams are not considered as early recollections.

Age	Incident (verbatim)	Behavior and Feeling Reactions
1. ___		
2. ___		
3. ___		
4. ___		
5. ___		

6. ____   _____   _____

_____   _____

_____   _____

STUDY QUESTIONS

Direction: Respond to the following in spaces provided.

1. What is meant by family constellation?

2. How do you distinguish between an early recollection and a report?

3. When you are completing the attributes portion of an Interviewer's Life Style Inventory, how might an oldest child respond compared to a middle or youngest child in the same constellation?

4. Ask a friend or acquaintance who has siblings within five years of his/her age to tell you about his/herself and each sibling. Pay particular attention to their age differences and who was most alike or different, played or fought, achieved or did not, etc. Do you observe patterns to the responses such as were described in Chapter 7? Can you see where rivals excel or have interests in different areas?

ACTIVITIES FOR INDIVIDUALS AND GROUPS

In Chapter 6 several concepts and assumptions about Adler's Individual Psychology for understanding behavior are put into practice. Some of the major concepts include the following:

a. Humans are socially oriented toward other people.
b. Behavior is goal directed, i.e., purposive and useful to the individual (even if the behavior isn't acceptable to others).
c. Individuals are self-determining, i.e., develop their own unique, private logic about life, themselves, and other people.
d. Emotions are tools which we use to achieve our goals.
e. Individuals can change their behavior whenever they perceive it as useful to them.
f. Whenever people "misbehave," they do so out of discouragement, i.e., lacking confidence first in themselves and second in others to be positive towards them.

Using these assumptions, one can recognize that understanding behavior means understanding *motivation*, understanding *goals*, understanding one's *intentions*. Motivation, goals, and intentions can be changed. Therefore, this is a very optimistic, encouraging outlook to understanding how we can help people of all ages. Young people tend to be more flexible, open, and amenable to change. Using this knowledge can help us to anticipate discouragement and actually avoid the misbehavior which often follows.

Another aspect to this approach concerns how one develops a private logic which guides one through life. Family, including extended family members, influence our notions about life, others, and ourselves. Adler noted that the person who influenced us most generally was the sibling closest to us in age but who was most different from us. You have been studying about the five ordinal positions in the family (oldest, second, middle, youngest, and only child). This exercise is designed to help you explore these concepts in relation to yourself and your siblings (brothers and sisters). Parents, family values, and conflict resolution also influence one's development. One's earliest recollections also help reveal how one perceives life. Data used here will be limited but not so much so that you cannot test the general concept of sibling influence and one's desire to be unique in some respect within the family group.

A. Listing Siblings

List all siblings in descending order (including yourself). Place your age next to your name and then indicate the years difference in age with + or — of each of your brothers or sisters.

		Name	Age (+ or —)	Comments
Siblings:	1	(Oldest) _____	_____	_____
	2	_____	_____	_____
	3	_____	_____	_____
	4	_____	_____	_____
	5	_____	_____	_____
	6	_____	_____	_____

B. Description of Siblings

Record your descriptions as you remember your siblings when you were a child of six to eight years of age or younger.

1. Who was most different from you? _____
   In what respects (if you are an only child, then compare yourself to others in general.)?

_____

_____

_____

_____

2. Who was most like you? _____In what respect?_____

_____

_____

_____

_____

_____

3. What kind of kid were you? _____

_____

_____

_____

4. Describe other siblings _____

_____

_____

_____

C. Ratings of Attributes

For each of the following attributes, place in the column the name or initial for yourself or a sibling you believe was the "highest" and who was the "lowest" for the respective attribute. If you were neither "highest" or "lowest," place your name or initial in the center column and draw an arrow to indicate whom you were most like.

	Highest Bob	Most Like me →	Lowest Jane
Example: sad			
1. Intelligent	_____	_____	_____
2. Hardest worker	_____	_____	_____
3. Best grades	_____	_____	_____
4. Helping around house	_____	_____	_____
5. Conforming	_____	_____	_____
6. Rebellious	_____	_____	_____
7. Trying to please	_____	_____	_____
8. Critical of others	_____	_____	_____
9. Considerate	_____	_____	_____
10. Selfish	_____	_____	_____
11. Having own way	_____	_____	_____
12. Sensitive—easily hurt	_____	_____	_____
13. Bossy	_____	_____	_____

	Highest	Most Like	Lowest
14. Temper tantrum	_____	_____	_____
15. Sense of humor	_____	_____	_____
16. Idealistic	_____	_____	_____
17. Materialistic	_____	_____	_____
18. High moral standards	_____	_____	_____
19. Most athletic	_____	_____	_____
20. Most artistic	_____	_____	_____
21. Strongest	_____	_____	_____
22. Tallest	_____	_____	_____
23. Prettiest	_____	_____	_____
24. Feminine	_____	_____	_____
25. Masculine	_____	_____	_____

D. Relationships of Siblings

1. Who took care of whom?_____

2. Who played with whom? _____

3. Who got along best with whom?_____

4. Who fought most with whom? _____

E. Grouping

Now using the previous data plus any other you can recall from your childhood, compile characteristics for you and your siblings.

Note: In large families or in families which have children six or more years apart, you may have more than one oldest or youngest child or two or more only children, e.g., Bob 18 and Mary 8 equals two only children. Therefore, only consider siblings 6 years or closer in age to you to decide positions.

Siblings   *Characteristics Compiled*

Oldest   _____

              _____

Second　　_____

　　　　　_____

Middle　　_____

　　　　　_____

Youngest　_____

　　　　　_____

Only (me)　_____

　　　　　_____

Others　　_____
(close cou-
sin, friend,　_____
or children
in general　_____
at that
time)　　　_____

F. Discussion

Discuss as a group or with an interested friend the following:

- The extent to which you see a pattern of similarities and differences among children?
- To what extent is the oldest, etc., similar to the descriptions which you found in the readings, even though you and your siblings have matured?
- Can you remember incidents in your childhood which reveal influences each had on the other?
- Can you recall when you decided to stop being the "boss," the "responsible one," the "baby," the "judge," etc., within your family?

G. Final Notes

The significance of this exercise can reveal that all people want to have a place in every social situation important to them. Belonging, being secure, and feeling cared about are all signs of this inclination.

People bring notions to school and work about what they have to do to belong. Some expect to be liked, others do not. Some expect to cooperate, others do not. Through encouragement and use of other specific methods and techniques, we can help all people to learn to like themselves better and to enjoy being co-operative and responsible members of our community.

CHAPTER 8

COUNSELING PROCESS

THE ORDER TO INTERVENTION

For the purposes of this chapter, a distinction between Adlerian counseling and psychotherapy will be made on the basis of life style and behavior change. Adlerians note that the life style of the individual is a unique, unconscious, cognitive "map" which facilitates his/her movement through life (Mosak & Dreikurs, 1973). Life style is a unifying set of convictions which permit the individual to evaluate, manage, and predict events within his/her experience. Adlerian counseling contains a combination of beliefs about self, others, and the world upon which his/her expectations are based. These self-determined notions become the source of direction and movement by which the individual establishes his/her place in the world.

Within each individual's life style is latitude for behavioral choice, i.e., one's convictions may result in a variety of behaviors. For example, the belief that "only a real man can cope with life's challenges" may result in a vocational choice as military officer, mountain climber, astronaut, or, particularly if combined with "I am only a ordinary man," defeated dropout, submissive husband, or philandering gigolo. The potential for pursuing socially useful or useless life activities lies within the same life style.

The distinction between counseling and psychotherapy processes can be made in relation to the goals of each (Dreikurs, 1967; Nikelly, 1971). *In the case of counseling, behavior change within the existing life style is the goal. In psychotherapy, a change in life style is the desired outcome.* While this goal can be construed as a moot point for distinguishing between two processes, considering the differences is valid. Granted that changes in attitude can result in changes in behavior and vice versa, usually counselors, teachers, social workers, or related community specialists will not have the training, experience, or time required to use life style analysis successfully for significant changes in the life style, per se.

Attitude changes result
in behavioral changes

As will be illustrated later in this chapter and in Chapters 10 and 12, successful use of basic Adlerian methods and techniques to help influence behavior change does not require advance graduate training in education or psychology. The counseling and consultation methods and techniques have been tested many times with much success by practitioners who in addition to their professional training, know and use Adlerian Psychology.

Success in psychotherapy by Adlerians, however, requires motivation modification. Dreikurs (1963) stated that:

> We do not attempt primarily to change behavior patterns or remove symptoms. If a patient improves his behavior because he finds it profitable at the time, without changing his basic premises, then we do not consider that as a therapeutic success. We are trying to change goals, concepts, and notions. (p. 79)

The author has experienced instances in which this distinction with behavior modification was clearly justified. An illustration of this was found in the life styles of some individuals in the counseling related professions. The motivation for some individuals being a "helper" was intimately intertwined with their concept of self-worth and justification for belongingness in the social world. When unsuccessful as a helper or when they received no signs of appreciation for being helpful, discouragement and disappointment developed. A change in behavior was not necessary, but an examination of why they wished to help was undertaken to determine how such notions were self-defeating.

Individuals in counseling, for example, often have hidden goals which are to prove that they are beyond help—that their situations are hopeless. To defeat the counselor is unconsciously a sign of success. The counselor who believes that he/she must be successful to maintain his/her self-esteem is already at a disadvantage when the interview begins. Counselors aware of their own motivation, then, can help themselves anticipate potential pitfalls as a helper (Mosak, 1965). A change in life style per se was not necessary in these cases but the confrontation with clients' own mistaken notions facilitated a freeing of counselors from feeling defeated or inadequate as persons.

Many youngsters strive daily to please their parents, teachers, and others. They are rewarded for being "good" children. Although a change in behavior may not be necessary, the motivation for doing well deserves serious examination. The child striving for perfection is a discouraged person whose goal can never be attained. Encouragement for simply participating in life, including acceptance of their mistakes, could be one objective for helping such youngsters.

On the other hand, changes in behavior can open new alternatives to behavior and attitude change. For example, the counselor's knowledge of the goals of disruptive behavior can help to suggest alternative behaviors to youngsters without conducting a life style analysis. Similarly, Dreikurs' (1971) four steps for problem solving can be implemented in establishing a new agreement between marriage partners without changing basic life goals. Therefore, for the purposes of this chapter, Adlerian counseling will be defined to include those methods and techniques used within the helping relationship which encourage situational, attitude, and/or behavior changes which free the individual to function more fully as self-determining, creative, and responsible equal within his/her environment.

STAGES OF ADLERIAN COUNSELING

The assumption is made that counseling will be with individuals who are seeking assistance with concerns of an immediate social nature. Assistance will be more preventative and educative in orientation than psychotherapeutic, therapy being more corrective and remedial in the sense that discouragement is noticeably pervasive and persistent, suggesting a need for reorientation of the individual's characteristic movement through life (life style).

The stages used in the counseling are as follows: (1) Relationship, (2) Psychological Investigation, (3) Interpretation, and (4) Reorientation. Each of these stages is alluded to or illuminated upon in other chapters as they relate to other methods and aspects of this approach. What follows is a brief exposition of these stages as they relate specifically to the counseling process with individuals or groups.

Relationship

A hallmark of the Adlerian relationship is its equalitarian quality. Adlerian counselors, while actively using their knowledge and experience to help others, also maintain respect for the individual's capabilities and power to make independent choices. They tend to assume that their counselees are capable of finding satisfactory alternatives to old predicaments if they are freed of some faulty notions. The counselor, therefore, is likely to dispel any notions of superiority by showing a genuine, nonpossessive caring for the individual, not unlike that of a friend.

Early in the conference the counselor will invite the individual to discuss his/her reasons for seeking assistance. A question which will be asked at some point during this period is, "How would life be different for you if this problem did not persist?" Other variations on this question include "What would you be doing now?" or "What could you do that you cannot do now if there were not a problem?" The significance of this question has to do with whether or not the counselee is avoiding some basic life tasks by having a "problem."

Dreikurs (1967) noted, for example, on occasions an individual may have a medically-related problem unknown to the counselee or even his/her physician. Nonmedical personnel are obviously not qualified to practice medicine. When asked, "What would be different in your life or what could you do that you can't do now if your problem was removed or resolved?"; some individuals simply say, "Nothing, except I wouldn't have these headaches," or "I'd be rid of these backaches!" Adlerians have asked such people to pursue medical evaluation before pursuing counseling in depth. On more than one occasion, the physicians inquired as to how the counselor knew that a physical problem existed when initial tests or a routine physical had not revealed it. Simply stated, when basic life tasks are being met adequately, then counseling probably is not necessary.

The author had one instance in which a man asked for assistance related to desire for food. He reported an almost insatiable appetite. When I observed that his weight seemed quite satisfactory, he indicated that this fact was true because of great restraint and careful selection of food. He had been quite overweight at one time but overcame this condition after he became convinced it was unhealthy and unsightly. He had been examined by a physician but the advice he received was to seek professional counseling.

When he enumerated that he had consumed four steaks, a whole chicken, two fish filets, salad, potato, and bread without feeling satisfied, I, too, was impressed! Exploring his work and personal relationships revealed no apparent problems. He was a willing and open counselee who showed a sense of humor even in the face of his predicament.

Further discussion of bothersome behavior revealed a tendency to nap at inappropriate times including while driving! Consultation with two physicians by the author revealed no known condition which would contribute to these behaviors. Convinced that more medical evaluation was needed, I strongly recommended attention by specialists at a clinic or hospital with the resources required to evaluate his condition thoroughly. After three days of hospitalization and clinical evaluation, the counselee was diagnosed to have a relatively rare condition know as narcolepsy. The counselee's relief and acceptance of the physician's recommendations were gratifying.

In another instance, a mother reported concern for her child who seemed to inflict injury upon himself through carelessness. Both parents reported great concern to the child's pediatrician. Accustomed to overindulgent parents, he chided them and recommended that they seek counseling. After talking with them and their children, the author observed some of the unnecessary parental over indulgence but basically met two happy, cooperative pre-schoolers.

Upon following the family to their car, the child was noted to have difficulty negotiating the steps to the parking area. At first I wondered if the child might have vision difficulty. Through follow up, the determination was that the youngster had a neurological disease, rare but insidious in its damage to the child's coordination. The parents, indeed, had good reason to be concerned.

Teachers and parents also should be alert to problems which may be responses to undiscovered difficulties with eyesight, hearing, teeth, diet, insufficient rest, and such (Smith, 1976). Physical growth during early adolescence also can be especially stressful for youngsters (Compton, 1973; Eichhorn, 1973). Adlerians are watchful of similar circumstances which might be helped more effectively by means other than counseling.

In Chapter 1 were a discussion and a graphic illustration of the difference between low and high social interest, i.e., characteristic differences of movement through life. Adlerians believe that low social interest is evidence of one's lack of self-confidence and esteem. Behavioral evidences of this social interest can be detected in persistent

> blaming,
> complaining,
> excuses,
> fears, and
> disability reports.

If the counselor perceives the counselee as using one or more of these as a means of avoiding responsibility for his/her role in life situations, all the more important will be encouragement to the total process. Dreikurs indicated that whenever one hears another person using these tactics to cope with life, that person is preparing not to cooperate. Dreikurs' observation can be equally true for the counseling process unless the counselor is aware of the here-and-now aspects of the counseling relationship.

Counseling requires cooperation to work toward common goals. Some Adlerians establish contractual agreements concerning the goals of counseling which are renegotiable (Pew & Pew, 1972). More frequently, a verbal understanding of what the individual hopes to attain is established including some indication of his/her expectations for the counselor's role. While Adlerians tend to be active participants in the counseling process, they are not miracle workers nor do they wish to be expected to have all the answers. They will assure the individual of their interest and commitment to use their knowledge and skill for the individual's benefit. Success, however, requires an equal willingness by the counselee. Rapport, therefore, is established and nutured throughout the counseling relationship on a basis of mutual respect, cooperation, and desire to achieve agreed upon goals.

Psychological Investigation

The second stage, psychological investigation of the process, will vary according to the nature of the presenting problem, the counselor's knowledge of the counselee prior to seeking counseling, and availability of data from such sources as tests, case histories, family, and so forth.

What the counselor attempts to do during this stage is understand the streams of conscious and not-so-conscious thoughts which guide individuals in understanding, predicting, and attempting to manage their environment. This action is a nonevaluative activity. You are formulating a type of word picture of the individuals' movement through life. They are active participants in this process. It is somewhat analogous to painting an individual's portrait with one important distinction, the portrait is not static. This aspect of movement can elude the counselor new to this method.

Individuals respond behaviorally somewhat differently to the same convictions in their private logic when confronted with different environmental conditions. For example, concern with appearing foolish before others may evoke shy retiring behavior in one situation and appearance of sophistication in another from the same individual. The ability to laugh at one's predicaments and not be impressed with situations which cannot be controlled could be a desirable goal in counseling. For the counselor to understand the movement toward a goal, e.g., to be in control or to avoid participation, is to begin addressing the underlying issues rather than symptoms of them.

Life style assessment is one means of achieving a gestalt or holistic view of the individual's movement. Private logic is uncovered by self-disclosure and personal validation of the construct by the counselee. By this time, rapport is based solidly upon respect, understanding and caring.

Interpretation

Adults. The third stage, interpretation, of the Adlerian counseling process involves the use of tentative inferences and observations made by the counselor. Having listened to the individual discuss concerns, possibly explore family constellation and/or early recollections, and having observed behavior in counseling and/or elsewhere, the counselor tentatively will offer observations which are descriptive of the individual and may have implications for meeting the individual's life tasks.

When family constellation information and recollections are used, this may take the form of an interview in which the counselor sketches a verbal portrait of the individual. This summary is based upon the information which the individual has shared. It would reveal the characteristic ways in which the individual views him/herself, life, and others.

The counselor may outline what he observes as the individual's assets in coping with life tasks including work, friendship, and love. The Adlerians also would present mistaken and self-defeating perceptions which, if accurate, could contribute to problems for the individual.

Without the detailed information, the counselor would be observing and listening to the counselee to derive some means of understanding his/her goals, and reflecting these to him/her. Whatever the source of data, the counselor usually would present it tentatively with a phrase such as "Could it be . . ."

In addition to using this technique with individuals, Pew and Pew (1972) described the use of life style in marriage counseling. Dreikurs (1946) noted that the very characteristics which attract individuals often lead to some of their later conflicts. The author has observed this as well. The same information in both marriage and premarital counseling has been received very well by couples. An example may help to illustrate. Early in the counseling session, each partner observes while the other partner has his/her life style developed. They are each asked what qualities or attributes particularly attracted them to the other.

In one case, a couple reported that they were having a conflict over the husband's work and where they would live. Both were only children with two children of their own. The wife indicated that the husband left all of the decisions and responsibility for the home to her. The husband worked long hours and seemed more concerned about advancement than family welfare.

She was attracted to him because he was reliable, serious-minded, industrious, and ambitious. He was attracted to her because he thought of her as more intelligent, i.e., a better decision maker, a good homemaker, and a good companion. Unlike some marriages, their love had not faltered, but their confidence was shaken by the strain of recent events relative to job and family.

They were quick to see how each reinforced the other's mistaken notions of how to maintain their equilibrium.

Dreikurs (1946) also noted that we often have a vested interest in maintaining the faults of our partners. Through counseling, even before marriage, such notions can be discovered and anticipated to a considerable degree.

Older Adults. Merriam and Cross (1982, p. 39) noted that "reminiscence, or recalling the past, is a behavior common to all ages." It is viewed as particularly important for older persons as they attempt the universal process of achieving ego integrity (Coleman, 1974; Erikson, 1950). Though not a new concept, study of reminiscence in older persons has accelerated over the past two decades as growing numbers of older people have stimulated increasing interest in gerontology.

Butler's (1963) research on the role of the life review among older individuals was the starting point and remains the focal point of much research and clinical practice using reminiscence. Research on the effectiveness of this technique has yielded equivocal results. Based on Adlerian theory, the technique of using early recollections provides an opportunity for structured reminiscence and offers several advantages over the traditional life review therapy referred to in the gerontological literature (Sweeney & Myers, 1986).

A variety of researchers have obtained positive outcomes in investigations of structured reminiscing in relationship to life satisfaction and ego integrity among older persons (Boylin et al., 1976; Havighurst & Glasser, 1972; Hughston & Merriam, 1982; Merriam & Cross, 1981; Revere & Tobin, 1980-81). It has proven to be effective for stimulating cognitive functioning (Hughston & Merriam, 1982) and for improving relationships between staff and residents of long term care facilities (Lawrence & Lehman, 1979). Szapocznik and others (1980) found life review to be an effective therapy with depressed individuals for whom meaninglessness in life was a central problem.

Some of these same researchers also reported negative and/or conflicting results using life review therapy approaches. Lawrence and Lehman (1979) found that depressed persons did not benefit from the therapy. Perotta and Meacham (1981) determined that reminiscence made no difference in levels of depression or self-esteem in a random sample of community-dwelling older people. Coleman (1974) found no evidence to support the hypothesis that reminiscing is an adaptive feature of old age in the presence of severe life change. He did determine, however, that life review is adaptive when accompanied by dissatisfaction with one's past.

Perhaps even more significant is the finding that marked negative effect can occur during the course of the life review process. This may be accompanied by heightened levels of anxiety that do not diminish until near completion of the review process, if at all. (Ziegler et al., 1981). As described in the literature, this process may be lengthy, leaving the individual older person in a depressed state for a varying amount of time, and perhaps permanently in the absence of professional intervention. This will not be the case from an Adlerian perspective.

Encouragement is used by Adlerians as the central concept to bring about change. Courage to be imperfect, courage to forgive oneself and others, courage to act even when one is very afraid, courage to do that which is no longer easy, and courage to make the very best of whatever situation develops are the basis for counseling. Adler believed that feelings of inferiority were a part of the human condition. How we cope with these feelings of inadequacy is reflected in our approach to life.

As noted earlier, the expert counselor can diagnose the degree of discouragement by the prevalance and persistence of reports of fears, excuses, complaining, blaming, criticizing, and disability. Some persons would contend that such behaviors are "normal" for "old" people. While aging does indeed bring many challenges, and any person who loses a loved one, for example, will experience grief and all of its ramifications. However, as to how well different individuals handle similar situations is still a matter of degree.

These differences can be uncovered, for example, through the use of early recollections. Adler noted, "Thus his memories represent his (Story of My Life); a story he repeats to himself to warn him or to comfort him, to keep him concentrated on his goal, to prepare him, by means of past experiences, to meet the future with an already tested style of action" (Ansbacher & Ansbacher, 1967).

The following recollection of a widow age 67, Ms. Sullivan, helps to illustrate the richness of information which even one recollection holds. At the age of five:

> I recall my mother getting ready to set out on our front porch, some of my dresses that were old and no longer fit. One of the dresses was my *very* favorite. I can remember my grandmother at the top of the stairs, my mother walking halfway down the stairs, and I was at the bottom of the stairs. I was begging my mother not to give away my favorite dress. She was telling me to stop making a fuss and being so silly and my grandmother saying soothing things to me.

> I hated both my grandmother and mother at the same time; my mother for giving away the dress and saying I was silly, and my grandmother for trying to make me feel better about the situation.

This woman provides us the opportunity to hypothesize about her outlook on life, herself, and other women. As a matter of practice, we also ask that a counselee report the feelings associated with such an experience. In this case, she noted:

> I was angry at mother and grandmother. I felt I was a baby and kept telling myself as I cried to stop and be intelligent about all this. If I act like a baby, my mother will really not take me serious. I also was angry at my grandmother because I felt I did not need to be taken care of.

This particular woman had lost her husband the year before due to an unexpected heart attack. She had appeared to have coped quite satisfactorily but was urged by her daughter who lived in an adjacent state to sell her home and move into a senior citizens' apartment complex. She agreed to this arrangement at the time but never seemed entirely accepting of it. The woman who was administrator of the apartment complex made friendly overtures to Ms. Sullivan but without much success; Ms. Sullivan was cordial but distant toward the administrator.

For someone not trained in Adlerian methods or aware of the implications of early recollections, such a report may seem interesting but inconsequential. In point of fact, when Ms. Sullivan was given the opportunity to discuss its meaning for her, she reported that it helped her rethink her position on some matters of much importance to her. Certain of the insights also would be important to anyone attempting to help her cope with loss, grief, and relationships with other women in her later years.

As time went on, other residents who came to know Ms. Sullivan expressed concern about the strong angry feelings which she had toward her daughter. Her son lived in California and was seen only at the time of the funeral for his father. The daughter had made more than a few efforts to visit her mother but seemed to have stopped trying of late. Those closest to her found it difficult to confront her because she would say something like, "don't be silly, I can take care of myself just fine"! Nevertheless, these folks did not believe that she was adapting well to her "new" circumstances.

Because of persistent headaches, Ms. Sullivan sought a prescription from her physician. Fortunately, he had known her for several years and recognized signs of depression during his time with her. At his insistence, she agreed to have a "couple of sessions to help her sort out her feelings and priorities now that she's a widow."

A few observations about the case of Ms. Sullivan can help to illustrate the practical usefulness of early recollections (ER) in counseling with older persons. First, even without using other life styles or ER data, we could guess that Ms. Sullivan may have difficulty with a woman counselor, unless the counselor was trained in life style methods. This is based on her reaction to her mother and grandmother in the ER and the perception of her mother being above her. This was corroborated at least in part by the female administrator's experience (potentially an authority figure) in attempting to befriend Ms. Sullivan. Also interesting to note is that she accepted her male physician's advice, rebuffed the women acquaintances who offered similar advice based on their experience, and seemed unusually hard on her daughter who tried to make at least some visits. On the other hand, her son was not known to even make an effort to come for a visit and her attitude toward him remained essentially positive.

Upon meeting with Ms. Sullivan, the counselor found a pleasant articulate lady who seemed quite self-sufficient in outlook and manner. When asked how life would be different if she did not get headaches, she stated that maybe she could be a bit more sociable with other residents. She later expressed disappointment with her relationship with her daughter as well. After a period of general discussion about her husband's death, adjustments since then, relationships with other family members, and similar matters, the idea of life style was introduced to Ms. Sullivan. She agreed quite readily to using this as a means of helping the counselor to know her better.

Life style assessment involving all the data about early relationships including siblings, parents, etc. and five or six ER's were developed into a kind of verbal narrative focusing on Ms. Sullivan's way of coping with work, friendship, and love relationships. Because the process of collecting life style information lends itself to rapport building and further information about current life coping, this is a positive empathic experience for the counselee. This is also an opportunity for reflection and corroborating or refuting impressions which the counselor has begun to formulate.

What caused her stress and how she coped with it was discussed. This was a give and take, interactive process. It involved a facilitative confrontation of life issues.

Ms. Sullivan acknowledged that for her, not feeling "on top" and in control of herself was very disquieting. Further, she recognized her pattern of being put off by anyone (but particularly women) who tried to "coddle" her. She was confronted by the counselor with the observation that "it could be" she was behaving toward her daughter exactly the way she had perceived her mother behaving toward her. This had never occurred to her before now. She reflected on this for some time and concluded that, indeed, she was probably more faithfully following that pattern than her mother had! On a subsequent visit her daughter joined her. They were both desireous of improving their relationship while there was still time.

No life review need end with on older person feeling depressed, defeated, or fearful without making an informed effort to confront the negative self-talk behind these feelings. The use of early recollections and life style assessment are not a panacea for all unhappy older persons. However, they can be viable alternatives or supplements to present methods (Sweeney & Myers, 1986).

If one can see the potential for only a single ER in revealing significant insight to an individual's outlook on life, self, and others, how much more will be realized with further data, counselee behavior in the interview and an opportunity to interact. The affect expressed in conjunction with the ERs is always important. The feelings reveal the meaning attributed to the events. In these comments, courage is revealed as present or not. Life is seen as fair or unfair, safe or unsafe. Life tasks are accepted as a challenge to be met or avoided. Others are seen as helpful or threatening. They perceive themselves as able or not able.

Two individuals from the same family having experienced the same event will assign different meaning to its significance. These perceptions of what happened and how they felt about it become our basis for understanding their "private logic." When we find discouraged attitudes and feelings in one's ERs, not surprisingly, we often find evidence of those attitudes and feelings popping up in their day-to-day lives. Normally this is revealed when the individual's typical way of perceiving and coping is ineffective or otherwise inappropriate for the present circumstances. Certainly, loss of one's spouse, friends, family, home, or slowing down or loss of physical faculties will bring on a test of one's ability to cope and grow in the light of new circumstances.

Using the other precepts of Adlerian Psychology also will increase the worth of these methods. They certainly have promise for work with older persons. Video tape illustrations of this technique are available for use with the curriculum in Myers, 1988 and Sweeney, 1988a, 1988b.

Children. In the case of children, parent and teacher reports of behavior can be sufficient data upon which to make some guesses. In Chapter 6, the goals of disruptive behavior were identified. While observation of the child's behavior before counseling can be helpful, effective counseling in many cases is not necessarily dependent upon those observations.

While talking with the teachers or parents, the counselor attempts to determine the child's mistaken goals and to obtain specific behavioral instances from which these goals are derived. The counselor may use these mistaken goals to confirm or refute his/her hunches while talking with the child. The counselor begins guessing, therefore, what the child expects to achieve by his/her disruptive behavior in order to help him/her assess these goals and behaviors. To have one's mistaken goals revealed can be very encouraging because what one intends to do can be voluntarily changed toward more mutually satisfying goals.

A major Adlerian technique can be described as *facilitative confrontation,* i.e., the counselor in a friendly, nonpossessive way shares what he/she observes to be beliefs which the individual pursues. In working with children, the counselor may ask and facilitatively confront as illustrated in the following (Co is counselor and Bo is Bobby):

Co: Do you know why you are here today?

Bo: Because I talked back to my teacher.

Co: That does seem to have been a problem. . .Have you talked back to her before?

Bo: Sometimes.

Co: Do you know why you talk back to her?

Bo: (Head shakes, no)

Co: You even feel mad right now. . .Would like to know why I think you talk back?

Bo: (Head nods, yes)

Co: I think you want her to know that she can't make you do anything. . . that you'll do what you want, when you want. . .fellow, you have a lot on the ball and nobody's going to tell you what to do without clearing it with you first. Could it be . . .

Bo: (Smiles and shakes head, no)

Co: Even now you're going to show me, you won't agree until you're ready! (Bobby smiles). . .Am I right? (Counselor smiles)

Bo: Yep!

In instances such as this the counselor may wish to cite one or two more specific instances in which the boy has demonstrated this same goal. The recognition reflex, in this case a smile, is a fairly reliable behavior clue that the boy's goal is power. If the counselor is mistaken, a lack of cues will be evident. In some cases, a more fundamental goal may be missed and the counselor must be prepared to revise his/her assessment accordingly. Only a few signs, e.g., those who practice being nonexpressive and those who laugh or giggle throughout a conference.

In cases such as this one, the counselor is not revealing so much about why the boy is being disruptive as he is revealing what the boy hopes to gain. The next question becomes one of how the boy can find his place in class without being disruptive. As was seen in Chapter 6, corrective and preventative action by the teacher and parents can facilitate the decision by the boy to try out new behaviors. Adlerians believe that discouragement, i.e., lack of self-confidence, moves individuals against others. Therefore, punishment is not appropriate nor is coercion. While the process described in words may seem to result in authoritarian manipulation, quite the opposite is true in practice. Respect for the individual and recognition that he/she cannot be required to cooperate are uppermost in the counselor's mind.

Before proceeding to the next aspect of the counseling process, a few guidelines for the interpretive stage is needed.

1. Labeling is to be avoided, goals (purposes) of behavior are sought.

2. Encouraging elaboration or modification of counselor observation is desirable. Sometimes the correct wording or phrasing cannot be captured accurately without assistance from the counselee. In other cases, they can document an observation with innumerable examples of how accurately it applies.

3. Being prepared to be incorrect and respecting the counselee's right to disagree are essential. Be particularly watchful of projecting personal biases into an observation, i.e., identifying counselor motives with counselee behavior.

4. Being aware of here and now behavior and feelings in the counseling relationships is invaluable. Behavior and feelings expressed in the interview also reveal life style data, i.e., methods of coping and goal orientation. Not infrequently, for example, the counselor can anticipate seductiveness, anger, or withdrawal by a counselee on the basis of life style information taken before the interpretation.

5. Setting a tone of encouragement including emphasis upon the assets of the person is an important part of the process.

6. Dispelling any mystical "analyst" aura which an individual may wish to ascribe to this process is essential. The counselor simply helps the individual bring to consciousness the fictive (as if) notions which are used to guide the individual and his/her feelings in life situations.

Reorientation

The final stage of Adlerian counseling is dependent upon a desire of the counselee to institute a change. Understanding the meaning of his/her behavior and the goal which he/she pursues, frees the individual to decide what other behaviors he/she might wish to try.

In the marriage case mentioned previously, each partner agreed to help the other in those areas which required encouragement. The husband began participating in home related decision making and the wife took more interest in the responsibility which he carried outside of the home. One behavioral agreement they had established early in counseling was to have an uninterrupted partnership meeting for one hour each week. One partner would speak for thirty minutes and then the other would speak for a similar period while the partner listened. They agreed not to speak about the topics between times but would alternate who had the first session each week.

The Pews (1972) have found this meeting technique particularly helpful to couples seeking to reestablish more intimate communications. Modifications of this process develop according to the need and desire of couples. In the beginning, however, a specific time, place, and procedure are agreed to in advance. The counselor may have the couples practice this meeting technique and similar techniques in the counseling interviews including role playing, problem solving, modeling, and goal setting.

In the case concerning talking back to the teacher, the counselor shared some suggested alternatives that he/she was prepared to make to the teacher. In every case, the issue that the boy had alternatives and choices was clear. The counselor then asked the boy if he wished to change and if he would like to use a written plan or agreement of what his intentions were, e.g., not to talk back but to find other ways of expressing his feelings to the teacher. Whatever the arrangement, the counselor was working toward realistic objectives which would greatly increase the probability of success by the boy.

In some cases, the time span for success may be short intervals, or only small changes in behavior may be attempted to constitute successful progress. Failure, per se, is minimized or eliminated by careful planning and patience with mistakes or lapses. Glasser (1969) described this progress particularly well for teachers and administrators alike. Encouragement, of course, is a key factor in assisting the person to change.

On occasions a person will pursue self-defeating behaviors which he/she seems resistent to change. Based upon "common sense," one would conclude that such behavior is illogical, useless, and clearly in need of remediation. Drawing on the private logic of the individual, however, reveals a rationale and purpose, to which the individual adheres without serious question.

In the case of a child who becomes characterized as a bully, fighting with other youngsters and adults becomes a source of many incidents. Punishment, lectures, and pleas for behavior change generally make little or no difference. Knowing that the child who fights is most often pursuing a goal of revenge and a private logic that "I may not be likeable but I can hurt you back," one can anticipate a rationale which makes fighting, for example, a necessary behavior in his/her repertoire.

By simply listening and actively reflecting what is said, you will discover, for example, that fighting is a noble thing to do. Not unlike Robin Hood or Knights of the Round Table, they are "correcting" or "evening the score" of others transgressions. The following is a case in point from an interview with a fourth grade boy (Co is counselor, Da is Daryl.):

Co: Do you like to fight, Daryl. . .?

Da: (He shakes head, no.)

Co: I think maybe sometimes you do. Could it be? (Daryl shrugs his shoulders) I think sometimes you like to show others that you can hurt them, too. . .that you can beat them up. . .

Da: (Smiles broadly and nods his head, yes.)

Co: So you like to fight, Daryl. . .and does that solve your problems. . .?

Da: (Now he's trying to cover his smile with his hand over his mouth.) Well, I hit them for teasing my sister, then they start picking on me!

Co: Oh, I see; so it really isn't your fault cause they were teasing your sister. . .

Da: (Nods, yes.)

You see a desire by Daryl to maintain self-respect. After all, who could fault the nobility of his intentions? The fact that his fights rarely involve his sister's honor is of no consequence in his private logic of being.

To move into the next stage, i.e., reorientation is a common error. At this point, we may understand Daryl's motivation better but asking or expecting him to change on this basis alone probably is insufficient. What I believe does help is (1) to pair the negative feelings associated with behavior which contributes to the individual feeling restored to control or satisfaction in the situation and (2) to introduce a new alternative with which only positive feelings can be associated. Using the previous illustration, the counselor may continue as follows:

Co: . . .and does this make you feel happy or sad. . .?

Da: Happy and sad. . .

Co: Happy that you got back at them but sad that they don't like you. . .(Daryl nods, yes). . .I wonder, do you really want other kids to like you and for you to like them . . . (He nods, yes) . . . I'm not so sure, Daryl. You see, I don't think you expect others to like you . . . (and that's a bad feeling . . . etc.) . . . and that's a bad feeling . . .so you want them to pay for your bad feelings. . .

Da: Well, I wouldn't hit them if they'd just treat me nice. . .

Co: You really feel bad when you're not included in games and stuff like everyone else. . .(Daryl looks down at the floor and fumbles with his fingers). . .and after a fight everyone talks about how bad you are and just makes you feel worse. . .(Daryl looks up with a little tear in his eye) . . .I wonder if you'd be willing to start over today on making and keeping friends. . .

In this case, Daryl was willing to start working on new behaviors but helping him to focus on his new goal and the satisfaction in making progress toward it was very important to the success. So long as he gained intrinsic satisfaction from his fighting, as he chose to see it, and did not believe others would like him anyway, winning him over to changing his behavior would be difficult. Adults are just as prone to continue using ineffective, socially useless behavior unless they are helped to associate the experience of negative feelings which are evoked by the consequences.

SPECIFIC TECHNIQUES

Convinced that individuals have the power to change if they choose to do so, Adlerians make suggestions and use techniques intended to illustrate this belief to counselees. Whether child or adult, individuals are encouraged to develop self-esteem and confidence in their ability to cope with life. The Adlerian is not impressed by fears, excuses, disabilities, blaming, or complaining.

Emotions which are used to distract others from the fact that the person wants freedom from his/her responsibilities are seen as tools which contribute to continued discouragement. Kindly but purposefully, the Adlerian will work toward avoiding the pitfalls of these expressions and instead emphasize the genuine assets of the individual's sense of belonging, security, and adequacy. Encouragement is the process the counselor uses to build the individual's confidence to cope with life.

In the author's experience, empathy, per se, has not been stressed by other Adlerians in their demonstrations or lectures. Persons of other theoretical persuasions sometimes are critical of this tendency. Because the Adlerian model is rationally based, i.e., mistaken evaluations or thoughts are the originating source of difficulties, feelings are not treated as an entity unto themselves. Feelings of the person are important, however, and serve as signposts for both counselor and counselee concerning the latter's intentions.

Listen for three levels of feelings

The author has found that listening for three levels of feelings is useful in counseling and consultation. For example, in what was essentially a vocationally-oriented counseling case, a high school senior expressed dissatisfaction with her part-time job. She had hoped to continue the position full-time after graduation but was not happy under her present supervisor. As the interview progressed, although carefully worded, it became apparent that she wanted more independence from her parents. Later in counseling, unexpressed doubt in her ability to be independent was revealed through avoidance of serious consideration of other alternatives to her present work and home situation. This was confirmed in subsequent interviews. The feelings heard at three levels were

1. present, obvious: dissatisfaction with work situation;

2. veiled: desire for independence; and

3. preconscious: self-doubt in ability to be independent.

Reasons and excuses for not considering alternatives to the presenting problem would defeat the most sincere counselor if the self-doubt was not confronted. Adlerians tend to deal with the doubts by helping to provide success experiences to overcome the doubts. Although aware of the present and veiled feelings, counselors choose to discredit the mistaken notions which contribute to the more persuasive feelings.

The reorientation stage, then, requires an awareness of the individual's thoughts and associated feelings which will affect his/her cooperation. Having cognitively decided to change does not make change happen. Therefore, a part of the counselor's function is to help distract the counselee from the advantages of his/her previous self-defeating notions and behavior.

Allen (1971c) and Mosak (1972) discussed various specific techniques which Adlerians use to (1) help the counselee catch him/herself at self-defeating behaviors, (2) become conscious of his/her control over his/her attitudes and feelings, (3) distract from the advantages of a hidden agenda in self-defeating behaviors, and (4) develop confidence in the individual's ability to cope successfully with life tasks.

Among the techniques, only a few will be mentioned to illustrate.

Spitting in the Soup

This is a vivid phrase for describing what happens when we expose the hidden agenda or goal for one's self-defeating behavior. When the counselor is accurate with his/her observation, *"could it be that. . ."* and can illustrate this clearly to the counselee, the counselee may continue this behavior but "it won't taste so sweet" any longer! The counselee is no longer innocent of its hidden meaning.

This technique is used very effectively as one means of disengaging the individual from previous behaviors. Children can understand the goals of misbehaviors quickly and will not repeat the same behaviors unless adults or other children make them useful. This technique also is quite effective with adults as in the case of the "good servant mother," the "super teacher," or "real man" images.

Antisuggestion

This technique, used by other than Adlerians as well, is used selectively to help illustrate that individuals have control of functions not otherwise accepted by them. For example, when a counselee says he/she gets tense talking to a member of the opposite sex and cannot help him/herself, the counselor may suggest that the next opportunity the counselee should get as tense as he/she can, i.e., try to get tense.

Occasionally this suggestion is used in the context of the interview, e.g., counselees attempt rehearsing the action as a variation of role playing. The irony, of course, is that when invited to do their "thing" they find themselves incapable of doing it. It has lost its value. Most counselees openly smile at their new predicament.

"If Only I Could . . ."

This phrase often follows the important question of "How would life be different for you if this problem did not exist?" An Adlerian counselor would suggest that the person behave *"as if"* he/she could, i.e., act as though you can.

This suggestion can be quite effective once the individual has some insight into the mistaken assessment he/she made before counseling. Not to succeed becomes less important, thereby minimizing disappointment.

Task Setting

Task setting is an important aspect of the counseling process although it certainly is not unique to Adlerian counseling. "Homework" assignment to try new behaviors, participate in a study group, or simply observe others in their daily living are employed often.

Generally, limited objectives are chosen and agreed upon by the counselee. The probabilities for success are high if properly selected. The method of successive approximation, i.e., to move the person toward an outcome in reasonable stages for him/her, is considered important. Naturally, follow-up is an important aspect of the total process. Generally, the counselor can determine in advance how cooperative an individual or couple will be on follow-up.

Adding Significant Modifiers

In addition to listening for excuses and other preludes to lack of cooperation mentioned previously, Adlerians practice reading between the lines and adding significant modifiers or conjunctions to counselee statements. For example, experience has shown that often when an individual says, "I will try," what they are thinking is "but I don't think it will work."

Mosak and Gushurst (1971) have an interesting, even amusing article on the topic of what individuals say and what they mean in counseling and therapy.

Assessing Probabilities

The counselor uses information obtained as a means of assessing the probabilities of certain suggestions being implemented. When encountering signs of discouragement, he/she tries other alternatives, smaller steps, or fewer expectations for the individual.

Examples of Task Setting

Task setting is illustrated in the following case.

For a young fellow who found a closeness lacking in his interpersonal relationships, particularly with a girl whom he liked, a variety of suggestions were explored including some developed by himself. A list was made and ordered according to his estimate of their value to him and his readiness to use them as tryout behaviors.

Among those listed first was smiling more often. He characterized himself as "Solemn Sam." More specifically, each day as he entered the office, he agreed to smile quite purposefully and again at some other point in the day. The result was so dramatic that it was not necessary to list it for the second week. A number of people approached him the first morning to simply chat. Luncheon invitations followed and he soon found reasons to smile.

Another item on his list was to impulsively buy something for himself which he would not purchase normally. This action was a little more difficult because he was usually "thrifty" and very deliberate in his purchases. He had carried a notion that self-indulgence would categorically result in terrible consequences. He gave himself permission to buy a record one afternoon that week and was delighted with the satisfaction he felt in being free to do what he had perceived as beyond his capability.

A more difficult item was to anticipate getting, doing, or saying something which would surprise and please his girlfriend. This item was not attempted in the first two weeks because he felt at a loss on how to proceed. The discovery of how to accomplish this task was the real challenge. He reported after successfully completing this item at least once, that he really had not been listening to her interests, aspirations, and desires. When he stopped worrying about how he was doing with her, he was freed to discover what they enjoyed together.

In my professional counseling, I have observed that the greatest prejudice discouraged persons hold against anyone, is the one they hold against themselves. The "punchline" in one cartoon said it well, "I know a lot of people who aren't as smart as they think they are, I just don't want to be as dumb as I think I am"! Not to believe in oneself is a terrible thing. Mahatma Ghandi said:

> Courage is the one sure foundation of character. Without courage there can be no morality, no religion, no love. One cannot follow truth or love so long as one is subject to fear. (Nehru, 1958, p. i)

A life lived in fear is no life at all. Our challenge is to confront in a caring way, for example, the mistaken meaning assigned by individuals to early life events as they present themselves in the here-and-now living of today. The process of growing, stretching, and risking can be approached with a new enthusiasm, new insight and new energy under the guidance of someone who cares too much to allow individuals to live their lives out with faulty self-evaluations and self-defeating behaviors toward others.

COUNSELING, LIFE STYLE, AND FAMILY CONSTELLATION

In the following interview, Dr. Harold Mosak demonstrated the integration of life style assessment with counseling. Published earlier (Mosak, 1972), it is presented in its entirety as an excellent illustration of an Adlerian clinician not only counseling a client but teaching other practitioners as well. You will note that the audience is used to encourage the young women rather than simply being observers.

LIFE STYLE ASSESSMENT:
A DEMONSTRATION FOCUSED
ON FAMILY CONSTELLATION [1,2]

HAROLD H. MOSAK, Ph.D.[3]
Chicago, Illinois

The phrase, life style, is currently used in many ways which Adler never intended. As Adler used it, life style refers to the "unity in each individual—in his thinking, feeling, acting; in his so-called conscious and unconscious, in every expression of his personality. This unity we call the style of life of the individual" (3, p. 175). While we agree with this definition of life style, we prefer one somewhat more limited, namely, a person's central convictions which, to oversimplify, describe how he views himself in relation to his view of life.

We formally assess a life style by interviewing the person regarding his family constellation and his early recollections, as Adler had emphasized the importance of birth order position and early recollections (3, p. 328). The family constellation part was described first by Dreikurs (4) and then by Shulman (7); the early recollections part has been described by this author (5). In an actual case we give equal importance to the two parts. In the present demonstration early recollections are merely touched upon during the last few minutes, while the emphasis is on the investigation of the family constellation. Dreikurs outlines the significance of this procedure in the following:

> The family constellation is a sociogram of the group at home during the person's formative years. This investigation reveals his field of early experiences, the circumstances under which he developed his personal perspectives and biases, his concepts and convictions about himself and others, his fundamental attitudes, and his own approaches to life, which are the basis for his character, his personality. (4, p. 109)

---

[1]The tape of the demonstration at the Fourth Brief Psychotherapy Conference, Chicago, March 25, 1972, was not available to the author. The demonstration reported here instead, was conducted the following day before the audience at a workshop of the Alfred Adler Institute, Chicago.

[2]Introductory statement and comments addressed to the audience are in large type; the interview proper is in small type.

[3]From *Journal of Individual Psychology*, 1972, *28*, 232-247. Reprinted by permission.

Some comments are in order regarding variations from our visual clinical procedure. At a demonstration such as the present, time is limited. Therefore, (a) we could not complete the assessment nor write the summary we ordinarily undertake in clinical practice, (b) we interpreted for the client as we proceeded whereas in actual practice the interpretive summary is postponed until data collection is complete, (c) the result is not necessarily a model of good interviewing. We also wish to mention that at a demonstration we use a blackboard to enter the main facts obtained through the interview as we go along, so that the audience may keep these before their eyes.

At the present session the client was a high school student, Ann, who I had never met before, and about whom I did not have any information. Her high school counselor, who attended the workshop, had invited her to serve as a subject for this demonstration before an audience, and she had agreed.

At the beginning of the interview we established that Ann was 17 years old, one of five children, with an older sister, Debbie, age 19; a younger brother Sam, age 13; and a pair of twins, Marty and Mary, age 10. One can start formulating hypotheses immediately. Thus I said, looking at this information, my best guess at this point is that Debbie, Ann and Sam form one subgroup and the twins, a second subgroup.

Dr. M.: How do you feel about this, Ann?

Ann: It's right.

Dr. M.: To confirm this, let me ask, who played with whom?

Ann: I played with Debbie. Sam usually played by himself, and Marty and Mary played together.

Here Ann may be suggesting that my guess of a two-group family was wrong, that it was actually a three-group family, 2-1-2. We shall keep this in mind and see which it might be. To help ascertain I shall ask:

Dr. M.: Who fought with each other?

Ann: Debbie and I fought constantly, and Sam and Debbie fought constantly.

Dr. M.: And who else fought?

Ann: The twins fought.

"Sam and Debbie fought constantly" would suggest that they are in the same subgroup. At this point I could ascertain more information about the subgroups, but I shall not go into that. These questions, and most of those which I shall ask can be found in the Dreikurs paper to which I have referred (4).

Regarding subgroups, psychologists have a difficult time with families beyond three children. They can more or less accurately describe an oldest, a middle, or a youngest child; but the fourth child is not described and the fifth certainly not. However, by dividing families into subgroups of children, it is possible to determine the psychological position of each child within the family. Sometimes, just on the basis of what we have so far here on the blackboard we can already begin to formulate some hypotheses, some alternatives.

Dr. M.: What kind of child was Debbie when you were growing up?

Ann: She was *very* studious all the time. . .Well, from my point of view, she was a goody-goody. . .It's hard to talk about your own sister.

Dr. M.: Especially if you have to say such nice things about her.

Ann: No, she was *very* reliable and *very* responsible. . .and *very* talkative.

Dr. M.: Did she get into trouble at school for that?

Ann: Occasionally.

Dr. M.: So, while she was a goody-goody, she still got into trouble occasionally. She wasn't quite perfect. What else was she like?

Ann: Well, she *always* tried to please my parents. And she was *very* sensitive. You know like she cried easily . . . that's about all.

Dr. M.: I'm going to invite you, Ann, to look at all of this on the blackboard. If you had one word to describe your sister, what word would you use? Let me give you an incomplete sentence. She was . . .

Ann: Responsible, I guess.

Dr. M.:   That's a good word.

Ann: I can't do it in one word.

Dr. M.:   I can. Would you like to hear my one word?

Ann: Yes .

Dr. M.:   She was *very*. . .(Audience laughter.) How does that sound?

Ann: *Very* good. (*Ann and audience laughter.*)

She was not just *very* studious, but *very* studious *all* the time. She always tried to please the parents. Even though Ann does not use the word "very" each time, she uses it quite consistently. Even when she doesn't use it, she still describes her sister as a "very," and a "very" is always something positive. *Very* responsible, good-goody, *very* studious, *always* wanting to please, and so forth. It must have been a hard act to follow.

Now one thing Adlerians observe is that when you have two children in competition (and when two children are this close in age, they generally are in competition), they operate as "teeter-totter twins." Where one succeeds, the other fails or does not even get into that area. He just decides, "The heck with it; its really not worth it. I'm going to do something else." They carve up the territory because every child in every family, you (*to audience*), Ann, and I, is striving for significance. We want to count; we want to belong; we want to have the feeling that people take notice of us, that we are part of it. We don't always use the best methods for gaining significance, but even sometimes with the poorest methods, people do take notice of us, as any teacher will testify. If that is the case, we can already begin to make some predictions in terms of probabilities with respect to Ann.

Dr. M.:   Since Debbie was "very", and "hardly ever." Let's find out, Ann, what kind of kid you were.

Ann: "Hardly ever" and not "very." (Ann and audience laughter) I wasn't studious, and I wasn't a goody-goody. Well I actually. . .

Dr. M.:   Very reliable? (Traits with which she described Debbie.)

Ann: No, I wasn't.

Dr. M.:   Very responsible?

Ann: No.

Dr. M.:   Very talkative?

Ann: No.

Dr. M.:   Always tried to please parents?

If you could see Ann as I can see her from this position, you would have seen the glimmer of a recognition reflex when I mentioned "always tried to please parents." And you are going to discover that she does not try to please them very much—although she wants to.

Dr. M.:   Right?

Ann: Right!

Dr. M.:   Very sensitive? Cry easily?

Ann: Yeah!

Sibling competition is one of the major factors leading to differences between children. Similarities occur in the area of the family values. A family value is one which both parents hold in common, and every child must take a stand, positive or negative, with respect to that particular value or behavior. You can well imagine because of the potency of the parents that most of the children will adopt positive attitudes to the parental values. If it's a family where both parents stress being good in school, all the children will do something about being good in school. They'll either be very good or very poor. Where the family values are not involved, the child may not take a stand at all. Consequently, one can suspect that both parents have some kind of stand in common on sensitivity, and Ann is now nodding her head, and consequences each child has to make up his mind whether he is going to be sensitive or not. It is not determined by the competition, because in terms of the competition, whatever Debbie does, Ann does the opposite.

Dr. M.: Anything you want to add to just the "minuses"?

Ann: I was athletic, whereas Debbie didn't even bother with sports.

Dr. M.: You were athletic and therefore Debbie was minus.

Ann: I think I was more interested—well maybe I was more generally creative than she was as a child.

You notice here the intensity of the competition. She does not merely say, I was athletic or I was creative. I was more creative, I was more athletic, which means that she grew up with one eye on her sister, watched how well her sister was doing and then compared herself to that. Since her sister was so "very," she had to feel inferior in most respects. Ann lives life comparatively.

Dr. M.: What was Sam like?

Ann: If you want to compare him between Debbie and me, he was more like Debbie. He was a good student, but at the same time he was athletic and enjoyed sports like my parents did.

Dr. M.: Both parents did? So you see we have another family value. Both parents enjoyed sports and every child is going to take a positive or negative stand on it.

Ann: He's athletic, very responsible for a kid his age, too, and likeable. That's about all.

That makes a good start. If you look at Sam, you will notice that he has many of the same characteristics that Debbie had, with one major exception. He's not "very." He's likeable, he's athletic, and he's a good student, but he's not "very." Only one time does she use the word "very" with respect to him. One reason that Sam could become these things is that Ann had already become discouraged and had defaulted. Therefore, he could become those things which she was not. Since Ann was a poor student, it was easy for him to become a good student, but, of course, as he became a good student, Ann found herself in the middle of a pincers movement—the two "good" ones, and herself in the middle. Not "very" good, not "very" accomplished, between two good kids! The squeeze was on. Now she said previously that Sam and Debbie fought, not Sam and she, but Sam and Debbie. And you can see the competition there, too, because Sam wanted to do the same things Debbie was doing, except she had a six-year head start. She could even like her six-year younger brother as long as he knew his place. If he occasionally decided to compete, she shoved him down.

Dr. M.: What kind of boy was Sam?

Ann: Well, he was the kind of boy that I suppose any father would like.

"The kind of boy any father would like." You see that Sam had a place merely by being a boy, so that while he competed, he didn't *have* to compete. But he wasn't merely content to take the place he could have had easily. He figured that you can't have enough of a good thing, so he would see if he could also intrude on Ann's territory a bit. She has not told us this yet, but she will (*Ann nods and bursts out laughing in confirmation.*) I sometimes tell my interns that someday I hope to get good enough at this so that I won't even need the subject. (*Audience laughter.*)

If *any* father would like a boy like this, then her father would like a boy like this. So, Sam must have been his favorite, at least his favorite in the old group. Perhaps when Marty arrived her father transferred his preference to the younger boy; but at least in the older group, we would guess that Sam was father's favorite.

Now, you have Debbie who was "very" and she must have been everybody's favorite—teacher's, parents'. I suspect when teachers got Ann after Debbie, the first day they said, "Gee, I hope you're like your sister."

Dr. M.: Did they?

Ann: Occasionally.

Teachers, incidentally, think that this is an encouraging remark (*audience laughter*) and they probably said to Sam, "I hope you're not like your sister, Ann." You can imagine what Ann must have felt like, growing up. Unless she had grandparents or an uncle or aunt or a favorite teacher, it must have been, "Why does everyone love everyone else but me?" (*Ann nods.*)

Dr. M.: Tell me a little bit about Marty.

Ann: He's very likeable.

Dr. M.: Does anybody know what the next word is going to be?

Ann: It's not going to be "very." (*Audience laughter.*)

Dr. M.: Don't let us intimidate you, please, Ann. If you want to use it, okay.

Ann: He's amusing.

Dr. M.: To whom?

Ann: To me, I like him. I think he's just a typical little kid with a big imagination.

Dr. M.: He's something like you?

Ann: Yes, he is in a way.

Dr. M.: And what about Mary?

Ann: Mary is a replica of my mother, sort of.

Now without asking a question about her mother, you're going to find out what her mother was like.

Dr. M.: What was Mary like?

Ann: She's very domestic, but she's intelligent. (*Audience laughter*).

Dr. M.: And your mother is not?

Ann: Well, I don't want to go. . .well, they're both domestic, yet they're both intelligent at the same time.

Dr. M.: Are you trying to say or indicate that these two don't ordinarily go together?

Ann: Not ordinarily, I was just. . .you know, you asked me what Mary was like and she's. . .

Dr. M.: Are you a candidate for Women's Lib?

Ann: Yes!

Dr. M.: I thought so.

Ann: Well, I was just trying to straighten you out that Mary. . .she tries to act like a mother. Like any ten-year-old girl, she tries to assume the tasks that my mother assumes. It's obvious to me.

Dr. M.: Is there much competition between her and Marty?

Ann: No, not really.

Dr. M.: Yet you said they fight.

Ann: Yes, they do fight, but. . .

Dr. M.: Go on, tell us how it is.

Ann: Well, I don't know. It seems like Mary has her own. . .well my parents expect one thing of Mary and one thing of Marty. I think the twins realize this and they don't cross in each other's territory, so to speak.

Dr. M.: Except, apparently when they do, and then they fight.

Ann: Then they fight.

If you look at the blackboard, you will see something interesting. You might not catch it if you did not write it down. Every person but one is "very" in something. Some more than others. If you look at the positive traits that Ann has described—studious, responsible, reliable, etc.—everybody has at least one "very," except Ann. She's the only "un-very" child in this family, except that she is not, because her parents probably regard her as "very" much of a problem.

Ann: Very true. (*Ann and audience laughter.*)

That is apparently the only way in which Ann makes sure that the family or school community take notice of her. She can't be "very" studious "all" the time; she can't please "all" the time; she's had "very" little training in responsibility. She figures that at least through—and I will use the word broadly because I have no more knowledge than you—some kind of "misbehavior," they take notice of her. They know she's there. I would also suspect that through her own "very," she keeps her parents and teachers busier than the other four kids together. Now, her hairdo is hiding her recognition reflex. (*Audience laughter.*)

Dr. M.: I know you have given us these descriptions as best you could, but let's round out the picture a bit. Who was the most intelligent, and who the least intelligent?[4]

Ann: Sam, I think, was most intelligent, and Mary, the least.

Dr. M.: I'll tell you what I'm going to do. Ordinarily I would ask you to rate all five of you. But because of the limited blackboard space, and since the twins are not in your group, I am going to restrict the rating to the older three who make up one group. Now then, the most intelligent is Sam, and the least intelligent is?

Ann: Well, me.

Dr. M.: You say that almost proudly.

Ann: Well, no.

Dr. M.: Who got the best grades in grade school, and who the poorest?

---

[4]All the "most" and "least" questions, as well as other pairwise questions, were asked separately, but we combined them here for more compact presentation.— Ed. note.

Ann: Debbie got the best grades. Yours truly got the poorest.

Dr. M.: What were your favorite subjects in grade school?

Ann: Art, gym, and English.

Dr. M.: And you didn't like?

Ann: Math, science, and social studies.

Yesterday, at the Brief Psychotherapy Conference, I discussed with some of you the meaning of achievement or underachievement in school subjects. Unfortunately I don't have time to go through all subjects today, but let me take math as an example. Math is a problem-solving activity. To do math or arithmetic isn't, like spelling, a matter of just putting it in your head and when the teacher says, "Okay, spell 'dog,'" grinding it out for the teacher. You must be able to use past experience to solve the current problem. You have to use your brain as a filter. You have to know what solutions seem to be on the right track (even if eventually they are not) and to discard immediately those which you know aren't going to work at all.

Adler had noted, "arithmetic demands the greatest degree of independence. In arithmetic, apart from the multiplication table, there is no security; everything depends on free and independent combinations" (2, p. 10). The child who does poorly in math, assuming he's had reasonably good instruction is not self-reliant. Faced with a problem, he says, "I'll never figure that out. Gee, I hope someone will help me. Maybe somebody will get me out of this jam, or maybe fate will do it, but I don't trust my own abilities to do it." So, apparently Ann had already made up her mind very early that all the capability in the family lay with her siblings and there was none left over for her.

Dr. M.: Who's the most industrious, and who the least?

Ann: Debbie, the most; me, the least.

Dr. M.: Who's the "goodest", and who rebelled openly?

Ann: Debbie was the "goodest," and I was the rebel.

Dr. M.: Proudly?

Ann: Yep!

Dr. M.: Who was the covert rebel, never fought openly, just did what he wanted?

Ann: Sam.

Dr. M.: Who demanded his own way, and who got it?

Ann: I demanded it, and Debbie got it.

Dr. M.: And Sam?

Ann: Sam got his way also.

After all, if you're the kind of boy that any father would like, you get your way. Besides which he was the baby of the older group. And that isn't going to hurt your chances of getting your own way. If you look at these two things in combination—who demanded and who got his way—you know the answer to the next question. Who felt sorry for himself? And the answer, of course, has to be Ann. She demanded most and got least. Or perhaps, she felt she got nothing. (*Ann nods.*)

Dr. M.: Who has a temper?

Ann: I do.

There are only two major reasons for temper. One reason is to announce to the world, "I want to have my own way. You better do it or I'm going to intimidate you." In the words of Adler, "Children make use of outbursts of temper to conquer by terrifying" (1, p. 59). Such a child throws himself on the floor, bangs and kicks, turns purple, hoping that you'll come across. The other reason is righteous indignation. "I'm the custodian of the right, and how dare you do something as wrong as that?" From Ann's answers it would seem that her temper was in the service of enforcing her own way. "I'm going to do what I want; I'm going to get what I want, and nobody's going to tell me how to do, what to do, when to do, and if they don't like it, too bad."

Ann: Exactly!

Even though she says, "Exactly," I should like to take a stab also at the second reason for temper. "This family may have its set of values, but I have my set of values, and my ethic is higher than theirs. Therefore, if they don't come across, they are wrong. Those old fogies over thirty don't understand, etc." She already told you she is a candidate for Women's Lib so she has her own ethic there, and I am quite sure that what started out as "I want my own way," as she got older, was tied in with "and I'm right, besides." And because she is right, nobody can tell her anything. Is that the problem?

Ann: It seems to be.

Dr. M.: Who's considerate of others, and who's inconsiderate?

Ann: Debbie is considerate, and I guess I am inconsiderate.

Dr. M.: Who is most sensitive, and who is least sensitive?

Ann: I'm probably the most sensitive, and Sam the least sensitive.

Dr. M.: I think we have forgotten to tell them something. Were you a tomboy?

Ann: Yes.

Ann was the tomboy. She was the tomboy for several reasons. One is, it was the opposite of what her folks wanted. Ann is what I call a "reverse puppet." With a regular puppet, if you pull the right string, the right hand goes up; but with a reverse puppet, the left hand goes up. It doesn't stop you from being a puppet. Yet many kids think, "Look how free I am when I am defiant." But actually they are still puppets. The person who is free decides for himself; he does not just do the opposite. If he does, he is still a puppet; he is merely wired wrong, i.e., his left hand goes up instead of his right. You can well imagine that at one level Ann was a tomboy because this is what she should not have been according to her parents. For another reason, it was easier to compete with Sam than with Debbie. At least in competing with Sam she had a chance. With Debbie, there was no chance. So she tried to tackle him on his home grounds, and of course this was reinforced by the fact that the parents were athletic and fostered or encouraged athletic behavior. So it was not a total disaster. She was doing something her parents wanted, and maybe, just maybe, her parents would be pleased with her if she were athletic. She almost had to be a tomboy. Let's get back to the ratings.

Dr. M.: Who had the most friends and who the fewest?

Ann: Sam probably had the most friends, Debbie the fewest.

Dr. M.: This is the first area we find where you did better than Debbie. Except for one thing. do you want to tell the audience? According to your family, you didn't have the *right* friends?

Ann: Exactly, exactly. (*Audience laughter.*)

Even where she did find some significance, where she did outdistance her sister, it still did not gain her what she really wanted, namely the feeling of belonging. Even though she had more friends and outdid her sister, they really were not the friends a girl like her ought to have, as far as her parents thought.

Dr. M.: Who was the most shy, and who the least shy?

Ann: Maybe Sam was most shy. I was least shy.

Dr. M.: Who was most neat and who was least neat?

Ann: Debbie was the neatest, and I was least neat.

There are many more of these ratings but time will not permit me to continue with them; yet each one we have so far, seems to follow in the same pattern. You can almost predict the sequence. As you have seen, as I say these things, Ann says, "exactly." I am going to have to, at this time, move on to her parents.

Dr. M.: How old is your father, and your mother?

Ann: My dad is 46; my mother is 42.

Dr. M.: So you had relatively young parents. Now, when you were growing up, let's say during your grade school period, what was your father like?

Ann: Well, my Dad was the type of person that expected a great deal from everyone, including all of his children.

She tells us here that her father was a discouraging individual in the guise of an encouraging individual. He was the type of man who had such high standards that people had to push and push to achieve them, and probably feeling that they could not achieve them, they became more or less discouraged.

Ann: He is a business man, *very* industrious, *very* responsible. (*Audience laughter.*) He tried to be understanding.

"He tried to be. . ." Ann just said about her father. Now, in therapy, in counseling, you hear people say, "I tried," "I'm gonna try," "I will try," and so forth, especially when you ask them to do something. "I try" or "I will try" has an implicit ending to that sentence. The ending is, "but I don't have the feeling that I will succeed." And when a person starts trying without expecting any success, he usually makes his anticipations come true. He does not succeed. So Ann feels that her father did not succeed in understanding. He merely "tried" to be understanding. Perhaps, father himself, despite his tremendous ambition and varied successes, was discouraged like the rest.

Dr. M.: Did your father have many friends? Was he respected in the community?

Ann: Yes, both.

Dr. M.: We know he favored Sam, but was Sam his very favorite?

Ann: I don't think he made it that obvious. I don't think he did that to the rest of us kids. He's very fair. (*Ann and audience laughter.*)

Dr. M.: Yes, he had to be *very* fair.

Ann: He tried to be fair. (Audience laughter.)

Dr. M.: And he didn't succeed at that, either.

In a recent paper, Dr. Gushurst and myself (6) described these phrases that patients use, and what they really mean. Most of us are not tuned in. I would suspect that most people in this room if they heard "he tried," would write it down on their sheet dutifully without realizing what it really means. He did not expect to succeed, and probably did not succeed.

Dr. M.: Okay, he tried to be fair and therefore, he never expressed favoritism.

Ann: He seemed to. . .Well, he was a strong person. At least he wanted to live up to the reputation that he was strong, so he concealed any emotion that he might have. He did not allow things to faze him, because he had to be the strong individual. By the same token he also believed that his was the role of the father of the house. His authority should not be questioned.

Here you see a strong masculine value. This is not a family value unless shared by mother. I don't know yet. With such a strong, masculine value, you can imagine the pressure on Sam and Marty. The girls, at least, to some extent, escaped this. However, now Ann is ready to give father his comeuppance.

Dr. M.: Women are just as strong as men, aren't they? (Ann nods). What was mother like?

Ann: Mother *tries* to be understanding. (*Audience laughter*). Okay, she isn't either. She's pretty weak, weaker than my father. In fact, she's everything that he is not. They fit together perfectly for that reason.

Dr. M.: A sort of master-slave, superior-inferior relationship?

Ann: No, I think it's more of a what she doesn't have, he fills in, and what he doesn't have, she fills in. I think she fills in for the emotional part of the relationship.

Dr. M.: Yes, I buy that, but what about the strong-weak bit? You know if father married a strong women, they would "kill each other."

Ann: No, she's *not* strong.

Dr. M.: So, on that basis, they have a sort of covenant—he's the head of the house, and she knows the proper responses to make so they don't run into trouble.

Ann: Probably.

Dr. M.:   But other than that you see them as rather complementary? What he has, fills in for what she doesn't have; and what she had, fills in for what he doesn't have?

Ann: If she's a slave, I think she enjoys being one. She's happy.

Dr. M.:   Tell me some of the things that she is.

Ann: She's creative.

Dr. M.:   That sounds like somebody else in the family.

Ann: She's very emotional.

Dr. M.:   Like somebody else in the family. And it isn't Mary. You mean you grew up weak like mother? Is that what you've been thinking the whole time? That you're creative and sensitive and in other ways like mother, instead of strong, "I can do anything I want and people better listen to me," father? I am going to ask you to look out into the audience a minute, Ann, because I'm going to ask them a question. I don't know the answer but we're going to have to take our chances. Willing to risk it?

Ann: Sure!

Dr. M.:   (*To audience.*) I want you to give an honest answer. I don't want you to please me nor Ann. How many of you feel that creativity and sensitivity are negative traits? Not one. How many think that they are positive traits? All. Well, they are neither intrinsically positive nor negative. Either can be used negatively. Of course, one can use, as many delinquents do, his creativity to make all kinds of mischief. As Dr. Dreikurs has said, "Neurosis is a testimony to man's ingenuity." (*Audience laughter.*) What do *you* think?

Ann: I think I realize that creativity and sensitivity aren't bad things to have; it's probably just my way of looking at it. It's the thing I associate with my mother's weakness and inability to cope with my father, or my inability to adjust in school.

Dr. M.:   You know, Ann, those people in the audience are creative and sensitive, but since they don't know your mother, they don't worry about it. They just enjoy being creative and sensitive. But you associate it with your mother's weakness and don't want any part of it. May I suggest what you might do with that vote you got out there? How you might interpret it? There's an old Hungarian proverb: If one person tells you you are drunk, laugh it off. If two people tell you, give it some serious thought. But if three people tell you, you better go home. (*Audience laughter.*) Now there are at least three people out there who say that your creativity and your sensitivity can be used as *positive* traits. You might want to think about it. (*Ann smiles and nods.*) What's the nature of the relationship between your parents? I know we discussed that just a little while ago in terms of complementarity.

Ann: Well, basically they both have great ambitions, materialistic ambitions. They want to make money. They *are* making money. They enjoy eating out. They enjoy playing golf.

Ann is now telling the family values. *They* enjoy. Not *he* enjoys, but *she* does not; not that *he* would prefer, but *she* would not prefer. *They* are materialistic, and so forth. These are the family values.

Ann: They are united in what they are supposed to accomplish. I don't know, I guess their relationship is . . .it's mutual what they want, and I think money is a big factor, even bigger than happiness, sometimes.

Dr. M.: Who's mother's favorite?

Ann: I think I am.

Dr. M.: Why?

Ann: Maybe it's because she recognizes that I have some of the same traits that she has. Creativity and sensitivity.

Dr. M.: In other words, we two people who have nothing going for us have to stick together.

Ann: (*Reflectively.*) Maybe. I never thought of it that way.

Dr. M.: I hope you will because it's a myth. It's just as much a myth as the belief that Zeus is sitting atop Mt. Olympus. It's something you believe but it just isn't so. We'll have to stop here with respect to your family. I would like to use my last few minutes getting your early recollections.

From all the things which a person can remember from his early childhood, each of us remembers about a half dozen incidents. It is not important whether these things actually happened or happened the way the person says they happened.

What is important is that the individual says and feels that he remembers them. A person engages in this selective process and believes that these things are so because they describe how the individual right now views himself in relationship to life.

Dr. M.: I want you to think back as far as you can. What is the first incident you remember? Something about which you can say, "One thing I remember. . ."

Ann: I remember my First Communion.

Dr. M.: Okay, please tell us about your First Communion.

Ann: It was about 7 o'clock in the morning and we all had to get up real early to get down to the church on time.

Dr. M.: And, what's going on? Supposing you are making a motion picture right now of what's going on at 7:30 in the morning on the day of your First Communion.

Ann: I remember I was half asleep and my mother was pulling curlers out of my hair, telling me what I had to do and what I had to say, and all that kind of stuff.

Dr. M.: And you were feeling. . .

Ann: I was feeling tired and I was scared, too.

Dr. M.: Scared of what?

Ann: Of walking down the aisle in front of all those people.

Dr. M.: And. . .and you were just lying in bed and mother was pulling curlers out of your hair?

Ann: It was like everyone was making a big fuss over me and I was supposed to feel something and I didn't feel anything.

Here you see, first of all, her role in life. She is the person they do it to. Secondly, she tells you their standards are quite different from her standards. They are making a big fuss, and she feels, "I'll be darned, I don't know what everybody is excited about, because I sure am not." Third you see her own reflection of her own lack of self-reliance. "I'll have to walk down that aisle, and I'm scared."

Dr. M.: What is the next thing you remember?

Ann: I don't remember anything specifically, but I just remember soon after I made my communion, I joined a speed skating club. One day I cracked my head open, because I slid into the wall.

Dr. M.: How did that happen?

Ann: I was racing. I was about ten years old, and it was up in Minneapolis. Somehow I just cracked my head open, and I remember that my Dad was real upset about it, and I probably felt sort of guilty, you know, for him for letting this happen to me.

Dr. M.: How did he let it? I'm not quite clear. How did he let it happen to you?

Ann: I was going to get into that. When I got home, my mother was aghast that my father had. . .She blamed the fact that I cracked my head open on him.

Dr. M.: But how was he responsible for it?

Ann: Because he had encouraged me to go out for speed skating. He had taken me up there against my mother wishes.

Dr. M.: In the first part of the recollection what are you trying to do? What do you do on a speed-skating team? What's the whole goal?

Ann: To get there first.

To get there first, to get ahead, to win. Even when she tries, it does not happen. I can't go into any more recollections with her, but you see, she sees herself as a victim of life. She is also a victim, as is mother, of father's encouragement or neglect, or something or another. She is the victim; whether she tries to get ahead, or to be first, or to succeed, all she is going to get for her troubles is a split head. Actually, what she is saying is she is discouraged. Why try if you can't win? Since she is working with a counselor now, her counselor will have to encourage her. At this moment she does not believe in herself.

Dr. M.: We can see, Ann, why you would not believe in yourself, growing up the way you did I guess if I grew up in that spot, I would feel pretty much the way you feel. The question is, is it necessary now? Or do you want to stop being a "reverse puppet" and decide what *you* want to do in life? Not, "what *they* want me to do which I will not do." That's the issue you and your counselor will have to work out together. Is there anything you would like to add, ask, or comment on?

Ann: I think you are just remarkable, I mean the way you can. . . (*Audience laughter and applause.*)

Dr. M.: Thank you, you are very kind. Other than that. . .

Ann: I guess I didn't realize that I was the victim of, what I was suffering from, I think I can accept myself a lot easier now.

Dr. M.: You are suffering from the ignorance that you are good, competent person. You *are* competent, you *are* good, but you are too busy looking at Debbie and your mother, and judging yourself negatively, instead of deciding what you want to do. Did you feel comfortable up here, Ann?

Ann: Well, no, to be perfectly honest, I didn't.

Dr. M.: Why?

Ann: I just feel self-conscious in front of all these people.

Dr. M.: But this thing itself did not make you uncomfortable or nervous or anything like that?

Ann: No, I enjoyed it.

Dr. M.: We didn't step on your toes in any way?

Ann: No!

Dr. M.: Thank you very much for coming.

STUDY QUESTIONS

Direction: Respond to the following in spaces provided.

1. What is the significance of motivation modification vs. behavior modification from the Adlerian view point?

2. What is the diagnostic value of the question: How would life be different if this problem or situation were solved or corrected?

3. What do persistent blaming, complaining, excuses, fear, and "disabling conditions" have in common from an Adlerian perception?

4. "Spitting in the soup" is a form of confrontation. Give an illustration of how you could use this technique. What conditions would be necessary for it to be effective?

MARK L. SAVICKAS
Northeastern Ohio Universities
College of Medicine

Mark L. Savickas, Ph.D., is Professor and Chairman of the Behavioral Sciences Department at the Northeastern Ohio Universities College of Medicine which is in consortium with The University of Akron, Kent State University, and Youngstown State University. He also serves as an Adjunct Professor of Educational Psychology, Administration, Technology, and Foundations in the College of Education at Kent State University.

Mark became dedicated to the discipline of career counseling during the five years he served as a college counselor. Each semester for the last 17 years, he has taught career counseling to graduate students in community counseling, rehabilitation counseling, counseling psychology, and college student personnel. His approach to the practice of career counseling emphasizes helping clients make educational and vocational choices by integrating their subjective interpretations of their lives with objective assessments of their abilities, interests, and opportunities. He has concentrated his research activities on vocational maturation and the process of career decision making. Currently, he serves on the editorial boards of the *Career Development Quarterly* and the *Journal of Vocational Behavior*. Mark has frequently presented his ideas to colleagues at professional meetings and has presented over 300 in-service workshops to career counselors and educators.

CHAPTER 9

CAREER-STYLE ASSESSMENT AND COUNSELING

Mark L. Savickas, Ph.D.
Behavioral Sciences Program
Northeastern Ohio Universities
College of Medicine
Rootstown, Ohio.

Adler's Individual Psychology offers a perspective on vocational development that enriches the classic career counseling model (Watkins, 1984). The present chapter contains an elaboration of this assertion and a presentation of methods and materials that career counselors can use to bring the Adlerian perspective to their work. The chapter begins with a review of the strengths and weaknesses of the most widely used approach to career counseling: matching persons to occupations. What follows is a discussion of four ways in which Adler's Individual Psychology elaborates this matching model to be more useful to counselors. The chapter proceeds with a brief section describing how Adlerian counselors apply Individual Psychology materials and methods to implement the matching model when they do career counseling as an adjunct to life-style counseling.

The remaining two-thirds of the chapter contains a presentation of Individual Psychology materials and methods specifically designed for Adlerian career counseling or, more precisely, career-style counseling. The presentation of career-style counseling is divided into three sections. The first section consists of a description of a structured interview that counselors use to collect data about a client's career style; the second section holds ideas on how counselors think about these data to assess the client's career style; and the third section contains a description of a five-stage model for career-style counseling.

THE MATCHING MODEL

The classic model for career counseling (Parsons, 1909) is based on the psychology of individual differences. Counselors use individual differences to match people with suitable and viable occupations. The fundamental proposition of the matching model follows the wisdom of the familiar maxim, "birds of a feather flock together." Counselors measure clients' interests and then identify corresponding occupations in which their interests may be enacted and rewarded. These congruent occupations offer clients opportunities to integrate personal needs with job demands and thereby experience job success, satisfaction, and stability.

Career counseling that follows the matching model can be likened to a translation service. A linguist translates Spanish into English; a career counselor translates a client's identity into occupational titles. For example, if clients identify themselves as nurturing and dominant, then the counselor may translate their self-concepts into occupational titles such as teacher, counselor, minister, nurse, or other occupations in which the worker helps people. The counselor then encourages clients to explore these occupations.

The matching model is embedded in the major career counseling instrument, **interest inventories.** These inventories automate the translation task. In responding to interest inventory items, clients describe themselves in terms of the constructs provided by the inventory's author. The scoring keys for the inventory comprise theoretically or empirically derived descriptions of successful workers in a variety of occupations or work environments. The results profile a client's similarity to workers in different occupations. In effect, results plotted on the profile sheet translate the client's self-concept into occupational titles. Test interpretation is the prime counseling method that counselors use with the matching model and materials (Crites, 1981). Counselors interpret interest inventory results to clients in ways designed to encourage vocational planning, guide occupational exploration, and structure career decision making.

The matching model with its inventory materials and interpretation methods is very popular with both clients and counselors. In fact, many clients begin their initial interview by requesting an interest inventory because they have heard from others that inventories are useful. Counselors like interest inventories because they provide occupational titles to discuss with clients. Few counselors deny that interest inventories can be used effectively with clients who are ready to translate their self-concepts into occupational titles.

Readiness, however, is essential if the use of inventories is to be effective. A great many clients have not crystallized their self-concepts and so they are not ready to respond meaningfully to interest inventories, especially those that present occupational titles as items. When asked to respond, they do their best, yet, their indecision and confusion in dealing with inventory items produces inconsistent, undifferentiated, and unstable profiles. Every career counselor has experienced frustration while interpreting flat or inconsistent profiles to disappointed clients.

Most counselors soon learn that interest inventory interpretation does not help clients who lack a clear and stable picture of who they are and what they want from life. These clients benefit from help that develops their self-concepts and clarifies their career goals. Career counselors need materials and methods that ease clients' identity development and goal selection. Such techniques make clients consider their own experiences and opinions instead of just reacting to interest inventory items.

Adler's Individual Psychology (IP) can broaden the classic matching model as well as its methods and materials to accommodate the needs of these clients. IP elaborates the core constructs of the matching model. It also offers methods and materials that widen the range of clients which the model addresses. **IP's attention to life goals and styles can help clients develop their identities.** This self-knowledge prepares them to make occupational translations that capture their spirit, not just their stereotypes of the world of work.

ADLERIAN ENHANCEMENT OF THE MATCHING MODEL

IP counselors appreciate matching for fit, yet view it as static. Therefore, they expand the classic matching model, beyond predicting occupational fit based on individual differences in traits such as interests and abilities, to include how people *use* the traits they possess. IP counselors agree with Uncle Remus who said to Briar Rabbit, "it ain't what you got, *it's how you use it.*"

Like trait-and-factor counselors who apply the classic matching model, IP counselors inventory clients' abilities, interests, and values. However, they concentrate on how their clients **use** these traits to fit in, that is, **belong, contribute,** and **cooperate.** Adler's psychology of use can elaborate the classic matching model in at least four ways because it:

1. expands the core construct of fit,

2. focuses on uniqueness,

3. explains how interests develop along a career path, and

4. explicates the career decision-making process.

Elaboration 1: From Fit to Belongingness

Individual Psychology elaborates counselors' conception of occupational fit and enhances their ability to communicate it to clients. In describing the classic matching model, vocational theorists present occupational fit as the core construct for psychological and pragmatic reasons (Dawis & Lofquist, 1984; Holland, 1985a). Empirical evidence shows that goodness of fit

between a person and occupational position relates to job satisfaction and success (Spokane, 1985). IP theorists agree and add
social and philosophical reasons to support person-position fit
as the criterion for career choice.

The IP elaboration of the fit construct rests on ideas about
belongingness and social interest. Each individual is born into
the stream of history. When a baby arrives, the community
already exists. The toddler's experience can be likened to someone being pushed to center stage as the curtain rises for Act II.
Without knowing what occurred in Act I, the actor must try to
fit into the ongoing story and relate to the characters who share
the stage. The successful actor moves toward the other characters, learns to cooperate with them, and thus carves out a role.
In life, the child should move toward the family and community.
They in turn must welcome the child in order for the child to
feel *belongingness.*

When the child feels belongingness, the child can form att-
achments and develop social interest. The child then responds
to *social expectations* (also called developmental tasks) to
become somebody in relation to other people. To thrive, children
must make a place for themselves in the community through
work, friends, and love. Thus, fit leads not just to earning personal payoffs like success and satisfaction but also to making
social contributions. People must ask both selfish and selfless
questions in trying to fit in: Where can I make my place? and
How can I contribute? To answer these questions, people
should consider their unique goals and talents.

Elaboration 2: From Similarity to Uniqueness

In the classic matching model, interest inventories deal
with how the client is similar to workers in different occupations. The Adlerian perspective addresses these similarities yet
also deals with individuality. IP emphasizes the uniqueness of a
life in progress because Adlerian counselors believe that people
design their own personalities. A person is both the artist and
the painting. People shape and channel their movement
through an ever widening social context by structuring personal goals and means. To understand clients, IP advises that
counselor learn *what clients intend* and *how they propose to*

do it. Clients' *goals and means* reveal their uniqueness more than do interest inventory profiles. Inventories measure how clients feel about occupations, not how they intend to use them to achieve their goals and become more effective and complete.

Elaboration 3: From Interest to Career Paths

Once a counselor understands a client's life goal, the counselor knows the client's orientation to life and the general direction in which the client is heading (Csikszentmihalyi & Beattie, 1979). Adlerians call the client's way of moving to a goal *guiding lines* (Griffith & Powers, 1984). Knowing a client's goal and guiding lines allows the counselor to envision the client's career path. Think of a real path that you can walk along in your own neighborhood. What you meet along the path can attract or repel you. You have to react to what you encounter even if the reaction is disinterest or boredom. Objects on a different path require no reaction, assuming that you even know they exist. By analogy, *only occupations along our guiding lines can become interesting to us.* We recognize these occupations and, if we evaluate them as potentially useful, may become interested in them.

Life goals preoccupy us. They shape our outlook, that is, how we approach a subject. From this subjective starting point, we look out for environmental opportunities to objectify our life goals. When we see them, we subjectively link ourselves to these objects by forming an interest. To paraphrase Angyl (1941, p. 55), an interest is not what defines the direction, but on the contrary, the direction defines what can become an interest.

This view of the origin and development of interests fits best for careers in the professions. Blue collar workers often do not have an opportunity to select work based on their interests. They may have to select from job alternatives narrowed by the opportunity structure in their community. Often they must settle for the job they can get or choose the job that pays the most. These workers express their interests through leisure activities and family roles rather than through work.

Elaboration 4: From Choice to Decision Making

The classic matching model and its interest inventories focus on occupational choice, not the career decision-making process. *Adlerian counselors distinguish between occupations that clients choose and how they make their choices.* This expands the focus of vocational counseling to include the career decision-making process. From the perspective of IP, the career decision-making process denotes clients' search for a synthesis between their dreams and reality, that is, an integrative solution to the problems of growing-up. Counselors evaluate the success of clients' attempts at synthesis by comparing their private sense (dreams) to common sense (reality).

Adlerians refer to *private sense* as the "private logic" that clients use to orient themselves to life and answer questions such as (1) Who am I? (2) What is this world like?, and (3) How and where do I fit in? In contrast, Adlerians refer to *common sense* as answers to these questions that make a contribution to the community. The degree of congruence between a client's private logic and the community's common sense indicates the probability that the client will adapt successfully to the challenges of occupational choice and work adjustment.

Clients' *private logic* include their "guiding fictions," that is, their conclusions about what they need to feel less incomplete and more secure. Guiding fictions also are called *fictional goals* because they define a client's ideal self-concept and conception of success. In the process of career decision making, clients use their private logic to evaluate occupations and to select ones along their guiding lines that move them closer to their fictional goals. An occupation that evokes interest, initially attracts a person because in some way it deals with that person's guiding fiction. Thus, the occupations that interest clients have a personal meaning for them. Typically people have unexamined ideas about how certain occupations will help them reach their fictional goals and become more complete. Knowing clients' guiding fictions enables counselors to understand the *hidden reasons* (Dreikurs, 1973) or meanings behind their career goals and occupational interests.

In discussing their occupational interests with other people, clients talk in common sense terms about the public meaning of their occupational interests. Rarely do clients spontaneously articulate the guiding fictions that direct their careers or the hidden meaning behind their occupational interests. For example, several of my clients have wanted to become physicians. They all gave the same common-sense explanation of their interest in medicine: they liked people and science. Yet each client invested medicine with a different fictional goal such as being in control, overcoming clumsiness, playing with winners, being right, or pleasing father. Their hidden reasons for choosing medicine expressed guiding fictions about what it would take for them to actively master what they passively suffered.

Common sense understands this idea of occupational choice as a means of turning problems into opportunities. We all have heard stories about a person overcoming stuttering to become an orator, a girl overcoming polio to become an Olympic track star, a boy overcoming shyness to become a famous actor, or a woman overcoming her lisp to become an accomplished newscaster. Although these are dramatic examples, they are not rare. IP contends that everyone forms guiding fictions as they grow up and that everyone's private logic distorts reality to some degree. Thus, in facilitating a client's career decision making, **Adlerian counselors always attend to private logic and uncover guiding fictions in general and hidden reasons for occupational interests in particular.**

For example, a girl grew up with the guiding fiction that she could belong only if she could please other people. In most instances, she was able to get along well. However, with regard to career choice, her father and grandfather were displeased when she considered anything other than law. Although she wanted to become a teacher, she felt completely lost and worthless when her father was displeased. She sought career counseling for the first time during her final year in law school. She asked the counselor to help her understand why she hated law school and to predict how she would fare as a lawyer. The counselor helped her to examine her fictional goal of pleasing other people and her hidden reason for choosing law. She ultimately became a law professor to integratively resolve her problem in growing-up.

ADLERIAN CAREER COUNSELING

Because of their concern with belongingness, uniqueness, usefulness, and private logic, *Adlerian career counselors typically do not use interest inventory materials or test interpretation methods.* They implement an IP matching model through prototypal Adlerian materials such as found in Chapter 7 or the *Family Constellation Interview Guide* (Dreikurs, 1954, 1973; Shulman, 1962, 1973), *Early Recollection Report Forms* (Dreikurs, 1954; Mosak, 1958), and the *Life Style Inventory* (Ekstein, Baruth, & Mahrer, 1982; Mosak & Shulman, 1971; Shulman & Mosak, 1988a). IP counselors use these materials to elicit clients' unique experiences and opinions so that they may assess clients' life goals and styles. Characteristic IP methods for interpreting the assessment to clients and facilitating their decision making (life style management) or reorientation (life style modification) are presented in Chapter 7 and 8 of the present book. Examples of how other IP counselors use these generic Adlerian counseling materials and methods with career clients can be found in McKelvie and Friedland (1978, 1981), McKelvie (1979), and Manaster and Perryman (1974).

Counselors who try them usually report that IP materials like the *Life Style Inventory* are extremely useful as they work with clients to facilitate identity development, enhance self-awareness, and translate identities into occupations. However, they also report three disadvantages in using the *Life Style Inventory* and similar materials with career-choice clients. First, the questions lack face validity for career clients. When clients begin career counseling they do not expect to be asked about their childhood experiences, family relationships, or early recollections. Although, communication and rapport engage them, career clients hesitate before discussing these topics. Second, the materials are extensive, taking two and sometimes three sessions to complete. Third, much of the data gathered with the *Life Style Inventory* pertain to career-adjustment counseling, that is, helping clients cope with problems at work. Although enlightening, data about family constellation and early recollections are not needed for career-choice counseling. To eliminate these disadvantages, some counselors do more than adapt life style counseling materials and methods to address career choice. They have developed IP materials and methods specifically for career-choice counseling.

Collectively, I refer to these materials and methods for implementing an Adlerian approach to person-position matching as *career-style counseling.* The rest of the present chapter contains a description of career-style counseling materials and methods, starting with interview materials designed to elicit career-style data from clients, continuing with assessment methods to interpret career-style data, and concluding with career-style counseling methods.

CAREER-STYLE INTERVIEW

The *career-style interview* consists of stimulus questions that seem valid to career counseling clients and elicit from them opinions and experiences relevant to their career choices. The questions elicit life goal and style information that reveal how clients think an interest can solve a problem or make them more complete. The stimulus questions are sequenced into a structured career-style interview. The topics flow smoothly and keep clients actively engaged in self-exploration while they describe themselves for the counselor. The stimulus questions deal with (1) role models, (2) books, (3) magazines, (4) leisure activities, (5) school subjects, (6) mottos, (7) ambitions, and (8) decisions.

Question 1: Models

Counselors begin the career-style interview by investigating a client's predicament in life as portrayed by role models. To identify a client's role models, the counselor might say "Whom did you admire when you were growing up?" If clients do not understand, then the counselor can ask them whom they respected a lot, maybe even enough to imitate. With clients who cannot think of anyone, the counselor may suggest that it does not have to be a famous person or fictional character. This often leads a client to name a relative or family member. After the client has named one model, the counselor asks for two other models. When the client has named three models, the counselor asks in turn for each model, "What did you admire about this person?" It sometimes takes prodding, so the counselor may ask the client to "just tell me about the person. What were they like?" The counselor closes this first topic by asking for each model, "How are you like this person and how are you different from this person?"

It is not unusual for a client to name a famous animal as a model. In fact, many counselors have said that they admired Lassie. Lassie was always able to help out and save the day. A crisis counselor said he admired Mighty Mouse for much the same reasons. A gentle and kind social worker reported that his hero was Ferdinand the Bull. He went on to explain what that meant to him in relation to his alcoholic father. Two different clients admired Peter Pan. Both clients had trouble accepting adult responsibilities and eventually chose occupations in which their childlike life styles were assets.

As clients discuss their models, counselors should **concentrate on what clients admire** about their models more than whom they admire. In attending to whom clients admire, counselors err by relying on stereotypes and what the model personally means to them. I recall a clear example of this mistake. I was doing a public demonstration of counseling with a disadvantaged student who said that he admired a football player. Several counselors in the audience jumped to the conclusion that the young man viewed professional athletics as his way out of the ghetto. In explaining why he admired the athlete, the young man told several stories demonstrating how the athlete was independent, artistic, and manly. This athlete modeled for him the self-confidence, independence, and vision that corresponded to his secret dream of being an architect. The young man chose his model because the athlete showed him that a person can be artistic without being effeminate. The athlete modeled a way for the young man to accept his mother's encouragement to be artistic and reject his father's admonition that, if he did, he would become homosexual.

As clients discuss role models, the counselor should think of what the models imply to form follow-up questions. Effective follow-up questions express inferences, not interpretations, so clients find them thought provoking and occasionally humorous. For example, someone who admires the Lone Ranger could be asked, "Are you a loner?" "Do you have a Tonto?" or "Do you like secrets?" and so on. The client's answers to follow-up questions increase the counselor's understanding of the client's career style.

In talking about their models, clients describe themselves. **A model shares the client's plight yet has found a way out of the predicament.** In responding to questions about models, clients tell counselors about the problems that they wish to solve above all else. Thus counselors may identify the problems which structure clients' goals as well as the means that they use to move toward these goals. In other words, *a client's model identifies a central life goal, articulates and labels the client's central concern, and reveals what the client thinks it will take to overcome that problem.*

Do not confuse role models with "gender guiding lines" examined by *Life Style Inventory* questions about parents (Griffith & Powers, 1984, p. 47). Parents guide clients' lines of movement because they are familiar with the course of life and offer their children continuous presence or direction about the way to proceed. In a life style interview, counselors ask clients to describe what kind of man was father and what kind of woman was mother. Clients respond by telling what impressed them about their parents' example. From their answers, counselors learn about parents as clients' standards for what it means to be a man or a woman and how to live. These archetypes are usually an unexamined part of a client's private logic. In contrast to the unexamined guiding lines that parents provide, people purposefully choose role models to show them how to work out a role and how to reduce their feelings of incompleteness or inferiority.

Experienced career counselors often ask their client to compare a role model to a guiding line. The differences between the guide and model reveal the link between that client's problems and goals and thus map the client's line of movement from passive suffering to active mastery. For example, one client described his father as tough and his mother as tender. He loved them both and felt torn between their contradictory styles of relating to other people and situations. His way of integrating these contradictory poses was to imitate Robin Hood whom he described as tough yet tender in defeating villains and helping people in need. The client eventually directed a social work agency, a role he enacted in a tough yet tender manner.

Question 2: Books

As the second topic in the career-style interview, counselors ask clients to describe their favorite books because a book usually includes another model, or more precisely, a life predicament and its solution. Typically, clients' favorite books portray clearly their central life problem and how someone else dealt with it. People are attracted to books in which a major character experiences a problem similar to their own problem. It comforts them to learn that other people have faced the same problem. They often find encouragement in how a character dealt with the problem and sometimes even imitate that character's coping strategy.

Some clients clearly demonstrate this idea. For example, a female pre-medical student frequently read *Gone With the Wind* because Scarlett O'Hara fascinated her. At an unexamined level, she was dealing with how to be a physician without deviating from her female gender guiding line. She found that this book addressed the fear that her needs for achievement and intimacy conflicted. Another client read Hemingway's *Old Man and the Sea* as a parable that addressed his creativity and hypersensitivity.

Sometimes discussing a favorite book draws the client and counselor to the core issue. A college freshman who had *Winesburg, Ohio* as his favorite book planned to major in chemistry. This story about a student writer corresponded to his dream but because of parental attitudes he sought a "real" career. He could not envision a person like himself becoming a writer because everyone in his family worked in a blue collar occupation. If a client cannot readily name a favorite book, then the counselor moves to the next topic without probing.

Question 3: Magazines

The third topic in the career-style interview is magazines. Counselors start by asking clients which magazines they enjoy reading. As prods, they ask clients if they subscribe to any magazine or read one regularly. Typically, counselors try to elicit two or three magazine choices before asking clients to describe what they enjoy reading in each magazine. It is useful to get some detail about the sections that clients like most, a favorite story from the last issue, or what attracts them to the magazine.

Counselors ask about magazines during a career-style interview because magazines vicariously immerse readers in an environment. Favorite magazines tell the counselor about the environments that fit the client's style. As they listen to a client's responses, counselors link them to the client's responses about role models and consider if the magazines represent environmental outlets for interest that the client finds useful. For example, the student who admired the athlete liked *Jazz Musician* and *Architectural Digest.* A client who emulated Lassie's helpfulness enjoyed *People, National Enquirer,* and *Psychology Today.*

Occasionally, a client does not read magazines. In these instances, the counselor may ask clients about favorite television programs. It usually turns out that they watch some television programs regularly. Favorite programs reveal some information about preferred environment, but rarely as much as magazines. Magazines immerse readers into an environment more completely than do television programs.

Question 4: Leisure Activities

The fourth topic in the career-style interview deals with self-expression. Role models and books reveal a central problem and suggest which interests may be useful. Magazines display which environments attract a client because useful interests can be enacted and reinforced. At leisure, clients manifest their interests.

Counselors begin to examine clients' leisure activities by asking them what they like to do in their free time and, if they need a prod, what hobbies they enjoy. If they still need prodding, counselors can ask clients what they did last weekend. After identifying their leisure activities, counselors discern the role clients play in these activities. Sample roles are partner, listener, performer, host, tourist, and member. Then, within the role, counselors determine the key functions and rewards. For example, bridge partners may cooperate to win. Listeners may experience feelings in response to music. Hosts may help guests relax in order to attract friends.

Sometimes clients say unexpected things. For example, one client loved bowling. I thought that physical competence or competition made the interest useful to her. Surprisingly, she said her favorite part of bowling was keeping score. Because leisure motives are intrinsic, counselors can form a clear picture of how clients prefer to interact with their environment.

In addition to self-expression, leisure presents opportunities for personal development. Through leisure activities clients can work on feelings of incompleteness or inferiority. Leisure can be autotherapeutic because in structured play, people can symbolically cope with activities or objects that they are unable to master in real life. Through leisure activities, people develop skills and strategies that eventually enhance their competence and confidence and enable them to cope with the problems in real life. In this sense, play is rehearsal. *So in examining a client's leisure activities, counselors consider both the self being expressed and the problem being addressed.*

An example may explicate the autotherapeutic function of leisure. A homemaker who was housebound and felt unproductive decided to learn to play tennis. She played every day during one summer. At the beginning she was pale, overweight, and clumsy. By the end of the summer she was tan, slim, and a tournament winner; that was what her playmates saw. They did not recognize her increased achievement motivation, competitiveness, and confidence. She had learned that not only could she compete with men, she could beat them at their own game. That fall, she started her own small business and succeeded. Through tennis she actively mastered what she had passively suffered by transforming her feelings of incompleteness and inferiority into feelings of competence and competitiveness.

Question 5: School Subjects

The fifth topic addressed in the career-style interview deals with clients' preferred work environments. Counselors investigate clients' school experience to sample this aspect of their career styles. Schools present fairly uniform work experiences that shape students' work habits and attitudes. Schools expose students to a variety of work environments. For example, English classes present different job demands than do shop or chemistry classes. Counselors ask clients about their success (grades) and satisfaction (happiness) in these different work environments.

Counselors inquire about school subjects during a career-style interview to find out which work environments clients liked best in high school. Counselors ask clients to separate teachers from subjects to avoid confusion. Sometimes clients report a particular subject as their favorite, yet this subject does not fit with their life story. On inquiry, it turns out that the client enjoyed the teacher. For example, one artistic and creative client loved ninth grade Latin. It turned out that he disliked the subject but admired the teacher. His favorite part of the course occurred when the teacher digressed from Latin instruction to relate life experiences and personal opinions.

After clients describe their favorite subjects, counselors ask them about disliked subjects. Then, they review each subject in detail by asking what clients liked about it, what grades they earned, and what effect it had on their career thinking. From these answers, counselors can picture work environments that clients prefer as well as their work habits and attitudes.

Question 6: Mottos

The sixth topic in the career-style interview deals with clients' favorite sayings or mottos. In a motto, counselors listen for how clients title their life story. Some titles that clients have used are "that which flows from the heart alone brings others to your own"; "you got a mouth, use it"; "better safe than sorry"; and "that shit happens." If clients do not have a motto, counselors can ask them to repeat a saying they remember hearing or create a saying. With encouragement, even reluctant clients can formulate something.

Question 7: Ambitions

As counselors approach the end of the career-style interviews, they ask clients to tell them about ambitions their parents had for them as children. This gives counselors some idea of the occupations to which clients have reacted. Occasionally, indecisive clients say that their parents wanted them to avoid trouble or a nervous breakdown. These clients have not reacted to positive images of themselves or occupations and usually they are extremely discouraged. When asked for a positive goal, they are silent because they have not developed a dream for their life.

In conjunction with the parental ambition question, some counselors ask clients about the ambitions they had for their lives when they were in elementary school. Another useful procedure is to ask which occupations they daydream about now. Playful daydreaming and fantasizing to conceptualize oneself in different occupations seems to be an essential component of effective career decision making (Crites, 1969, p. 167). Moreover, the content of occupational daydreams is about as valid in predicting career choice as are interest inventories (Touchton & Magoon, 1977).

Question 8: Decisions

At the end of the career-style interview, counselors ask clients to describe an important choice they have made and how they made it in order to discern their decision-making strategies. For example, a client described how he chose a college by saying:

> I think I chose it just by the fact that it was convenient. I really couldn't decide. I applied to a lot of schools and we couldn't really get financial aid from any of them. That was how I first decided it's not practical. You know if anybody gave me any money, I'd go there. I didn't get any money, so I decided to come here because it was close to home and it wasn't that expensive. I didn't want to go downtown. I wanted to go to a good place. You know, like I didn't want to go to a state college. I wanted to go to a good place, but I didn't want to go to an Ivy League college either. I wanted to stay in between. I don't know how I made the decision. I just kinda ended up here. I'm not sure how. I booted my girlfriend the same way. I just, one night I realized I didn't want to go out with her anymore, so I just stopped taking her out. It was like a very sudden thing. I didn't really sit down and rationally think about it. I just suddenly realized I didn't want to take her out anymore. It was more like intuition, a gut feeling. That's how I chose this college. It's more like a intuition, rather than a rational decision.

Counselors close the career-style interview by asking clients to think in between sessions about how they will eventually choose an occupation and by orienting them to the next session.

CAREER-STYLE ASSESSMENT

Before the first counseling session and after the career-style interviews, counselors analyze their clients' interview responses to assess clients' career styles. The following seven steps in summary form provide an Adlerian approach to career-style assessment.

First, they begin by reviewing a client's responses to the role model questions. In considering the responses, counselors attend to the central problem portrayed and the interests that seem useful in resolving this problem.

Second, counselors may consider the leisure question responses to discern manifest interests and identify the roles, functions, and rewards that intrinsically attract the client.

Third, counselors may review responses to the magazine questions to determine the prominence of data, people, things, and ideas in the client's preferred environments (Prediger, 1982).

Fourth, counselors may consider the client's schoolwork responses to compare the client's reaction to different work environments and analyze successful and satisfying experiences as well as failure and dissatisfying experiences.

Note that the first two areas that counselors review (models and leisure) deal with the self whereas the next two (magazines and schoolwork) deal with the environment.

Fifth, the area that they review next deals with occupational fantasies and decisional strategies: parental ambitions, childhood ambitions, occupational daydreams, and an important choice. Consideration of these topics allows counselors to envision clients' images of themselves at work and how they might choose an occupation. This consideration may also yield a better understanding of how private logic affects clients' decision making. After reviewing these five areas, experienced counselors usually can verbalize a client's career style.

Sixth, counselors relate the career style to the career-choice predicament that the client presented and then identify occupations that can continue the client's life story and lead to more completeness. Usually, counselors should start informally by thinking about the occupations that the client mentioned during the career-style interview. These occupations are reference points in the client's thinking and must be discussed with the client. After considering occupations explicitly mentioned by the client, some counselors use intuition and imagination to generate a list of occupational titles. Remember, that by knowing the client's career path, counselors can identify some occupations which may be useful and interesting to the client.

Seventh, after using these informal procedures to generate occupational titles for a client to consider, counselors may turn to more formal procedure. At this point, person-occupation translation materials devised to implement the classic matching model of career counseling are very useful, particularly those based on personality systematics (Dahlstrom, 1972) such as Holland's (1985a) typology of vocational personalities and work environments or Jung's theory of psychological types (Myers & McCaulley, 1985, Chapter 4). For example, with Holland's typology, a counselor can assign a type code to each hobby, magazine, school subject, and self-descriptive adjective that the client mentioned during the career style interview. Using clinical judgment, the counselor can sum the results to determine an occupational type code and then use the *Dictionary of Holland Occupational Codes* (Gottfredson, Holland, & Ogawa, 1982) to identify occupations that correspond to the client's occupational type code. When they have a list of occupational prospects in hand and the client's career style and fictional goal in mind, counselors have completed the career-style assessment.

Practice Case

The following case material may be used to exercise your skill at career-style assessment. Read the following career-style interview data and, before reading further, perform your own assessment of the client's career style, career path, interests, and occupational prospects. The client was a male, 19 year old, college sophomore who disliked the science courses in his pre-medical curriculum.

Models:	Lincoln because he (1) lost political campaigns yet never gave up, (2) got up and gave speeches, and (3) wrote speeches.
	Edison because he was (1) imaginative, (2) practical, and (3) told other people what to do.
	Walt Disney because he came up with and built imaginative things.
Books:	*Winesburg, Ohio*, about a boy who works for a paper and wants to write.
Magazines:	*Time* and *Newsweek* for movie reviews and politics.
	Jazziz for articles about jazz music and musicians.
Leisure Activities:	Play trumpet, build models, watch *Star Trek*.
School Subjects:	Liked history of how foreign policy was shaped and English, especially drama in plays. Disliked science and mathematics.
Motto:	The unexamined life is not worth living.
Parental Ambition:	Father said be an actor or use your mind; Mother said be a doctor.
Childhood Ambition:	Musician or teacher.
Important Choice:	Talked with parents about which college to attend; deferred to them and chose the one they preferred.

The counselor's goal in performing a career-style assessment is not "to be right." As Aristotle noted, there are so many more interesting things to be than right. Specifically, Adlerian counselors try to be useful to their clients. In comparing your assessment of the above data to the assessment which follows, do not get stuck in the dichotomy of right versus wrong. Instead, look at both assessments and ask yourself, "How useful would these assessments be to the client in easing his self-exploration and prompting occupational exploration and career decision making?

Career Style: He moves through life as a communicator who uses oral and verbal skills to entertain, report, persuade, supervise, and critique other people. His style includes the use of imagination, persuasiveness, and perseverance to identify and deal with practical problems or challenges.

Career Path: His future success and satisfaction may follow the line of writing or speaking about how to make decisions and solve practical problems.

Interests: He appreciates the usefulness of writing, politics, performing, teaching, human relations, managing, and consulting.

Occupational Prospects Along Career Path: He may want to investigate occupations such as journalist, author, lawyer, politician, actor, technical writer, human relations manager, performing arts manager, advisor/consultant.

Guiding Fiction: "If other people like me, then I will belong and feel secure ."

This client eventually completed a bachelor of arts degree in journalism and entered law school.

CAREER-STYLE COUNSELING

Having completed a career-style assessment, the counselor is ready to begin career-style counseling with the client. Career-style counseling has a structured agenda that deals with five topics:

1. career style and path,

2. decision-making difficulties,

3. interests,

4. occupational prospects, and

5. choice barriers.

Usually, counselors can address career style, decision making, and interests during the first counseling session. During a second counseling session scheduled about a week later, they discuss occupational prospects and how clients can explore them. About a month later, counselors use a final session to confirm a client's choice or deal with barriers that block a choice. The pace of counseling can vary. Occasionally, counselors may deal with the first four topics during one session or deal with only the first topic during one session.

In pursuing the career-style counseling agenda, Adlerian counselors use the IP counseling methods described in Chapter 8. Their methods differ for the two dimensions of counseling. Along the **relationship dimension,** they use *empathy, encouragement,* and *humor* to maintain collaboration and keep the client's attention on what needs to be done. Along the **communication dimension,** they use *interpretation, facilitative confrontation, suggestion, teaching,* and *clarification* to increase self-knowledge and vocational development as well as to facilitate career choice and commitment to that choice.

Topic 1: Career Style and Path

The first counseling session begins with a direct presentation of a summary of the client's career style. In presenting this summation of understanding, Adlerian counselors follow principles taught by Dreikurs (Powers & Griffith, 1987, Part 4). Counselors thoroughly address the strengths and limitations in clients' career styles. They relate clients' ways of doing things to their work habits and attitudes in general and their educational-vocational successes and failures in particular.

Two techniques make the discussion concrete. One technique is to *identify examples of clients' career styles* as expressed in their present behavior, preferably during the last five minutes or, if not, some things they said or did during the career-style interview. The other technique is to *ask clients to cite an example* of something they have done during the last week that also expresses their career styles. Clients are so embedded in their own style, that they do not realize they have a style. Counselors must be sure that clients recognize their career styles before discussing where they are heading.

Counselors may move the discussion from *career styles* to *career paths* by explaining to clients that the more clearly they envision where they are heading, the more evident will be their choices. They may begin by telling clients that path is the basic meaning of career. In fact, the term career path is somewhat redundant because the word career denotes course or passage having evolved from the medieval Latin word "carraria," meaning road for vehicles and the middle French word "cariere," meaning street. Counselors may continue by describing clients' current career decision-making task as choosing a direction at a crossroads or turning point. Then counselors may relate this metaphor to clients' vocational experiences by describing the career paths that they have already traveled and project the paths over the horizon. Of course, a most useful procedure is to use simple words and specific examples to describe clients' career paths and crossroads so that they can recognize and understand them.

To make a client's career path concrete and memorable, some counselors use success formula materials to describe a career path. I use the contents of Table 9.1 to help clients state their success formula. Together we select the three roles that best

TABLE 9.1
SUCCESS FORMULA ELEMENTS
GROUPED BY ORGANIZATIONAL ROLES*

DOER

WORK WITH TOOLS
THINK WITH MY HANDS
MAKE OR REPAIR THINGS
USE MECHANICAL ABILITY
APPLY PHYSICAL SKILL
WORK OUTDOORS
WORK WITH ANIMALS
WORK WITH NATURE

HELPER

HELP OTHERS
WORK WITH PEOPLE
PROVIDE A SERVICE
BE OUTGOING AND PLEASANT
HELP CHILDREN
HELP THE ELDERLY
TEACH
COUNSEL
ADVISE

THINKER

SOLVE PROBLEMS
WORK WITH SCIENCE
WORK WITH MATH
USE LOGIC
RESEARCH IDEAS
FIGURE OUT HOW THINGS WORK
READ
ANALYZE PEOPLE

INFLUENCER

MAKE DECISIONS
CONVINCE OTHERS
LEAD A GROUP
USE POWER
ACT WITH ENTHUSIASM
SELL THINGS
BE THE CENTER OF ATTENTION
BE DYNAMIC
HAVE A LOT OF VARIETY

CREATOR

BE INDEPENDENT
SHARE FEELINGS
BE SENSITIVE
PAINT
PLAY AN INSTRUMENT
WRITE
APPLY ARTISTIC FLAIR
DECORATE
DESIGN

ORGANIZER

BE PRECISE
BE PART OF A TEAM
RECORD DATA
TYPE
ORGANIZE FILE MATERIAL
HAVE A SET ROUTINE
KNOW WHAT IS EXPECTED
CARRY OUT ORDERS

*For more information about the six roles, consult Holland (1985a).

characterize the client's career style and fictional goal. Then I ask the client to complete the following sentence with one phrase from each of the three role clusters: "I feel successful and satisfied when I _____ ." The client picks the phrases and together we arrange them into a success sentence which the client can use to identify and evaluate prospective occupations. For example, one client selected solve problems from the thinker role cluster, help others from the helper role cluster, and share feelings from the creator role cluster. She combined them into her success formula: "I feel successful and satisfied when I help others solve their problems and feel better."

Topic 2: Decision-Making Difficulties

After clients recognize their career styles and envision their career paths, counselors direct their attention to how clients' use private logic to process career decision-making tasks. On the one hand, if common sense can comprehend and validate their private logic, then counselors may reinforce clients' private logic and apply it to their career decision-making tasks. On the other hand, if common sense cannot comprehend or validate their private logic, then counselors reveal this to clients and explain how the guiding fictions in their private logic cause their career indecision or unrealism. Invalid ideas in a guiding fiction usually take the form of preemptive distinctions, over-simplifications, or over-generalizations (for examples see Shulman, 1973) in a client's fictional goal (e.g., If I were _____, then I would be safe, secure, and significant). The more exaggerated these invalid ideas become, the more they delay or distort career decision making.

An example of how a client's private logic can delay or distort career decision making may be useful here. I recall one client whose ambition was to be respected. However, in his fictional goal he oversimplified respect to mean control: "If people obey me, I will be safe, secure, and significant." He succinctly expressed this mistaken idea in his motto, "my way or the highway." This exaggerated distinction distorted his career decision-making process in that he considered only occupations that offered him respect in the form of power, possessions, and prestige. Because it was irrelevant to his goal, he had not considered how he would contribute to society or how his need to control other people would impair his relations with coworkers and family members.

A client's private logic enters common sense when two people talk about it during a counseling session. By representing common sense, counselors help counselors reevaluate mistaken ideas. A counselor may begin by explaining to the client that the mistaken idea is understandable but not necessary. This may take the form of explicating where the idea came from and why it is no longer needed. With clients who mistake respect for control, a counselor might explain how the need to control people served an adaptive purpose earlier in their lives yet how it is now maladaptive. Thus, the need to control people is understandable in light of past circumstances but not necessary in present situations.

In confronting the previous client's mistaken idea (i.e., respect equals control), the counselor should use a phrase that captures the client's imagination and compels him to reconsider the idea. For example, the counselor might impress upon the client that "our way is the highway" leads people to respect him whereas "my way or the highway" leads people to fear him. Adlerian counselors might also consider *spitting in the soup* by telling the client that his equating respect with control causes something he dislikes; maybe his hypertension, insomnia, or free-floating anger (Mosak, 1977).

Another Adlerian method that a counselor might use is to confront the client with a negative picture of his future if he continues to dominate other people (Shulman, 1971, p. 174). Other counseling methods for correcting mistaken ideas have been presented by Adlerians in writing about mistaken assumptions (Shulman, 1968), basic mistakes (Dreikurs, 1973), or interfering ideas (Powers & Griffith, 1987), and by other counselors in writing about neurotic convictions (Horney, 1945), irrational ideas (Ellis & Greiger 1977), private rules (Krumboltz, 1983), or irrational expectations (Nevo, 1987).

Topic 3: Interests

The third career-style counseling topic deals with interests as criteria in making occupational choices. After helping clients recognize their career styles and examine their private logic as it affects decision making, counselors discuss interests that clients can use to move toward their goals. Counselors may start by explaining that interests are not simply feelings, they have meanings, both public and private. Then counselors may discuss how an interest connects a career style to the environment. This lays the groundwork for naming clients' interests, discussing the hidden meanings that their interests hold, and explaining how these interests can be useful to them. In discussing how well various interests serve fictional goals and express career styles, counselors should be as specific as possible and cite examples from the client's life experience.

Next counselors explain to clients how they can use their interests to identify occupations to explore. No one has time to explore every occupation so each client must identify a set of plausible occupations to investigate. Some counselors help clients do this by systematically describing their preferred work roles, activities, and settings. This discussion develops implicit interests into explicit criteria for screening occupational prospects. For example, following a discussion of this type, one client came to say that he was interested in a job that would allow him to play a leader role, use intellectual and persuasive abilities, and work in a entrepreneurial setting.

To keep clients actively involved in the career decision-making process between counseling sessions, counselors close this first counseling session by assigning two tasks as homework. The first **homework task** has clients think about what they discussed during the counseling session because the next session will begin with a discussion of their reflections on their career styles, career paths, and interests so as to reinforce, refine, or clarify their self-knowledge as it relates to career choice. The second homework task has clients learn an occupational classification system and prepare a list of occupations to discuss during the next counseling session. Counselors can select one of four different materials to assign as client homework: (1) *The Self-Directed Search* (Holland, 1985b), (2) *Career Decision-Making System* (Harrington & O'Shea, 1982), (3) *The Career Key* (Jones, 1987), or (4) *Individual Career Exploration* (Miller-Tiedeman, 1976). Counselors may augment this assignment by asking clients to examine the *Encyclopedia of Career* and *Vocational Guidance* (Hopke, 1987) or the *Occupational Outlook Handbook* (U.S. Department of Labor, 1988). An alternative to this assignment is to ask clients to work through computer-assisted career exploration programs such as *SIGI* or *DISCOVER* (Harris-Bowlsbey, 1984).

Topic 4: Occupational Prospects

The second session in career-style counseling is devoted to selecting a short list of occupations to investigate and devising an exploration plan. Counselors start the session by discussing clients' reactions to the previous session. This discussion usually leads naturally to the occupations that appeal to clients. At this point, counselors inquire about the second homework assignment by asking clients to relate the occupations that they considered and to share their thoughts about how each one implements their success formulas. Then counselors may ask clients to think aloud about each occupation that they mentioned during the career-style interview which they have not commented on during this counseling session. Next, counselors may add to the discussion, occupations identified in the career-style assessment. This first half of the second counseling session usually will produce a list of about six occupations for clients to explore in-depth and another six occupations to hold in reserve.

Having a short list of occupations to investigate allows the counselor and client to collaborate on constructing an exploration plan during the second half of the counseling session. A plan consists of activities that will help clients see choices clearly so that their ability to decide is enhanced. Most clients do not know how to explore and clarify their choice alternatives. Therefore, counselors must teach them about exploratory behavior in conjunction with suggesting specific activities that will increase the clarity of their choices. Stewart (1969, pp. 218-221) prepared materials that are particularly useful to counselors who wish to teach clients the principles of exploration as they collaborate on constructing an exploration plan. The materials consist of four pages which counselors may give to clients. One page presents examples of information sources, two pages explain how to get helpful information, and the fourth page structures a process for using information in career decision making. To end the second counseling session, counselors use Adlerian encouragement methods to move clients to enact their exploration plans. Counselors schedule a third career-style counseling session about a month later to allow clients time to enact their exploration plans.

Topic 5: Choice Barriers

When the client and counselor reach the fifth topic (usually during the third counseling session) career-style counseling concludes, one way or another. For most clients this final session is almost casual. They tell the counselor how exploration clarified their alternatives and led them to a choice. Counselors reinforce that choice and discuss practical matters that will increase clients' commitment to their choices and help them implement their choices.

For other clients, this final session is far from casual; in fact, it may be the most moving of all sessions. They begin this session by announcing that they still cannot make a choice. In these instances, distinguishing between a preference and a choice helps counselors recognize the decision-making difficulty. A *preference* expresses what a client would like to do whereas a *choice* expresses what a client probably will do (Crites, 1969, p. 129). for example, a person may prefer vanilla ice cream yet choose chocolate to make it easier for the server.

The fact that some people make choices that they do not prefer makes the distinction between preference and choice critical in career counseling. If a barrier blocks turning a preference into a choice, then career-style counseling is complete because clients can state viable and suitable occupational preferences. The client and counselor spend the session problem-solving how to deal with the barrier. The most frequent barrier encountered is *family opposition.* This occurs when family members press clients not to choose the occupations that clients prefer.

Other common choice barriers include *financial strain, training* or *entry requirements, prejudice,* and *dilemmas* involving consorts or children. Common solutions include talking to the family in the counselor's office, moving out from the parents' home, getting a part-time job, or letting some time pass. If the client cannot state a preference during the third session, then counselors try to determine whether the inability to decide on a preference is **situational undecidedness** or **trait indecisiveness** (Cooper, Fuqua, & Hartman, 1984). In the case of indecision, many counselors recommend to clients that they engage in specified maturational or self-development experiences. In the case of indecisiveness, Adlerian counselors recommend life style counseling and, if the client agrees, begin by collecting family constellation information and early recollections.

SUMMARY

The present chapter asserted that Adler's Individual Psychology enriches the classic model for career counseling by elaborating its constructs and extending its applicability to a wider range of clients. Furthermore, the chapter explained how an approach called career-style counseling resolves problems that arise in adapting Adlerian life style methods and materials for clients who want to make a career choice. In describing career-style counseling, the chapter dealt with the assessment of career styles, the identification of career paths, and the recognition of private logic in career decision making. It presented counseling methods for interpreting clients' career styles to them and correcting mistaken ideas that delay or distort their career decision making. It also presented materials which counselors may use to perform and assess career-style interviews with clients and articulate their success formulas. Hopefully, as more counselors do career-style counseling, they will increase its effectiveness by developing its methods and devising additional materials.

STUDY QUESTIONS

Explain how the rationale for the Adlerian Matching Model of career counseling expands the classic Parsonian Matching Model.

Why is Adler's "psychology of use" an improvement over the "psychology of possession" that is manifest in interest inventories?

Use Adler's Individual Psychology to explain the origin of interests.

The essence of Adlerian career counseling is to clarify choices so that a client's ability to decide is enhanced. How does Career Style Counseling clarify choices?

ACTIVITIES

Perform a Career Style Assessment with a client and administer your favorite interest inventory to that client. Before looking at the results of the interest inventory, predict the results, in as much detail as possible, based on the Career Style Assessment.

Write your own "Success Formula" using the procedures and materials discussed in the Career Style and Path part of the Career Style Counseling section in this chapter.

CHAPTER 10

MARRIAGE
COUNSELING

Love is the third and most difficult of the life tasks for individuals to master. This tends to be so because of the courage and cooperation which it requires of both parties involved in the relationship. In Dreikurs' (1946) classic book on marriage, he noted that "tradition" had not prepared us for the democratic revolution which brought greater equalization into the marriage relationship. Contrary to others of that day, he was not discouraged by signs of the family's, and hence marital relationship's, demise. Our shortcomings, however, were most notable in the marriage relationship.

> We suggest that the family is not disintegrating, but is rather faced with a serious dilemma. . .We do not know how to resolve conflicts and classes of interests in the spirit of mutual respect, a requisite for living in a democratic atmosphere. Our cultural inability to live with each other as equals, which we have become in fact, is most painfully felt in our closest relationship, in marriage. (p.v)

In Adler's article (1936), *"Love is a Recent Invention,"* he observed that, "There is no doubt that we know more about sex than our fathers did." He goes on to ask, ". . .But do we know more about love?" These same observations could be made today. He even used a now familiar story of the father asking his son if he knew the "facts of life", to which the boy replied, "Yes, Papa, what is it you would like to know?". Humorous, yet, telling is the fact that *our attention fifty years later is still more oriented to the physical relationship than to the spiritual/intellectual/social dimensions of our most intimate of relationships.*

This by no means is intended to distract from genuine sexual problems found in some marriages and the need for their remediation or the substantial value to be found through planned sex education of our youth. Rather, like Adler and Dreikurs, this chapter is intended to provide an introduction to the concepts and methods central to achieving a healthy marriage relationship. Of course, entire books are written on marriage counseling and therapy. The information provided in this chapter should prove useful as a basic position on which to build the theory and methods of other approaches. Unlike many other references on methods and techniques, the Adlerian model provides a value system as a basis for assessing progress in counseling or therapy as well as goals considered desirable in any such relationships.

LOVE: THE ANTECEDENT AND BY-PRODUCT OF A HAPPY MARRIAGE

The reader may be distracted by the subtitle of this section. Contrary to popular belief, however, the emotion of love is not the "cause" for a satisfactory "love" relationship. This in no way minimizes its power or significance. Dreikurs (1946) noted that,

> The realization of being loved is a moment of high importance psychologically. It is characterized by a desire to give oneself and to accept the other one by a sustained and exclusive interest in the other one, by a longing to be together. . .The existence of love (however) is threatened whenever our attitude toward the other one changes. (pp.15-16)

Individuals, based upon their personal goals and desires, direct their affection according to how well they perceive their needs being met by the subject of their attention. While this process is generally an unconscious one, it operates just as deliberately as if it were by conscious intent. After considerable elaboration on the subject, Dreikurs (1946) characterized love as being highly subjective.

> Love is what one calls love—. . .be it created for devotion or domination, for heaven or hell, for happiness or misery. (p. 18)

Therefore, love depends upon the intentions of the lover. Left with only this assessment, we might conclude that very little practical value can come from defining love for other than poetic purposes. However, Dreikurs and Adler offer further elaboration in the context of social interest.

Adler defined love in marriage as ". . .the equal partnership between a man and a woman—where two are merged into one, a human dyad, reconciling the sex urge of the individual with the biological needs of the race and the demands of society" (pp. 148-9). To achieve the "the perfect dyad of love", Adler (1936) offered the following "rules" for consideration:

1. Don't look up to your mate and don't look down: approach love as an equal.

2. Don't expect an impossible perfection in others, of which you yourself are incapable: love a woman, not an angel; a man, not an eidolon (phantom, ideal).

3. Don't think of yourselves as one or two, but as a twosome.

4. Don't take without giving, nor give without taking, in love.

5. Don't pick out a partner who does not entice you physically, but do not entangle your fate with one who appeals to you only on a physiological basis.

6. Don't fail to cooperate with your mate on every plane, socially, economically, intellectually, spiritually, emotionally and biologically.

7. Don't lose yourself in by-paths and blind alleys: There is always a way out of emotional labyrinths—potentially all humans are fundamentally normal.

8. Be a slave neither to convention, nor to your own ideosyncrasies: remember you are not merely an individual, but a unit of your social group and the human race. (p. 149)

From these recommendations, the reader may conclude that Adler was not much of a romantic! Based upon anecdotes of those who knew him well, he was fun loving, personable and probably quite romantic as well. However, we must remember that emotions are our tools and love is no exception! We can surmise, therefore, that Adler's admonitions would be practical and free of the entanglements into which poets would lead us.

Love, therefore, is both an antecedent and by product of a successful marriage partnership. Two people decide to contribute to the other's comfort, convenience, preferences, and so forth even when it requires discomfort, inconvenience, and overlooking of one's own preferences at any given moment. Within this process of giving, intrinsic rewards are joy, satisfaction, and peace. Under such conditions, happiness with the relationship no doubt follows. How do we establish relationships? Dreikurs offers a psychological explanation.

CHOOSING A MATE

Dreikurs believed that the secret personal anticipations of individuals guided them in the selection of their perspective mates. These are translated into impressions of physical, social, and psychological characteristics. They are unconscious in most respects but predictable in satisfying unspoken wants, desires, and expectations.

From the first impression until the outward expression of commitment, each individual weighs minute behaviors into a pattern of anticipations which either fit, or do not, a prototype of the "desired characteristics for me." An important Adlerian concept is imbedded within this perspective. Dreikurs (1946) believed:

> There are deep personal demands which influence the final decision; and unbelievable as it may sound, everyone gets from his mate just the treatment that he unconsciously expected in the beginning. The demands which are gratified when we suddenly or gradually accept one person as our right mate are not conventional—not those of common sense. We feel attracted when we have met somebody who offers through his personality an opportunity to realize our personal pattern. . .to continue or revive plans which we have carried since childhood. (p. 68)

Therefore, as Dreikurs described it, we see that mating serves "secret personal anticipations." These are often unspoken, even unconscious, expectations and wants of the individual. When we "feel" the person is right for us, we tend to say that we are in "love." Conversely, when we no longer perceive that the person meets our "needs," we tend to say that we have "fallen out of love." Thriftiness prior to marriage becomes characterized as miserliness; generosity as extravagance; or interest in family as dull domesticity.

As strange as the continuation of an abusive relationship may seem, when an abused partner refuses to leave at the urging of friends, families, and counselors, often what is missed is the pattern of anticipations which are being met by the abusive partner. This is not intended to minimize the real physical danger which such partners often experience as a threat to leaving. Often, however, the abused partner would benefit from life style therapy (the abusive spouse as well) as a means of changing unhealthy attitudes, goals, and behaviors which sustain them in the abusive relationship. With such changes, the courage and conviction needed to accept the help and support of others to leave the abusive partner become the foundation for more and better changes.

Dreikurs (1946) characterized such a tendency as an "appeal to deficiencies." Unwittingly, some individuals are attracted to a person who offers the least possibility of a harmonious union.

> Two secret tendencies are chiefly responsible for this: the desire to maintain one's superiority, and hope of suffering. The one induces the selection of an inferior mate; the other the choice of someone who, despite certain qualities, brings dissatisfaction or even torture, granting only the solace of martyrdom. (p. 80)

The purpose associated with this inclination is to choose a partner for his/her faults. A partner who is inclined to be irresponsible, unproductive, asocial or otherwise "socially inferior", offers no challenge to the individual caught in a private logic requiring continual affirmation of their superiority. In point of fact, more than no challenge, the erring partner provides a readily available stark contrast for all to see how notable, competent or long suffering the "victim" or "martyr" is in their relationship. Again, however, we must avoid stereotypes of what categories of individuals seek specific types of relationships. More importantly the counselor needs to come to understand the private logic of the individual.

Less obvious but just as destructive are signs of discouragement revealed through marriage counseling, for example, where one partner makes small disrespectful comments, withholds intimate disclosures of love, or exhibits nonverbal evidence of condescending behaviors. These become the grounds for divorce.

Another basic concept useful in counseling relates to the observation that whatever characteristics attracted us in courting also will contribute to our conflicts in intimate relationships. In fact, the very qualities which bring us together also tend to contribute to our conflict. For example, a fellow marries a woman because she is intelligent, charming, home loving, independent, and fun loving. She marries him because he is intelligent, ambitious, hardworking, dependable, and gregarious.

While over simplified, the scenario becomes one of her feeling trapped at home or, more recently, limited career wise by a hardworking, hardly at home, successful but too busy husband who may or may not show much appreciation for the sacrifices she makes to have his career take precedence over other aspects of their relationship.

One seeks companionship to
complement private logic.

Each partner feels justified in this discontent. They may accept some responsibility for their tension but neither may understand how fundamentally each got exactly what they sought in the other person! For marriage counseling to be effective both partners need an understanding not only of their goals, convictions, and attitudes but also of how their present relationship tends to reinforce mistaken notions which bring conflict.

MARRIAGE COUNSELING

Counselors must ask themselves at some point when one or more partners approaches counseling, what is the status of the relationship? Are both partners committed to the relationship? Are both prepared to enter counseling with a desire for success in achieving a "twosome" or dyad? Of course, assessment instruments are available to pinpoint trouble spots and areas of discouragement. The measure of commitment to continue the relationship, however, is not so easy to determine.

As Vaughan (1987) found from interviews with 103 individuals of various types, ages, and description who went through what she called the "uncoupling" process, discernable stages and patterns can be identified which can be useful for the counselor to recognize. She characterized the unhappy member as the *initiator* and the other as simply the *partner.* She notes that often counselors are confronted by a situation in which the initiator has unsuccessfully tried to communicate unhappiness and, only after the initiator had considered the relationship "unsaveable", does the partner realize the depths of their predicament. At this juncture, the initiator already has begun the process of leaving, psychologically if not physically. She notes that when a counselor is sought:

> Partners will push for a professional whom they believe will be committed to saving the relationship. . .Initiators on the other hand, will lobby for a counselor with no apparent bias toward keeping relationships together. . .Both compete for support of this third person who has now entered the fray. . .All things are possible. . .Nonetheless, counselors note that in most cases by the time a couple seeks counseling, it is too late. (pp. 176-177)

"Too late" is not an Adlerian viewpoint, however, from which to approach counseling. First, many couples join parent study groups and discover that they could learn much to improve their marriage relationships. Many discover through programs such as *Marriage Encounter,* a Christian couples enrichment program, that much benefit can be obtained from outside assistance with improving their relationship. Second, if in doubt, an Adlerian counselor would inquire about the probabilities each partner would predict that they would still be married in five years. So long as each offers any prospect that they will be married in the future, no matter how small, then hope exists and is worth pursuing. If no hope is present, then the assistance expected by one or both partners may be divorce counseling. This most certainly needs to be as clear as possible from the outset.

Establishing the Relationship

Getting started will be more difficult for some couples and partners than others. Initiators are likely to be more anxious than their partner because their own motivation is in question, i.e., they harbor thoughts that the relationship probably is not saveable. Conversely, the partner still hopeful of saving the relationship is emotionally distraught over the prospect of the marriage ending. Worth noting is the fact that Vaughan found instances where partners had been initiators on other occasions or in other relationships. One can imagine over the life of a relationship how each member may have become discouraged enough to think of terminating it.

The uncoupling process is a natural evolution when one or more partners becomes so discouraged, so fatigued by fighting, thinking, arguing, trying, etc. that, at some times, they feel too physically and emotionally drained to imagine continuing for even five more minutes, let alone five more years. As a consequence, they begin to explore other alternatives, if not in fact, at least in their mind. They tend to begin disengaging themselves from the frustration, guilt, hurt, anger, and related feelings associated with this relationship by pulling away from their partner.

In effect, the initiators have begun the opposite process to how they originally became engaged with their partner. Now you can guess, they can think more quickly of the partners' faults than they can of what is attractive, encouraging, and desirable. Empathizing with these feelings, reassuring them that these are normal and understandable feelings under the circumstances, and offering support to both partners can do much to diffuse the discouragement.

The counselor, then, strives to put both parties at ease by establishing rapport with each in a genuine way. This is not as difficult as it may seem if you can imagine that both parties are most likely emotionally in pain and yearn for empathic understanding. Without taking sides, simply asking each person to describe what has brought them to this point and what they have been doing to resolve their differences gives the counselor sufficient basis for empathizing with each partners' predicament.

Establishing rapport includes reaching some agreement on goals and process. One goal with which both partners can usually agree is that the outcome should result in the promise of a happier life for each of them. At this juncture, the assumption can be expressed that they are there because the relationship needs to be improved and that counseling possibly could move each of them toward this goal.

Even though one partner may obviously resist, some agreement is desirable for short term goals. For example, you can explain the value of life style assessment. This is true for both partners, whether or not they continue counseling or the relationship beyond the sessions needed to complete it. Assuming that they are agreeable to participating in this process, then they should be agreeable to scheduling another four or five sessions with an opportunity to renegotiate after that point.

Assessment

The assessment process can be done formally or informally. As was noted previously, the counselor need to be alert to unspoken words as well as nonverbal cues between the couple. These are important to the counseling relationship.

The process includes determining what they hope to achieve through counseling. When the relationship seems in serious question, asking the partners to individually write what they consider to be the likelihood of the marriage surviving five more years can be asked. Each writes the percentage (e.g., 20% chance) on a piece of paper and gives it to the counselor. How closely they agree may give an indication of how much discussion has preceded seeking counseling. It also can indicate who the initiator is (i.e., unhappy and has begun the process of leaving) and which partner is still believing that the relationship is saveable.

The individual with the lowest percentage often poses the greatest challenge to cooperation. Their discouragement is likely to have begun a long time before and they have exhausted much of their hope for a happy resolution. As a consequence, they may unwittingly, if not deliberately, attempt to prove that really no hope still remains. If you suspect that this is the case, then kindly but deliberately raise the issue. This can be done in such a way as to explain how the process of "uncoupling" works.

In the initial interview, issues related to finances, in-laws, parenting, shared responsibilities, and expressions of love (sexual as well as otherwise) are common. These are an expression of the issues related to cooperation. Most often, these reveal the areas where the partners have focused their unsuccessful efforts at cooperation. Decision making, problem solving, and conflict resolution strategies are teachable. In the homework/reorientation phase of the counseling process, these can be developed. The real issues, however, concern clashes of the life styles. For this to be uncovered, life style assessment is helpful.

The counselor also must listen for what is not said as well. Serious symptoms of lack of success will be found in alcohol abuse, other substance abuse, spouse or child abuse, and triangulating by one or both partners. *Triangulating* may seem relatively innocuous as when a parent is overinvolved with a child or one is overly ambitious at work. But both are at the expense of the marriage relationship and both erode its foundation.

Obviously, when alcoholism and other more serious conditions are involved, the challenge to successful counseling is just that much greater. These are frequently "secrets" which the couple keep to themselves. The counselor must be alert to uncovering them when they are not presented by the couple. In some cases, the uncovering process is as easy as asking how much and how often they consume alcohol or what ever the interfering object/substance is. Depending upon the family background, and values, they may see their abusive drinking behavior, for example, as perfectly normal. In other cases, they will attempt to minimize or deny it.

Another serious impediment to a successful counseling relationship is triangulation by the partners with others outside of the marriage. These can be well intended friends or relatives or a lover of one of the partners. If the precipitating crisis for counseling came from an affair of one of the partners, the type and length of the relationship and availability of the third person should be determined. These can be indices for the likelihood that one partner will be tempted to seek refuge at that person's residence when counseling is difficult or seemingly unsuccessful. The affair itself, however, is usually an expression of the discouragement in the marriage. Statistically, few of the "third party" persons ever enter into the lives of the partner even after a divorce. They definitely can be a factor, however, during this fragile time in the life of a struggling marriage.

The relative or friend who supports the partner against the other is also a problem. What both partners need are friends who support their efforts to be a couple and are willing to do so in a genuine loving way. As a consequence, the counselor may need to spend some time helping the couple identify such people and consider how to involve them in their social lives at this point in time. Some of these may be old mutual friends who were dropped as the relationship deteriorated, co-workers with common interests, church members looking for couples of like age, family life, or persons newly met through a recreational activity like dancing, card playing, or bowling. Such persons and couples can constitute a social support network for normalizing their relationship.

Life Style Assessment for Couples

Life style assessment and the interpretation of what this means in relation to their conflicts provides a nonthreatening pairing of beliefs, behaviors, and feelings. These pairings become the basis for new understandings, trying on new behaviors, and dissipating of negative feelings. As noted in Chapter 7, it provides a method for uncovering, for example, the views we hold about men, women, and the way that they relate to one another in resolving conflicts and meeting life tasks. This method provides a useful way of constructing the individual's unique patterns which can be made immediate, relevant, and concrete to a counselee.

The process followed includes the childhood family constellation and early recollections. In each case, the partner is present during the collection of data and interpretative observations of the counselor. This activity itself tends to diffuse some of the anxiousness of both parties and generally evokes some greater hopefulness. It may be one of the few truly cooperative, nonthreatening activities that they have done together in some time.

Prior to collecting the life style information, you may wish to ask each of the partners *to write on a piece of paper how their relationship would be made better if their partner were different in certain ways.* These should be shared with the counselor but not the partner until later in the interpretative phase of counseling. At the point when the counselor has enough insight to see the connection between the individual's life convictions and the "offending" behavior, then they, counselor and client, can disclose this to the observing partner.

Another technique described by Pew and Pew (1972), allows a quick assessment of trouble spots early in the counseling process. *Partners are asked, first to rate him/herself on seven areas of life tasks,* i.e., occupation/work, love and marriage, friendship, getting along with oneself, finding meaning in life, leisure and recreation, and parenting. They do this using a scale of 1 to 5 with 1 as high. *Next, partners are asked to indicate where they believe their partner would rate them in each of the areas.* This results in three rating for each person. These are plotted on a paper or board for all to see.

The discrepancies as well as agreements become the focus of attention. Depending upon the couple and circumstances, this technique can be used to have partners rate other areas such as coping with finances, in-laws, or spiritual issues.

THE CASE OF NEL AND MARK

Mark and Nel came for counseling after referral by their pastor. He had talked with them and concluded that they would benefit from a professional counselor's assistance. Mark was wary and not altogether communicative. Nel was obviously distraught and very tense. Early in the first session a disclosure was made that Mark had had an affair with a woman where he worked. The woman did not work near him and had changed shifts since Nel had confronted Mark with her suspicions. Nevertheless, Nel was not sure that it was really over or simply waiting to start again.

When asked how their relationship would be better if their partner were different, Mark wrote that Nel would be more fun to be with if she was less bossy and less task oriented. Nel said that she would like for Mark to be more responsible and more sensitive to her feelings and desires. Based upon what had been said, the counselor was inclined to think that Mark was the initiator and Nel was only now realizing the potential loss of their relationship.

The need for structure and encouragement to help them get unstuck from the emotionally draining dialogues which had been continuing for the last several days seemed evident. Prior to beginning life style assessment, a revealing procedure is to have the couple describe a typical day. The counselor listened for cues as to how roles were structured, unspoken rules, and ways of relating to one another, children, co-workers, in-laws, and similar things. These helped the counselor develop notions about the unconscious goals and movement of each partner in this relationship as well as how external influences maybe important. This was the counselor's first opportunity to assess the possibility of later family counseling including in-laws when their influence impinges on the success of the marriage.

This was a tension relieving activity for the couple, both of them got involved and showed some evidence of cooperation. As will be revealed a little later, the counselor's hunches about the priorities of this couple were corroborated by the life style assessment.

As the life style assessments progressed, both Mark and Nel became engrossed in the process itself and let down their defenses. Occasional laughter came into the telling of childhood stories, recalling friends, relating family situations, and supplying other information requested in the assessment process.

Mark was a youngest child. he had been doted by his mother and taken care of by his sometimes reluctant sisters. Two of his recollections:

> I remember Beth (+4 years), my oldest sister, telling me that I'd have to wait until Mom got home to get my dessert. When she wasn't looking, I got it anyway. I thought, I'm old enough to get my own dessert. I felt good. I don't think she ever knew that I got it.

I remember Beth and Nancy (+2 years) holding my hands between them. We were going somewhere and I didn't want to go. They held on tight and dragged me along. I didn't like it and they knew it, too!

Mark is telling us a lot about his approach to life and his priorities. Adler characterized four types of number one priorities: **ruling, getting, avoiding,** and **socially useful.** Not to be confused with categorizing, they offer one way of attempting to understand the dominate themes in an individual's life. The counselor revealed to Mark that what he perceived and decided was "I should get what I want, when I want it and not before!" or words to that effect (Mark smiled agreement).

Building on the prior theme, the counselor continued, "No woman can stand in my way of getting what I want". Nel could not resist saying that this had certainly been true in their relationship. What may be a surprise to some people, Mark was not defensive about this, indeed, he was proud of it! For him, it was true, so what's wrong with that?

You might guess by now that Nel was an oldest child. She had a younger brother, Bill, by four years. Both had a special position within their family. While she had helped with her brother, she had not considered it a problem. He was "a pretty nice little kid" and aside from getting into her stuff sometimes, he really was kind of fun to have around.

Now for a couple of her recollections:

> One evening, Billy was suppose to be helping me do something in the kitchen, as it turned out, I think I did all the work but I remember he was so funny clowning around that I didn't mind.

> One Sunday we were at church and I remember the minister talking to my mother and father out on the front steps. It was a lovely day. The grass was green, the trees were in bloom (it must have been Spring), the sun was shining, everything was just great. And I remember overhearing the minister say what a delightful little girl I was, how fortunate my parents were to have a child so

responsible that she could go to the adult church and never be noticed. My parents agreed and I know that it made them feel really good. Me, too.

Interpretation

Without getting into a great deal of detail, we can already do some guessing about this relationship. Unless, for example, it was a family value to go to church in Mark's family, guess where he would resist "being dragged" by Nel? This guess was on target and both were fascinated by this small insight. It had been a bone of contention between them since the early days of their marriage. We also can guess who has taken on the responsible and "pleasing" role within this family, Nel, of course.

Mark, on the other hand, is suppose at least to come home and help lighten up the weary work environment of the home and provide some entertainment. Nel readily acknowledged, if there was to be any fun or social activity, it was up to Mark to be the "social director." He, however, tired of this expectation. At this point, they were invited to share what was on their, "how our relationship would be different list". With a little prompting, both could see how Nel's preoccupation with being "responsible," "seen but not heard" and in charge of "pleasing" were heavy burdens and impediment to their relationship.

While Mark had married Nel because she was pleasing, responsible, and so forth, he didn't like her bossiness when he came home. She countered that a little help around the house and with the kids could make it possible for her to be less bossy. At this point, I intervened to ask if they would like to do something about it. This redirected the energy and we began to move into the next phase of the counseling process.

This is not a lock step process, however. Many more insights were gained from the family constellation, images each developed about how men and women behave toward one another, how they had learned either to cooperate and collaborate or merely cohabitate, how they handled disagreement, conflict, and the like. Likewise, these and other early recollections provided additional useful insights. And throughout the process of counseling, we would occasionally refer back to the life style material.

Reorientation

Reorientation is the process of reframing old outlooks and attitudes such that they produce new and better feelings and behavior. The case of Mark and Nel is used to illustrate reorientation.

For Mark's, we had to confront the mistaken, adversarial role he assigned to women in general, and Nel in particular. An interesting aside to Mark's insight was the realization that a recurring difficulty that he had with a woman coworker was rooted in his private logic about women. In relation to Nel, helping him to gain intrinsic satisfaction in a role as helpmate and willing companion was going to take time. On the other hand, the trust that Nel had lost in him was to be regained only after some emotionally, soul searching experience. Time and deliberate effort were necessary for these and more to be accomplished.

Adlerians have observed that couples tend to be attracted by patterns. For example, if one partner is concerned with power, the other will be concerned with control or one in pleasing and the other in comfort and being served (Kefir & Corsini, 1974). In this case, Nel and Mark could see that each of them had contributed to the growing discontent with their marriage. Nel was clearly tired of the domestic role alone, and yet it was comfortable to her and a lot safer than stepping outside of the home. She had felt satisfied in pleasing Mark and her children.

Now Nel was needed less by the children and Mark was not happy with her efforts to please him. Mark could be a source of support and encouragement. This was to be a new role for him as Nel had always been the one to listen to his concerns at work, plans for promotion, and so forth. For the first time in a long time, and maybe ever, Mark and Nel were going to collaborate on working toward mutual goals. Until now, each contributed to the household by performing different tasks in conjunction with different people, using different resources, and on different time schedules. Each succeed in their own endeavors with the cooperation but not necessarily collaboration of their partner.

Mark meets people easily. One of his contributions was to help Nel learn to do the same for herself. Nel agreed that she would like to "lighten up" and be able to enjoy more recreational time with friends as a couple. She also expressed a desire to take an adult continuing education course to see how that would do for finding new activities outside of the home. Mark acknowledged that he would work alongside Nel to get evening chores done so that they could have more quality time together.

In the process of counseling, Nel had willingly characterized herself as "Super Mom." While that image served her purposes previously, she was ready to take off the proverbial cape (and apron, too!) to see herself as a person, not as one in a perfectionistic stereotypic role. One assignment which they, like many couples found difficult but necessary to their relationship, was dialogue/communication time. Many variations may occur on this as a method but the goals are the same, to establish or reopen authentic communications between the partners.

One recommendation to a couple is to establish a *mutually agreed upon time to share feelings* about anything that they care to share. One way to do this is by one person talking first for a fixed time such as fifteen to thirty minutes without response from the partner. The partner then talks an equal amount of time. They alternate who starts first each time. A variation on this is to have *partners write a letter to each other*, to share the letters, and then to dialogue on the messages in each letter for a specified period of time. Topics of the letters can be suggested by the counselor until the couple catches on and can create their own.

Because the purposes of these activities are to increase intimacy and to cultivate better communication skills, the counselor will need to **teach or review basics of such communication.** For example, when attempting to communicate feelings, the person should learn to use feeling vocabulary such as is found in Chapter 5. A quick technique for descriminating between "feeling" and "thinking" communication is by substitution of the word "think" for the word "feel" in the sentence. If the sentence makes good sense, then it is not a "feeling" communication. For example:

Not a feeling communication;

I feel that we should stop pointing out each others faults!

I think that we should stop pointing out each others faults!

A feeling communication;

I feel so hurt everytime you say something ugly in front of our friends!

I think so hurt everytime you say something ugly in front of our friends!

The use of **I-Messages** described in Chapter 5 are also an important addition to many couples communications skills. These can be reinforced by participation of such couples in **marital group counseling** or, as they have a stable foundation, in **marriage enrichment groups.**

The counselor can be a resource and/or direct assistance in many other topical areas. These include child rearing attitudes and practices, financial management strategies, coping with in-laws, former spouses, blending families, and encouraging career and other life planning. The foundation for all of these are basic life coping strategies. Conflict resolution, democratic decision making, and encouragement techniques such as found in other chapters of this book are fundamental to the repertoire of successful couples.

On the other hand, the counselor must be prepared to let go of the relationship as the goal of counseling when and if separation or divorce become clear as the goal of one or both of the partners. In these cases, the process of coping with all that moving apart entails will be important. Both parties will have emotional, social, physical, and financial challenges before them. In the event children are part of the family, they, too, will have need of support, encouragement, and ideas of how to cope.

Of course, many issues will need to be considered related to legal separation and divorce which are beyond the scope of this chapter. The book by Kranitz (1987), *Getting Apart Together,* is an excellent example of an Adlerian type approach to dissolution by couples who agree to cooperate at least in separation. Dreikurs said that it takes an agreement to have a fight. If a couple can see that turning the agreement to cooperation, at least for the purpose of minimizing hurt to themselves, their children, careers, and other aspects of their lives, then they may learn from this experience what they never could learn when they were together.

Even in separation and divorce, some good can come from the experience which can follow them into another relationship. This is an important point to understand for partners intent upon ending the relationship. The relationship most often has a life of its own beyond the legal termination. Emotionally, financially, and familywise, when children are involved, partners continue to experience the presence of the old relationship. The longer the marriage or relationship, the deeper, more long lasting the impressions and memories. As a consequence. the more "unfinished" business of an emotional nature is sorted out and directly confronted, the better off both partners will be in the future.

SUMMARY

Adlerian counseling has an essential ingredient within it that all marriages require: hopefulness. Without hope, no successful marriage counseling can occur. Hope can be cultivated with genuine, uncompromising encouragement. The business of counseling persons in troubled relationships is challenging and fraught with pitfalls. In spite of one's very best effort, the ultimate responsibility for the hope of success rests with the individual partners. Adlerian counselors strive to use all of their knowledge, skill, and caring to nurture whatever hope exists within the partnership. If the relationship changes from that of marriage or living together, still positive work can be done to help all of the parties involved to cope with the inevitable changes and adjustments.

STUDY QUESTIONS

DIRECTIONS: Respond to the following in the spaces provided.

1. Why does the author believe that Adlerian philosophy and methods related to marriage relationships are even more relevant today than in generations past?

2. What is meant by, "Love is an antecedent and by-product of a happy marriage?"

3. How can the fact that one got exactly what he/she wanted in a partner result in marital discord?

4. Why do you think Adlerians maintain an optimistic outlook when a marriage relationship may seem almost hopelessly lost?

CHAPTER 11

FAMILY COUNSELING AND CONSULTATION

Adlerians work in a variety of settings and deal with many kinds of problems, persons, and situations. Dreikurs noted on different occasions that no significant or unresolvable social problems would exist if persons had confidence in their own equality. Without the courage to be imperfect, small problems become large ones. He also taught that the issues which disagreeing parties bring to a counselor or consultant are most often not the real source of their difficulty. The major source of difficulty is most often who wins and who loses. Whatever the social conflict, who gets the upper hand or who loses respect is the hidden agenda in negotiations.

To solve conflicts requires an awareness of the hidden agenda and a strategy for establishing a new agreement in which no one wins or loses. For this reason, Dreikurs recommended four steps in problem solving:

1. Establish mutual respect, i.e., grant each the legitimacy of his/her stand.

2. Pinpoint the real issue(s), i.e., personal concerns about one's relative status or loss of it.

3. Change the agreement from one of fighting to a genuine concern for what the situation or task requires, i.e., the facts of the situation, what I am doing and how I can change my behavior to help provide for the welfare of others in the resolution of the problem situation.

4. All parties participate in making the decision, i.e., listen to each other, help each other, decide together how to solve our problems, and each assume responsibility for a part of the new agreement.

Adlerians, therefore, approach different social relationships, e.g., teacher-student, employer-employee, husband-wife, parent-child, with essentially the same problem-solving strategy. In addition, Adlerians tend not to make a distinction between counseling and consultation, per se. Whether a counselee or consultee, the individual involved will be conscious of the fact that how he/she thinks, feels, and acts are subject to influence and change as a part of the resolution of a situation. A definition of consultation, however, may be useful as a means of distinguishing between it and other methods of helping relationships.

Consultation involves three or more persons.

Adlerian consultation involves:

1. At least three persons, directly or indirectly; the consultant, consultee, and the consultee's clients, students, or children.

2. A problem or situation among persons which could benefit from a third party's view and expertise.

3. An equalitarian, collaborative relationship in which the consultee is free to accept, reject, or alter consultant suggestions.

4. The same facilitative conditions necessary in any helping relationship, e.g., genuineness, caring, empathy, and facilitative confrontation.

The consultant, then, is a third party who provides assistance on an ad hoc basis. The consultant's goal is to effectively share his/her knowledge and skills in such a way that further referral for similar concerns is no longer necessary.

Unlike counseling, the focus of attention in consultation tends to be directed more toward resolving conflicts with a person and a group (e.g., supervisor-supervisees) or between groups (whites and blacks, union-management). An exception, however, can be when the counselor consults with parents about how to cope more effectively with their children. Later in this chapter, such a case is illustrated. Distinctions between Adlerian counseling and consultation with parents about child rearing, therefore, tend to be more academically than clinically relevant.

ADLERIAN AND SYSTEMS THEORY

In the book *Family Therapy*, Nichols (1984) correctly noted that Adler and Dreikurs were among the earliest community group practitioners. Particularly noteworthy are Nichols' observations about Dreikurs' contributions to family therapy:

Dreikurs's technique with families combined emotional support and encouragement with interpretations and suggestions about modifying unhappy interactions. He encouraged families to discuss their mutual problems in an open, democratic spirit, and he urged them to institute regular "family council," in order to carry the model of family group therapy into the family's daily life.

Despite the fact that his approach anticipated many later developments in family therapy, Dreikurs work did not gain wide attention, nor did it have much influence on the field. . .he is one of those people who possess foresight and imagination, but whose ideas do not take hold because they are not developed in a receptive professional context. (p. 232)

Systems theory essentially builds on the idea that individuals influence and are influenced by the human *systems* within which they live and work. The systems proponents believe that the *identified patient* (IP) is simply an expression of a dysfuntional family of which the IP is a part. Depending upon which approach to systems theory one follows, the practitioners variously use communications methods, strategies to restructure family interaction, or techniques to help their counselees reframe their perceptions of the family dynamic.

These variations on systems offer a different and potentially complementary way of conceptualizing and intervening with families from an Adlerian perspective. While not developed as a systems approach, as noted by Nichols, Dreikurs preceded most of the current theorist-practitioners by several years. On the other hand, systems proponents like Minuchin (1974); Minuchin and Fishman 1981) have made contributions to family therapy from which Adlerians can benefit.

In Minuchin's approach, research has demonstrated particular effectiveness with family situations involving anorexia nervosa, adult drug addiction and similarly difficult to treat cases (Minuchin, Baker, Rosman, Liebman, Milman, & Todd, 1975; Minuchin, Rosman, & Baker, 1978; Stanton & Todd, 1979). Because structural theory and methods are well suited to comparison with Adlerian concepts and methods, a brief discussion follows.

Minuchin, like Dreikurs, worked in intercity, low income (slum) areas. He found that establishing rapport involved what came to be known as **joining** with the family. While not becoming a part of the family system (as some other theorists propose), Minuchin makes a quick assessment of whether the family is dysfunctional or simply transitional in the life cycle of a family, e.g., when children are born or leave home.

Like Adlerians, Minuchin prefers to have the entire family present in order to assess their here and now functioning. However, he has young children and the parents together. Rather than a distraction to the process, he sees the child-adult interactions as an essential part in the early assessment of the family's functioning. If he concludes that the family is disfunctional, he moves quickly to intervene as his assessment dictates. Like Adlerians, he is very conscious of **normal developmental** family concerns. He cautions others to be slow to categorize a family's functioning as dysfunctional. He accepts a broad range of coping behaviors and interactions as "normal", at least in light of stages and circumstances that a given family is facing.

One important tenet is related to what he terms **subsystems** within the family. If the mother-child subsystem is treated without consideration for its purpose in relation to the other subsystems (e.g., father-mother), then the intervention is not likely to result in a lasting change. Subsystems are elements of the family based upon function. Therefore, if the mother's goal is to maintain distance from the father or if the father is aligned against the mother with another child, presenting techniques such as **going to the bathroom** to sidestep excessive attention or power struggles (as Adlerians often do) will only address a part of the problem.

He believes that subsystems are circumscribed and regulated by emotional **boundaries.** Normal families have clear enough boundaries to protect individuals and the subsystems but all receive freedom for autonomy and mutual support as well. Interpersonal boundaries regulate the amount of contact with others. With not enough boundaries, individuation is hampered. With too much, individuals experience little or no emotional support.

With what he terms **enmeshed families,** the boundaries are diffused. Such families "smother" the individuality of its less powerful members. The enmeshed subsystem offers a heightened sense of mutual support but at the expense of autonomy. The challenge to the counselor is to help members of the family to think, feel, and behave independently. This is certainly consistent with Adlerian goals as well.

Disengaged families have rigid boundaries. These families have members who literally go their own way and "do their own thing". These members feel no loyalty, no support or commitment to the members of the family. Adlerians would move quickly to encourage family members toward greater emotional and related support. These are difficult families to help and Minuchin's techniques have been lacking with them as well (Nichols, 1984).

Having diagnosed a subsystem that works against a healthier environment for the family members, Minuchin attempts to restructure the family by activating dormant structures. For example, if he finds the mother and child in a subsystem distancing mother from the father, he may deliberately have the parents sit together and place the child at some distance away from them, possibly next to another family member or himself. He may ask the parents and children how this feels. He then reinforces the benefits of this arrangement and asks them to continue practicing until the feelings are comfortable.

Techniques like these are creatively developed to fit the situation. Then family members are encouraged to replicate these activities outside of the counseling office. An Adlerian counselor often recommends a discussion or counseling group for parents or couples to help deal with some of these issues.

Minuchin notes that family structure involves a set of **covert rules.** Like Adlerians, he brings these to the awareness of the family members to be examined. When necessary, these rules are exposed as counterproductive to the best interests of the family. Because they are covert, when left unexamined, they tend to be self-perpetuating.

While only speculative, I believe that Adler would have enjoyed exchanging points of view with Minuchin. Likewise, Adler would have been interested in the work of others as well. Unfortunately, the state of the art of family counseling is only beginning to reach the point where different proponents ideas are being crossed referenced with others. This also is true of Adlerians and systems approaches. However, the process has begun (Sherman & Dinkmeyer, 1987).

Adlerians will continue to follow the basic tenets of Adler. However, the value of extending the family history to include generational issues (e.g., history of alcoholism, person abuse, health conditions, and so forth); assessing the subsystems within the family beyond mother-father-child (which Dreikurs did as well); studying ethnicity as an influence on values, feelings, and behaviors both within the nuclear and new families; and, potentially, adopting specific techniques which further the work of assessment and intervention will merit consideration.

For those interested in an overview of systems theory, research and techniques, Nichols (1984) provides an excellent resource. He brought a personal point of view together with a good review of not only the concepts but the people who are their proponents as well.

UNDERLYING ASSUMPTIONS OF ADLERIAN CONSULTATION

Among the assumptions underlying the Adlerian consultation process are the following:

1. We are all in the same boat, i.e., we share common human frailities and assets and can benefit from this fact as we work together to overcome common problems. No one needs to act on feelings of inadequacy or compensatory superiority if he/she understands and accepts the human condition.

2. What is shared by the consultant is basically educative in nature, i.e., he/she is teaching a philosophy and process of social democracy in which the logic of social living is predicated upon the equality of persons. Techniques and methods help to establish this approach as a useful way of living together for all people. Pathology or abnormality is not assumed to be the source of difficulty nor is therapy the modus operandi.

3. What is required is a willingness of the consultee to consider changing his/her behavior and attitudes first, i.e., an acceptance of responsibility for helping to establish a new agreement.

4. While many of the recommendations generally are effective with certain types of problems, the consultant is prepared for the unexpected, e.g., most children respond to specific recommendations in a particular way but you can be equally sure that some will not and this, too, should be expected.

5. Encouragement is a keystone to the entire process. Attentiveness, friendliness, and general supportiveness are fundamental to the relationship. When recommendations are made, they are offered in a clear, concise manner without harsh evaluative implications that everything done before was wrong. In fact, the consultee is encouraged to build upon his/her strengths to help prescribe new alternatives to behaviors which he/she considers potentially more useful than others.

6. With proper consultation and desire by the consultees, they will make innovations upon the consultant's suggestions; and eventually, will function independently of the consultant quite successfully.

INTERVIEW

The one area in which Adlerians have had the most experience is adult and child relationships. Dreikurs (1971) did refer to other situations, including labor relations, in which he used Adlerian methods successfully as a consultant. Likewise, the author has used Dreikurs methods successfully as a consultant and workshop leader in business and organizational circumstances. The remainder of this chapter, however, will be devoted to illustrating Adlerian intervention primarily with parents and children.

From the author's experience, observations of demonstrations by other Adlerians, and descriptions of Rosenberg (1959), the following section outlines the major sequential stages of the interview. In this case, the illustration is based upon parent-child consultation. The family and marriage relationship are fundamentally healthy. As a consequence, rather than counseling the family, per se, the counselor functions as a consultant to the parents in helping them learn more effective attitudes and methods of working with the children.

With minor modifications, teacher-pupil examples could be used as well. Because demonstrations or large group participation are common with Adlerian methods, reference is made as to how this is taken into consideration by the counselor-consultant. A full, only partially edited, family interview is in Appendix A.

PROCESS STAGES

Establishing Rapport

Whether in the counselor's office or in a group setting such as a family education center, the counselor-consultant will be concerned at the beginning with helping to put parents at ease. Friendliness and sensitivity to the newness of a group situation for parents can reduce their apprehension early in the conference.

Generally Adlerians work with parents in a **group setting** only after parents have had one or more opportunities to observe a similar demonstration. In any case, **structuring statements** often are used to help establish ground rules for the group conference and to clarify the parents' expectations for the conference as well.

Because experience has shown that families have much in common concerning parent-child relationships, the counselor uses his/her knowledge and experience to dispel the notion that this family and these parents are more troubled or less competent than others. While being aware of and empathizing with the parent's concern, the counselor attempts to provide a new perspective on family living for them. If necessary, he/she helps to unite them with the larger body of parents who experience similar problems but also have begun to learn new methods for coping with problems.

Among the types of ground rules for a group setting consultation are the following:

1. Parents and children are invited to ask questions of the group as well as the counselor whenever they desire.

2. The group may ask questions or comment but the parents may choose not to respond and/or the counselor may intervene if he/she believes that is necessary.

3. Labeling, evaluating, or otherwise categorizing the family or its members into static terms is definitely avoided.

4. Support and encouragement from the group members is used whenever appropriate, i.e., to show solidarity, common concerns, validate usefulness of methods from others' experience, or help reduce distance among participants.

5. What is discussed with the family remains within the group although most of what is discussed will be behavior relatively public to others as well, i.e., neighbors, friends, and even strangers often know about the problems of a given family. On the other hand, respect and

even admiration can be shown best by limiting discussion or comments about the family to the group of which they are a part.

6. Questions or comments relating to others families are not discussed.

7. The method of teaching by demonstration is explained and the fact that therapy, per se, is not the orientation for helping is clarified if necessary.

Parent Interview

Once the preliminary aspects of the relationship are established, the counselor will begin by requesting information about the family constellation. This information requires a listing of the children by name, age, and sex, including any children who are deceased, stillborn, or miscarried. The latter information can be significant with respect to special or unusual treatment of living children.

Other children living in the same household or significant other adults with whom the children interact regularly may be noted. Grandparents, for example, who keep the children while mother and father work have a substantial influence upon the children.

Frequently, the mother will be seated nearest the counselor and will tend to answer the questions as they are asked. This may suggest that the mother is considered to be more responsible for the children. This is one reason why an effort should be made to include both parents in all phases of the process as much as possible. Fathers, obviously, can be be a very important part of any success with the children's development.

Some Adlerians take notes as they talk with the parents. If this is the case, a mention of the fact and how it is helpful in recalling important information may allay concerns the parents feel about this process. The counselor may decide in some cases to set his/her notes aside if they are a distraction.

Family constellation information is
essential in consultation.

Generally the parents are quite prepared to report their reasons for seeking assistance. One or more of the children are a source of difficulty and they feel unable to cope successfully with it any longer. On the basis of the initial family constellation information including birth order, the counselor may make a guess about the characteristics of one or more of the children after hearing the parent's description of the presenting problem. Based upon probabilities, the counselor often can determine who among the children:

1. Tries to please
2. Gets best grades
3. Helps out at home
4. Tries to be consid-
   erate
5. Is happy-go-lucky
6. Is cute
7. Gets own way easily

8. Demands own way
9. Is rebellious
10. Is critical of others
11. Is easily hurt, sensi-
    tive
12. Is bossy
13. Fights with whom
14. Takes care of whom

As we noted in Chapter 6, such guesses are based upon the experiences of many families. The value of guessing is twofold: (1) It tests a working hypothesis against that of the family being interviewed. If it is incorrect, better that it be discarded as early as possible; (2) It can be a source of interest and encouragement to the parents that a relative stranger already understands their family in just a short time.

Although some general descriptions of the problem that they confront can be helpful, Adlerians find reports of specific incidents necessary to an adequate understanding of the parent-child interaction. For example, parents give general reports such as the following:

1. The two oldest are fighting constantly.

2. Someone is doing poorly in school.

3. They won't help out around the house without a big hassle.

4. They won't obey even simple requests to get up in the morning, to do their homework, or to get ready for bed at night.

On the other hand, the Adlerians will request a description of specific situations, representative of the type most troublesome to the parents. Frequently these come from events of the last twenty-four hours. The following excerpt from a group session will help to illustrate this technique. The parent is a mother of three boys: Joe, 6; Bobby, 4 ½; and Kevin, 2 ½ years.

Parent: I've been trying everything I know to get them to help out around the house but nothing seems to really work—even bribes of things I know they really want. Now they even talk back to me when I try to straighten out their fights . . .

Counselor: It's really discouraging to be trying your best and see things getting worse. . .could you give me specific examples of some incidents that have happened recently. . .

Parent: Well yes, uh, just this afternoon they started fighting over who could wear what coat as we were getting ready to come over here. . .

Counselor: Okay, what exactly did they do. . .just tell us how you remember the situation at the time. . .

Parent: Well, I was working in the kitchen when I heard the boys beginning to get into a fight. Evidently Joe was trying to help Kevin with his coat and Bobby felt that something was not being done properly. The next thing I knew, Bobby was shouting at Joe and they were getting into a fist fight. I went into the hallway to see what was happening and proceeded to scold the boys for the noise and their fighting. At this point,

Bobby turned to me and said that I had no right to stick up for them when he was the one who needed help. He promptly ran upstairs and began crying.

Counselor: So when the fight started, you found yourself going to find out what was happening. Bobby felt that you were interfering on behalf of the other boys. How were you feeling at that point?

Parent: Well, I was angry at first, but then I was shocked by his turning on me like that. I found myself feeling a little bad, like maybe I had jumped in too soon and made the assumption that he was the trouble maker.

Counselor: How did the other two boys react when Bobby ran upstairs crying?

Parent: Well, they just went on getting themselves dressed and didn't seem to bother too much about it.

Counselor: Do you have any other situations that are troublesome to you that we might be able to help you with?

Parent: Well, every morning I myself going through a routine of trying to get the boys up before their father gets off to work and I have to get down to the kindergarten with Joe. Generally, Joe's not too bad to get up in the morning, but he can be awfully slow about getting dressed. In fact, all three of them are quite a problem to get organized in the morning. I find that Joe will often try to help with his brother but it only becomes a fight because Bobby doesn't want to be helped and. . .well, that's only part of the problem because the boys don't like to have the same kind of breakfasts. Some mornings, I can make pancakes, and Bobby and Joe will be quite satisfied but the baby will want something besides what I fixed or I'll scramble eggs and Joe won't like the eggs and Bobby will eat all the eggs. . . and I just find that if it's not one thing it's another.

Counselor: So, from the time you get up in the morning, the boys begin a routine that manages to keep you pretty busy.

Parent: They sure do.

Counselor: Well, I think maybe we can help to get you out of that situation. We find that many families like yours start out with disagreements in the morning, some of which are small in nature, but nevertheless an aggravation. Sometimes these aggravations are more intense, and, as a result, becomes more important to us as we try to smooth out some of the bumps in daily living. I wonder how many parents here in the group have had similar problems to that described by our mother this morning. (At this point, the counselor turns to the members of the group who are observing.) I see we have several people here who evidently share some of the same problems that you have experienced with your boys.

Opportunities to bring the parents and group participants closer together are always important. It reduces the distance in such a way that the parents no longer feel self-conscious or concerned about the fact that they are the center of attention.

After the parents have had an opportunity to explain the concerns that they have for which they have come to this conference, the counselor generally will invite them to **describe the happenings of a typical day** in their family. This description begins with a report of getting up in the morning and how the day is typically started.

In most families, we find that the "good" mother is the servant par excellence. She is the first or one of the first persons to arise in the morning. It befalls her to begin waking up the younger members of the family, to prepare breakfast for the morning, and lunches as well. In the families such as the one we have just described, it's not uncommon for the mother also to be concerned about laying out the children's clothes, seeing that they have brushed their teeth, that they have their lunches, books, and other paraphernalia ready for starting school. For the youngster who's staying home, it's a matter of getting him/her ready for the day, including possibly an outing where he/she is entertained by the mother.

The typical day may be different to some degree for each family, but also it usually involves the children coming from school, leaving their materials, clothing, and other items wherever they find themselves as they enter the house, proceeding outside to play with friends and potentially coming in late for supper. This might be followed with some discussion and reminders about getting their homework done, preparing for bed, and finally, for the last hour of the day, hassling over going to sleep and being quiet. Most families experience these circumstances to a greater or lesser degree at any given time. It's when these become persistent and augmented by frequent fights, evidences of lying, stealing, or similar behaviors that parents seek consultation.

After the major aspects of a typical day have been covered, the counselor should have a fairly clear idea of (1) which parent feels responsible for the children, (2) what goals of misbehavior the children pursue, (3) what behavior the parents might be willing to change initially, and (4) which procedures to offer as alternatives to the children. If it is not already clear, the counselor might ask the parents if they would like to work on some particular behavior related to the children. The use of encouragement and humor (Mosak, 1987), if appropriate, can be very helpful in expressing confidence in the parents' ability and judgement. The counselor should not press for goals beyond the willingness of the parents to be consistent.

If resistance is encountered, often it helps to identify one recommendation that they would be willing to try for a week. This can be facilitated by asking, "Has what you've been trying worked? Have you anything to lose by trying this for one week?"

While the parents may have some doubts about the new recommendations, they are just as ready to admit that what they have been doing has not worked. This being the case, the parents realize that not trying something new will in all probability not change the situation, so why not give it a try?

The counselor might ask the parents if they know how the children are likely to respond in the interview situation. They also might speculate on whether the children know why they are coming in for the interview and how they are likely to respond to recommendations which have been discussed. In those instances when older children or adolescents are involved, the counselor may wish to indicate to the parents that suggestions by the youngsters may modify to some degree the goals and methods which have been discussed already. Unless the parents have further questions or comments, this portion of the conference ends and the parents are excused in order to allow the youngsters their opportunity to meet with the counselor.

Children Interview

As in the case of the parents, the counselor will note who among the children comes first, who leads and/or speaks first, and who supports whom among the children as they begin their discussion with the counselor. It's important for the counselor to realize that children deserve the same respect that we show for their parents. As a consequence, the counselor will talk with the youngster and not at them. The counselor will encourage the audience not to be overly impressed with the small size of the little children, or to any overt signs of fear and discomfort.

Persons not familiar with Adlerians psychology occasionally are critical of the seemingly adultlike expectations which the counselor holds for the children. Normally this direct, adultlike approach is accepted by even very young children. Baby talk or talking down to children is definitely not Adlerian. On the other hand, the same empathy and attentiveness shown to the parents is exhibited with the children. Being distant or otherwise stern with the children would be a misuse of this approach.

Putting the youngsters at ease, then, is the first order of business. With very young children, even getting names and ages may be a bit of a problem if a group of adults surround them. On the other hand, they usually forget their concerns quite readily and join in the discussion at the first opportunity.

An early question asked of the youngsters is, "Do you know why you are here? . . . Do you want to guess? (or say more about that?)" Generally the youngsters do know why they have come for this conference but may be reluctant to admit it. For this reason, the counselor may volunteer why the parents have chosen to come in for the conference. Then the counselor may say, "Do you know what your parents say about the problems this causes? . . . (you may tell them) . . . Do you feel that way too?" The counselor then may inquire about their feelings and attitudes concerning their parents' behavior toward them.

Youngsters can identify what
behaviors bother their parents.

Much to the surprise of many parents, the children understand the ground rules of family living quite well. For example, the youngsters usually know exactly how many times mother must call before they are to get up in the morning. In other cases, they realize that the inflection in the voice or choice of words is what determines when mother is at her wit's end. Equally important, the youngsters can discern when their fights are aggravating the parents even though they may not be in the same room. When asked what behaviors bother the parents most, the youngsters identify them without hesitation. This is not to suggest that the youngsters have consciously planned and plotted every one of their activities. Quite the contrary, they, too, operate very much on a day-to-day, moment-by-moment basis. On the other hand, when given the opportunity to examine their behaviors in relation to their parents, they have little difficulty identifying the key factors in their relationships.

After the youngsters and the counselor have had an opportunity to become acquainted, the counselor may ask, "Do you know why you do what you do? . . . Would you like to know what I think? . . . could it be . . .? The counselor has established some hypothesis about the goals of misbehavior for the children. He/she will have identified some specific behaviors which help to illustrate this point. On occasion, youngsters will not immediately recognize the significance of their behavior by a simple statement related to its goal. On the other hand, when given two or three instances which help to illustrate this point, the youngsters cannot resist a recognition reflex (smile) or other evidence which validates the counselor's observation.

The following excerpt can help to illustrate how this process takes place.

Counselor: Boys, I wonder if you know why you're here today? . . . Do you know why your parents have brought you down here with them today?

Joe: I think they don't like the fact that we fight.

Counselor: Well, Joe, that's very good. As a matter of fact that is one thing they had on their minds. Can you think of anything else?

Joe: (Shakes his head "no.")

Counselor: What about you, Bobby? Can you think of some things that your parents might want to talk to us about?

Bobby: (Shakes his head "no.")

Counselor: And what about you, Kevin?

Kevin: (Has his thumb in his mouth and is looking off at members of the group.)

Counselor: Do you boys feel that fighting is a problem for you?

Boys: (Nod their heads "yes")

Counselor: Are there any other things you feel your mother is concerned about?

Bobby: Mama doesn't like to get us up in the morning.

Counselor: Oh, I see . . . Is that a problem, too? (Bobby nods his head.) Are there any other things that you feel have been a problem for your family? (Boys seem uncertain.) Do you know why you do the things that you do? (Boys shake their heads "no.") Would you like to know what I think? (The boys nod their heads "yes.") Could it be that you like to keep Mom busy, and like Mom to know that you'll do things when you want to do them? (Both boys smile a little, and the younger one begins to pay attention.) Can you think of times when you managed to keep your mom pretty busy and also have your own way, too?

Bobby: I don't get to have my own way. In fact, I don't get to have my way at all.

Counselor: I see. You feel that you're the only one in the family who doesn't get to have his way. Life is just not fair to you . . . I wonder, Bobby, could it be that you'd rather be right than have your own way sometimes in order to let people know how unfair they've been?

Bobby: (Shakes his head tentatively "no.")

Counselor: I wonder . . . you might want to think about that, Bobby. Could it be that when Joe and Kevin are getting their way, you'd rather complain about not getting your way so that you can make mother feel bad, like she's done something wrong? Could that be? (Bobby looks on.) I think, Bobby, there must be satisfaction for you sometimes in seeing your mother uncomfortable and feeling that she's wrong and you know that she's wrong. What do you think about that? (Bobby smiles and nods his head "yes.") Tell me, Bobby, what would be more important to you, having your own way more often, or having the satisfaction of knowing that your mother was mistaken and that you know she was wrong?

Bobby: Having my own way more often.

Counselor: Well, that certainly is a possibility, Bobby, but it's for you to decide; and it may be hard, because sometimes in the past you've had some real satisfaction from knowing that your mother was wrong. Am I right? (Bobby nods his head "yes.") Would you boys like some help in changing some of the problems in your family?

**Bobby and
Joe:**   Yes.

Counselor: And what about you, Kevin? Would you like to see some things different in your family, too?

Kevin: (Nods his head "yes" also.)

The counselor then explains to the boys some alternatives which had been discussed with the parents. The boys are given an opportunity to discuss how they think it will help to improve their situation at home. In some cases, working out details with the children, for example, about getting themselves up in the morning, allows the counselor to ask them, "Do you think your parents will agree?" Such questions can help the counselor assess mutual confidence between the parents and children. it is also an indication to them of how people begin to improve their relationships. With young children, the counselor may conclude by summarizing aspects of what is to follow at home, indicating when they will return, and generally expressing friendliness and encouragement.

The counselor may express thanks to the youngsters for talking before the group if that is appropriate. As was true with the parents, the youngsters will have been given the opportunity before the conference to volunteer that they would be willing to speak before the group.

Consolidation

For the parents of young children, the remainder of the conference will be conducted without the presence of the youngster. When teenagers are involved, they frequently are included in the wrap-up session. This session is an opportunity to review behavioral goals and recommendations upon which agreement has been reached. It is also an opportunity to answer questions which the parents or youngsters may have. Details of how, when, and where the next conference will be held also should be covered. Comments from the group might be in order if they have had experience with the recommendations which the family is preparing to implement. Such responses often provide encouragement and general support to the family as evidence that they, like others, have it within their capability to make changes in a positive direction.

TYPICAL RECOMMENDATIONS

Because certain family situations are so common, Adlerians have found that many of the same recommendations are effective for different families. For example, among the recommendations which have been found to reduce the number of hassles in the family are the following.

Alarm Clock

Many families have discovered that one of the finest inventions of all time is the alarm clock. This is due in no small part to the fact that even young children can learn to set the alarm in the evening in order to get themselves up in the morning. Contrary to what many parents expect, children appreciate the fact that they are given the responsibility for taking care of themselves in the morning. This is a very basic way to demonstrate that the children can assume responsibility.

The parents often will feel that the youngster will sleep-in, in spite of the alarm clock. This action is not normally the case. In the event that it should happen, however, parents should be instructed to allow the consequences of the youngsters' behavior to follow just as it would if they had slept in. If the youngsters normally get themselves up but sleep over one morning because of a particularly late activity the night before, there certainly would be no reasons for not awakening them as one might do for a friend. The only concern would be with not establishing a pattern or expectancy that sleeping in is all right because someone else will take care of us.

Dress Before Breakfast

Many parents are surprised to find that a very simple change in the ground rules in the morning can save them a great deal of time and hassle. An illustration of this might be helpful:

> One mother reported that her five-year old son, Frank, was the last one to be dressed every morning. Because mother worked outside of the home, this presented a number of problems. The other children managed to get themselves dressed and come down for breakfast, but Frank would linger until the very last minute and then finally require that mother get him dressed. As a consequence, the mother would be late getting to work.

> After two or three evenings of discussing chapters in *Children the Challenge*, members of the group suggested that she might wish to consider a new ground rule for their family. The new ground rule was simply this: All members of the family, including Frank, would be expected to get dressed before breakfast in the morning. The logic of this was that mother was busy making breakfast and preparing for the remainder of the day while Frank should be getting dressed. If Frank was unable to get dressed, then it would be necessary for mother to help him, which took time from her day. The result would be that Frank would not have breakfast and would be going to the nursery without breakfast. This would be explained to the nursery teacher in the event that this should be necessary.

> The following week the mother returned to the discussion group quite delighted to report that Frank had gotten himself in the habit of dressing before breakfast in the morning. This did not happen the first morning however. The evening of the parent discussion group, the mother had tucked Frank into bed and said, "We will

have a new rule in the morning. It will be necessary for everyone to be dressed for breakfast in order that I can go about my chores, too."

The next morning Frank arrived in his pajamas as he had so many mornings before. The mother said nothing to Frank and he simply sat and waited for his breakfast to be served. The other children began eating and Frank received no breakfast. Shortly after sitting for a time, he proceeded to go back upstairs and returned with his pants and shirt on but no socks and shoes. He waited again for breakfast to be served and still no breakfast was served. During this time the mother said nothing.

Frank then proceeded up the stairs again and came back down with one sock and shoe on but not the others. It was again a short period of time and Frank was back upstairs, whereupon he returned completely clothed. He had to rush, but he did get his breakfast. The mother reported that every morning since he has dressed himself before breakfast.

The success was largely to the mother's credit that she did not remind Frank or in any way make a fuss over the fact that he had done what was expected of him. Many other examples could be sited in which the same recommendation was used and worked just as effectively.

No Reminders

What becomes increasingly obvious to the person using Adlerian methods is that a lack of effectiveness of recommendations is almost directly proportional to the amount of talking the parents do with the youngsters about a behavior. Parents have a tendency to want to talk about the aggravations that come about as a result of the youngsters' behavior, both past and present. An important lesson to be learned by all adults who work with children concerns the value of silence. Allowing the reality of consequences to operate is the key.

Although children have clocks and watches, parents are often in the position of being timekeepers. They remind the youngsters that it's time to get up, it's time for breakfast, it's time to get ready for school, it's time to put away their materials, it's time to study, it's time to stop watching TV, it's time to do the dishes, it's time to get ready for bed, it's time to go to bed, and it's time to go to sleep. In one parent discussion group of this author's experience, the group determined that a mother of five children was spending approximately twenty-nine hours a week telling her children what to do. Principal among the activities was reminders of when it was time for the children to accomplish the various items listed previously.

So the new rule is, no reminders. If there is an understanding of when it's time to get up, to go to school, to eat supper, and to go to bed parents of even young children may avoid the problem of having to remind them several times. Adults in the family can provide a routine and order which is very helpful to the children. The logic of the routine and order is based in no small part upon the social activities in which the family is engaged.

Generally no one needs to explain that the school bus arrives at a certain time, or that father or mother have to be at work at a given time, once the pattern is established. Equally so, if regular eating time and a regular time to go to bed has been established, then the parents will not need to continually remind members of the family. The logical and natural consequences which follow from one's behavior should be the source of learning. Persons interested in practical applications of this principle will find Dreikurs and Grey (1968) and Dreikurs et al. (1971) very helpful.

Bedtime

Bedtime is one of the most common problem periods for children and parents alike. Parents sometimes bribe the children to be good when they have company, or in other cases, threaten them with punishment of the severest sort. Unfortunately, these work some of the time, but certainly not all the time. As a result, the parents have a tendency to resort to them periodically with the hope and expectation that they might work again. This simply plays into the youngsters' expectations that if they apply themselves diligently, they can have what they want when they want it.

In most cases, the consultant can help the parents and children reach a new agreement about the time that the youngsters should go to bed. Upon agreeing that the time is satisfactory to both the parents and the youngsters, the youngsters will be responsible for getting themselves ready for and into bed. For the children who cannot tell time, the parent simply mentions the time without particular reference to going to bed. Once bedtime has passed, however, the parents are instructed to ignore completely any of the behavior of the youngsters which demand their time or attention. Another illustration from parent discussion groups might be helpful:

> The father of three youngsters was having difficulty with the youngest girl going to bed at night. She was four years old and, as a consequence, aware of when the other children were going to bed and when she should be going to bed also. She would slip out of bed when the lights were out and the parents were back downstairs to go about whatever activities they had before the evening was completed. At these times, she would talk to father and mother about things that they were doing or things that she had done during the day that would peak their interest in what she was saying. Usually the parents would tell her to go back upstairs and begin to ignore her behavior. However, she was quite persistent and, as a consequence, normally ended up having one or the other of the parents carry her upstairs.

> As is true of many families, the parents had tried many methods but had not been consistent in any of them. So it was recommended to the father that on the next occasion of the youngster getting out of bed, he and the mother ignore the daughter when she came downstairs.

> He reported at the next meeting of the group that the daughter had indeed come down that very next night and proceeded to talk to him while he tried to

complete some work that he had that evening. His wife was a teacher also and was grading papers. The daughter went from one to the other until she found that she was getting no satisfaction. She remained up for approximately forty minutes, alternately making distracting noises, playing and attempting to bring attention to herself.

The next evening, she came downstairs and tried even more persistently to distract her father. At one point, without saying a word, the father pointed to the room and went back to his work. The girl immediately returned to her room and that was the last evening that she got out of bed. What is noteworthy is that while the father did give an indication that he was aware of her presence, he said nothing. He simply emphasized that this was not the time for play or talk.

In instances such as this one, when the parents are advised to ignore the children, they are also informed that a very important aspect of the plan is for opportunities at other times to talk and play and generally have fun together. The parents can be important contributors to pleasantness during those times of day when the family members are all present. Very often, during breakfast in the morning, dinner in the evening, and just prior to bedtime, the parents can inject humor, pleasantness, and a general appreciation for each member of the family.

Establishing New Agreements

While the situation comes in many forms, the consultant often finds him/herself helping to negotiate new agreements between the warring parties in the family. Parents and children alike need to learn ways for resolving differences. As has been noted before, even when a conflict exists an agreement also exists. In fact, without an agreement, no conflict can occur.

Therefore, many of the recommendations involve a negotiation between the parents and the children. For example, at bedtime they can establish an understanding about what is a reasonable expectation for time, each others' role, and the advantages of such a change. Based upon this agreement, all parties know what is expected of them and generally act accordingly.

Another frequent problem of parents is establishing a satisfactory arrangement with respect to the children doing their homework. Often, parents believe they know what the best solution is for children. Time and again, however, children surprise their parents, when in the course of discussion with the consultant, children propose alternative ways of handling the homework situation which turn out to be quite satisfactory and even more effective than what parents had imagined. Building confidence in the children's ability to understand the problem and to propose solutions is one of the greatest lessons of the consultation process.

Very often children will recommend, for example, that on certain evenings they be given the option of completing their homework after they've had a chance to play with their friends. On other evenings, because of certain television programs that they especially like, they prefer to do their homework when they arrive home and then play for as long as time will permit before the television programs begin. Experiencing success with their solution becomes a significant source of satisfaction.

Helping with chores around the house is handled in a similar way. The children want to indicate that they have good sense and can determine when things need to get done. For this reason, when given the opportunity to decide when the dishes should be completed, when the garbage should be taken out, or when the grass should be cut, their attitude toward getting the job done changes and they find it much more agreeable to be contributing members of the family.

WHEN RECOMMENDATIONS FAIL

Frequently, parents will report that certain recommendations did not work for them. On such occasions the consultant should determine exactly what transpired in the situation to which the parent refers. Generally certain conditions have contributed to the recommendations's not succeeding. Some of the most common factors for the consultant to note are discussed within the balance of this section.

Talking

As noted earlier, adults have a tendency to talk too much and at the wrong time. When trying to utilize advantages of natural and logical consequences, parents must learn to not talk and to not draw attention to the fact that they are aware a youngster is experiencing the outcome of an ill-advised act. The most obvious example of this is the "I told you so" comment which many adults feel compelled to insert whenever they gain the satisfaction of having the upper hand. Such remarks only deepen the conflict and increase the probability that the youngster will learn how to get back when he/she has the opportunity.

The following example is taken from the case of a mother whose daughter, a teenager, was using her mother as a bus service. In this case, the mother demonstrates unusual patience and an awareness of the importance of not talking at important times. As a result, both she and the daughter learned a very important lesson.

Karen basically got along well with her family and friends. Her mother did have concern, however, that Karen was increasingly depending upon her as a source of transportation to school and other functions. The mother realized that Karen could not drive, but she was beginning to resent the fact that Karen would take advantage of her at times when it was not necessary. This contributed to words between the mother and daughter and was a source of increasing tension in other matters which were of lesser consequence. The mother did not work and felt that she was obligated to help Karen even though it was sometimes inconvenient for her.

The recommendation to the mother was simply that she give consideration to Karen as she would to any friend. When the mother found it not convenient or not in the best interest for Karen to have a ready taxi driver, the mother was simply to allow the consequences of Karen's behavior to follow as it might for a friend who had not planned sufficiently in advance.

The next week Karen was up late one night and slept in the next morning and missed her school bus. When this happened previously, the mother had rushed to get dressed and hurried to get the girl to school on time. On this particular morning, however, the mother decided to finish reading the newspaper and have a second cup of coffee. The girl stood by in disbelief until she finally went outside, slamming the door behind her, and sat in the automobile. The mother proceeded to straighten up the kitchen as she normally would before she left the house. As she approached the car, she could tell that Karen was quite upset with her.

On the way downtown, the mother mentioned that she had an appointment this morning and would be a little late unless she kept to her schedule. They conversed about one or two matters that concerned Karen and activities for the coming week. Because the traffic was heavy, the mother asked Karen to walk the last few blocks to school in order that she would not have to get out of the main flow of traffic. Karen looked surprised but agreed somewhat reluctantly.

That evening during supper, the mother found herself in a conversation with Karen about the events of the day. The mother reported that she caught herself just as she began to ask Karen if she had made it to school on time. The next morning, Karen was on time for the school bus and nothing was said about that particular incident.

The mother found that on subsequent occasions when Karen needed a ride she asked her mother well in advance. The mother found this much more agreeable and was inclined whenever she could without feeling resentment or, in other cases, guilty when she did not.

Inconsistency

Inconsistency in following through with recommendations of the counselor is another problem found in learning to apply Adlerian methods. This is why the counselor will attempt to insure that parents not only understand the recommendations but also are prepared to continue them in the event that recommendations should not be effective when initially applied.

What is acceptable to one parent as a recommendation can be quite unacceptable to another. Most parents find that allowing their children to get themselves up in the morning is quite acceptable. On the other hand, bedtime can be so important in the minds of parents, that they will be unwilling to negotiate the time for going to bed during the first few interviews. Later these same parents may find negotiating bedtime more agreeable because the methods recommended previously worked for them and served the purpose of a more cooperative, harmonious family life.

Integrating respect for others
and respect for self
is an art worth practicing.

Adler emphasized the importance of order and routine in the lives of children as a means of helping them to feel more secure. The fact that children test the limits to various rules of order might lead one to believe that they generally do not desire such guidelines. Quite the opposite is true of the rules related to the logic of living together.

Being able to make an exception to rules and still maintain the order is a fine art not always understood by parents. Kindness and firmness are needed in child guidance. **Kindness** might be characterized as respect for the other individual's well-being. This will involve making judgements that allow occasional exceptions to rules. **Firmness** indicates a respect for oneself which should preclude being manipulated or otherwise used in ways not in the best interests of the adult or the child. As new ground rules are established for interacting within the family, both of these ingredients will be important as parents learn to be consistent in their guidance of children.

Over Correcting

Parents and teachers sometime find that once they have begun to understand some of the principles of Individual Psychology, they become embroiled in situations involving two or three misbehaviors of children. The misbehavior on which adults focus initially becomes secondary as another behavior is exhibited. Adults inadvertantly take away the effectiveness of the first corrective measure by making mistakes on subsequent behaviors. The following illustration will help to clarify this error:

> Joey was outside playing with his friends. His mother heard a disagreement ensuing. As she watched the proceedings, Joey was attempting to boss the other members of the group and they would have no part of it. In his frustration, Joey grabbed his friend's truck and began to hit him with it. At this point, the mother called to Joey that he should come in. When Joey came in, she simply indicated that until Joey was able to play without getting into a fight, he would have to stay in the house.

> A few minutes later, Joey was throwing toys around the room. His mother then proceeded to scold him for making a mess. He talked back to her and said that he would do what he pleased. She became angry at this point and sent him to his bedroom and said that he would not have supper until he came out and apologized.

> In this case, the mother had begun to utilize principles and methods recommended by the counselor. Unfortunately, she did not understand yet that only one behavior can be dealt with successfully at a time. What Joey did until he decided to stop fighting should be ignored. Upon her return for consultation, this principle was pointed out to her so that in subsequent instances, she would not find herself frustrated by attempting to deal with too many situations at one time.

Self-Fulfilling Prophesy

Unfortunately adults often verbally or nonverbally communicate to children that adults do not expect children to behave in a way which would be helpful to the family or class. Adults also might indicate that they have little or no confidence in the children's judgement to handle a new situation. The children respond in kind and perform in much the way the adults indicated that they had expected.

As was indicated previously, it is important that adults believe that they can follow through on recommendations and be consistent. Having faith in themselves and in the youngsters is a critical factor in helping to bring about a change.

FOLLOW-UP

As is true with any attempt to be helpful to an individual or family, consultees must be given an opportunity to evaluate their progress since the last conference and to clarify any questions which might be in their minds. At this point the counselor has an opportunity to determine the extent to which the recommendations were understood and implemented properly. On the assumption that some recommendations will have been useful, new suggestions will be made as if sufficient progress has been made, however, the number of new suggestions will be limited so as to avoid overloading consultees with new tasks.

If the adults are not already in a *study group,* joining groups can be very helpful in providing the kind of insight and support needed to implement the recommendations of the counselor. Children also can benefit from discussion groups in their classes or in counseling groups which might be established through the school.

Occasionally adults and children alike tacitly agree to stop having conflict over original presenting problems. Although still not functioning in a spirit of genuine cooperation and equality, they settle for a new agreement of services and contingencies not far removed from their original problems. The counselor-consultant should attempt to help them anticipate this pitfall and overcome it by following through with the study groups, class/family meetings, and follow-up consultation or counseling as necessary.

Further Applications

As noted at the beginning of this chapter, as many applications of these methods exist as number of social conflicts. Family physicians and pastors often hear the plight of the frustrated mother. A physician's guide to some typical non-medical behavior problems for children will be found in Table 6.4 and excerpts from a family interview in Appendix A. These are provided as a means of extending the theory into practice.

With respect to adult relationships, the same steps are followed although techniques will vary. The most commonly violated aspect of conflict resolution concerns the first step, *mutual respect.* When we believe that someone else is mistaken or has done something wrong, we tend to begin our interaction by asking accusatory questions, blaming, or pointing out the error. In short, we tend to undermine the other persons sense of belonging, security, or adequacy. Action statements follow as to what should be done to correct the situation. Even though suggestions may address what the situation requires to correct it, the violation of step one almost precludes successful resolution. Winning and losing become the goal of such situations.

On the other hand, if mutual respect is established through active listening, good eye contact, and empathic communication, the other steps may not be executed optimumly but the situation can still be resolved satisfactorily. When others perceive openness, flexibility, and respect as elements of efforts to solve differences, a much greater probability of success exists in achieving a satisfactory outcome.

SUMMARY

The Adlerian uses principles and practices of Individual Psychology to help mediate differences between individuals and groups of various types. They approach each situation with a strategy for conflict resolution originally outlined by Dreikurs. In the area of adult-child relations a wealth of information is available with specific examples and recommendations for resolving problems (Dreikurs et al., 1971; Dreikurs & Grey, 1968; West, 1986).

Dreikurs was active particularly in demonstrating the effectiveness of the Adlerian approach in marriage conflicts, union negotiations, multicultural conflicts, and similar circumstances. By using his strategy for conflict resolution and the logic of social living based upon social equality, he taught how to apply the approach in a wide variety of situations. He would say that we are limited only by our imagination and our will to cooperate.

As is true with any approach new to us, it requires patience and a willingness to be in error in order to find out the most effective ways of using it in one's life. For this reason, the consultant is an important source of encouragement and instruction as others seek to use the new approach effectively in their lives.

STUDY QUESTIONS

1. Illustrate the four steps of social conflict resolution using a situation with which you are familiar. If the conflict was not resolved satisfactorily, explain why this was so from an Adlerian perspective.

2. What are the hallmarks of a consultative relationship?

3. Identify two or more of basic assumptions of the Adlerian consultative process which you consider particularly important and explain why.

4. What are some promising insights or methods from the family systems approach to complement Adlerian methods?

ACTIVITIES FOR INDIVIDUALS AND GROUPS

The following activities provide an opportunity for you to apply the techniques of conflict resolution. Please note that the situations in part "A" are especially well suited to group activity. Individuals working alone or with a study partner should review the first section and then, using the same principles and techniques, respond to the marital conflict vignette in part "B."

A. Role Playing Critical Incidents in Parent/Teacher Conferences

Following are several initial incidents which could occur in parent/teacher conferences. In each case, the approach used by the teacher could have a strong impact upon the parent/teacher relationship and upon the child's school progress. Follow the directions below and role play each of the situations. Try to act realistically, identify as much as possible with your role and attempt to reach a solution.

DIRECTIONS: Three roleplay situations are provided. Divide into groups of four persons and role play the situations. Each member of the group should select one of the following roles for each situation. After each activity, participants should rotate roles:

Role Play Activity 1	Role Play Activity 2	Role Play Activity 3
Teacher	Teacher	Teacher
Father	Parent	Father
Mother	Child	Mother
Observer	Observer	Observer

In preparation for your roles as the Observer and Teacher, you will find the following hints helpful:

Observer: Note as unobtrusively as possible which teacher responses are the most helpful in establishing a constructive atmosphere and, in general, observe the interactions of the group (note behaviors, dialogue, and so forth).

Teacher: Consider the following as you play the teacher's role:

- At the beginning of the conference, get up and greet the person(s) using his/her name(s).

- Be pleasant and look the person(s) directly in the eye.

- Avoid physical barriers between you, e.g., a desk.

- Speak quietly and listen carefully.

- Respond empathically, accepting feelings as non-defensively as possible.

- Attempt to establish what the situation demands. Be prepared to show examples of the student's work.

- Determine the willingness of the other person to cooperate in a plan of action.

- Establish a concrete plan of action.

- Summarize and establish follow-up contact.

Role Play Activity 1

Situation: A bright child in your class (select grade level) and parents have requested a conference.

Parent Role: Father and mother express concern (feeling) that the daughter/son is not receiving enough enrichment in the class. She/he seems bored, less interested in school than they think is good. They are eager for him/her to do well. They expect the teacher to do something.

Teacher Role: The teacher should reinforce the following concepts: listening skills, communicating feelings, clarifying (values)—what parents expect, encouraging child, and specific home/school cooperation tasks.

Following the role playing, responses should be given to the following:

1. *All Participants:* How did you feel in your role? Was it especially difficult or did it seem to come naturally?

2. *Parents:* Did the teacher seem interested and involved? How did he/she react to your expectations? Did he/she seem to understand your concern? Were you satisfied with the outcome? Would you have liked to have done something differently?

3. *Teacher:* How did you feel about the parents' expecting you to "do something?" Did you find yourself defending your position? How did you feel about the outcome? Would you have liked to have done something differently?

4. *Observer:* Share your perceptions of the parents' and teacher's roles. Which teacher responses did you note as being particularly facilitative? Can you suggest any different approaches to the teacher? In general, how did this group discussion relate to the principles presented in this and previous lessons?

Role Play Activity 2

Situation: The teacher has asked a parent to come in for a conference because the son has been a persistent problem in school. His level of achievement is below what his standardized test score indicate that he is capable of achieving.

Parent Role: Parent is at least initially defensive, and will observe that the son did not have this problem with other teacher(s) previously. Feelings of anger, resentment, and being uncomfortable in the school can be shown either verbally and/or behaviorally. This position can be modified at least somewhat if the teacher uses insight and skill.

Teacher Role: In addition to the suggestions listed earlier, the teacher should reinforce the following concepts: listening skills, accepting feelings, a shift from blaming to what the task requires (i.e., "how can we help you son?"), specific encouragement tasks for the son agreed upon by the teacher and parent.

Child Role: The son is present, but he says nothing unless asked. He is well behaved throughout and willing to respond to questions. He feels uneasy in this situation and will either quietly enjoy teacher's predicament with parent or become genuinely encouraged by the adults working together to help.

Observer: Note the interchange among the three. As much as possible note how, when, and by whom Adlerian concepts were utilized and how doing so affected the meeting.

Following the role playing responses should be given to the following:

1. How did you feel in your roles? Were you able, as you perceived your role playing, to utilize Adlerian concepts?

2. *Parent Role:* Did the teacher seem interested and involved? Did the teacher react to your comments as you expected? Were the teacher's comments helpful to you as a parent?

3. *Teacher Role:* Did you feel accepted in your interaction with the parent? Did you believe you were being helpful to the parent? How did you perceive the child's reaction to the meeting?

4. *Observer:* Shares your perceptions. How, when, and by whom did you see the Adlerian concepts being utilized?

Role Play Activity 3

Situation: The principal recently called the parents to ask their permission to refer their child to the school psychologist for diagnostic testing on the teacher's recommendation. The parents asked to talk with the teacher.

Parents Role: The parents (both) are distressed by the idea that something is wrong with their child. They want an explanation of why their child is being singled out as "defective" or not altogether "right." They don't see anything wrong with him at home. They're afraid that he may get labeled for life by psychological jargon.

Teacher Role: In addition to the suggestions listed earlier, the teacher should reinforce the following concepts: listening, empathy, expressing attitudes toward "slow" students (e.g., teachers position on mainstreaming all children), helping parent understand referral.

Observer: Same directions as for Activity 2

Following the role play activity responses should be given to the following:

1. *All Participants:* How did you feel about this final role? Which, of the three, was the most difficult for you? Can you explain why?

2. *Parents:* How did you think the teacher felt about your child? Were your fears allayed or are you now more anxious than before the conference? What kinds of information did the teacher impart? Is the psychological testing justified in your eyes?

3. *Teacher:* How effective did you feel in explaining your reasons for the testing? Did you find yourself defending your position? What might you have done differently to obtain more cooperation from the parents?

4. *Observer:* Share your perceptions of each member's role. Which teacher responses did you note as being facilitative? How, if at all, might the teacher have approached this situation in a more constructive manner? Share any other observations you have of the group's interaction.

B. Responding to a Marital Conflict Situation

Bob and Mary have been married a little over a year. Both are working and they have no children. Each night Mary comes home to cook supper. She cleans the apartment and does the laundry on weekends. Bob washes the cars and generally looks after their maintenance.

Due to increased responsibility at work, Mary has asked Bob to share more responsibilities with the chores. He says that he doesn't know how and besides, that isn't a man's work. Mary is developing deep resentment about this situation and has begun to show it in small but significant ways (e.g., "accidently" burning supper).

Bob brings the subject up. Mary immediately becomes defensive but looks to you for support. How would you respond to the following:

1. What is the real issue?

2. What can you do and say to remain a "friend" and help them understand the conflict?

3. What does the situation require to restore harmony?

4. How can that be achieved?

When you have completed the Marital Conflict Situation, share your responses with your study partner or an interested friend. Following your discussion compare your responses with those in the Answer Key.

Answer KEY for Learning Activity B

The following are illustrative of the kinds of answers which would reflect an Adlerian solution to Bob and Mary's conflict:

1. The real issue is Bob's fear of losing his masculinity and privileges as the "man of the house" and Mary's resentment at Bob's perceived disrespectful attitude toward shared responsibility. Bob's priority is comfort and Mary's has been in pleasing him.

2. You can follow the four steps of conflict resolution by (a) helping each person's position be stated and respected; (b) clarifying that each would rather not fight, i.e., prefer cooperation and harmony through mutual agreement; (c) facilitate establishing what Mary thinks she needs in the way of assistance; what Bob knows or can learn to do; what a new agreement can accomplish, and (d) reaching an agreement on what to do to establish a new arrangement.

3. A responsible, flexible, division of shared responsibility in keeping up the apartment, cooking, laundry, and related "chores" for daily living.

CHAPTER 12

GROUP PROCEDURES
FOR A
DEMOCRATIC SOCIETY

Probably no other methods are more compatible with Adlerian psychology than group procedures. From the assumption that people are understood best in relation to their social environment follows that in a variety of instances, group situations can be used to teach and encourage others in the logic of social living. Adlerians wish to dispel the notion that problems of social living require secrecy and one-to-one specialized treatment. For this reason, Adler and his followers established child and family education centers wherever Adlerians worked.

Frequently, audience or group observers will inquire about the effectiveness of these methods with other than middle-class families. In the absence of more empirical data, Adlerians note that in Chicago, for example, the earliest child guidance centers were established in inner city neighborhoods. Much of the work there was necessarily volunteered and many lay leaders were found to be at least as effective in discussion groups as the trained counselor. In fact, paraprofessionals have been the backbone of the Adlerian family education movement in working with participants who do not require therapy.

The author's experience, like Dreikurs', also indicates that economically advantaged persons will request participation in discussion groups on child rearing and marriage at least as readily as any other persons. Marriage discussion groups at any socioeconomic level, however, have not been nearly as prominent in the activities of Adlerians as the child rearing groups. In the author's judgement, a decided increase has and will continue to occur in marriage education and counseling among Adlerians.

TYPES OF GROUPS

Types of group methods used most often by Adlerians can be classified as **discussion, consulting,** and **counseling** although **psychodrama** (Nikelly, 1971; Starr, 1971) and **group therapy** (Corsini, 1971) are notable additions. Common elements in these methods relate to principles in Individual Psychology. Whether working with children or adults, in consulting, counseling, or discussion groups, participants are

1. inherently equal and may expect to behave as such, i.e., have a place which no one can rightfully challenge;

2. considered to be capable of assuming responsibility for their behavior;

3. individually understood best in a holistic, unified way as creative, purposive beings;

4. considered as social beings meeting the same life tasks as others;

5. capable of changing their attitudes and/or behavior; and

6. able to help as well as be helped in the process of giving meaning to life.

The climate or conditions which exist in these groups are typically those of any helping relationship. Expectations are for sincerity, caring, trust, empathy, support, cooperation, and honesty in transactions between members. In addition, a good measure of humor and friendliness also are present. In counseling or consulting groups, confidences are kept among members out of respect for the context within which information was shared, i.e., among those with common interests or concerns who have a commitment to assisting each other. In public demonstrations, such as described in Chapter 10, respect for participants is uppermost in the leader's mind.

The amount of training and/or knowledge a leader needs in Individual Psychology as well as in group procedures varies with types of groups and their objectives. In discussion groups, for example, leadership can be shared or rotated among members for a session or more. This rotation is particularly possible when the group is using a common reading source to provide structure and information.

In consultation or counseling groups, portions of sessions may be influenced significantly by one or more members but the leader would likely maintain a share of the responsibility for clarifying, summarizing, or otherwise directing the group. **Co-leadership** is recommended whenever possible for it increases the probability that what one person might overlook, another person would not. Compatibility of co-leaders in these cases requires cooperation and a general sense of equality but not necessarily similar training or background. In some cases, a counselor and teacher or parent might co-lead a group with considerable effectiveness because of their complimentary insights and experiences.

DISCUSSION GROUPS

Discussion Groups for Children

While the same observations can be made for persons in any of the Adlerian groups, one of the most important outcomes for children concerns their realization that individually and col-lectively they can use their intellect to solve problems that they experience in their daily living. Gordon (1967) observed in his review of the Coleman Report that

> In addition to the school characteristics which were shown to be related to pupil achievement, Coleman found a pupil characteristic which appears to have a stronger relationship to achievement than all school factors combined. The extent to which a pupil feels he has con-trol over his own destiny is strongly related to achievement. This feel-ing of potency is less prevalent among Negro students, but where it is present "their achievement is higher than that of white pupils who lack that conviction. (p. 175)

To believe in their own capabilities, to mobilize and cooperate in the use of other's capabilities, and to expect that problems can be solved in constructive, rational ways are important lifelong lessons to be learned through group discussions. These discussions can help to counteract some adults' tendency to overemphasize the importance of subject matter in school. Discipline, per se, can be a subject of learning instead of an adjunct in the sense that "good" pupils know how to behave and others must be shown through rules, merits, demerits, lectures, and punishment. Discouraged pupils misbehave or do poorly in school because that appears to them to be their best solution. They need guidance in learning alternative behaviors and attitudes.

Classroom Meetings

Unfortunately, school and home tend to reinforce mistaken notions of discouraged children by emphasizing their shortcomings and overlooking opportunities to offer new or different alternatives. Classroom meetings are one important way to ensure that each child has opportunities to discover his/her unique talents and strengths. This meeting is an excellent way for children to overcome whatever real or imagined limitations they perceive as roadblocks to a more satisfying life for themselves and others.

Responsible behavior is possible
for all children.

Glasser (1969) provided valuable principles and specific procedures on classroom meetings for counselors and teachers. While Glasser refers to his approach as Reality Therapy, principles that he uses are very compatible with Individual Psychology and his methods are equally helpful. He believes that responsible behavior is possible for all children when they are given the opportunity to become involved, to learn the significance of valuing, and to make commitment to activities which provide a sense of worth and belonging or love.

Glasser discussed and illustrated three types of classroom meetings: *open ended, educational diagnostic,* and *special problem solving.* A discussion of each follows.

Open-Ended Meetings. Children are invited to discuss any thought-provoking question which interests them. In these discussions the teacher wishes to stimulate both the creative and rational thinking capabilities of the children.

Fact or known answers are not the major focus of an open-ended meeting. For example, this author has asked the following questions of second grade elementary school pupils:

> Have you ever wondered what would happen if we could not buy toys in stores? Do you think that would be good or bad?
>
> Have you ever had a toy that was made especially for you? Would you like that as well as a store bought toy?
>
> Have you ever made a toy or pretended you had a toy? Did you enjoy playing with it?
>
> Have you ever made someone else a toy? How many of you would like to make a toy you could share with a friend? What kind of toys could we make?

In this case, the teacher could follow up with discussions on giving and receiving or on what makes us happy or sad, and possibly with activity time devoted to making toys for others out of pipe cleaners, common household articles, or materials readily available in the children's neighborhoods. On the other hand, such sessions do not have to be planned, followed up, or scheduled. In fact, some of the most meaningful sessions for the children will be spontaneously suggested by them or by events in the news which cannot be programmed in advance. As the pupils learn that "correct" answers are not the goal, they will look forward to these opportunities.

Educational Diagnostic Meetings. These sessions are related to what the class is studying. The teacher can determine quickly whether or not what the class is studying is being understood by the pupils. Glasser particularly emphasized the need for relevance of curriculum to the pupils. Without relevance, motivation to learn the subject is lost or misplaced on values unrelated to the subject itself, i.e., grades to show superiority.

Challenging the pupils to examine concepts and to transfer their knowledge to current events is often the focus of these sessions. This author found the following questions useful in helping a seventh grade teacher evaluate the class's use of concepts and facts being studied in social studies.

Why do you think we have never had a woman president?

What role have women played in the history of our government? Can you name a few women who have made a significant contribution to this country?

Can you name other countries who have women as the recognized head or leader of their country.

Do you know of any women who may have an opportunity in the future to run for president? What knowledge or experiences which women traditionally have had might contribute to their being a good leader and president?

At the time of the previous meeting, the primary election campaigns were in progress. Students had been studying current events as well as history. After class, the teacher reported some disappointment in their responses to the questions. Approximately six weeks later, after an average of two or more class meetings a week for twenty-five minutes each, the author observed a substantial improvement in the quality of their discussions and a noticeable increase in responses from the quieter, less academic students.

The author usually co-leads with the teachers on at least two occasions and simply observes at other times. Normally a demonstration and assistance on a few other occasions is sufficient help for teachers to carry on the activity. Learning to listen and respond empathically, to withhold evaluation, and to encourage any genuine effort to participate are the key ingredients for success of group activities. The author concurs with Glasser that if possible, teachers probably will find the educational-diagnostic meeting most informative when someone else leads the discussion. Sharing time for this purpose as in team teaching could be a meaningful way for teachers to assist one another.

Social Problem-Solving Meetings. These meetings are held to discuss and potentially solve individual and group educational problems of the class and the school. Social problem-solving meetings are more difficult for an outsider to lead than they are for the teacher. This fact tends to be true because problems often cannot be solved in one meeting and follow-up with involvement by outsiders is difficult, even if pupils accept them as members of the group. A few rules of thumb taken from Glasser (1969) and this author's experience can help to identify the hallmarks of the social problem-solving meetings:

1. All problems relative to the class as a group and to any individual in the class are eligible for discussion. Home problems may be included if the pupil or parent wishes to bring them up.

2. The discussion should be directed toward solving the problem. Fault finding or punishment should never be a part of the discussion of the solution.

3. The teacher remains nonjudgemental but the class may be judgemental and then work toward positive solutions. The teacher helps sustain the understanding that everyone has value and a place in the group—even the misbehaving individual. Class members, however, have a right to decide how they will respond to a lack of cooperation by members in the class.

4. Meetings should be conducted in a tight circle with everyone visible to everyone else. This arrangement is also important in other types of meetings.

5. Meetings should be relatively short for younger children (10 to 30 minutes) and increased in length for older pupils (30 to 45 minutes). Meeting regularly, however, is more important than undue concern for the length of the meetings.

6. The principal can be an important partner in the possible alternatives open to the class. The principal may be involved in discussing a problem situation of a class or individuals. His/her role would include helping them to examine what they did which contributed to a problem, encouraging discussion as to what they can do to solve the problem, and asking for a commitment to follow through on a plan to resolve the problem. With punishment completely out of the question, frank discussions are entirely possible.

7. No one problem or individual should be allowed to dominate these meetings one session after another. Once the negative aspects of a situation are identified, future attention should be directed to progress and positive steps which can be taken. Behavioral problems, per se, should not be the only basis for discussion. Concerns with friendship, loneliness, vocational choice, sportsmanship, dating, and many other topics can be discussed quite profitably.

The author was invited to join a teacher of high school seniors in a family living class to discuss student attitudes toward male/female roles in our society. The teacher reported a problem of overt reactions directed at her by some of the boys because of her presentation of women's equality, opinions, information, and so forth. She became upset by the boy's comments, including what she considered disrespect for women, in general, and her, in particular.

While the class had had discussions before, they had not met in the circle nor had they known the author. A noticeable tenseness was in the group as they entered the room and a few audible comments suggesting that, although the teacher had asked if a visitor could join them, a few of those boys were less than ecstatic about the prospects. A few of these boys resisted joining the tight circle initially but became full-fledged members as the meeting progressed.

After the teacher's opening comments concerning her perceptions of the problem, the author was asked to help lead a discussion which might allow them to take a fresh look at their feelings and attitudes. Indicating that even though a hidden agenda may be suspected by some members of the class, assurance was provided that none existed other than an open attempt to have them discuss their true attitudes and feelings. To facilitate this process, they were invited to share their opinions and ideas of the following:

"What does it mean to be a human being?" The first remarks came from a few of the more academically inclined students. The reluctance to participate by a few of the boys was still obvious but they were attentive. Nonevaluative, reflective, and clarifying comments were the primary responses to the remarks of the students.

They sought to distinguish human beings from animals and other living things. They identified characteristics and abilities which they considered important aspects of being a human being. Living cooperatively and responsibly was mentioned among the qualities of being a human being.

Then they were asked, *"What does it mean to be a person?"* The discussion was much more relaxed and counter questions followed comments. To be a person meant different things to different people but all agreed that to be a person was important to them. Persons are human beings and they have many qualities which are held in common.

The discussion then moved to, *"What does it mean to be a man?"* and following that *"What does it mean to be a woman?"* At this point in the discussion, the reluctant participants were actively sharing their views. No signs of hostility or disregard for others' views were observed. Quite the contrary, much agreement occurred on the general equality of men and women as persons and human beings. On the other hand, three of the boys stated that they still didn't like to consider women as equals even though they agreed with the logic of the discussion.

The period was about to end as their attention was turned to considering prejudice. The view was offered that being aware of our prejudice can be a significant step toward examining it. They were not being asked to change their views, only to be honest in accepting them as their own. On the assumptions that we all hold unexamined values, attitudes, and prejudices, further discussions might be helpful to everyone in the class.

The teacher reported further discussions were held and a unit on careers allowed the class to consider the issue further but from a different point of view. Of importance to the teacher, the behavior of the boys improved noticeably and she found them more cooperative in the class.

Dreikurs (1968) and Dreikurs et al. (1971) discussed and illustrated several considerations important to the training of children for effective discussions. They believe that children need specific training in group participation. Natural leadership from within the group usually will emerge in a few weeks so that the teacher can relinquish leadership to members of the group. The teacher functions as a consultant once the members have learned fundamentals of group discussion. In the beginning, she provides guidance by doing the following:

1. **Helping to establish ground rules,** i.e., to talk about what it means to have friendly discussion and how a few simple rules can help participants work and play together in a cooperative, friendly way. Order is important to a democratic setting but it evolves from the logic of the situation and respect for self and others.

2. **Insuring total group participation,** e.g., there are topics, questions or issues about which any pupil can safely express an opinion. By observing which children are not participating, the teacher can ask a question and invite the quiet pupils to share their views. Any genuine effort by these pupils to participate can receive recognition by

the teacher's responses to them. Normally, these pupils will slowly but willingly join in the class discussions.

3. **Modeling through initial leadership,** i.e., the teacher's leadership is directed toward relinquishing the responsibility for leading. The teacher models how the children can think through their own experiences, how they can question and evaluate what they have heard in order to reach a conclusion or solve a problem.

4. **Handling touchy problems,** i.e., keeping the discussions focused on constructive thinking and devoid of meaningless or derogatory comments, this is particulary important when pupils discuss the misbehavior of other pupils. Fighting, lying, stealing, or cheating can be topics which bring about lively discussions (Dreikurs et al., 1971). As pupils become experienced in dealing with such matters, certain ones will become the moderators in the sense that they will intervene when unnecessary or unkind comments are made. Until that time, the teacher will redirect comments or suggest other alternatives in a friendly but purposeful way.

5. **Stimulating ideas,** i.e., to introduce problems, questions, or ideas which require the pupils to observe, evaluate, and reach conclusions are important functions of the teacher. In the activities of a year, pupils will have ideas or topics which they will wish to discuss. At other times, and especially when they are still learning how to participate in a discussion, the teacher can anticipate topics which will motivate them and possibly be of help in acquiring the confidence to deal with situations which face them in the future.

6. **Encouraging group decisions and avoiding premature interventions,** i.e., learning to make group decisions and to accept the consequences of them are the necessary ingredients for democratic living. Some groups make ill-considered decisions and the teachers prematurely intervene to save the class from the consequences of their choice. If the class chose to disregard

suggestions or otherwise overlooked important considerations, better that they discover the outcome for themselves. Equally important, the teacher can increase the satisfaction gained from the many occasions when sound decisions help individuals or the class as a whole.

An example of how group decisions, whether soundly considered or not, can be valuable sources of learning to pupils is illustrated in the following situation:

A sixth-grade class had had enough experience with classroom meetings that they were feeling some expansiveness in their ability. They had decided that if they could get all their week's work accomplished by Friday noon of that week, they would like to have a "free" afternoon for a class picnic at a nearby park.

The teacher injected that permission notes from their parents and approval for a picnic by the principal would be needed. She also suggested that they check with the principal as early as possible to avoid any problems. The teacher observed that they seemed confident of their ability to get along quite well without her suggestions.

The following week plans moved along enthusiastically and they worked diligently in all of their studies. They requested permission slips for their parents' signatures from the teacher and proceeded to collect them.

On Thursday afternoon, they sent a committee to the principal for permission. The committee returned in a short time with their faces revealing a dilemma. The principal willingly gave them permission and hoped that they enjoyed the picnic as much as the other children enjoyed the surprise circus visit planned for Friday afternoon!

Needless to say, a reassessment of their alternative was made and they decided to see the circus and work diligently for a second week in order to have the picnic.

This time they agreed to gain permission and check on conflicts ahead of time. The teacher was asked if she had any suggestions or thoughts on how to plan more effectively. to the teacher's credit, she never said "I told you so" or mentioned her earlier admonitions.

7. **Summarizing and evaluating progress made,** i.e., groups should make an assessment periodically of their performance and consider plans for the future as well. They might ask, "What have we done?" "In what ways has it been of value?" and "What other things might we do which could be helpful or needed?"

Guidelines

The use of stories with young children and role playing with all age groups are valuable methods to be incorporated into group problem solving. Dreikurs et al. (1971) provided specific examples and resources for using them. In addition, these authors outlined guidelines for teachers of the democratic classroom. Among them are the following:

1. A group cannot run democratically without order and ground rules.

2. Limits are necessary.

3. Children should participate in establishing and maintaining rules necessary for functioning in an orderly group.

4. The group needs leadership and the teacher needs to know how to exert democratic leadership.

5. Without mutual trust and faith in each other, a class cannot function democratically.

6. The teacher must know how to win the cooperation of students.

7. A spirit of cooperation must replace competitiveness in the classroom.

8. The teacher needs the skill to integrate the class for a common purpose: each child has to have a sense of belonging to the whole class.

Dreikurs and associates (1971) also emphasized the encouragement of creative and independent thinking in young people. These authors were critical of adult behavior which stifled the intrinsic curiosity and the desire to learn of children.

> Teachers who insist on the exact answers that they prepared or the ones that come from the book are dull teachers, responsible not only for the boredom of their students, but for many discipline problems that come up because of rigid, stale, and antiquated method of teaching. Not uncommon is to find children who, because of such teaching, decide that they don't like social studies, arithmetic, or some other subject. (Dreikurs et al., 1971, p. 176)

One structured program of materials based on Adlerian concepts is Dinkmeyer and McKay's *Developing Understanding of Self and Others* (DUSO). Used in thousands of elementary school classrooms in this country and abroad, these materials have been found effective as an aid to teachers in creating positive learning climates and improving behavior in the classroom. Once familiar with the basic concepts and methods, children and teachers alike can create and innovate to suit their purposes.

Dreikurs believed that the means of producing more effective education lay in teaching adults as well as children the methods of democratic living. Whenever children have the opportunity to move from autocratic to democratic settings, they do not know how to behave in responsible ways. Equally important, adults do not know how to guide children in the methods of democratic living.

As in the experiments of Lewin (1948), Dreikurs noted that laissez faire leadership as an alternative to autocratic leadership is very poor. And yet, in the search for more human, child-oriented methods, many teachers and parents mistakenly subscribe to these methods and create even more havoc in their lives. When autocratic methods are set aside, adults and children alike require guidance and a period of training.

Glasser indicated that observing another lead classroom meeting and then actually leading thirty or more meetings was necessary before substantial competence could be expected. Similarly, parents are not likely to lead family meetings successfully without some instructions and encouragment. For this reason, Adlerians have experienced some of their most enthusiastic support from participants in the parent discussion groups.

Soltz (1967) drew upon the experience of others as well as her own in preparing a *Study Group Leader's Manual* for use with parent groups using *Children the Challenge*. She noted that parent study groups use a self-help method involving the following:

1. Parents gather together in groups under the leadership of a lay person (who may or may not have previous acquaintance with the material). "This is not meant to exclude those trained in Individual Psychology . . .We want to emphasize that those with no previous training in Individual Psychology can and do help themselves."

2. They mutually examine problems, concepts, and values.

3. They share in stimulation and encouragement.

4. They learn new basic principles and their application in the art of democratic family living. (p. 8)

In discussing the role of leaders, Soltz noted that they are not impartial, i.e., they are recommending a definite viewpoint. The leader of a study group, however, is simply to facilitate the discussion, help avoid pitfalls of digressions, and leave responsibility to members for accepting or rejecting what is presented through the readings. She offers many practical guidelines and rules of thumb for leading groups, organizing the first meeting, and studying the text. In addition, she has outlined questions for each chapter and included suggested supplementary readings.

In the author's experience, groups usually meet for ten sessions of approximately one and one-half hours each. Group size varies from eight to twelve persons. Evening sessions allow working persons to attend although daytime sessions have been well attended by nonworking parents. A male co-leader seems to help increase the probability that men who come to the first session continue to attend. Having both parents participate is very helpful but not necessary if one or the other desires to benefit from the sessions.

Leadership for the individual sessions can be rotated among those willing to do so by sharing the leader's manual. This procedure seems to contribute to the confidence of participants and increases their interest in the discussion. Frequently, persons who participate in their first group can be encouraged to lead or co-lead groups for others who desire this opportunity. Because every group is somewhat unique, new ideas are discovered or learned ones reinforced. Therefore, an individual can reread and discuss principles and examples many times and continue learning from the group discussion.

Zucherman et al. (1978) also has a useful leader's guide which supplements *Children the Challenge*. Experienced counselors and lay leaders will find Dinkmeyer and McKay's (1976) *Systematic Training for Effective Parenting* (STEP) program a valuable extention to an outreach program. The authors reported significant positive results for participants in their program. A similar program for teachers by the same authors is *Systematic Training for Effective Teaching* (STET).

Another program which has proven effective in teacher training is the telecourse, *Coping with Kids* (Sweeney, 1978). Studies of graduate and undergraduate classes (Appalachian Community Services Network, 1979, 1980; Kibler, 1978; Rush, 1978) and in-service education of teachers (Kerney, 1980) revealed significant positive changes in child guidance attitudes toward methods consistent with Adlerian concepts and these were sustained over periods of at least three months after participation in the programs.

Family Meeting or Council

The family meeting or council is a logical extension of the democratic process into the home. Dreikurs and Soltz (1964) and Rigney and Corsini (1970) described important attitudes and suggested procedures for the family council. Rigney and Corsini (1970) defined the family council as

> . . . a regularly scheduled meeting of all members of the family who want to attend. Its purpose is to take up the business of the family, such as: to give information, make plans, establish rules, express complaints, settle quarrels, come to agreements and make decisions. It is an open forum in which everyone in the family can express his ideas, his opinions, and/or his complaints without any interruption. (p. 3)

Each family establishes its own rules for meeting. Sometimes these rules are elaborate; in other cases, they are minimal. Recommended considerations include the following:

1. Establish a mutually agreeable time and place to meet.

2. Establish a procedure for keeping minutes and chairing the meeting. A rotation of chairing is often effective.

3. No one is urged or required to attend.

4. Anyone can enter or leave at any time.

5. Decisions can be made which affect absent members.

6. Decisions can be changed at other meetings.

7. Decisions are made by consensus. When consensus cannot be reached on an issue, consensus should be reached on voting and abiding by the majority vote or the issue is tabled until another time.

Parents and teachers alike who are new to these methods sometimes worry that the children will be irresponsible and uncooperative in these meetings. With patience and a willingness to learn together, such concerns will pass away. A foundation in principles is important, however, if adults are to help the children in this process.

In the following excerpt from a family meeting, an important principle is introduced by the oldest daughter (9 years old) at the first meeting. She has a rule for father, but the family discovers, rules are for everybody!

Father: Is there anything else to discuss today?

Mother: No.

Son: No.

Oldest Daughter: Yes, you should tell us the days that you're going to come home late so that we can have things fixed for you and dinner and such. . .

Father: Well, what do you think I ought to do; I'm not sure what you are saying. Are you saying I should tell you when I'm coming home?

Oldest Daughter: Uh huh, so we'll know. And sometimes Mother cooks food and she doesn't expect you home and you come home. And she has to cook more supper after she's all done.

Father: Well, I see . . . that's a good point. would that . . . is that a rule for everybody then? In other words, when Mother's out and she's coming home late, she should let us know? And when you're out, you should let us know when you're coming home so we knwo? Is that what you're saying, too?

Oldest Daughter: Not exactly.

Father: I mean it is just a rule for me, or is it for everybody?

Oldest Daughter: It should be sort of like be a rule for you.

Second Daughter: I think it should be a rule for everybody. Cause everybody doesn't know when everybody else is coming home.

Mother:	Yes, that's right because it sometimes gets dark before you children decide to come in. I've called and called. Right?
Second Daughter:	Yeah.
Father:	How about that . . . is it a good rule for everyone? (All nod their heads, yes) . . . Does anyone want to say more about it before we go on? . . . (no) . . . We'll want to put that in our minutes and I'll make a point of calling if I'm not coming home on time. Will everyone try it? (nods)

In this case, important lessons have been learned by parents and children alike. First, the children now know that they can safely confront the parents with behavior that they believe needs improvement; second, they also have learned that rules are for everyone and they are not to be applied in a discriminatory manner; and third, the parents have learned that the children are capable of not only observing and reporting behavior which the parents need to improve but also they are very rational about how to resolve it successfully. Equality is well illustrated in this case and from it, more open dialogue can be expected. Appendix B has a full typescript of the family council from which the previous excerpt was taken. Because such an example is not available elsewhere, parent study group leaders should find it a useful reference for parents interested in starting their family council.

As was true of the classroom meetings, the ages of children and the agenda items which evolve generally determine the length of meetings. When members consistently leave early or begin complaining about the meetings, the meeting may be too long. Other common contributors to unsuccessful family meeting are listed by Rigney and Corsini (1970, p. 6):

> not starting on time
> cancelling meetings
> meeting at mealtime
> parental domination
> getting discouraged
> not following through on agreements

Parents, like teachers, must realize that learning to participate in a democratic meeting with children requires experience
and an inclination to be patient. Some excellent meetings with
outstanding progress will occur and some others will be relatively poor meetings with regression to old ways. The meetings
can improve the quality of living significantly when the spirit
behind them becomes an integral part of the family's way of
relating to one another.

Marriage Discussion Groups

Because the principles of Individual Psychology apply to all
interpersonal relationships, participants in parent groups often
see its implications for their marriage relationships as well. As a
result, marriage discussion groups, organized and conducted
much in the same manner as the child-rearing groups, are
formed to satisfy the interest of those individuals wishing to
pursue study further.

Marriage discussion groups are not counseling or therapy
groups, although some individuals may be in counseling outside of the group. When questions are asked in the meetings, no
attempt is made to relate them to problems or concerns of
members in the group. Members may volunteer examples of
behaviors which illustrate certain principles when they fit into
the flow of the discussion however.

As was true of the parent groups, participants may be
encouraged to record questions or concerns that they hope will
be answered through the discussion. If at the end of ten sessions their questions have not been answered, they may bring
them up for discussion. Occasionally, a member of the group
will volunteer to tell how the application of these principles has
improved a specific situation which was troublesome for husband and wife. An illustration of such improvement is the
following:

> A husband had a habit of calling his wife (a group
> member) late in the afternoon to announce that he was
> bringing home a visiting business associate for dinner.
> This habit was a source of regular anguish to her
> because the food might not be what she considered

suitable for a guest or she simply had other things to do. Being a dutiful servant, however, she would do what she thought was expected and then feel resentment because of his insensitivity.

After reading sections of *The Challenge of Marriage* with the discussion group, she decided to discuss her observations with her husband and propose an alternative. She suggested that in the future, if it was inconvenient for her to do the cooking, he should be responsible for the meal. Much to her surprise, he was very agreeable and actually enjoyed cooking for the guests he brought home. She was then able to meet the guests, enjoy the conversation before dinner, and gain a new appreciation for the work her husband had chosen as a career.

Another case involved a husband who frequently came home late for dinner. The wife would be angry because "supper was ruined" and many an evening was ruined as well. She decided that trying to keep supper warm beyond the time which was agreed upon was unnecessary. She discussed this fact with him saying simply that if he was late, she would first put it in the refrigerator for him to warm up when he got home. After the first two occasions when she did this but made no complaint or comment, he came home much more regularly. Equally important, their evenings together were friendlier and more enjoyable.

Dreikurs' (1946) book on marriage has been a useful reference for discussion groups even though it was written in the mid-forties. Participants often are surprised at the accuracy of his predictions with respect to social change and relevance of his suggestions for today's marriages. The organizer and/or leader of the group will need to develop a few questions for each session which will help the group to discuss the principles involved. After the first few meetings leadership can be rotated to members of the group as they show a willingness to assume it.

CONSULTING GROUPS

Dinkmeyer (1971) had developed consulting groups for parents and teachers to the extent that he refers to them as *"C" groups.* He made great use of Adlerian theory and techniques in these groups. The purposes of these groups are threefold:

1. To help adults understand the practical application of Individual Psychology in their relationships with children.

2. To help them understand their feelings and behavior in adult-child conflicts.

3. To help them integrate their understanding into beliefs and values which help them to work more effectively with children.

Groups vary in size from four to six persons for teachers to slightly more in parent groups. They meet for approximately an hour a week for six or more times depending upon their previous background and experience with Adlerian methods. Through group experiences, participants are taught four procedures for improving communication. They are particularly attuned to the fact that they communicate emotional as well as intellectual messages. The procedure involves

learning to communicate empathic responses,

stating own feelings about the impact of the child's behavior on them in a facilitative way,

learning conflict resolution to reach mutual agreement, and

utilizing logical consequences when children choose not to help in conflict resolution.

Dinkmeyer refers to his groups as *"C" groups* because the factors that tend to make them effective begin with a "C":

1. *Collaboration:* the group works together on mutual concerns.

2. **Consultation:** the group consults by sharing ideas about the specific application of the new approaches they learn. They are consultants to one another.

3. **Clarification:** the group clarifies for each member what it is he/she believes and how congruent his/her behavior is with those beliefs.

4. **Confrontation:** each person is expected to seek an understanding of him/herself and his/her behavior and to confront others in a manner which helps them achieve the same goal.

5. **Communication:** empathic understanding is a hallmark of the group interaction.

6. **Concern and caring:** members and children are valued and considered deserving total group interest.

7. **Confidential:** trust is a high priority value to the group.

8. **Commitment:** after each session, members are expected to set a specific behavior goal that they intend to fulfill before the next session.

The leader must be the one who is competent in group process as well as Adlerian methods. Group interaction can stagnate or otherwise remain inconsequential without appropriate leadership. For this reason, the goals of the group must be clear and agreed upon before starting. Attention to the effective development of the group is essential.

Generally, after some period of getting to know one another through structured exercises, groups begin by learning how to establish alternative approaches to the disruptive behavior of children. Those methods and procedures described in Chapter 6 are involved in this process. For example, the group uses a specific teacher-child or parent-child conflict to identify goals of misbehavior and alternative corrective and preventative actions for the adult.

Taylor and Hoedt (1974) in their study reported that teacher and parent groups using *Encouraging Children to Learn* (Dinkmeyer & Dreikurs, 1963) and *Children the Challenge* (Dreikurs & Stoltz, 1964) as references were significantly better than no treatment or eclectic group counseling with elementary school children in bringing about significant change in the children's classroom behavior. While these authors referred to methods as group counseling, their purposes appear to be more descriptive of the discussion or consulting groups described previously. They reported (p. 4) "Both parent and teacher groups focused upon identifying children's discouragement and subsequent 'misbehaviors' and then applied the appropriate principles of encouragement as suggested by Dinkmeyer and Dreikurs" (1963).

Platt in his study (1971) sought to determine if Adlerian group counseling with the children and consultation with their parents and teachers were more effective than no treatment. In this case, classroom meetings with the children for thirty minutes over a period of ten weeks was combined with fine weeks of thirty-minute sessions with the teachers. Parents were in a ten-week discussion group using *Children the Challenge*. "The results showed that all children in the experimental groups made significant progress as rated by their parents. Similarly, the teachers rated all of the children except two, in a way implying that they all had made significant progress" (Platt, 1971, p. 89).

Children's behavior in the placebo groups was rated as the same as or, in a few cases, worse than prior to the experiment. While for research purposes the results are less definitive with regard to which methods were most effective, the study illustrates how a counselor could maximize the influence of the Adlerian model in a school program.

A study of Hoffman (1975) sought to determine the effectiveness of Adlerian counseling with disruptive high school students compared to teacher consultation groups and combinations of both compared to no treatment groups. All were more effective than no treatment, however, significant differences occurred among the methods. In order of effectiveness: teacher consultation combined with group counseling of the students;

teacher consultation alone; group counseling alone. These results suggest that working with teacher groups can be a good use of counselor and teacher time.

As noted previously, the need for further research in all areas of Adlerian methods is required (Kern et al., 1978). As authors of these studies observed, an inherent limitation of their methodology lay with the nature of the programs. Limitations are based upon the volunteer groups working and living in relatively uncontrollable environments for research purposes. Nevertheless, studies tend to confirm and validate the experiences of Adlerians who have been told over the years that their assistance was helpful.

The research reported in Chapter 6, although not specifically identified as Adlerian in origin, does deserve further mention here. Research on cooperation as a superior method to competitive group activities is clearly support for the teaching of Dreikurs. More such, literature can be expected in the future.

COUNSELING GROUPS

Although a distinction between counseling and consulting has been made for the purposes of this introduction to Adlerian methods, much of what had been presented under consultation and discussion groups also applies here. Actually, very little has been reported in the literature on Adlerian group counseling per se. For example, classroom meetings (Platt, 1971), parent and teacher study and consultation groups (Platt, 1971; Taylor & Hoedt, 1974), and parent consultation groups (Sonstegard & Dreikurs, 1967) have been referred to by others as forms of group counseling.

LIFE STYLE GROUPS

The author's experience with groups employing life style as a means of self-exploration and potential change suggests that a difference my exist in these groups from others, primarily in the degree of emphasis upon discovery of one's life plan. Purpose of the life style groups include:

1. to help each member understand the application of Individual Psychology in his/her own development;

2. to help each member discover his/her characteristic ways of approaching and perceiving his/her basic life tasks;

3. to help each member test his/her perceptions of self, others, and life with those of others in the group while also validating the life style technique; and

4. to help each member resolve any specific conflicts with which he/she desires assistance.

Starting Life Style Groups

Usually the first group session is concerned with ground rules for establishing trust, cohesiveness, and administrative details necessary in any group which expects to involve self-disclosure for promoting personal growth. Structure and task orientation are provided for early sessions by the educative function present in learning theory and technique. The author's bias is similar to that of Patterson (1971) and others who speak of "training as the preferred mode of treatment."

The leader of the group interviews and presents a life style analysis for one of the members of the group in the first sessions. Members of the group are asked to record the information and ask for collaboration or clarification as co-participants in the process. In this manner, they are actually involved in learning how to collect and use information. This also facilitates the collection of their own life style information on forms which they can complete at home. Examples of forms are the one presented in this book and the LSI (*Life Style Inventory*, Shulman & Mosak, 1988a). For a member unfamiliar with Individual Psychology, recommended readings and instructional sessions on basic principles are conducted. Shulman and Mosak (1988b) have provided a *Manual for Life Style Assessment* which describes the process in detail.

Life Style Sessions

As members become more familiar with the process and theory, they are asked to preview the life style information of one or more members of the group, to interview them in teams of two, and to develop from that a life style summary that includes the following:

1. characteristic ways of making their place;

2. characteristic ways of approaching work, social relationships, and love relationships;

3. characteristic attitudes about self, others, and life; and

4. possible self-defeating notions as well as notions which will contribute to their coping successfully with life circumstances.

Members of the group have access to the life style information of a member one week before the session at which the individual's life style is presented for reaction. All such information is treated as confidential and is in a secured location.

Individuals who interviewed the member usually present their observations first, although questions and observations from other group members are always in order. Observations are offered tentatively, i.e., "It seems as though. . .," "Could it be that . . .," rather than as dogmatic statements of fact. Generally interpretations can be validated by direct reference to the life style information as well as by the individual's behavior within the group.

The group is watchful of presenters projecting to other members attributes possessed by the presenter. The "recognition reflex" has proven to be a valuable index to accuracy of an observation. The smile or laugh of recognition comes readily in these groups because the genuine caring and empathy which develop make defensive maneuvering quite unnecessary.

Genuine caring and empathy make
defensive maneuvering unnecessary.

Facilitative confrontation becomes a natural adjunct to the relationships which develop. After two or three life styles are completed, the level of self-disclosure and trust are established to a degree that honestly offering or rejecting observations is not a threat to the warmth and supportive nature of the group.

At the beginning of the group, members are asked to write as specifically as possible any concerns or relationship problems which they may wish to resolve through the group. After all of the life styles have been completed, members are asked if any of these recorded concerns have been resolved by the group activities. If there is "unfinished business" of this nature, then they may wish to bring it to the group's attention. Depending upon the circumstances, the group may reexamine the life style summary to discover how the individual may be experiencing difficulty because of mistaken notions. Behavioral homework goals, role playing and other similar techniques may be suggested or used in the process.

Usually six to eight individuals compose a group. They meet a minimum of once a week for two hours. Everyone is expected to attend each session and to participate actively in the group, although leading a session on someone else's life style is voluntary. When used with counselor, psychologist, or social worker trainees, members of the group also are better prepared to judge the value of the theory and technique. For those solely interested in personal insight and development, reports indicate that the process is highly valued and considered useful in coping more effectively with basic life tasks.

When do life style sessions cease? When the group perceives no further business, the group will cease to meet.

Abramowitz and Jackson (1974) reported on a study which examined methods of group procedures. They concluded that a combination of certain methods (i.e., discussing early childhood antecedents and present behavior, attitudes and feelings) was superior to other methods, although only modestly so compared to the problem discussion procedures. Abramowitz and Jackson's procedure of discussing early childhood antecedents referred to as "there and then" group procedure was similar to those used in life style groups. The procedure of discussing present behavior, attitudes, and feelings referred to as "here and now" group procedure also is used in life style groups. Another method these authors examined, therapist interpretations, per se, was not demonstrated to add significantly to the general procedures involved in the group interactions. These authors did not refer to the specific use of Adlerian methods and appear to have not taken full advantage of such procedures. Also if the life style group was utilized, group members' interaction would tend to minimize the significance of leader contributions.

SUMMARY

The significance of group work in the growth of Adlerian methods is apparent. Most illustrations of principles and methods in the literature are taken from reports of parents, teachers, and others who have shared their experiences in discussion, consultation, or counseling groups. One reason why lifestyle technique, per se, may have remained somewhat obscure is that it apparently had not been adapted to group work. This likely will be less true in the future as its use in public demonstrations (Mosak, 1972), in marriage counseling (Pew & Pew, 1972), and in groups such as have been described by the author becomes more common.

STUDY QUESTIONS

Direction: Respond to the following in the spaces provided.

1. Identify three or more characteristics of all Adlerian groups whether with children or adults and whether the focus is therapy or discussion.

2. What are relative strengths and weaknesses of open-ended, educational-diagnostic and problem-solving classroom meetings?

3. (a) If family meetings are to succeed, what are some rules of thumb to follow?

   (b) What are some precautions?

4. What are some distinctions between study groups and consultation or counseling groups?

APPENDICES

Appendix A

FAMILY COUNSELING

The following typescript is taken from an interview by the author with a family: mother, father, and four children. The oldest is a girl, Teryl 11 years, John 8, Paul 3 1/2, and Michael 2 1/2. Michael has braces on his legs because of a birth defect. In this interview, the two youngest were at home with colds.

The interview is conducted in the presence of a graduate class of approximately forty persons. This is the first opportunity that the parents have had to talk with the counselor, therefore, the preliminary remarks help serve the purpose of providing an orientation to both the parents and class. After talking with the parents, the children are interviewed, and then the session concludes with the parents.

PARENT INTERVIEW

Counselor: We're sending around pictures of Mr. and Mrs. F's youngest children because they have the flu today. Mr. and Mrs. F have four children. Of the two oldest children, Teryl is 11 and John is 8. The other two boys you'll see in pictures are Paul and Mike. Paul is 3 1/2 and Michael is 2 1/2. He is the fellow with the braces.

Now, we want you to be as comfortable with us as we can possibly make it. These class members are for the most part a group of teachers and counselors and a couple of school administrators. But, more important, also many parents are here. As a matter of fact my wife, Elizabeth, is over there and we have four children also. Our purpose in being here is to discover together what others have found to be some principles that relate to living together as families, and as groups in classrooms and other social places. We know from experience that there's a great deal that you experience in your family that's just as true in our family. As a matter of fact as we go along, on occasion I'm going to ask these folks how many of them have something like this going on in their families, and I think you're going to be surprised to find out you've got a lot of companions here. Most of the things that we think are hassles in our family, other people experience as well. There's nothing terribly unique about it. As a result of that, we can learn a lot from each other. We really appreciate the fact that you're willing to come in and talk to us about what's happening in your family because it allows us to learn something about our own. There may be some things that these folks might want to know, and I'm inviting them to ask questions although I may censor it and say I don't think it's going to move us in the direction that we want to go; or you may say "I'd just rather not answer that," or "I don't know," and that's perfectly fine. There's absolutely no expectation that you talk about anything you don't want to talk about. You may ask them questions if you like. You may say, "Well, what would you do about this?" and see what they say. I've found out already that they're very willing to correct me! (laugh)

Now, I see here, an oldest child—a girl and three boys. Ron, you did mention that you were having difficulty with one of the boys but that didn't surprise me. It wouldn't surprise this group either because we have been looking at other families and we know that when you have an oldest child who is a girl, she tends to get along better with the parents than the second child right behind her. Does that tend to be true in your family?

Mother: Yes.

Counselor: OK. (We got a nice smile there.) Again, I don't know Teryl, but we'll see if we're wrong and if we are its OK to correct us. Teryl's probably a girl who would be helpful to her mother. She won't always do what you ask her to do, but she will follow through and do things more readily than the other children. In fact, she'll try to be a pleaser; she'll go along with what your expectations are, Mother and Father, in terms of how an oldest child should be, helping out with the younger children. She will probably get along pretty well in school. In fact, she might even be a model child in school. She may try very hard to do a good job, and, if she has difficulty, it will probably be with that second boy. That's where we're likely to have fights, but with the younger children she'll try to help out as much as she can. Now how does that sound to you?

Mother: Pretty good!

Counselor: O.K. Now, we know one of the children is having some difficulty with John. It may be that all of them do. In fact, I think you're going to discover that all of them work together to keep both of you pretty busy. You're smiling again. But, in all probability, John, will be the most rebellious and independent. Most likely he'll look at the other side of the coin. If there's a rule for the family, he'll find an exception to the rule. He'll try to say it's not fair, that this rule applies to him only in certain situations. Does that sound like something John would say?

Father: Absolutely!

Counselor: This is not to say that John is what is sometimes called a bad child, in fact, we don't even think about bad kids. We're thinking about kids who experience some discouragement. By discouragement we mean that they feel that life is such that right now they're not getting their way—they think the way things "ought to be." They may feel defeated and become very discouraged. I suspect that because you're in here and interested in talking to us, there may not be serious discouragement. You're probably concerned enough to want to try and help out and see that the children are given love and attention and care. But, none the less, in most families you'll have one youngster like John who, because the other kids seem to be having their way by doing well and helping out, chooses to make his place by being troublesome at times.

In the case of Mike, he's special in a couple of ways. He's the youngest and, because he has braces, he has some disability that requires that he receive special attention. Maybe even at birth, it was known that he was going to need some special help and special attention. You see, he won it right away. Paul gets his attention very likely by being cute. He smiles, he's charming, he gets along with just about everybody, and he gets his own way pretty well because others will take care of him. Is that what it's like?

Mother: Yes. It seems like you have known them for years!

Counselor: Well, in a manner of speaking, that's true. It's because your family is like my family, and it's like other families here, too. I guess one of the important things to realize from this is that what works in helping my children may help your children, too.

Mother: I think the group here know that we didn't tell you about the children.

Counselor: I didn't have any foreknowledge of these kids; hadn't met them before they came in the door. This is something which is not unusual, but it sometimes surprises people. Some may think that I'm simply saying this and you're being agreeable because you feel you must. I think they can see the smiles on your faces showing that I'm not putting words in your mouth!

Now, knowing that you have a lot in common with others, let's become specific because, frankly, every family is different from every other family. Now, that may sound contradictory to what I just said, but it's true. I believe that not one of your children is like another and, that you folks aren't like any of us in some respects. We're each unique. As we talk about your kids, I want you to know that we're going to be trying to understand how the kids are unique and how your family is unique. OK?

Father: OK.

Counselor: All right. Would you tell me why you choose to come in this morning?

Father: Well, we thought it would be a different type of experience. We're having some problems with John and it has raised some questions about what we should do; should we encourage him to knock somebody's teeth out; should we encourage him to be a tattle-tale; how should we we treat him? We haven't got any drastic problems, but John gets the idea he wants to run away from home once in a while. He had those ideas when he was a year and a half old!

Counselor: Are there some specific behaviors that you can think of; something that happened recently or persistently that you think you'd like to get some help in working with?

Mother: John? He has been a problem on the bus. I think he's well-controlled in class. Maybe he's worn out by the time the bus gets there. I'm not sure. Awhile ago there was a little boy whose birthday came up and John was very determined that he was going to the birthday party. He didn't have an invitation and when it got a little closer we suggested that they call to invite John to the party. Well, then it's, John, you can't go. Teryl always gets to go to parties. Then, John wasn't going to get on the bus at school until the principal assisted him. When he got off the bus, he was quite upset and wanted to run away. I said, "Well go ahead. It's rather cold out." He packed his suitcase and out the door he went. I watched and thought, "I wonder how far he's going to go before I have to get him." He's a very strong-willed child. He doesn't like to back down when he's done something. Pretty soon he came back and snuck in the door. When I looked out to see which way he went, there he was.

Counselor: So now we know for sure that he won't go too far in his efforts to impress you. Let's see if I can help you by starting with a typical day. How do things proceed with breakfast and getting dressed and things of that sort?

Mother: Well, just since last Christmas, I started working at the day care center in New Lexington. Ron usually wakes up first and tries to get me up. Then he usually gets Michael and Paul up. They're usually awake. It's just a matter of getting them up out of bed and taking them out to the table. Breakfast is served . . .

Counselor: Excuse me a minute. You said you get Mike and Paul up. Are they on a high bed?

Father: Michael can't get up by himself. He's totally paralyzed from the waist down. Usually between five-thirty and six-thirty, he hollers, "Daddy, come and get me, I want my cereal." And I usually take Paul and Michael out, set them up at the table, and give them something to eat. Then Pam (Mother) gets up and gets dressed and makes her bed. I make a pot of tea and she comes out and has some breakfast. Then, about a quarter till seven Teryl and John get up before their mother leaves. They come out and although I don't insist that they eat right away, usually by five of seven they're having their breakfast when she's leaving.

Counselor: Do they make their breakfast or do you?

Father: We're changing that right now. This is a mistake I suppose we've been making. We have never felt that our kids ought to pour their own cereal in the bowl but this is one of the things they're teaching Michael and Paul at school. We've cut their meat up and put it on the plate and things like this. In the last two weeks we've started to put their meat on their plate and although they didn't know what to do with it, they're finding out.

Mother: It was ridiculous. They were finished eating by the time we were starting. We could all be eating together. It really works.

Counselor: Letting them learn to take care of themselves really works.

Mother: It does! (Laughter) I've learned quite a bit in just a little while at the day care. We've had an eating problem with Paul. He just didn't want to eat anything at all. He liked snacks but not basic good food. And now that he's serving himself he's eating real well. They have a counselor at school who suggested that we don't make any kind of a fuss if he doesn't eat. We do brag when he's cleaned his plate. Now that we're not talking about it, he's eating. So serving themselves has worked.

Counselor: If you had come in two month ago before you had had this experience and I had said this to you, I think you would probably have thought I was out of my head. Right?

Mother: Well, that was my first reaction. I thought, "They just can't do it. They're too little." But they can!

Counselor: Sure. They can do a lot more than you realize. When Paul wanted his food differently, he was getting attention and a special service. The youngest children generally know how to press other people into their service. While John feels its hopeless, he can't get what he wants, Paul's convinced he can get everything. All he has to do is want it and it will be taken care of. (Mother smiles and nods agreement.) On the other hand, they can now learn the satisfaction of being able to care for themselves. But it does require that you work with them early. Now what I'd like to suggest is that when you see the youngsters doing something that is showing progress toward taking care of themselves, self-reliance, more independence, more responsibility, and so forth, think not so much about *how* they're doing as about *what* they're doing. If you can just make that distinction, not *how* they're doing but *what* they're doing, and say for example, to Paul when he's just finished eating, "My goodness, you must have really enjoyed what you ate," rather than "Oh, I see you ate everything on your plate." There is a difference because the process of eating can give you a great deal of enjoyment and satisfaction; you like what you eat and feel some satisfaction upon eating a good meal.

The reason for this is it avoids the chance that kids will compare themselves. You know, Teryl didn't finish, John didn't finish, *I* finished; therefore, I did better. You don't want to encourage the competition between kids. So if you simply say, "Hey you really seem to have gotten enjoyment out of eating that meal," or when they bring a report card home, "You seem to like your reading better than you do your math," emphasizing the areas in which they have the strengths; or saying, "Maybe you would like some help with this or that." And, "What has the teacher said about these other areas," or "Do you have any concern about it?" You'll find that by not being terribly impressed by grades, they'll do as well as they can with proper encouragement.

Mother: Teryl is an all A student. She does quite well without any effort. It's really disgusting! (Laughs) She doesn't work up to her capacity and she's still getting straight A's. She isn't, she isn't . . .

Counselor: Challenged?

Mother: Right, she can do it without an effort, and I'm afraid it's going to make her not work quite as hard as she really could. I think this is another conflict for John because he does have a harder time with his lessons. It is *work* for him to get the grades that he gets, and he sees she can do nothing and get good grades.

Counselor: Just another confirmation that life is unfair. (Mother murmuring assent.) "Look how hard I have to work." I would like to say that I'm not so concerned and this may influence what I say to you about trying to get Teryl working harder.

Let's go back to breakfast. So we've got Paul who had something of an eating problem, but now he's taking care of himself and the whole eating pattern for the family is beginning to change and get better.

Father: Right. Then following breakfast, Pam has gone off to work, and Teryl and John are usually dressed by 7:30, and they have had their breakfast. Then Teryl usually goes and makes her bed. John is beginning to make his bed and get it done. Then he goes on to Paul and Michael's beds and usually makes them.

Mother: Teryl practices her piano usually in the morning before she goes to school.

Father: Right. She practices her piano between 8:30 and 9:00 when I'm not there to see whether it's happening or not. I think it's happening.

Counselor: Now one thing here, Ron. You're at home with the kids. Pam, you've gone off to work. Michael and Paul are still there?

Mother: No, they go with me.

Counselor: In terms of Teryl and John getting dressed, do you have to remind them about that?

Father: No, I don't think there's much of a problem there.

Mother: They've dressed themselves for quite some time. Usually we have to remind John to comb his hair . . .

Father: He combs his hair, but not good enough. Or he comes out with a short sleeved shirt in zero weather.

Counselor: Isn't that beautiful, he just leaves a bit of something, just one little thing so you have to be sure to remind him about it.

Mother: Thursday they went on a field trip and it was really surprising. He came out and he had every hair right where it belonged. So he can do it.

Counselor: Yes, he knows how to do it.

Father: Usually I leave for work about 8:00 and leave Teryl and John home for an hour by themselves. They've done real well. There have been no problems there. Teryl usually packs her lunch in the morning while John makes the other two beds. She does that on her own.

Counselor: And John?

Father: Well, she fixes John's also. John has some trash to take out. There's usually a couple of diapers from Michael that he takes out and puts in the trash for me.

Counselor: Now, he does this without you telling him?

Father: No sir! (Laughter)

Counselor: I'd have been surprised if you'd have said yes.

Student: Dr. Sweeney, I have a question. (To Mother) When you decided to go to work, did you talk this over with the two older children and decide what they would do differently in order for you to work? Or, was this just a decision made between you and your husband? Were the children involved in it?

Mother: Somewhat, yes, I told them that I had an opportunity to go to work and that they were going to have to accept certain responsibilities. We didn't sit down and say, "We're going to have a discussion about going to work."

Father: I don't know that there was much discussion between Pam and me. I wasn't too sure I could agree with it in the beginning, but it hasn't been bad leaving the children by themselves.

Mother: He obviously doesn't want me to work.

Father: I wasn't against her going to work; I just wasn't sure what it would do to the family relationships. We have so many commitments with Michael. What happens if the kids get sick? It's working out though. I guess they understand at the Day Care because they work with children. John and Teryl watch Lassie in the morning on television. I'm so drastically against TV, but I do let them watch Lassie in the morning. When Lassie goes off they have to turn the TV off and come back upstairs. I would say that TV is John's number one love. He does enjoy it and this is what we pull away from him as his main punishment. I think this hurts him worse than anything that we could do. They turn off the TV at 8:30 and the bus comes at ten after nine . . .

Counselor: OK, so they're off to school by now, and you're off to work. Who comes home first and what happens then?

Mother: I do. I'm home by four before Teryl and John get home. They come home from school at about 10 after four, and come in and have a snack and watch TV in the afternoon. Then we usually have dinner around six.

Counselor: Are there any fights between home time and dinner time?

Mother: Not usually. It's usually pretty quiet. There are certain programs they like to watch on TV and they'll go down and watch those. Paul's beginning to watch some program. There for a while he would go down and stand in front of the TV to see if John would yell. But he's beginning to watch, too. We have a large basement and they have their riding toys. They play on their toys usually until dinner time. Teryl doesn't watch too much TV; she likes to read quite well. She has scouts one day a week. We usually have dinner about six.

Counselor: Is it pretty quiet at dinner time?

Father: The children want to talk.

Mother: It's more of a . . .

Father: . . . complete runaway during dinner. They want to relate everything. John wants to tell you everything he's seen on TV.

Mother: I've had to tell him, "If I wanted to see what the program was I'd be down there sitting with you. I don't want to hear it." And so we hear it all the more.

Counselor: Excuse me. Isn't it interesting. Dad hates that TV and what's John want to talk about? (Laughter) So at supper time the TV talk is a nuisance. How do you usually handle that?

Father: Well, it's not always TV. John talks about everything.

Mother: Everything that has gone on through the day. It's like a competing thing. Paul may be talking and John interrupts because he's got something really important he has to say. And then Paul talks a little bit louder so that he can get in what he wants to say.

Father: Teryl is challenging, also, at this time.

Mother: It goes back and forth between each of them—talking about nothing important, just babbling to hear themselves.

Counselor: Is that enough of a problem that you'd like to change it?

Father: I don't know. We've been trying to listen a little bit to what they're saying but it's difficult to know what's important to an eight-year-old. We try to listen to part of it and try to stop them enough so they have time to eat their dinner.

Mother: This is the thing that has really caused most problems. They have so much to say that they don't eat.

Counselor: So what do you do?

Mother: Just say, "Well, why don't you eat your dinner," and "We'll talk about it later."

Counselor: What are you doing while all this is going on?

Mother: Usually we have dinner when Ron comes home, so there's talking that we would like to do. I think they realize this, and I think maybe this is the reason why they're talking.

Counselor: Everybody wants to talk at the same time and they know that you two want to talk. Would you like to know some things to do about that?

Mother: Right.

Counselor: OK. Let's move on and finish the day and we'll come back to this talking at the table. I don't want to flood you with too many things. Actually, we just want to come back to one or two. There are a few situations that you've mentioned that you said you'd like some help with. One is how to handle the fights. You've mentioned that all the kids are in the fights. Paul's bedtime. Talking at the table. Can you think of any others that stand out in your mind that you especially want to work on?

Mother: Teryl just the last little while has been putting off bedtime with her reading. Is there a way that we can work around this, or should we just say, "This is the time that you're supposed to go to bed. Whatever you're doing has to be stopped." Or should we allow her more time? Maybe she's not requiring as much sleep.

Counselor: I suspect that the answer that I might give you would not be acceptable, but let me suggest this. You might consider finding out what time the kids think they should go to bed. In other words, ask them what time they should be in bed at night. I mean, "What time do *you* feel that you should be in bed at night? Is that an agreeable time?" And, once they know the time, then you really shouldn't have to talk about it any further. Now the younger children won't know how to tell time but they'll know by the routine what time to go to bed. I think we can ask Teryl what time she thinks she should be in bed, and then she is responsible for it. One of the mistakes that we often make is that bedtime becomes a big struggle with some families. If it's an occasional problem, I don't think I would make much of it. Can she read in her own room?

Mother: Yes.

Counselor: I think if she goes to her own room and reads, she's the one who's going to be tired the next day. I just wouldn't make too much of it. Do they have their own alarm clock?

Mother: No. Well, built in. There's not an oversleeping problem.

Counselor: Well, I thought if they had a clock they would know the time.

Mother: She has a clock-radio in her room but she doesn't use it for that purpose.

Counselor: You're most fortunate that they get themselves up. With many families that's where we start—with an alarm clock.

Well, let's focus then for the moment on the fighting and the table talk, because these seem to be two big items. With regard to fighting, you need to appreciate first of all that the fighting is done for your benefit. And, because it is for your benefit, you've got to get yourself out of the situation. Now, one of the things that's recommended is that for example, you go to the bathroom. If you're home alone and the kids are fighting, go to the bathroom, have a magazine, have a transistor radio and just be oblivious of what's going on. You don't want to say anything about it.

Now, that may sound like its going to be very difficult, and it may well be, until you understand they're fighting for your benefit. Now, I'm going to tell the kids this. We're going to talk about how they are all conspiring together, and how Teryl will allow certain things to happen so that she'll come out looking good; how Paul will have the satisfaction of knowing John got in trouble; and how Mike stands by enjoying the whole free-for-all. So, you want to remove yourself from that situation. Now, if this happens, for example, at a time when you're watching your favorite TV program, then everybody goes to their room and they can fight all they want to until they're ready to come back, either individually or in a group. Now, in mind of the fact that you're really not that keen about TV anyway, I could see how you could very well turn off the TV and when the kids have left, talk or read or do whatever you choose to. If it's a program that you want to watch, or if you are where you need to be, then its for them to remove themselves physically. Now, what I'm saying is, the kids know that it bugs you. You may have to talk about this together.

From what we've heard so far, the fighting probably won't happen when you are there by yourself, Pam, so the bathroom technique may not need to be used. But it may happen when you've all had supper and both of you have sat down to watch TV, read the paper, or do whatever you do. They may start their fussing and fighting, but we've set a new rule in the family, "When you fight it takes place in your room, not in our room. The TV room is our room and we're not involved in fights, so you must leave the room. When you're ready to come back you can." Well, who wants to fight if nobody's going to pay attention.

Mother: I do the books for a company, and I've been doing this in the basement. The table's separate from the TV room but usually when I go down there, the children are right there. This is upsetting and I think they could play there when I'm not there. Yesterday, I had gone down and finished my work. They were playing and didn't upset me, but when I went upstairs to do something every one of them, Michael included, trooped up. I thought, "Gee, I'm being followed." How would you combat that?

Counselor: Which part? The part about going . . .

Mother: All of it.

Father: Ignore them again?

Counselor: Well, have you gone into an area where they usually play in order to do your work? Is that what you're saying?

Father: Well, yes, that's usually their playroom. But they don't go down there to play unless she's down there.

Counselor: OK, so they wait until you're there to hassle you. It may be that if the rule applies to everybody, maybe you need to find a space where you're not where they are. The kitchen might be a better place to do your work. Could that be?

Mother: No, I think they would be in the kitchen.

Counselor: Well, no. They can't have it both ways. See, I can ask them a question: "Where should you be when your mother has her work to do?" and let them decide where they should be.

Mother: OK, I see what you're saying.

Counselor: They can't have it both ways, so what I can do is help you find a place where they won't bother you.

Mother: OK.

Father: About this squabbling situation, Paul just teases John enough that John hits him on the back or pats him a little hard. I don't think he ever hurts him. You say ignore them, but Paul, you don't ignore him. He comes and climbs up or stands up on top of me or bangs into me to make sure I know that he's crying.

Counselor: Paul comes to you?

Father: Right.

Counselor: So you go to the bathroom or your bedroom. Even children understand the bathroom is a place where you get privacy. It's sacred.

Father: Not at our house.

Counselor: Well, it is when the door is closed and locked. The same thing can be true of your bedroom. If both of you want to go, then you can go in the bedroom and lock the door, put your music on and do your work or read your books or whatever. Now many parents have images of being locked in a room for hours. It doesn't happen and it requires confidence. Now, if you don't want to do this, that's fine. Just let us know right from the beginning that you don't see yourself doing that. Then we won't work on that.

Father: Mmm.

Mother: We can try.

Counselor: It will be important to be consistent, because most parents find it will take one or two times. We've had kids who stop and say, "Don't go in the bathroom." . . . (Laughter) . . . It really happens.

Mother: Even at the dinner table, if they're squabbling, you're saying . . .

Counselor: Oh no, at table time we've got another suggestion.

Father: I think I'm not so concerned about feeling locked in my room all the time, but I feel that I ought to be accessible to those kids at any second that I'm there. It would hurt me that they couldn't get to me.

Counselor: We've got the "good father" here. "At any moment they may need me."

Father: We've never shut ourselves out from them when we're there and no matter where we are, they know they can come to us.

Counselor: You're not shutting yourselves out except to the extent that they want you to be shut out. That's the message. They decide. All we're trying to do is win their cooperation. They've decided they're going to throw a fit in order to get your attention and you've said, "You can get my attention in other ways. This way I won't let you have it." And you just withdraw. As soon as they stop the noise, and stop making the cries and so forth, you can go back out. You've seen cartoons I'm sure where kids walk blocks to get home to be able to cry and complain about what happened at the playground. They can wait that long. They can turn it on and off just as . . . we call it "water power." It's a way of managing other people. So, how do you feel about this now. If you're uncomfortable with it, it's OK.

Father: Now I am, but I'll try it and see.

Counselor: Okay, let's take a little break and then I'll talk with the children.

CHILDREN INTERVIEW

Counselor: Now, do you know why you came down today?

Teryl: (Murmers) "No."

Counselor: You have no idea at all?

Teryl: Not really.

Counselor: Do you want to guess? (Silence)

What about you, John, would you like to guess? You don't want to guess at all. Well, your parents have some situations at home that they're not real sure how to handle. They think that the situations that deal with you kids fighting, for example, they're not sure how to handle. So they don't know what to do with you kids. How about that?

(Silence)

Do you know what to do with your Mom and Dad? (Some nonverbal response) Ah, I think I know better than that, John. OK. Well, what are some things that you consider to be kind of a hassle at home? Do you have any problems that you can think of?

John: Brothers bugging you when you don't want bugged.

Counselor: OK, brothers bug you. All the brothers? One more than the other?

John: Mostly the middle one.

Counselor: Mostly the middle one.

John: Yeah, Paul.

Counselor: Is that Paul? OK, Paul wants to get your attention a lot, huh?

John: He takes things away from me.

Counselor: OK, so Paul takes things that you want to play with and that bugs you. Any other kinds of things?

John: He bites.

Counselor: He bites you, too? Uh, hum. Does he bite hard?

Teryl: Yes.

Counselor: Does he bite *you*, too? . . . Not so much I think. I think he bites John more. Right? Yeah, OK. You guys, do you have fights in the family? So you agree with your mom and dad, Hum? How many times a day do you fight?

Teryl: At least once every day.

Counselor: At least once a day. John doesn't think so. Is that right John? Does once a day sound right?

John: Maybe.

432   *Adlerian Counseling*

Counselor: Yeah, maybe. You're trying to think back on how many times you get bit, I think. You don't always get bit, but there are some hassles. About one a day. What happens when you have a fight? Can you describe a fight that's just gone on recently?

Teryl: One wants to watch one TV program, and another another.

Counselor: OK. So then what happens?

John: We get to arguing, and finally one walks off and lets the other watch it. Then the other turns it to the channel the other one wants to watch.

Counselor: Ah ha, so when one guy walks off then another guy enters the fight. He'll come in and change . . .

Teryl: No, the guy that you were fighting with will change the channel to the one you wanted to watch.

Counselor: Oh, I see. OK so you resolve that yourself then? Huh? OK. Do you have any fights where you don't resolve it yourself? (Nods, Yes) OK, what happens? Can you think of a fight like that? Something that maybe's happened recently?

Teryl: You can get sent to your room.

Counselor: OK. Oh, you can get sent to your room. Who sends you to your room?

Both: Usually our mother.

Counselor: Oh, I see. Is Mom generally the one who comes in and helps with the fight?

Teryl: Hmm, not al . . . No.

Counselor: Not always.

John: Not usually.

Counselor: Not usually.

John: Paul fights the most.

Teryl: Yeah, he comes in and decides to fight.

John: He comes in and he'll knock me down on to the floor and start wrestling me.

Counselor: Paul comes in. Now lets see, Paul is what, he's 3 1/2. Is that right?

Teryl & John: Hm, hmm.

Counselor: Paul comes in and knocks down . . . and you're about eight?

John: Hm, hmm.

Counselor: He knocks you down, and beats you up.

Teryl: Really, John lets him knock him down.

Counselor: Oh, I see. Is that right, John?

John: No.

Teryl: He knocks you down, and beats you up.

Teryl: Really, John lets him knock him down.

Counselor: Oh, I see. Is that right, John?

John: No.

Teryl: I think he really likes to fight with Paul though.

Counselor: Uh, huh. What do you think, John? (Laughter) John's smiling again. I think you like to fight, John. Sometimes, hum?

John: Not really.

Counselor: OK. All right. So sometimes when you have your fights, your mother or maybe your father more often, comes in on a white horse and like the Lone Ranger saves you? What does he do?

Teryl: Gets mad.

Counselor: Does he get mad?

Teryl: Sometimes.

Counselor: Uh, hum. So, it really bugs Mom and Dad when you guys get into a fight then. Uh, humm. Why do you think you get into fights?

Teryl: Humm? (Murmurs I don't know)

Counselor: Don't know why? What purpose would be served by it?

John: If I want to watch a different cartoon than she wants to watch, she will end up flipping the channels 'til we finally decide on one.

Counselor: Uh, hmm. But when you don't flip the channels and find one?

Teryl: We get in a fight.

Counselor: Uh, humm. Do you want to know what I think? . . .

Well, you said, yes, John said no. I guess I have a choice. Do I have a choice? I think, John, that you like to get in a fight because it gets your mom and dad involved. I think it keeps them busy with you. Could that be?

(Silence.)

Teryl thinks "maybe, yes." What about you John?

John: I agree with *her*.

Counselor: You'll agree with her, you won't agree with me though, right? So fights are very often to keep Papa and Mama busy. You know what I've suggested to your Mom and Dad? I've suggested that they not get involved in your fights. What do you think about that?

John: I think that's better.

Counselor: You think that's better. I don't really think you'll like that,
            John. If Mom and Dad don't enter into your fights, you
            won't have anybody to bother with you. Oh, you think
            Teryl will? Teryl, are you going to come in on your white
            horse and save the day? (Nods, no!) Teryl says she's not
            going to do it, John. How about that?

John: Well, she'll . . . I don't think she'll give up the minute I
            hit her.

Counselor: Oh, you're going to hit her, is that it? Well, Teryl . . .

John: We always get hitting each otner.

Counselor: Well, let me tell you what I've suggested to your Mom and
            Dad and maybe Teryl might do this too. I've suggested to
            your Mom and Dad that if you guys are downstairs and
            you're into your own fight that they just closet themselves
            away somewhere, or do something that they want to that
            takes them completely out of the noise range, and com-
            pletely out of any being bothered by it all. They won't
            even know you're fighting. They won't even be concerned
            about it.

John: They won't even hear it. I know how they'll do it. They'll
            run the vacuum. It makes too much noise.

Counselor: Oh? They'll run the vacuum and ignore whatever it
            happens to be. There will be no reason to come in and get
            involved in your fights. I don't think you're going to like
            that John. What do you think? . . .

            (Silence)

            Not so sure. No. You see, John, there are a lot of
            things that go on that are to get your folks involved but
            from now on they won't. They'll let you kids take care of
            it yourselves.

            OK, one other thing that Mom and Dad talked with us
            about is the fact that dinner time sometimes gets to be kind

of a hassle. Everybody wants to talk at the same time. Is that true?

Teryl: Hmmm.

Counselor: Well, I suggested maybe there'd be a new rule at dinner time. The new rule is that everybody will get a chance to talk, one at a time. And if somebody wants to talk and get loud, and begin making it difficult for everyone else to be able to eat and enjoy dinner, then they leave the table until they're able to come back and join in with the rest of the family.

John: My mom and dad already know that.

Counselor: Do they already know that? Do they tell you to leave the table, John.

John: Uh, hum.

Counselor: OK. Can you come back to the table when you want to?

John: Hmmm?

Counselor: Kind of. OK. Well, we're just clarifying that so you know that when you leave you can come back. Now, this applies to Mike and to Paul also. There is one other thing that maybe you can help with. That could be true of any of these things by the way. If you see some things you'd like to see handled a little differently, we would like your suggestions. Mother reports that she has work to do at home, and her place to do it so far has been down in the TV room where you kids play very often. She said sometimes it's difficult to work because she wants to work when you kids are down there playing.

John: Maybe we could go in and watch TV while she's working, and not get on the toys that make a racket.

Counselor: OK. Now is the TV in the same room where she works?

Teryl: No.

Counselor: Oh, it's in another room. OK. The toys are in that room?

Teryl: No.

John: The toys are in the room where the TV is.

Teryl: They end up in the other room though.

Counselor: Oh, I see. They end up in the other room where she needs to work, and that becomes a part of the problem then. I didn't understand that. Well, let's see if I understand now, John. I understand you're saying that maybe when Mother has to work you kids will watch the TV quietly and not play with any toys that would be noisy. Does that sound like it would be possible?

Teryl: It would be a little hard.

Counselor: And how would that be hard, Teryl?

Teryl: Paul and Michael.

Counselor: You don't think they would go along with this rule?

John: Yes, but there's another problem with the TV. When Mom types it messes up the TV and it makes a racket.

Counselor: Oh, I see. So when she's running the typewriter it interferes with the TV. Could it maybe be that you kids could go outside or go up to your bedrooms, or play someplace else besides down there while she's working? Would that be a reasonable solution to suggest?

John: Yes, but I don't think Paul and Michael would.

Counselor: You don't think they'll go along with that?

John: Um, nhh.

Teryl: They might.

Counselor: They might, though. Maybe the family could sit down and talk to the boys and see how they feel about that? I guess you two would have a chance to show them how to do it. That way they could learn how from you guys. Do you think so? (They nod, yes.) Well, I'll tell you what, John. I'll tell your mother what you've suggested. It seems like Teryl's agreeing. Maybe you can talk as a family with Mike and Paul when you get home and see what they think about that.

Are there any things that you would like help with? Is there something that's going on at home, or some things that Mom and Dad do that you wish they didn't do. (Silence) Nothing? John, what about you? . . . OK. Well, I get the feeling that you really have a nice family, that your Mom and Dad really care a lot about you. They pointed out some things that I was really pleased to hear, for example that Teryl helps to make John's lunch in the morning, and that John takes out the trash. We really need to do these kinds of things for each other in a family. One of the things that I suggested to your Mom and Dad is that a couple of times a week you kids all plan together with your Mom and Dad what you can do to have a good time together as a family. Maybe you will choose some place to go, or a game to play, or some way to have a good time together. Would you like that? Do you think Mike and Paul would? (They nod, yes.) We want to include them.

You really have folks who care a lot about you kids. They want to have you grown up being able to take care of life and take care of yourself. I have a feeling they're going to be doing everything they can to help you find ways that you can deal with your life situations and have a good time. They're going to be looking for you to give them some ideas to help them out and it's going to be important that you talk to them about it. Now, this thing about fights and talking at the table. It's simply a matter that if we're going to live together we need to find ways to do it so that we're not hassled. So, they don't bug you and you don't bug them. Do you think this conference has been helpful? (Both smile and nod, yes.)

PARENT INTERVIEW RESUMED

Counselor: ... About the fighting thing, Teryl and John didn't really like the idea that you wouldn't get into it. You may be surprised to know that John knows that you run the vacuum when you don't want to hear him.

Mother: Gee!

Counselor: Well, he knows that. He said, "She'll run the vacuum and then she won't know we're fighting." So he already understood. I think I've said to you before that kids sometimes know how many times they have to be called, and so forth. They know also how you're likely to respond.

Student: Is it a coincidence that you're busy and you run the vacuum cleaner or do you really turn it on to drown out the noise?

Mother: Oh, I don't think I ever have!

Counselor: Well, it's occurred to him that you have. In his mind he wanted you to come in and save him and you were busy with that darn vacuum. He was not too keen about the idea that you're not going to come in on your white horse and save him. What he said was that Teryl would do it. Well, of course Teryl's hearing everything we're saying. Being a good surrogate momma, she will probably pick up on this, and if she doesn't then you can point this out to her the next time.

About the table talk, they said that you've already done this, probably with the one difference that when they left the table maybe they could come back, but not always. Now, if someone leaves the table and doesn't come back, you clean up and put away the food. One of the outcomes is that someone misses supper so there's some motivation for wanting to come back and fit in. You want to take advantage of that by not leaving the food so that they get to eat some more later. Follow me? In other words if they act up at the table, you say, "Hey, if you're going to be that way, you know the rule." Now, on some occasions, especially with the little people if they're into a power kind of thing, you may actually have to remove them. That's unusual, and I don't think you'll have to do it with your kids. So don't do that first. First is simply, "Hey, you know the rule. Leave. When you're ready to come back you may." Now if they leave the table and dilly-dally, and you leave the food, you've made it easy for them not to experience the full consequences. It's not punishment. It's just what happens when dinner's done. We clean up. Now, I didn't say anything about the cleaning up yet. I think that if you make straightening up after dinner a fun thing to do, they'll swing right into it. They really care for each other, and they like you. It's obvious they really don't want to hassle you too much, just a little bit. So, its really a low level of hassling that you've got. That's really a good sign. It's going to be very easy to deal with these things.

Counselor: Now, the question about mother working, where could she be, where could they be. I think they concluded that they couldn't be downstairs while you're working because the TV gets interference from the typewriter, and the other boys wouldn't go along. That part they really shared in most. If you talk with them a little further about it you may find other alternatives, but allow them to help decide where they can be while you're working. The point is, Mom has to have time to be able to get her work done so that she can cook the supper, so that she can have time to play with them, and so that you can have time to be together. And I did mention to them, that I had also suggested that you plan one or two times a week when you're going to play together. It may be Sunday after Church, or Friday night when everybody's at home and the work is behind you. Whatever is a mutually good time for all of you. They liked that. They felt good about that, and that's very promising.

Parents: (The parents responded with comfort in the recommendations and pleasure with what they learned.)

Note: Subsequent interviews involved the younger children. The youngest boy's solicitation of special service was quickly identified and corrective recommendations implemented. Parents and children alike reported fewer "fights," greater cooperation on helping mom get her work done, and the parents found playtime with the children a good time investment with fewer hassles.

Appendix B

FAMILY COUNCIL

What follows are excerpts from the actual typescript of the first family council meeting of the author's family. Besides mother and father, there are three children. The oldest daughter (Elizabeth Rose) was almost nine, the second daughter (Ann), seven, and the youngest, (Tom), 3 years. This session was video taped in the home.

The oldest daughter is about to leave on her first Girl Scout camp adventure for one week. At one point in the meeting, she gives an indication of being uncomfortable with leaving but it was more nonverbal than verbal. The reader will note the youngest child leaves the group periodically, made faces at the camera, and finally evoked a response from the middle child (second daughter) who responded in a characteristic way. Even the typescript revealed how skillfully the youngest gained attention.

This was a first and by no means model family meeting. As relative neophytes to the Adlerian approach, mother was reading the section in Dreikurs' on family meetings *Children the Challenge* while father was giving the children an introduction to the purpose of the meeting. You'll note that the oldest daughter catches on quickly to the equalitarian concept and starts in on "new rules" just for Dad! The second daughter is a willing, if not enthusiastic, participant.

For families who regularly talk over events and problems during the course of a week, a meeting such as this one is probably rarely if ever needed. On the other hand, for the family where members tend to see each other rarely altogether, the family meeting has merit. While the recommendation is that a time be adhered to regularly, our experience suggests that once everyone learns how to participate in a meeting, these skills carry over and can be called upon even on an irregular meeting time basis, i.e., meeting occasionally.

Father: Do you remember us talking about a family council before?

Children:	Yes . . .

Father: Well, I wanted to do this now because I was hoping that before you got away, Elizabeth Rose, we would be able to talk about it and get out of the way whatever things we needed to so that the next time you came home, we'll be able to meet again. Your mother's still reading the book now and trying to find out something about . . . What are you laughing about?

Mother: I'm just laughing because I'm reading here—This is the way to do it. Read the directions as you "fly the plane!" (Laugh)

Father: Got to find out what you're supposed to do. (Laugh)

Mother: Yeah.

Father: Well, you know Mom and I have attended discussion groups where we've been talking about how to rear children and also how to have a better family. A lot of the things that we've done, and still do for that matter, we feel are not good for you children or us. So we're trying to find better ways to do it and we think that the best way to do it is for you to help us. Now one of the things that is really important is for us to learn how to treat you as equals, like real people, and also how to, for us as a family, to work together cooperatively. You know I've said a lot of times, you've got to cooperate. We have always felt as though we have a good family, we've always been happy, but we do have problems at times and you have problems with us. (Children nod agreement) So, if we get together at a fixed time when we agree say every week, then anybody who's got something they want to talk over with the whole family, knows that they'll be able to do it at that time.

Father: One of the things we need to do is to learn how to listen to each other and for Mom and Dad not to talk so much. We should listen. The only reason I'm talking so much today is because I feel I need to tell you about the meetings to help us get started.

One of the things they say is really important is everybody has an equal vote. I thought one of the ways we could show that, just to show that we're all equals, I have these five pieces of paper and they are all the same size. Just for fun we can start by putting your name on one, Elizabeth, put your name on one, Tom, Ann's name on one, put Mother's name on one and I've got one. Now, if there's anything that we need to vote on or that would be helpful to vote on, then we all have the same vote. In other words, oldest daughter's, second daughter's and son's and Mother's and mine are all the same.[1]

From what I can tell from people who have done this kind of thing before, it is important that we not use this as a gripe session alone. It isn't for me and Mother to tell you girls what you're doing wrong. It's just a good time for us to sit down and talk to find out how each other's doing and things that are on our minds.

Oldest
Daughter: And what's going on.

Father: Right.

And if somebody's not cooperating in the family, we can talk about that. One of the things that we can do is talk about it and decide what might be the best solution for us as we see it. Not as I see it or as Mother sees it.

Second
Daughter: I don't get the voting.

Father: You don't understand the voting?

Second
Daughter: No.

Father: What would we vote about? Is that what you mean?

---

[1]Note: Dreikurs in his works later concluded that voting is not conducive to the spirit of cooperation desired. There always tend to be winners and losers.

Second Daughter:	No. I don't understand how you do it.
Father:	Well, let's pretend for a moment that we all felt that the dishes ought to be cleaned up, or that there ought to be a time when we all get together. Let's try one for real right now. I know that I keep real bad hours in terms of work and things I do, I can't always be depended upon to be at home. I'd like to be here. How would you feel about meeting on Sunday mornings?
First Daughter:	Don't we always?
Father:	Well, I mean that would be the time that we would meet for our council. This is generally when I'm home. I go to church with the family, whether it's morning or evening, but we agree that we meet on a Sunday, probably on Sunday morning after breakfast.
Mother:	Instead of just sitting around the house, we would make it a point to sit down together and talk together and we would call it our council. We would call it our family council time, even though you are right, we are always all here on Sunday morning.
Second Daughter:	Almost.
Mother:	Well, yeah. Usually, we're all here, but we're all doing something else. You're watching TV, he's reading the paper, and Tom's playing so we would make . . .
Son:	Will we be taping next time?
Father:	Maybe, maybe we will. Now, if you don't like the taping, we can always stop. We don't have to do that.
Children:	No, no I don't care . . .
Father:	Well, is Sunday OK with you girls?
Daughters:	Uh huh, yeah.

Mother:	Then we need to vote on it to make sure.
Father:	Right. All right, everybody who's in favor of meeting on Sunday put your hand up. All agreed?
Mother:	Four in favor and one abstaining. (Son had left the group) You've come back. Maybe we ought to ask him.
Father:	All right. Son, do you, would you like to meet on Sundays like we're meeting today? Would this be an OK day for you?
Mother:	OK, that's your vote. You can put it down on the table.
Father:	Yours is just as good as everybody else's. Now do you understand? Sometimes we may not want to just vote, we may say that we agree, and that constitutes a vote. I guess when it would be critical would be when we didn't agree, then we would vote. When we vote, if three people say it ought to be one way and two say it ought to be another way, the three would have the say as to how it should be.
	And if we make mistakes, that's OK. In other words, if we decide to do something and find out in between times it is not such a good idea, at the next family meeting, the next Sunday, we can talk about it and change our decision.
Mother:	It doesn't have to stay.
Father:	Right, but during that week we decided to do something, we'll have to try the best we can, and . . .
Second Daughter:	But how long will we meet? We won't have time.
Father:	Do you think it best, that there be a time that would be better to do it than mornings?
Second Daughter:	What times does everybody get up?

First
Daughter: That's a good question.

Second
Daughter: Because when there's some that get up at seven and some that get up at eight and then some that get up at ten and nine.

First
Daughter: And eleven, too.

Father: Do you have any suggestions?

Mother: Some at twelve, go ahead and say it. (laughs)

Father: Sometimes, huh?

Daughters: Yeah. (smiles)

Father: Sometimes, and you know who it is, don't you? (laugh)

Daughters: Yeah.

Father: The last one out of bed.

First
Daughter: Everybody's just got this habit of getting up when they. . .

Mother: How about if we make the point of getting up at ten o'clock.

Father: Be up by ten?

Mother: Be up by ten and that will give us a chance to get ready for twelve o'clock Mass.

First
Daughter: And then we could vote on those that would make the breakfast.

Second
Daughter: Yeah!

Father:	You'd like that, wouldn't you?
Mother:	That sounds like a winner already!
First Daughter:	First we got to vote on me.
Second Daughter:	If we would start off like Sunday, we'd vote first on who would do it and then, that same Sunday, we'd vote on who would do it next week and so on.
First Daughter:	Of course, you're not going to go alphabetically!
Mother:	You don't think so, huh? (laughs)
Second Daughter:	No.
Mother:	I think I'll make that suggestion!
Second Daughter:	No, no!
Mother:	I suggest we go alphabetically!
First Daughter:	Okay.
Mother:	I wouldn't have even thought of it 'till you opened your mouth!
Second Daughter:	Okay, first daughter, you can go ahead and do it first!
Father:	Well, are we saying that we're going to meet at ten o'clock on Sunday mornings, then?
Daughters:	Um hum.
Father:	Is that all right with you, son?

Son:	And from ten to ten thirty. It doesn't have to be that long.
Father:	In other words, it doesn't have to be the exact time.
Son:	Yeah.
Father:	Well, we'll be meeting next week on Sunday.
First Daughter:	We'll vote next week who makes breakfast!
Father:	For whoever's here.
Second Daughter:	Not me!
Father:	I just remembered that I'm likely to be out of town next week, so you folks make it to the meeting without Rosie (oldest) and me. Do you have any questions about the council?
First Daughter:	Not about it, but—it wouldn't make any sense anyhow.
Father:	Well you can ask. You know, in this instance, for example, Tom is making noises to get our attention and so far we've been able to ignore him. Now if he interferes with your being able to think or talk, we can ask him to . . . (no one seems bothered) Well, can we think of anything else we need to talk about?
First Daughter:	The dogs.
Father:	What about the dogs?
First Daughter:	Well, ever since you started feeding them, I remind you about the dogs and you say—um, like at night, I think, this is only what I think, I hear the car drive up, and then, I hear a click-click at the door, and after that I hear some footsteps and I think that after I hear the car come

in, I should hear something go like plunk, like the garbage can being opened to get the dog food.

Father: And you listen for it and you don't hear it?

First
Daughter: Um huh.

Father: You're thinking I don't feed the dogs.

First
Daugher: Right, just like you did with . . .

Father: In other words, what I was getting after you about, not feeding the dogs, now you notice that I'm not feeding the dogs.

First
Daughter: Yeah!

Father: Okay. I don't know. Mom and I have talked about this and this is something we didn't get real clear. In fact, I think we thought we would meet sooner than just now, but you remember that we said to you one day . . . We're the ones that bought the dogs, you didn't. In fact, at that point, you were young enough that we didn't expect you to do anything about the dogs. And along the way, we said that they were your dogs, or at least one of them was your dog, and that you should take care of them. Well, we decided as we began to learn about how to be fair about this as parents that we had really stuck you with that job and that we were making you feel bad about it when it really wasn't fair. It wasn't fair of us to expect you to do things when we were the ones who bought the dogs, so we should take care of them if anybody did.

Now, what Mom and I decided was that we had been threatening to get rid of the dogs as a way of trying to make you feel bad . . .

First
Daughter: Making me feed them . . .

Father:	Right, and so we said that that isn't right. So, we'll take care of the dogs because we got them and if we got them, then it's our responsibility. Now, if we can't take care of the dogs, then we have to decide what to do about it. In other words, if we should get rid of the dogs then we'll do it, but we shouldn't make you feel bad about us getting rid of the dogs . . .
Mother:	Right, we can't really say "We're gonna get rid of the dogs because you don't take care of them." That's not really fair. If we get rid of the dogs, it's because *we* don't take care of them.
Father:	Right. And we don't really want to get rid of the dogs. We'd like to keep them, too. We really love them. I think you have every right to say to me, "And you're not taking care of these dogs either!"
Second Daughter:	You know when I got "Boots," I thought it was unfair if I had two pets and the rest had one, and Tom didn't have any, so I gave "Mac" to him.
Father:	Yeah, now he feels better knowing he's got a dog and you've got a cat. And yet it's still Mom and my responsibility to take care of the dogs. Now I'm tickled to death to have you help. You know, just like everybody else, sometimes I forget and sometimes I don't get around to doing it, but I have been doing this, if I don't feed the dogs at night, I try to be sure and do it in the morning before I leave for work. So it may be that you haven't heard me because you're asleep in the mornings.
First Daughter:	Except for this morning.
Father:	Yeah, well, I fed them last night.
First Daughter:	Yeah, I know. I watched you!
Father:	Right. And I'll feed them tonight again. But you're right, I've missed a couple of times and Mom knows, she's

told me about it. Now, Mom has fed them a couple of times for me and I've been keeping the dog pen pretty clean, I think, and I'm trying and I see it's a lot harder sometimes when you don't get credit for it.

First
Daughter: Yeah.

Father: It's kind of good to know the problem, isn't it? To know where you are, too.

First
Daughter: Um huh. (Teary eyed over first time leaving for Scout camp shortly.)

Father: You know, we really do love you, don't you? Sometimes I don't act like that, do I?

First
Daughter: One thing, Dad . . .

Father: We're going to miss you, too. (Speaking to her expression and tears)

Mother: You're going to write us and tell us what you're doing aren't you?

First
Daughter: Um huh.

Mother: Are you going to write us postcards?

First
Daughter: Um huh, and letters.

Mother: Okay. Are you going to write to your Grandmas and Grandpas. Now be sure to write Grandma and Grandpa a card, though, because you know they'll be going off on the twentieth.

First
Daughter: Okay.

Father: We'll have to give you some stamps before you go.

Daughter:	No, I can get them at camp.
Mother:	She can get them up there at the trading post. I gave six dollars credit, and a dollar and a half, I think, is for . . .
Son:	Look at my name!
Mother:	And seventy-five cents is for . . .
Son:	Look at my name!!
Mother:	So that leaves about four dollars . . .
Son:	Look at my name, Daddy!!!
Second Daughter:	I have something to complain about. He keeps interrupting people when they're talking. That bothers me.
Mother:	What are we going to do?
Father:	I think he feels like he's being left out. Do you feel like you are being left out, Tom? That's not a good feeling to be left out, is it? I think what happens, Tom, is that when you start making noise people try to, you know, keep on with what they're doing. But if you want to talk to us about something that's on your mind, we'll sure give you our attention. We'll be glad to listen to you.
Mother:	We'd be glad to. The only reason we don't pay any attention to you is because when you're making noise we don't want to encourage you, to make you think that's the thing to do.
Second Daughter:	That's the way to get attention!
Mother:	Right. If you have something to talk about, we'll listen to you.
Father:	Now he feels put out.
Mother:	Well, don't. We just want you to know.

Father: If you want to say something, Tom, you just do what Annie does. Put your hand up to let us know.

Mother: Hold it up this way. And we'll listen to you.

Father: Your paper is just as big as mine, did you notice that? See here. Okay, is that what you wanted to say?

Second
Daughter: Yes.

Mother: Now, how do you end one?

Father: When everybody feels like they've said everything they wanted to say. Is there anything else that you need to bring up?

Mother: No.

First
Daughter: You?

Father: I'm trying to think. I feel like there probably ought to be, but I don't know.

Mother: Are you finished, Tom? You don't have something to say do you? Okay.

Father: When you want to come back, Tom, you come on back.

First
Daughter: You should tell us the days that you're going to come home so that we can expect you and we'll have the place clean for you and we can have a good meal, besides coming in at twelve and ten and one.

Father: Well, what do you think I ought to do. I'm not sure what you're saying. Are you saying I should tell you when I'm coming home?

First
Daughter: Un huh, so we'll know. And sometimes Mother cooks food and she doesn't expect you home and you come home. And she has to cook supper, after she's all done.

Father:	Well, I see. Would that, is that a rule for everybody then? In other words, when Mother's out, and she's coming home she should let us know and when you're coming home you'd let us know. Is that what you're saying too?
First Daughter:	Not exactly.
Father:	I mean, is it just a rule for me, or is it for everybody?
First Daughter:	It should be sort of like a rule for you.
Second Daughter:	I think it should be a rule for everybody. Cause everybody doesn't know when everybody's coming home.
First Daughter:	Yeah, like if Daddy comes home from work, nobody knows.
Mother:	Yes, that's right because it sometimes gets dark before you children decide to come in. I've called and called. Right?
Second Daughter:	How about the time Daddy came home and the door was unlocked and he scared Lucy and you.
Mother:	Yeah.
Father:	You mean the time all the doors were locked and you were supposed to be in the house and you couldn't get in?
Second Daughter:	No, I'm talking about the time you . . .
Mother:	No, don't you remember the time you came home, we didn't expect you and I was sitting in here and Lucy was in here and I saw this shadow going down the hall and you really scared the both of us. Lucy, too. You really scared us! We didn't know who was in the house. Nobody else was supposed to be here.

Father:	I didn't remember that one. I remember one night I called the children and nobody came home and I locked all the doors cause I figured everybody was gone. Nobody answered and, then, everything was locked up and I had the TV on and everything.
Second Daughter:	He was back in the back room.
Father:	Yeah, that's right.
Second Daughter:	I was banging on the windows, saying, "Daddy, let us in!"
Father:	Well, I guess the way I feel about it is this: If you're asking me to let the family know when I'm going to be home on any given day, I'll try it. I also know that there are going to be days when I'll have to change it, but if what you're asking me is to call and tell you, I'll be agreeable to doing that if everybody else is agreeable to it. In other words, if you're going out and you're going to be playing and say it's six-thirty or seven o'clock and you say, "Mother, I'll be home before dark," when you're going out the door you let her know that; then, if we all do that I think that would be very good. I think your suggestion is very good.
First Daughter:	Cause there was one time when everybody went off. So I turned on the light, walked in, and I locked all the doors and turned on the TV, and nobody was there. Somebody knocked on the door so I asked who it was, I just heard footsteps and so I didn't know what to do, so I called the neighbors.
Father:	So if you'd known when we were going to be home, it would have helped you not to be scared.
Daughter:	Yeah.
Father:	Well, you know, Ann said something a little different there, too. Ann was saying, maybe I ought to set a time when I'm going to be home. Is that what you were saying?

Daughter: Un huh.

Father: It'd be a little hard for me, Ann. I mean, there are certain days, now, for example, in the Fall, when I know what my schedule is, I could say I will be home. Otherwise I can call and say I can't make it. But I have been very loose about this in the past. A lot of times I wouldn't even tell Mother at all when I was going to be home and I would come early sometimes and sometimes I'd come in late. You're right, she didn't know. And you didn't know either.

Daughter: And she didn't expect you and you knew she would have supper for all of us and you walk in the door and say, "Where's supper?"

Father: Yeah . . .

Daughter: And there we are, eating.

Father: Right. So, Okay. Now, are we saying that we're all in favor and we're all voting for keeping the whole family informed when we're coming home and stuff.

Mother: Why not . . . I hate to leave notes on the door in obvious places. If you want to leave notes, then leave a piece of paper like this cause it's so handy, why not—and everybody knows where the Scotch tape is—why not.

Daughters: We don't.

Mother: You know where the masking tape is.

Daughters: Yeah.

Mother: What differences does it make whether it's Scotch tape or whatever?

Daughters: Un huh.

Mother: Okay. Why not leave notes on the inside of the first door, where the drawers are, on the inside of that door.

Second Daughter:	Yeah, but what if the door's locked?
Mother:	What door?
Second Daughter:	Any door. I mean if the whole house is locked.
Mother:	No, a note to tell you what time I'll be back.
Daughter:	Oh! Outside the door.
Father:	And if we come home and we don't know where they are we'll look behind the door.
Mother:	Exactly.
Father:	Okay. And . . .
Mother:	On the inside of the door.
Father:	Okay. Then the other thing is that if we have left a written note and we find that we're not getting home for some reason, then we could call.
Mother:	We call. Yes.
Father:	Right. Okay.
	Any more suggestions?
Daughter:	We could also keep records of our meetings. Me and Ann have these record things.
Second Daughter:	And Mother has already used a couple of them. She typed them and she uses them.
First Daughter:	We've got little folders and we can just have, you know, what we voted on and the dates, and the times that we missed the meetings. And we could go during the week and make it up for that.

Father: Who's going to ask for that . . .

Second
Daughter: And then while they are gone we would pick up things and, you know, think about what goes on and during the meeting . . .

Mother: That's right. We would be able to tell you when you're not here on a Sunday, what we decided last Sunday.

Daughter: And then . . .

Father: That would be important wouldn't it? That's a good point.

Second
Daughter: I have a notebook . . .

First
Daughter: And then, the person that's been gone, why they would know what's been going on there.

Father: All right. Maybe we ought to write down some things we decided today so that we won't forget them.

Second
Daughter: I have a notebook. It has paper in it. I'll go get it.

Father: Do you have a pencil, too?

Second
Daughter: I think so.

Mother: A little note. That would be a way of tallying them up. Cause I won't even remember.

Father: I bet you they will!

Mother: I know they will!

Daughter: If we don't, we'll use the back of Mother's paper.

Father:	Tom, We're going to write down the things we decided to-day if you want to join in with us, we'd be pleased to have you.
Mother:	You want to sit down with us?
Son:	Daddy, let's do it on TV. Let's bring the stuff down there.
Father:	You think it was a lot of fun.
Son:	Let's watch us up there in the air and watch me on TV.
Daughter:	I have a pen.
Daughter:	Okay.
Father:	It's a lot more fun when everybody doesn't want to be serious, huh?
Mother:	Did you get your notebook?
Father:	We should have it in color, do you think?
Son:	Please!
Mother:	Okay, now what were the things we decided?
Father:	We can't open that up now, Son. We're not finished yet.
Mother:	First of all, we decided what day we were going to have our meeting. That I remember.
Daughter:	Yeah, Sunday. Okay, second.
Mother:	What time everybody should be up by. Ten-thirty.
Daughter:	Okay, third. About Tommy, wasn't it?
Daughter:	Umm, about calling, about writing the notes.
Mother:	Yeah, where to put the notes. If you're going to be going off and nobody's home, or if somebody's—notes to be left . . .

Daughter: Put where?

Mother: Inside the first storage door. Is that what you call it?

Father: Okay. I think I was asked—what it started with was Ann saying to me that I ought to have a time to come home and we were agreeing that we would call . . .

First
Daughter: That was me.

Father: Oh, that's right. It was you.

First
Daughter: Yeah, I said Daddy . . .

Mother: Okay, then put down, he agreed he would call and let us know.

Father: Well, but that was for everybody.

Mother: Yeah.

Father: It wasn't just me. We agreed to let the family know when we would be home. That's worthy of note, I think.

Mother: Well, put in all.

First
Daughter: Okay. There.

Mother: Okay. What was the fifth one?

Father: Well, was there a fifth one?

Second
Daughter: I think there was.

Mother: I don't know . . .

Second
Daughter: Yeah. About Tommy. Remember about interrupting?

First
Daughter: Oh, not that.

Second
Daughter: You know when Tom started to . . .

Mother: That's another topic. I'd like to wait.

Father: You're saying you don't want to do more today?

Daughter: We don't have to limit. Because if we did limit then we'd
             have to say Okay, we can stop right now!

Mother: We might cut somebody off.

Father: It might be a good idea to set a time limit, though. In
             other words, we might agree to spend no more than forty-
             five minutes or an hour. Do you girls want to continue
             talking a little longer or would you like to finish as soon
             as we can? (This was the beginning of the end!)

Daughters: Finish it.

BIBLIOGRAPHY

BIBLIOGRAPHY

Ambrowitz, S.F., & Jackson, C. (1974). Commemorative effection of there-then verses here and now: Therapist interpretations in group psychotherapy. *Journal of Counseling Psychology, 21*(4), 274-6.

Adler, A. (1907). *Study of organ inferiority and its contribution to clinical medicine.* (S.E.. Jelliffe, trans.). New York: Moffat-Yard.

Adler, A. (1936). Love is a recent invention. *Esquire Magazine,* (4), pp. 36 & 128.

Adler, A. (1938). *Social interest. London: Faber & Faber.*

Adler, A. (1954). Understanding human nature. (W.B. Wolf, Trans.). New York: Fawcett Premier. (Original work published 1927)

Adler, A. (1956). *The Individual Psychology of Alfred Adler.* Ed. by H.L. & Rowena R. Ansbacher. New York: Basic Books.

Adler A. (1963). *The problem child* (1930). New York: Putnam Capricorn Books.

Adler, A. (1964). *Problems of neurosis.* (1929). New York: Harper Torchbooks,

Affleck, G., Pfeiffer, C., Tennen, H., & Fifield, J. (in press). Attributional processes in rheumatoid arthritis. *Arthritis and Rheumatism.*

Allen, T.W. (1971a) The individual psychology of Alfred Adler: An item of history and promise of a revolution. *Counseling Psychologist, 3*(1), 3-24.

Allen, T.W. (1971b). A life style. *Counseling Psychologist. 3*(1), 25-29.

Allen, T.W. (1971c). Adlerian interview strategies for behavior change. *Counseling Psychologist, 3*(1), 40-48.

Allport, G. (1955). *Becoming.* New Haven, CT: Yale University Press.

Altman, K.E. (1973). The relationship between social interest dimensions of early recollections and selected counselor variables. Unpublished doctoral dissertation, University of South Carolina.

American Institute for Character Education (1986). *The character education curriculum (an evaluation with principals and teachers)*. San Antonio, TX: American Institute.

Angyl, A. (1941). *Foundations for a science of personality*. New York: Commonwealth Fund.

Ansbacher, H.L. (Ed.). (1969). *The science of living: Alfred Adler*. Garden City, NY: Doubleday Anchor Books.

Ansbacher, H.L. (1970, February). Adler, individual psychology, and Marilyn Monroe. *Psychology Today, 3*, 42-44; 66-67.

Ansbacher, H.L., & Ansbacher, R.R. (Eds.). (1967). *The individual psychology of Alfred Adler*. New York: Harper Torchbook, Harper and Row.

Antonovsky, A. (1987). *Unraveling the mystery of health*. San Francisco: Jossey-Bass.

Appalachian Community Services Network, (1979 and 1980). *Evaluation of Coping With Kids Telecourse*. Lexington, KY.

Bandura, A. (1977). Self-efficacy: Toward a unifying theory of behavior change. *Psychological Review, 84*, 191-215.

Bandura, A. (1986). *Social foundations of thought and action: A social cognitive theory*. Englewood Cliffs, NJ: Prentice-Hall.

Bar-Tal, D. (1978). Effect of an innovative science program on perceptions of locus of control and satisfaction. *Science Education, 62*, 349-357.

Bar-Tal, D., Raviv, A., Raviv, A., & Bar-Tal, Y. (1982). Consistency of pupils' attributions regarding success and failure. *Journal of Educational Psychology, 74*, 104-110

Baracks, B. (1979). The passion of recollection; A living history group. *Teachers and Writers Magazine, 11*,(1), 2-5.

Baruth, L., & Eckstein, D. (1978). *Life style: Theory, practice and research*. Dubuque, IA: Kendall Hunt Publishing.

Beck, A.T. (1976). *Cognitive therapy and the emotional disorders*. New York: New American Library.

Beck, A.T. (1984). Cognitive approaches to stress. In R.L. Wollfolk & P.M. Lehrer (Eds.), *Principles and practice of stress management* (pp. 255-305). New York: Guilford Press.

Belloc, N.B. (1973). Relationship of health practices and mortality. *Preventive Medicine, 2*. 67-81.

Belloc, N.B. & Breslow, L. (1972). Relationship of physical health status and health practices. *Preventive Medicine, 1*, 409-421.

Benson, H. (1975). *The relaxation response.* New York: William Morrow.

Benson, H. (1987). *Your maximum mind.* New York: Times Books.

Benson, H., with Proctor, W. (1984). *Beyond the relaxation response.* New York: Times Books.

Berkman, L., & Syme, S.L. (1979). Social networks, host resistance, and mortality: A nine-year follow-up study of Alameda County residents. *American Journal of Edidemiology, 109,* 186-204.

Berne, E. (1964). *Games people play.* New York: Grove Press.

Bland, G. (1972). *Success: The Glenn Bland method.* Wheaton, IL: Tyndale House Publisher, Inc.

Borysenko, J.Z. (1985). Healing motives: An interview with David McClelland. *Advances. 2,* 29-41.

Boylin, W., Gordon, S.K., & Nehrke, M.F. (1976). Reminiscing and ego integrity in institutionalzed elderly males. *Gerontologist, 16*(2), 118-124.

Bradley, G. (1978). Self-serving biases in the attribution process: A re-examination of the fact or fiction question. *Journal of Personality and Social Psychology, 36,* 56-71.

Bradley, R.H., & Gaa, J.P. (1977). Domain specific aspects of locus of control: Implications for modifying locus of control orientation. *Journal of School Psychology, 15,* 18-23.

Brill, P. (1978). Work satisfaction best predictor of longevity. *American Medical News,* December 1, *16.*

Bulman, R., & Wortman, C.B. (1977). Attributions of blame and coping in the "real world": Severe accident victims react to their lot. *Journal of Personality and Social Psychology, 35,* 351-363.

Burkman, E., & Brezin, M. (1981). Effects of expectation level on achievement in high school physical science courses (ISIS) employing a quasi-mastery teaching method. *Journal of Educational Research, 75,* 121-126.

Burnett, P.C. (1988). Evaluation of Adlerian parenting programs. *Individual Psychology, 44,* 63-76.

Butler, R.N. (1963). The life review: An interpretation of reminiscence in the aged. *Psychiatry, 26,* 65-76.

Butler, R.N. (1964). Successful aging and the role of the life review. *Journal of the American Geriatrics Society, 22* (12), 529-535.

Butler, R.N. (1968). The facade of chronological age: An interpretative summary. In B. Nergartern (Ed.) *Middle age and aging.* Chicago: University of Chicago Press.

California Department of Mental Health, Office of Prevention (1979). *In pursuit of wellness.* San Francisco: 2340 Irving Street, 108.

Campbell, A. (1981). *The sense of well-being in America: Recent patterns and trends.* New York: McGraw-Hill.

Carkhuff, R.R. (1969). *Helping and human relationships. (Vol. 1).* New York: Holt, Rinehart and Winston.

Carkhuff, R.R., & Berenson, B. (1967). *Beyond counseling and therapy.* New York: Harcourt, Brace, and World.

Carnegie, D. (1964). *How to win friends and influence people.* New York: Simon and Shuster.

Carter, H.D. (1940). The development of vocational attitudes. *Journal of Consultive, 4,* 185-191.

Cartwright, W.J. (1980). *Reminiscence: Therapeutic memories.* Paper presented at the Southwestern Sociological Association, Lubbock, Texas.

Cauly, K., & Murray, F.B. (1981). *Structure of children's attributes of school.* Paper presented at annual meeting of the American Education Research Association at Los Angeles, CA.

Cepek, L., & Teaff, R.R. (1977). *Adult education looks at life in America 1900-1950. Lifelong learning: the adult years. 1* (3), 4-7.

Chandler, T.A. (1980). Reversal peer tutoring effects on powerlessness on adolescents. *Journal of Adolescent Counseling, 15,* 15-22.

Ciricelli, V.G. (1982). *Similarities and contrasts in quality of child and sibling relationships with elderly.* Paper presented at the Annual Scientific Meeting of the Gerontological Society, Boston, MA.

Cohen, S. (1988). Psychosocial models of the role of social support in the etiology of physical disease. *Health Psychology, 7,* 269-297.

Coleman, P. (1974). Measuring reminiscence characteristics from conversation as adaptive features of old age. *International Journal of Aging and Human Development, 5* (3), 281-294.

Compton, M. (1973). Characteristics of the early adolescent learner. In N.P. Atkins & P. Pumerantz (Eds.), *Educational Dimensions of the Emerging Adolescent.* Washington, D.C.: Associations of Supervision and Curriculum Development and Educational Leadership Institute.

Cooper, K.H. (1983). *The aerobics program for total well-being.* New York: Bantam.

Cooper, S.E., Fuqua, D.R., & Hartman, B.W. (1984). The relationship of trait indecisiveness to vocational uncertainty, career indecision, and interpersonal characteristics. *Journal of College Student Personnel, 25,* 353-356.

Coopersmith, A. (1967). *Antecedents of self-esteem.* San Francisco: Freeman.

Corsini, R. (1971). Group psychotherapy. In A.G. Nikelly, *Techniques for behavior change.* Springfield, IL: Charles Thomas.

Coster, K., & Webb, B. (1979). *Gray and growing.* Program packages for the older adult. A manual and supplement. Towson, MD: Baltimore County Public Library.

Cousins, N. (1979). *Anatomy of an illness as perceived by the patient.* New York: W.W. Norton.

Crandall, V.C., Katkovsky, W., & Crandall, V.J. (1965). Children's beliefs in their own control of reinforcements in intellectual-academic achievement situations. *Child Development, 36,* 91-109.

Crandall, V.J., Katkovsky, W., & Preston, A. (1962). Motivational and ability determinants of young children's intellectual acheivement behavior. *Child Development, 33, 643-661.*

Crites, J.O. (1969). Vocational psychology. New York; McGraw-Hill.

Crites, J.O. (1981). Integrative test interpretation. In D.H. Montross & C.J. Shinkman (Eds.), *Career development in the 1980's: Theory and practice* (pp. 161-168). Springfield, IL: Charles C. Thomas.

Csikszentmihalyi, M., & Beattie, O.V. (1979). Life themes: A theoretical and empirical exploration of their origins and effects. *Journal of Humanistic Psychology, 19,* 45-63.

Cunningham, J.D., et al. (1978). Effects of success and failure on children's perceptions of internal-external locus of control. *Social Behavior and Personality, 6,* 1-8.

Dahlstrom, W.G. (1972). *Personality systematics and the problem of types.* Morristown, NJ: General Learning Press.

Danner, S., & Dunning, A. (1978). Spared alluence. they've lived past 90. *Medical World News,* January 23, 42.

Dawis, R.V., & Lofquist, L.H. (1984). *A psychological theory of work adjustment: An individual-differences model and its application.* University of Minnesota Press: Minneapolis.

Devin-Sheehan, L., Feldman, R.S., & Allen, V.L. (1976). Research on children tutoring children: A critical review. *Review of Educational Research, 46,* 355-385.

Dillon, K.M., Minchoff, & Baker, K.H. (1985). Positive emotional states and enhancement of the immune system. *International Journal of Psychiatry in Medicine, 15,* 13-17.

Dinkmeyer, D.C. (1971). The "C" group: Integrating knowledge and experience to change behavior, an Adlerian approach to consultation. *Counseling Psychologist, 3*(1), 63-72.

Dinkmeyer, D.C., & Carlson, J. (1973). *Consulting: Facilitating human potential and change processes.* Columbus, OH: Charles E. Merrill.

Dinkmeyer, D.C., Dinkmeyer, Jr., D.C., & Sperry, L. (1987). *Adlerian counseling and psychotherapy.* (2nd. edition). Columbus, OH: Merrill Publishing.

Dinkmeyer, D., & Dreikurs, R. (1963). *Encouraging children to learn: The encouragement process.* Englewood Cliffs, NJ: Prentice-Hall.

Dinkmeyer, D.C., & Losoncy, L.E. (1980). *The encouragement book.* Englewood Cliffs, NJ: Prentice-Hall.

Dinkmeyer, D.C., & McKay, G.D. (1976). *Systematic training for effective parenting.* Circle Pines, MN: American Guidance Service.

Dinkmeyer, D.C., & Muro, J.J. (1971). *Group counseling: Theory and practice.* Itasca, IL: F.E. Peacock.

Dinkmeyer, D.C., Pew, L.L., & Dinkmeyer, D.C., Jr. (1979). *Adlerian counseling and psychotherapy.* Monterey, CA: Brooks/Cole Publishing.

Dreikurs, R. (1946). *The challenge of marriage.* New York: Hawthorn Books.

Dreikurs, R. (1951). Family group therapy in the Chicago community child-guidance centers. *Mental Hygiene, 35,* 291-301.

Dreikurs, R. (1952-53). The psychological interview in medicine. *American Journal of Individual Psychology, 10,* 99-122. Also in *Psychodynamics, psychotherapy, and counseling,* 1967, pp. 125-152. Chicago, IL: Alfred Adler Institute.

Dreikurs, R. (1953). *Fundamentals of Adlerian psychology.* Chicago: Alfred Adler Institute.

Dreikurs, R. (1954). The psychological interview in medicine. *American Journal of Individual Psychology, 10,* 99-122.

Dreikurs, R. (1963). Psychodynamic diagnosis in psychiatry. *American Journal of Psychiatry, 119,* 1045-1048.

Dreikurs, R. (1967). *Psychodynamics, Psychotherapy, and Counseling.* Chicago: Alfred Adler Institute.

Dreikurs, R. (1968). *Psychology in the Classroom.* (2nd ed.). New York: Harper and Row.

Dreikurs, R. (1971). *Social equality: The challenge of today.* Chicago: Henry Regnery.

Dreikurs, R. (1973). *Psychodynamics, psychotherapy, and counseling.* (Rev. ed.) Chicago: Alfred Adler Institute.

Dreikurs, R., & Grey, L. (1968). *Logical consequences.* New York: Hawthorn Books.

Dreikurs, R., Grunwald, B.B., & Pepper, H.C. (1971) *Maintaining sanity in the classroom.* New York: Harper and Row.

Dreikurs, R., & Soltz, V. (1964). *Children the challenge.* New York: Hawthorn Books.

DuCette, J., & Keane, A. (1984). Why me? An attributional analysis of a major illness. *Research in Nursing and Health, 7,* 257-264.

Dweck, C.S. (1975). The role of expectations and attributions in the alleviation of learned helplessness. *Journal of Personality and Social Psychology, 31,* 674-685.

Eckstein, D., Baruth, L., & Mahrer, D. (1978). *Life style: What it is and how to do it.* Dubuque, IA: Kendall Hunt Publishing.

Eckstein, D., Baruth, L., & Mahrer, D. (1982). *Life style: What it is and how to do it.* (2nd ed.). Dubuque, IA: Kendall/Hunt Publishing.

Eggleston, L.P. (1973). A study of the role and importance of interaction in a high school setting. Unpublished paper.

Eichhorn, D. (1973). Boyce medical study. In N.P. Atkins & P. Pumerantz (Eds.), *Educational dimensions of the emerging adolescent.* Washington, DC: Association of Supervision and Curriculum Development and Educational Leadership Institute.

Ekman, P. (1975). Universal smile: Face muscles talk every language. *Psychology Today. 9*(4), 35-39.

Ellenberger, H. (1970). *The discovery of the unconscious.* New York: Basic Books.

Ellis, A. (1962). *Reason and emotion in psychotherapy.* New York: Lyle Stuart.

Ellis, A. (1970). Humanism, values, rationality. *Journal of Individual Psychology, 26,* 37-38.

Ellis, A., & Greiger, R. (1977). *Handbook of rational-emotive therapy.* New York: Springer.

Erikson, E. (1950). *Childhood and society.* New York: Norton.

Fahey, D.A. (1984). School counselors and psychological aspects of learning disabilities. *School Counselor, 31,* 433-440.

Feldman, R.S., Devin-Sheenan, L., & Al]]en, V.L. (1976). Children tutoring children: A critical review of research. In V.L. Allen (Ed.), *Children as teachers: Theory and research on tutoring* (pp. 235-252).

Ferman, L.A. (1982, October). *Some health aspects of unemployment.* Ann Arbor: A public address, University of Michigan.

Fine, R. (1973). Psychoanalysis. In R. Corsini (Ed.), *Current Psychotherapies.* Itasca, IL: F.E. Peacock.

Flanagan, J. (1978). A research approach to improving our quality of life. *American Psychologist, 33,* 138-147.

Frankl, V.E. (1959). *Man's search for meaning.* New York: Pocket Books.

Freedman, J.L. (1978). *Happy people.* New York: Harcourt Brace Jovanovich.

Friedman, M., & Ulmer, D. (1984). *Treating type A behavior and your heart.* New York: Alfred A. Knopf.

Friend, J.G., & Haggard, E.A. (1948). Work adjustment in relation to family background. *Applied Psychology Monographs, 16.*

Fry, W.F., & Salameh, W.A. (Eds.). (1987). *Handbook of humor and psychotherapy.* Sarasota, FL: Professional Resource Exchange.

Furtmueller, C., & Wexberg, E. (1922). Heiland and Bilden (2nd ed.) of A. Adler (1904).

Gandy, G. (1974). Ordinal position research related to vocational interest. *Journal of Counseling Psychology, 21*(4), 281-287.

Gartner, A., Kohler, M., & Riessman, F. (1971). *Children teach children: Learning by teaching.* New York: Harper and Row.

Gaylin, W. (1979). *Feelings, our vital signs.* New York: Harper & Row.

Gerfo, M. (1980-81). Three ways of reminiscence in theory and practice. *International Journal of Aging and Human Development, 12* (1), 39-48.

Gerler, E.R., Jr. (1985). Elementary school counseling research and the classroom learning environment. *Elementary School Guidance and Counseling, 20,* 39-48.

Getzel, G.S. (1982). Helping elderly couples in crisis. *Social Casework, 63* (9), 515-521.

Gillis, C., & Wagner, L. (1980). Life writing: Writing workshops and outreach procedures. Paper presented at the Annual Meeting of the American Educational Research Association, Boston, MA.

Glasser, W. (1969). *Schools without failure.* New York: Harper and Row.

Gnagey, W.J. (1981). High school facilitators and inhibitors. *Clearing House, 54,* 370-375.

Goldstein, K. (1939). *Organism: A holistic approach to biology derived from pathological data in man.* New York: American Book Company.

Goodall, K. (1972). The line: Big brother and the presidency. *Psychology Today. 5*(11), 24.

Gordon, E. (1967). *JACD Bulletin.* Ferkauf Graduate School, Yeshiva University, *3*(5).

Gordon, T. (1975). *Parent effectiveness training.* New York: New American Library.

Gottfredson, G.D., Holland, J.L., & Ogawa, D.K. (1982). *Dictionary of Holland Occupational Codes.* Palo Alto, CA: Consulting Psychologists Press.

Greene, D., & Lepper, M.R. (1974). Intrinsic motivation: How to turn play into work. *Psychology Today, 8*(4), 49-59.

Greene, J.C. (1985). Relationships among learning and attribution theory motivational variables. *American Educational Research Journal, 22,* 65-78.

Green, J.C. (1976). Choice behaviors and its consequences for learning. A T I study. Unpublished dissertation, Stanford University.

Griffith, J., & Powers, R.L. (1984). *An Adlerian Lexicon.* Chicago: Americas Institute of Adlerian Studies, Ltd.

Griggs, S.A. (1983). *Counseling high school students for their individual learning styles.* (ERIC Document Reproduction Service No. ED 273 879).

Griggs, S.A. (1985). *Counseling students through their individual learning styles.* Ann Arbor, MI: ERIC/CAPS.

Growald, E.R., & Luks, A. (1988, March). Beyond self. *American Health,* 51-53.

Gushurst, R.S. (1971). The technique, utility, and validity of lifestyle analysis. *Counseling Psychologist, 3*(1), 30-39.

Harman, W.W. (1988). *Global mind change: The promise of the last years of the twentieth century.* Indianapolis, IN: Knowledge Systems.

Harrington, T.F., & O'Shea, A.J. (1982). *Career decision-making system.* Circle Pines, MN: American Guidance Service.

Harris, T.A. (1969). *I'm OK, you're OK.* New York: Harper and Row.

Harris-Bowlsbey, J. (1984). The computer as a tool in career guidance programs. In N. Gysbers (Ed.), *Designing careers* (pp. 362-383). San Francisco: Jossey-Bass.

Harrison, C.L. (1980). Therapeutic art programs around the world: XIII. Creative arts for older people in the community. *American Journal of Art Therapy, 19* (4), 99-101.

Havighurst, R.J., & Glasser, R. (1972). An exploratory study of reminiscence. *Journal of Gerontology, 27* (2), 245-253.

Heppner, P.P., & Krauskopf, C.J. (1987). An information processing approach to personal problem solving. *The Counseling Psychologist, 15,* 371-447.

Herr, E.L., & Cramer, S.H. (1988). *Career guidance and counseling through the lifespan* (3rd ed.). Boston: Little, Brown.

Herzberg, F. (1966). *Work and human nature.* New York: World.

Hill, N. (1970). *Think and grow rich.* Greensburg, PA: Manna Christian Outreach.

Hine, F. & Pfeiffer, E. (1972). *Behavioral science: A selective view.* Boston: Little Brown.

Hoffman, F.J. (1975, June). Efficacy of the Adlerian model in secondary school counseling. Unpublished doctoral dissertation, Ohio University.

Holland, J.L. (1985a). *Making vocational choices: A theory of vocational personalities and work environments.* Englewood Cliffs, NJ. Prentice-Hall.

Holland, J.L. (1985b). *The self-directed search.* Odessa, FL: Psychological Assessment Resources.

Hopke, W. (1987). *Encyclopedia of careers and vocational guidance (7th ed.).* Chicago: Ferguson Publishing.

Horney, K. (1945). *Our inner conflicts.* New York: Norton.

House, J.S., Robbing, C., & Metzner, H.L. (1982). The association of social relationships and activities with mortality. *American Journal of Epidemiology, 116,* 123-140.

Hughston, G.A., & Merriam, S.B. (1982). Reminiscence: A nonformal technique for improving cognitive functioning in the aged. *International Journal of Aging and Human Development, 15*(2), 139-149.

Izard, C.E. (1977). *Human emotions* New York: Plenum Press.

Johnson, D.S. (1981). Naturally acquired learned helplessness: The relationship of school failure to achievement behavior, attributions, and self-concept. *Journal of Educational Psychology, 73,* 174-180.

Johnson, D.W., Maruyama G., Johnson, R., Nelson, D., & Skon, L. (1981). Effects of cooperative, competitive, and individualizing goal structures on achievements: A meta-analyst. *Psychological Bulletin, 89* (1), 47-62.

Jones, L.K. (1987). *The career key.* Chicago: J.G. Ferguson Publishing.

Kefir, N., & Corsini, R. (1974). Dispositional sets: A contribution to typology. *Journal of Individual Psychology, 30,* 163-178.

Kelly, E.W., & Sweeney, T.J. (1979). Typical faulty goals of adolescents. *School Counselor, 26*(4), 236-246.

Kennedy, J.F. (1956). *Profiles in courage.* New York: Harper & Row.

Kennelly, K.J., & Mount, S.A. (1985). Perceived contingency of reinforcements, helplessness, locus of control, and academic performance. *Psychology in the Schools, 22,* 465-469.

Kern, R., Matheny, K., & Patterson, D. (1978). *A case for Adlerian counseling: Theory, techniques and research evidence.* Chicago: Alfred Adler Institute.

Kerney, E.J. (1980). The efficacy of an Adlerian child guidance study group on changing teachers' attitudes toward students' behavior. Unpublished doctoral dissertation, Ohio University.

Kernodle, R.L. (1982). Sharing the past: Themes and values from early life. Paper presented at the Annual Scientific Meeting of the Gerontological Society, Boston, MA.

Kerr, J., & Pratt, C. (1982). "Back to the farm": Stimulating reminiscence and interaction among the institutionalized elderly. *Activities, Adaptation, and Aging, 3* (1), 27-35.

Kibler, V. (1978). The persistence of reported attitude change following completion of an Adlerian guidance course using two methods of instruction. Unpublished doctoral dissertation, Ohio University.

Kibler, V.E., Rush, B.L. & Sweeney, T.J. (1985). The relationship between Adlerian course participation and stability of attitude change. *Individual Psychology,* 354-362.

Kiecolt-Glaser, J.K., Garner. W., Speicher, C., Penn, G.M., Holliday, J., & Glaser, R. (1984). *Psychosomatic Medicine, 46,* 7-14.

Kobasa, S.C. (1979). Stressful life events, personality and health: An inquiry into hardiness. *Journal of Personality and Social Psychology, 37,* 1-11.

Kobasa, S.C. (1982). The hardy personality: Toward a social psychology of stress and health. In G.S. Sanders & J. Suls (Eds.). *Social psychology of health and illness.* Hillsdale, NJ: Erlbaum.

Kobasa, S.C., Maddi, S.R., & Kahn, S. (1982). Hardiness and health: A prospective study. *Journal of personality and Social Psychology, 42,* 168-177.

Kohn, A. (1986a). *No contest: The case against competition.* Boston, MA: Houghton Mifflin.

Kohn, A. (1986b). How to succeed without even vying. *Psychology Today, 20*(9), 22-28.

Kranitz, M.A. (1987). *Getting apart together.* San Luis Obispo, CA: Impact Publishers.

Krumboltz, J. (1988). The key to achievement: Learning to love learning. In G.R. Waltz (Ed.), *Proceeding on Building Sound School Counseling Programs.* Alexandria, VA: AACD Press.

Krumboltz, J.D. (1983). *Private rules in career decision making.* Columbus, OH: The National Center for Research in Vocational Education.

Lawrence, J.H., & Lehman, E. (1979). Oral history as a motivating factor among adult learners. Paper presented at the American Educational Research Association Annual Meeting, San Francisco, CA.

Lazarus, R.S. (1984). On the primacy of cognition. *American psychologist, 39,* 124-129.

Lazarus, R.S., & Folkman, S. (1984). *Stress, appraisal, and coping.* New York: Springer Publishing.

Lefcourt, H.M. (1976). *Locust of control: Current trends in theory and research.* Hillsdale, NJ: L. Erlbaum.

LeShan, E. (1982). *On living your life.* New York: Harper & Row.

Lewin, J. (1948). *Resolving social conflict.* New York: Harper and Row.

Lightel, D. (1974). The effectiveness of the Adlerian model in elementary school counseling. Unpublished doctoral dissertation. Kent State University.

Lissandro, P. (1979). The great depression: Were you there? *Social Science Record. 16* (2), 20-21.

Locke, S.E., Kraus, L., Leserman, J., Hurst, M.W., Heisel, J.S., & Williams, R.M. (1984). Life change stress, psychiatric symptoms, and natural killer cell activity. *Psychosomatic Medicine, 46,* 441-453.

Lombardi, D.N. (1973). Eight avenues of life style consistency. *Individual Psychologist, 10*(2), 5-9.

Lorig, K., Holman, H.R., O'Leary, A., & Shoor, S. (1986, Sept 28-Oct 2). Outcomes of a patient education experiment to increase self-efficacy. Paper presented at the 114th Annual Meeting, American Public Health Association, Las Vegas.

Losoncy, L.E. (1977). *Turning people on.* Englewood Cliffs, NJ: Prentice-Hall.

Lynch, J.J. (1985). *The language of the heart.* New York: Basic Books.

Lynch, J.J. (1977). *The broken heart: The medical consequences of loneliness.* New York: Basic Books.

Maddi, S.R., & Kobasa, S.C. (1984). *The hardy executive: Health under stress.* Chicago: Dow Jones-Irwin.

Madsen, C.H., & Madsen, C.K. (1970). *Teaching discipline.* Boston: Allyn & Bacon, Inc.

Maltz, M. (1960). *Psychocybernetic.* North Hollywood, CA: Wilshire Book.

Manaster, G.J., & Perryman, T.B. (1974). Early recollections and occupational choice. *Journal of Individual Psychology, 30,* 232-237.

Maqsud, M. (1980). The relationship of sense of powerlessness to antisocial behavior and school achievement. *The Journal of Psychology, 105,* 147-150.

Marmot, M.G., & Syme, S.L. (1976). Acculturation and coronary heart disease in Japanese-Americans. *American Journal of Epidemiology, 104,* 225-247.

Marsh, H.W., (1984). Relationships among dimensions of self-attribution and dimensions of self-concept. *Journal of Educational Psychology, 76,* 1291-1308.

Marsh, H.W. (1986). Self-serving effect (bias?) in academic attributions: Its relation to academic achievement and self-concept. *Journal of Educational Psychology, 78,* 190-200.

Marsh, H.W., Cairns, L., Relich, J., Barnes, J., & Debus, R. (1984). The relationship between dimensions of self-attribution and dimensions of self-concept. *Journal of Educational Psychology, 76,* 3-32.

Maslow, A.H. (1968). *Toward a psychology of being (2nd ed.).* New York: D. Van Nostrand.

Maslow, A.H. (1970). *Motivation and personality (2nd ed.).* New York: Harper & Row.

Matthews, E.E. (1972). Mature adulthood and old age. In E.A. Whitfield (Ed.), *Counseling girls and women over the life span.* Washington, D.C.: National Guidance Association.

Mayers, P.L., Csikszentmihalyi, M., & Larsen, R. (1978). *The daily experience of high school students.* (ERIC Document Reproduction Service No. Ed 159 583).

McClelland, D.C., Ross, G., & Patel, V. (1985). The effect of an academic examination on salivary norepinophrine and immunoglobulin levels. *Journal of Human Stress, 11,* 52-59.

McGee, P.S., Kauffman, J.M., & J.L. Mussen. (1977). Children as therapeutic change agents: Reinforcement, intervention, paradium. *Journal of Review of Educational Research, 46,* 215-237.

McKay, G.D., & Hillman, B.W. (1979). An Adlerian multimedia approach to parent education. *Elementary School Guidance and Counseling, 14*(1), 28-35.

McKelvie, W. (1979). Career counseling with early recollections. In H.A. Olson (Ed.), *Early recollections: Their use in diagnosis and psychotherapy.* Springfield, IL: Thomas.

McKelvie, W., & Friedland, B.U. (1978). *Career goals counseling: A holistic approach.* Baltimore, MD: F.M.S. Associates.

McKelvie, W., & Friedland, B.U. (1981). The life style and career counseling. In L. Barut & D. Eckstein (Eds.), *Life style: Theory, practice, and research* (2nd. ed.) (pp. 57-62). Dubuque, IA: Kendall/Hunt.

Medway, F.J., & Lowe, C.A. (1980). Causal attribution for performance by cross-age tutors and tutees. *Americans Educational Research Journal, 17,* 377-387.

Mehrabian, A. (1968). Communication without words. *Psychology Today, 2,* 52-55.

Merriam, S.B., & Cross, L.H. (1981). Aging, reminiscence, and life satisfaction. *Activities, Adaptation and Aging, 2* (1), 39-50.

Merriam, S.B., & Cross, L.H. (1982). Adulthood and reminescence: A descriptive study. *Educational Gerontology, 8* (3), 275-290.

Messer, M.H. (1973). Suicide prevention: Adlerian contributions. *Journal of Individual Psychology, 59*, 54-71.

Miller, M.J. (1980). Cantaloupes, carrots, and counseling: Implications of dietary interventions for counselors. *Personnel and Guidance Journal, 58*(6), 421-424.

Miller-Tiedeman, A. (1976). *Individual career exploration student inventory booklet.* Benesville, IL: Scholastic Testing Service.

Miller-Tiedeman, A. (1988). *Lifecareer: The quantum leap into a process theory of career.* Vista, CA: Lifecareer Foundation.

Minuchin, S. (1974). *Family therapy techniques.* Cambridge: Harvard University Press.

Minuchin, S., & Fishman, H.C. (1981). *Families and family therapy.* Cambridge: Harvard University Press.

Minuchin, S., Baker, L., Rosman, B., Liebman, R. Milman, L., & Todd, T.C. (1975). A conceptual model of psychosomatic illness in children. *Archives of General Psychiatry, 32*, 1031-1038.

Minuchin, S., Rosman, B., & Baker, L. (1978). *Psychosomatic families: Anorexia nervosa in context.* Cambridge: Harvard University Press.

Mischel, W. (1981). A cognitive-social learning approach to assessment. In T.V. Merluzzi, C.R. Glass, & M. Genest (Eds.), *Cognitive assessment* (pp. 479-502). New York: Guilford Press.

Mitchell, J.V., Jr. (1979). Causal attribution and self-assessment variables related to grade point average in high school. *Measurement and Evaluation in Guidance, 12*, 134-139.

Mize, J., Ladd, G.W., & Price, J.M. (1985). Promoting positive peer relations with young children: Rationale and strategies. *Child Care Quarterly,* Vol. 14, 222-237.

Montagu, A. (1955). *The direction of human development: Biological and social bases.* New York: Harper.

Montagu, A. (1981). *Growing young.* New York: McGraw-Hill.

Mosak, H.H. (1958). Early recollections as a projective technique. *Journal Projective Techniques, 22*, 301-311. Also in G. Lindzey & C.S. Hall (Eds.). (1965). *Theories of personality: Primary sources and research.* New York: Wiley, pp. 105-113.

Mosak, H.H. (1965). Predicting the relationship to psychotherapist from early recollections. *Journal of Individual Psychology, 21*, 77-81.

Mosak, H.H. (1972). Life style assessment: A demonstration based on family constellation. *Journal of Individual Psychology, 28*, 232-247.

Mosak, H.H. (1977). *The controller: A social interpretation of the anal charac-ter, On purpose: Collected papers of Harold H. Mosak.* Chicago: Alfred Adler Institute.

Mosak, H.H. (1987). *Ha ha and aha: The role of humor in psychotherapy.* Muncie, IN: Accelerated Development.

Mosak, H.H., & Dreikurs, R. (1967). The life tasks III, the fifth life task. *Individual Psychologist, 5*(1), 16-22.

Mosak, H.H., & Dreikurs, R. (1973). Adlerian psychotherapy. In R. Corsini (Ed.), *Current psychotherapies.* Itasca, IL: F.E. Peacock.

Mosak, H.H., & Gushurst, R.S. (1971). What patients say and what they mean. *American Journal of Psychotherapy, 25,* 428-436.

Mosak, H.H., & Mosak, B.A. (1975). *Bibliography for Adlerian psychology.* New York: John Wiley & Sons.

Mosak, H.H., & Shulman, B.H. (1971). *The lifestye inventory.* Chicago: Alfred Adler Institute.

Murray, H., & Staebler, B.K. (1974). Teacher's locus of control and student achievement gains. *Journal of School Psychology, 12,* 305-309.

Murray, J.N. (1980). Understanding and use of chemotherapy by learning dis-abilities and behavior disorders teachers. *Journal of Learning Disabilities, 13,* 356-360.

Myers, I.B., & McCaulley, M.H. (1985). *Manual: A guide to the development and use of the Myers-Briggs Type Indicator.* Palo Alto, CA: Consulting Psychologists Press.

Myers, J.E. (1988). *Curriculum guide: Infusing gerontological counseling in counselor preparation.* Alexandria, VA: AACD Press.

Naisbett, J. (1982). *Megatrends: Ten new directions transforming our lives.* New York: Warner Books.

Nehru, J. (1958). *Toward Freedom.* Boston: Beacon Press.

Neisser, E. (1950). *How to live with children.* Chicago: Science Research Associates.

Neuenschwander, J.A. (1976). *Oral history as a teaching approach.* West Haven, CT: National Education Association.

Nevo, O. (1987). Irrational expectations in career counseling and their confront-ing arguments. *Career Development Quarterly, 35,* 239-250.

Nichols, M.P. (1984). *Family therapy: concepts and methods.* New York: Gardner Press.

Nikelly, A.G. (1971). *Techniques for behavior change.* Springfield, IL: Charles C. Thomas.

Nowicki, S., Jr.. (1982). Competition-cooperation as a mediator of locus of control and achievement. *Journal of Research in Personality, 16,* 157-164.

Orstein, R., & Sobel, D. (1987). *The healing brain.* New York: Simon and Schuster.

Paffenbarger, R.S. Jr., Hyde, R.T., Wing, A.L., & Hsieh, C. (1986). *New England Journal of Medicine, 314,* 605-613.

Palmore, E.B., (1969). Physical, mental and social factors in predicting longevity. *Gerontologist, 9*(2), 103-108.

Paolitto, D.P. (1976). The effect of cross age tutoring in adolescents: An inquiry into theoretical assumption. *Journal of Review of Educational Research, 46,* 215-237.

Parsons, F. (1909). *Choosing a vocation.* Boston: Houghton-Mifflin.

Patterson, C.H. (1971). Education and training as the preferred mode of treatment. *Counseling Psychologist, 1971, 3*(1), 77-78.

Peale, N.V. (1956). *The power of positive thinking.* Englewood Cliffs, NJ: Prentice-Hall.

Pearl, R., Bryan, T., & Donahue, M. (1980). Learning disabled children's attributions for success and failure. *Learning Disability Quarterly, 3* (1), 3-9.

Peck, M.S. (1987). *The different drum: Community-making and peace.* New York: Simon and Schuster.

Pelletier, K.R. (1981). *Longevity: Fulfilling our biological potential.* New York: Delacorte Press/Seymour Lawrence.

Pelletier, K.R. (1984). *Healthy people in unhealthy places: Stress and fitness at work.* New York: Dell.

Perrotta, P., & Meacham, J.A. (1981). Can a reminiscing intervention alter depression and self-esteem? *International Journal of Aging and Human Development, 14* (1), 28-30.

Pew, M.L., & Pew, W.L. (1972). Adlerian marriage counseling. *Journal of Individual Psychology 28* (2), 192-202.

Platt, J.H. (1971). Efficacy of the Adlerian model in elementary school counseling. *Elementary School Guidance and Counseling, 6*(2), 86-91.

Powers, R.L., & Griffith, J. (1987). *Understanding life-style: The psycho-clarity process.* Chicago: The Americas Institute of Adlerian Studies.

Prediger, D.J. (1982). Dimensions underlying Holland's hexagon: Missing link between interests and occupations? *Journal of Vocational Behavior, 21,* 259-287.

Psychology Today (1978, May). What you really want from your job. 53-65, 118.

Reuben, D. (1978). *Everything you always wanted to know about nutrition.* New York: Simon & Schuster.

Revere, V., & Tobin S. (1980-81). Myth and reality: The older person's relationship to his past. *International Journal of Aging and Human Development, 12* (1), 15-26.

Rigney, K., & Corsini, R.J. (1970). *The family council.* Chicago: Family Education Association, (pamphlet).

Rogers, C.R. (1951). *Client-centered therapy.* Boston: Houghton Mifflin.

Rogers, C.R. (1961). *On becoming a person.* Cambridge, Massachusetts: Riverside Press.

Rose, J.S., & Medway, F.J. (1981). Teacher locus of control, teacher behavior, and student behavior as determinants of student achievement. *Journal of Educational Research, 74,* 375-381.

Rosenberg, B. (1959). The counselor. In R. Dreikurs, R. Corsini, R. Lowe, & M. Sonstegard, *Adlerian family counseling.* Eugene, OR: University Oregon, University Press.

Rotter, J.B. (1966). Generalized expectancies for internal versus external control of reinforcement. *Psychological Monographs, 80.* (1, whole no. 609).

Rotter, J.B. (1975). Some problems and misconceptions related to the construct of internal versus external control of reinforcement. *Journal of Consulting and Clinical Psychology, 43,* 56-67.

Rubin, L. (1985). *Just friends: The role of friendship in our lives.* New York: Harper & Row.

Rush, B. (1978). Evaluation of teacher attitude change due to involvement in an Adlerian child guidance course. Unpublished doctoral dissertation, Ohio University.

Sadowski, C.J., & Woodward, H.R. (1981). Teacher locus of control and students' perceptions and performance. Paper presented at the annual convention of the American Psychological Association, Los Angeles, CA.

Saunders-Harris, R., & Yeany, R.H. (1981). Diagnosis, remediation, and locus of control: Effects on immediate and retained achievement and attitudes. *Journal of Experimental Education, 49*, 220-224.

Schachter, S. (1963). Birth order, eminence and higher education. *In Social. Rev. 28*, 756-757.

Schaefer, C., Coyne, J.C., & Lazarus, R.S. (1982). The health-related functions of social support. *Journal of Behavioral Medicine, 4*, 381-406.

Scheir, M.F., & Carver, C.S. (1987). Dispositional optimism and physical well-being: The influence of generalized outcome expectancies on health. *Journal of Personality, 55*, 169-210.

Scherwitz, L., Graham, L.E., & Ornish, D. (1985). Self-involvement and the risk factors for coronary heart disease. *Advances, 2*, 6-18.

Schumacher, E.F. (1981). Good work. In J. O'Toole, J.L. Scheiber, and L.C. Wood (Eds.), *Working, changes, and choices* (pp.25-32). New York: Human Sciences Press.

Schunk, D.H. (1987). Peer models and children's behavior change. *Review of Education Research, 57*, 149-174.

Schweitzer, A. (1965). *The teaching of reverence for life.* New York: Holt, Reinhart and Winston.

Seaman, B., & Seaman, G. (1977). *Women and the crisis in sex hormones.* New York: Rawson Associates Publishers.

Selye, H. (1974). *Stress without distress.* New York: New American Library.

Sherman, R., & Dinkmeyer, D.C. (1987). *Systems of family therapy: An Adlerian integration.* New York: Brunner/Mazel, Publishers.

Shulman, B.H. (1962). The family constellation in personality diagnosis. *Journal of Individual Psychology, 18*, 35-47.

Shulman, B.H. (1968). *Essays in schizophrenia.* Baltimore: Williams and Wilkins.

Shulman, B.H. (1970). (Revisor and Annotator), Wexberg, Erwin. *Individual treatment.* Chicago: Alfred Adler Institute, (Originally published, 1929).

Shulman, B.H. (1971). Confrontation techniques in Adlerian psychotherapy. *Journal of Individual Psychology, 27*, 167-175.

Shulman, B.H. (1973). *Contributions to individual psychology.* Chicago: Alfred Adler Institute.

Shulman, B.H., & Mosak, H. (1988a). *LSI—Life Style Inventory.* Muncie, IN: Accelerated Development.

Shulman, B.H., & Mosak, H. (1988b). *Manual for Life Style Assessment.* Muncie, IN: Accelerated Development.

Shulman, B.H., & Nikelly, A.G. (1971). Family constellation. In Arthur G. Nikelly, *Techniques for behavior change.* Springfield, IL: Charles C. Thomas.

Siegel, B.S. (1986). *Love, medicine and miracles.* New York: Harper & Row.

Sime, W.E. (1984). Psychological benefits of exercise. *Advances, 1*(4), 15-29.

Simon, S.B., Howe, L.W., & Kirschenbaum, H. (1972). *Values clarification.* New York: Hart.

Simonton, O.C., & Matthews-Simonton, S. (1978). *Getting well again.* Los Angeles: J.P. Tarcher.

Slavin, R.E. (1980). Cooperative learning. *Review of Educational Research, 50,* 315-342.

Slavin, R.E., & Karweit, N.L. (1981). Cognitive and affective outcomes of an intensive student team learning experience. *Journal of Experimental Education, 50,* 29-35.

Smith, L.H. (1976). *Improving your child's behavior chemistry.* Englewood Cliff, NJ: Prentice-Hall.

Soltz, V. (1967). *Study group leaders manual.* Chicago: The Alfred Adler Institute of Chicago.

Sonstegard, M., & Dreikurs, R. (1967). *The teleoanalytical approach to group counsling.* Chicago: The Alfred Adler Institute of Chicago.

Spencer, H. (1885). *Education-intellectual, moral, physical.* New York: P.D. Alden Publisher.

Spokane, A.R. (1985). A review of research on person-environment congruence in Holland's theory of careers. *Journal of Vocational Behavior, 26,* 306-343.

Stanton, M.D., & Todd, T.C. (1979). Structural family therapy with drug addicts. In E. Kaufman & P. Kaufman (Eds.), *The family therapy of drug and alcohol abuse.* New York: Gardner Press.

Starr, A. (1971). Psycho drama. In Nikelly, A.G. *Techniques for behavior change.* Springfield, IL: Charles Thomas.

Steingiser, S. (1981). Optimism as a meditating variable in the management of stress. Unpublished doctoral dissertation, Ohio University, Athens.

Stewart, N.R. (1969). Exploring and processing information about educational and vocational opportunities in groups. In J.D. Krumboltz & C.E. Thoresen (Eds.), *Behavioral counseling: Cases and techniques* (pp. 213-234). New York: Holt, Reinhart, & Winston.

Stipek, D. & Hoffman, S. (1980). A causal analysis of the relationship between locus of control and academic achievement in first grade. *Contemporary Educational Psychology, 5,* 90-99.

Stipek, D.J., & Weisz, F.R. (1981). Perceived personal control and academic achievement. *Review of Educational Research, 51,* 101-137.

Stone, A.A., Cox, D.S., Valdimarsdottir, H., Jandorf, L., & Neale, J.M. (1987). Evidence that IgA antibody is associated with daily mood. *Journal of Personality and Social Psychology, 52,* 988-993.

Strickland, B.R. (1978). Internal-external expectancies and health-related behaviors. *Journal of Consulting and Clinical Psychology, 46,* 1192-1211.

Sturdevant, A.D. (1979). Stress: The relationship of social interest to life change and well-being. Unpublished dissertation, Ohio University.

Sweeney, T.J. (1973). Adult models for the emerging adolescent. In N.P. Atkins, & P. Pumerantz (Eds.), *Educational Dimensions of the Emerging Adolescent.* Washington, DC: Association of Supervision and Curriculum Development and Educational Leadership Institute.

Sweeney, T.J. (1977). *Coping with kids.* Telecourse and films. Athens, OH: Ohio University.

Sweeney, T.J. (1978). *Coping with kids: Guided learning resources.* Appalachian Educational Satellite Program, Lexington, KY.

Sweeney, T.J. (1986). The secret power of encouragement. *Suzuki World, V*(5), 14-15.

Sweeney, T.J. (1986). The three R's for guiding young children: Respect, reason and responsibility. *Suzuki World, V*(3), pp. 22-23.

Sweeney, T.J. (1988a). Video tape study guide. Listed in J.E. Myers, *Curriculum guide: Infusing gerontological counseling in counselor preparation.* Alexandria, VA: American Association Counseling and Development Press.

Sweeney, T.J. (1988b). Series of five video tapes on counseling older persons: A supplement to the current guide as source. As listed in Myers, J.E., *Curriculum guide: Infusing gerontological counseling in counselor preparation.* Alexandria, VA: American Association Counseling and Development Press.

Sweeney, T.J., & Moses, M.A. (1979). Parent education topical bibliography. *School Counselor, 26,*(4), 254-263.

Sweeney, T.J., & Myers, J.E. (1986). Early recollections: An Adlerian method for use with older persons. *Clinical Gerontologist, 4*(4), 3-12.

Sweeney, T.J., & Shafe, M.C. (1978). Competency-based career guidance for the classroom. *American Vocational Journal, 53*(4), 53-56.

Szapocznik, J. (1980). *Life enhancement counseling: A psychosocial model of services for Cuban elders.* Coral Gables, FL: Miami University.

Tart, C.T. (1986). *Waking up: Overcoming the obstacles to human potential.* Boston: New Science Library, Shambhala.

Taylor, W.F., & Hoedt, K.C. (1974). Classroom-related behavior problems: Counsel parents, teachers or children? *Journal of Counseling Psychology. 21*(1), 3-8.

Terner, J., & Pew, W.L. (1978). *The courage to be imperfect: The life and works of Rudolf Dreikurs.* New York: Hawthorn Books.

Thayer, S. (1988). Close encounters. *Psychology Today, 22*(3), 31-36.

Tiger, L. (1979). *Optimism: The biology of hope.* New York: Simon and Schuster.

Toffler, A. (1980). *The third wave.* New York: Bantam Books.

Touchton, J.B., & Magoon, T.M. (1977). Occaptional daydreams as predictors of vocational plans for college women. *Journal of Vocational Behavior, 10,* 156-166.

Trachsel, R., Rebeka, L., & Gregg, R. (1978). Life odyssey: Life review. Paper presented at the Association for Humanistic Sociology, Akron, OH.

U.S. Department of Agriculture and U.S. Department of Health and Human Services (1985). Dietary guidelines for Americans (2nd ed.). Home and Garden Bulleting, No. 232.

U.S. Department of Labor (1988). *Occupational outlook handbook, 1988-1989 edition.* Washington, DC: U.S. Government Printing.

USA Today. (1988, February 29). A wife adds satisfaction to man's life, p. 10.

Vaihinger, H. (1965). *The philosophy of "as if."* London: Routledge and Kegan Paul.

Vaillant, G.E. (1977). *Adaptation to life.* Boston: Little, Brown.

Vasquez, J. (1973). The relation of teacher locus of control to teacher characteristics and student learning gains. Doctoral dissertation, University of California at Los Angeles.

Vaughn, D. (1987). *Uncoupling: How relationships come apart.* New York: Vintage.

Waitley, D. (1983). *Seeds of greatness.* New York: Simon & Schuster.

Watkins, C.E. (1984). The individual psychology of Alfred Adler: Toward an Adlerian vocational theory. *Journal of Vocational Behavior, 24,* 28-47.

Weiner, B. (1976). An attributional approach for educational psychology. In L. Shulman (Ed.), *Review of research in education* (Vol. 4). Itasca, IL: F.E. Peacock.

Weiner, B., Frieze, I.H., Kukla, A., Reed, L., Rest, S., & Rosenbaum, R.M. (1971). *Perceiving the causes of success and failure.* Morristown, NJ: General Learning Press.

Weiss, R.S. (1988). Loneliness. *The Harvard Medical School Mental Health Letter, 4*(12), 4-6.

West, C.K. (1986). *Parenting without guilt.* Springfield, IL: Charles E. Thomas.

West, C.K., Jones, P.A., & McConahay, G. (1981). Who does what to the adolescent in the high school: Relationships among resulting affect and self-concept and achievement. *Adolescence, 16,* 657-661.

Witmer, J.M. (1985). *Pathways to personal growth: Developing a sense of worth and competence.* Muncie, IN: Accelerated Development.

Witmer, J.M., Rich, C., & Barcikowski, R.S. (1988). *Optimism as a mediating factor in coping with stress.* Manuscript submitted for publication.

Witmer, J.M., Rich, C., Barcikowski, R.S., & Mague, J.C. (1983). Psychosocial characteriscs mediating the stress response: An exploratory study. *The Personnel and Guidance Journal, 62,* 73-77.

Wolf, S., & Goodell, H. (1976). *Behavioral science in clinical medicine.* Springfield, IL: Charles C. Thomas.

Wolfe, W.B. (1982). *Alfred Adler: The pattern of life.* New York: Cosmopolitan Book.

Wrenn, C.G. (1980). The importance of believing in yourself or building a more positive self-image. *The School Counselor, 27*(3), 159-167.

Wrye, H., & Churilla, J. (1977). Looking inward, looking backward: Reminiscence and the life review. *Frontiers, 2*(2), 98-105.

Wurtman, J. (1986). *Managing your mind and mood through food.* New York: Rawson.

Yandelovich, D. (1978, May). The new psychological contracts at work. *Psychology Today,* 46-50.

Yankelovich, F. (1981). *New rules.* New York: Random House.

Young, M.E., & Witmer, J.M. (1985). Values: Our internal guidance system. In J.M. Witmer, *Pathways to personal growth* (pp. 275-289). Muncie, IN: Accelerated Development.

Zarski, J.J., Barcikowski, R., & Sweeney, T. (1977). Counseling effectiveness and social interest. *Journal of Counseling Psy chology, 24*(1), 1-5.

Zarski, J.J., Bubenzer, D.L., & West, J.D. (1980). Social interest, life changes and mood states. Unpublished Research Report, West Virginia, College of Graduate Studies.

Ziglar, Z. (1977). *See you at the top.* Gretna, LA: Pelican Publishing.

Zuckerman, L., Zuckerman, V., Costa, R., & Yura, M. (1978). *A parents' guide to children the challenge.* New York: Hawthorn Books.

Zuckerman, M. (1979). Attribution of success and failure revisited, or: The motivational bias is alive and well in attribution theory. *Journal of Personality, 47,* 245-287.

INDEX

INDEX

G

Gaa, J.P. 469
Gandy, G. 474
Garner. W. 54, 75, 478
Gartner, A. 150, 474
Gaylin, W. 17, 474
Gemeinschaftsqefuhl 6
Genest, M., 481
Gerfo, M. 474
Gerler, E.R., Jr. 475
Gesundheit 31
Getzel, G.S. 475
Gillis, C. 475
Glaser, R. 54, 75, 478
Glass C.R., 481
Glasser, R. 248, 476
Glasser, W. 3, 24, 178, 180, 257, 386, 389, 475
Gnagey, W.J. 147, 475
Goal 239
    aggression 162
    assess 167-8
    beauty 163-4
    central 33
    charm 163-4
    clients' 294
    conformity 160-1
    counseling 239
    defiance 162-3
    disruptive behavior, *Table* 172
    faulty 160-5, *Table* 173-5
    fictional 33, 295
    guiding lines 294, 296
    inadequacy 162-3
    intellectuality 164-5
    popularity 160-1
    promiscuity 162-3
    psychotherapy 240
    superiority 160-1
Goldstein, K. 11, 475
Goodall, K. 24, 475
Goodell, H. 489
Gordon, E. 385, 475
Gordon, S.K. 248, 469
Gordon, T. 123, 475
Gottfredson, G.D. 307, 475
Graham, L.E. 75, 485
Greene, D. 23, 185, 475
Greene, J.C. 147, 475

Gregg, R. 488
Greiger, R. 314, 474
Grey, L. 83, 94, 162, 278, 364, 373
Griffith, J. 294, 300, 311, 314, 475, 484
Griggs, S.A. 475
Group setting 349-50
Groups
    "C" 404-5
    children 385-6
    counseling 384, 407
    consulting 384, 404-7
    discussion 384, 385-403
    life style 407-11
    marriage 402-3
    procedures 383-411
    psychodrama 384
    therapy 384
    types 384-5
Growald, E.R. 72, 475
Grunwald, B.B. 178, 364, 373
Guide
    physicians, *Table* 182-4
Gushurst, R.S. 263, 476, 482
Gysbers, N. 476

H

Haggard, E.A. 474
Hardiness 50
Harman, W.W. 34, 476
Harrington, T.F. 315, 476
Harris, T.A. 18, 476
Harris-Bowlsbey, J. 316, 476
Harrison, C.L. 476
Hartman, B.W. 318, 471
Harvard University 61
Havighurst, R.J. 248, 476
Health 31, 72-7
    habits 59-64
Heisel, J.S. 54, 479
Helper, *Table* 312
Heppner, P.P. 47, 476
Herr, E.L. 66, 476
Herzberg, F. 476
Hill, N. 476
Hillman, B.W. 480
Hine, F. 476
Hoedt, K.C. 25, 406, 407, 488

T

U

ABOUT
THE
AUTHOR

ABOUT THE AUTHOR

THOMAS J. SWEENEY
Professor, Consultant, Author
Executive Director, Chi Sigma Iota Counseling Academic
and Professional Honor Society, International

Dr. Sweeney became interested in Adlerian concepts and methods as a father of five children and professionally as a counselor and consultant. As a second son in a family of two, he perceived the validity of Adler's observations and teaching in his own development. His history of "trying harder" as the second child is readily discernible in his accomplishments.

He has been president of state, regional, national, and international associations in his chosen field of counseling and guidance. A state licensed and nationally certificated counselor, he also has been a certificated teacher. Formerly a junior and senior high school teacher and counselor, he has been an administrator in higher education for over eighteen years as well as a professor for over twenty-four years.

The author of numerous articles, reviews, and monographs, he also authored the American Personnel and Guidance Association/American Association for Counseling and Development (APGA/AACD) positions on counselor licensure and accreditation. He chaired each of these respective activities for AACD to move them forward for the profession.

The recipient of numerous awards and consultant/lecturer in this country and abroad, he reports his greatest satisfaction with the award winning telecourse/film series based on Adler's and Rudolf Dreikurs' teaching, *Coping With Kids*, with over four thousand participants in just five years. More recently, he produced a nationally distributed video series on counseling older persons which incorporated Adlerian methods and techniques into the programs.

Dr. Sweeney has not limited his professional commitment to Individual Psychology or its many applications. A consultant to the General Electric Foundation Educators in Industry Programs for over 18 years, he served the National Vocational Guidance Association/National Career Development Association (NVGA/NCDA) as Field Services Coordinator for three years and elected Trustee for three additional years. He is a past-president of the Association for Counselor Education and Supervision and APGA/AACD. A founding member of the Association for Adult Development and Aging and its governing council representative to AACD, he also helped to establish the International Association for Marriage and Family Counseling. Since completing his term as the Founding President of Chi Sigma Iota Academic and Professional Honor Society International, he continues as its Executive Director to promote the recognition of excellence within the counseling profession.